The Literary Humor of the Urban Northeast

D1555401

Edited, with an Introduction, by David E. E. Sloane

❧ The Literary Humor ❧
of the Urban Northeast
1830–1890

Louisiana State University Press, Baton Rouge and London

Copyright © 1983 by Louisiana State University Press
All rights reserved
Manufactured in the United States of America

Designer: Joanna Hill
Typeface: Linotron Sabon
Typesetter: G & S Typesetters, Inc.
Printer: Thomson-Shore
Binder: John Dekker & Sons

Library of Congress Cataloging in Publication Data
Main entry under title:
The Literary humor of the urban Northeast, 1830–1890.
Bibliography: p.
1. American literature—Northeastern States.   2. American wit and humor—Northeastern States.   3. American literature—19th century.   4. City and town life—Literary collections.   5. City and town life—Anecdotes, facetiae, satire, etc.   6. Northeastern States—Literary collections.   I. Sloane, David E. E., 1943–   .
PS538.L57 1983   817'.3'08   82-12688
ISBN 0-8071-1055-8

This one's for Wolf

2223472

Contents

🦢 Illustrations 🦢

✳ Preface ✳

The texts for this edition are taken from the available contemporary sources. Because dialect and phonetic spellings figure in the humor of many pieces, inconsistencies in spelling and punctuation have been retained.

Illustrations formed an important component of American humor. Famous illustrators of American humorists included D. C. Johnston, F. O. C. Darley, Thomas Nast, and N. C. Wyeth, among others. It may be that several of Neal's best stories, including "The News-boy," were written to accompany Darley's drawings. The young Thomas Nast proposed, as a joint venture, to illustrate Mark Twain's lectures on-stage while the humorist spoke. Nast had previously illustrated newspaper stories by Doesticks and had created the image of Petroleum V. Nasby for Nasby's *Swingin' Round the Cirkle*. Books by Marietta Holley and Mark Twain were sold door-to-door by subscription and were profusely illustrated to appeal to the popular market. Comic papers were likewise lavishly illustrated. A particularly good collection of illustrations and political cartoons of major American political and historical events appears in Roger Butterfield, *The American Past* (New York, 1947).

The illustrations in this book are intended to show a spectrum representing important images of the changing Northeast in the nineteenth century. The objective has been to give an indication of the visual expectations of readers of northern comic literature rather than to collect political or social cartoons following a formal historical progression.

I am indebted to many people for this book. Walter Blair's *Native American Humor* (1937) first defined this field for me. "Books" Messenger's Book Barn in Tatamy, Pennsylvania, provided more than one of the sources. I am particularly grateful to two valued colleagues and friends, Louis Budd of Duke University, who has made many Twain items available to me from his own research and has always been unstinting in his encouragement, and Jean Henry of the University of New Haven, who saw in my ramblings about northeastern humorists the continuity that defines them as a school and encouraged me to bring together this introductory study. I am also grateful to Linda Senkus, Eric Johnson, and Carol Harker of the University of New Haven Library for careful attention to details of this study. Qui Tran painstakingly proofread the selections, in addition to commenting on oriental customs in relation to Paulding's sketch reprinted here. Douglas Robillard of the University of New Haven, Mary Farnum of Albertus Magnus College, and Marcuss Oslander of the Paier College of Art all read versions of my introduction and made useful comments on it. My brother Tom Sloane, by introducing me to the word processor on which this material was written, gave me valuable aid for which I am grateful. Thanks are also due to Myra Morse, Betty Bucar, Christine Nastri, and Pinky Fox for aid in completing the manuscript. I am also very grateful to my parents Ted and Elaine Sloane for encouragement above and beyond the call of parental duty.

The encouragement of the University of New Haven and its president, Phillip Kaplan, through sabbatical leave and research support, including a Connecticut Visiting Faculty Mellon Fellowship to Yale University, are particularly appreciated. LSU Press and its fine staff, and especially Judy Bailey, have also been, as always, wonderfully helpful. The staffs at Yale University's Sterling and Beinecke Libraries, the Pennsylvania Historical Society, Houghton Library of Harvard University, the New York Public Library, and the Cambridge, Massachusetts, Public Library have also given me considerate aid and attention, as has the entire staff of the Marvin K. Peterson Library, University of New Haven.

The Literary Humor of the Urban Northeast

❧ Introduction ❧

For the past forty years or more, scholars have been preoccupied with humorists of the American Southwest, who have been seen as heartily and naturally American because of their depiction of country ruffians speaking in low-class, or "vernacular," dialect and expressing frontier viewpoints. The political vision of the federalist founding fathers and the social values of the Protestant ethic and Jeffersonian democracy are central components of American comic literature. Yet, almost no attention has been paid to the large number of comic writers in the Northeast who sought to integrate these values with the growing village, urban, and commercial experience of the capitalist and industrialist Northeast. The Knickerbocker and Yankee humorists have received attention in a handful of excellent studies, but there has not yet been a fair and comprehensive representation of the full range of northeastern humorists as a consistent school of writers. Writers in the Northeast covered as broad a range of classes and dialects, from the top to the bottom of the social scale, as did their counterparts in the Southwest. But the literary humorists of the North, rather than punishing vice in violent action, also resorted to irony and burlesque in their class-conscious, literary-conscious writings. These techniques linked them to their British roots and freed them to combine the long-standing tradition of ethical humanism in Puritan New England and Quaker Philadelphia with the emerging world of industrial and urban America in the 1830–1890 period. In the 1860s Mark Twain, the greatest writer of the northeastern school, raised this tradition from a regional to a national and international vision. He continued to insist on the interrelationships between political, social, economic, and moral terminology even as the postindustrial modern age emerged in the 1890s, and, seemingly, made much of his comic terminology obsolete. As these examples from a broad range of the most important northeastern humorists will show, the humor of the urban Northeast was grounded in American idealism, and it was from the idealist's perspective that these writers viewed the changing landscape of the urban Northeast and subsequently of all America.

The Northeastern Background

By 1830, Boston, New York, and Philadelphia, preeminent among American cities, were emerging from their colonial and federal origins into modern American cosmopolitanism. By the 1850s, urban newspapers, from the New York *Tribune* to the Cleveland *Plain Dealer* contained a now-familiar mix of items ranging from advances in weapons to political alliances, economic news, and local robberies, rapes, and murders, not infrequently mixed with comic stories. The South's commitment to the cotton economy after the invention of the cotton gin in 1793 impeded social change in that region. But in the North heavy-machine manufacturing, transportation industries, and mills proliferated; public education advanced rapidly; and municipal services appeared in modern form. In the American city of the middle and late nineteenth century, cash as such became a focus for commercial and political action, and masses of men in the form of civic associations, social clubs, or bodies of troops during the Civil War achieved preeminence over the frontier ideal of individualists like the Mississippi flatboatmen. New figures emerged in the North at every point in the social scale.

Throughout Yankee North America, from the shores of Thomas Chandler Haliburton's Nova Scotia to Madison Tensas' Mississippi, the boasts of expansionist democracy dominated the humor of a nation that saw its natural boundaries as the equator to the south, the aurora borealis to the north, and to the west nothing less than the setting sun. The creation bear of Thomas Bangs Thorpe's "The Big Bear of Arkansas" may have ruled in the backwoods, but Yankee exaggeration was just as likely to rub an Englishman's nose in America's greatness in the shadows of New York's Bowery as in the frontier encampments of the old Southwest. One Englishman who knew the Yankee habit of bragging is reported in *The American Joe Miller* (1865) to have seen some huge watermelons at a fruit seller's stand in New York. Walking up to look at them, he said disappointedly, "What! don't you raise bigger apples than these in America?" The woman looked at him for a moment and then retorted, "Apples! any body might know you was an Englishman. Them's huckleberries." [1] Vulgar dialect, naturalistic motifs, and exaggeration show up even in the northern marketplace. The bear hunter of Arkansas has much in common with the bar haunter of New York City.

The somewhat arbitrary date of 1830 might be taken as a starting point when northern industrialization and transportation began the cultural and physical transformation of the region from farming country to settled urban community. Boston, New York, and Philadelphia were sizable cities, and figures in various American almanacs indicate another twenty or thirty smaller cities as large as or larger than any one of the South's state capitals. Only the shipping centers Baltimore and New Orleans showed populations that compared to those of the major cities of the North. Northern cultural and physical patterns began in 1830 to diverge from those of the expanding southwestern cotton regions. Southwesterners continued to depict their region as a milieu for an upper class of hunter-outdoorsmen and aristocrats and a lower class of slaves and untutored frontiersmen, which was increasingly at variance with the world of farmers, merchants, and lawyers in the economically diversified northern states. The Northeast began to notice its own middle class, an expanding group in every city, whose livelihood was solely dependent on the percentage of cash flow they retained from their employment as traders and merchants, publishers, bankers, manufacturers of intermediate and finished products, and agents handling goods rather than producing raw materials. A lower stratum of the same class was composed of shop clerks and mill girls, and the comic writers of Boston and New York in the 1840s and 1850s readily identified the differences between these commonplace daily lives and the lives of the Mazeppas and other heroes and heroines of melodrama who were wept over in the theaters of the day. Northern village life also continued to be more socialized than its southern counterpart. At a still lower level, the emerging American city of the Northeast brought out grotesques from many points on the social scale: the hard-core urban misfit, the petty pickpocket, the witch or fortune-teller, or the rising middle-class *arriviste*, all of whom were in moral decline in a competitive business and social world. Democratic idealism could even be blended into the double-talk of the acquisitive professional sharper, an entrepreneur who profited from

1. Robert Kempt (comp.), *The American Joe Miller* (London, 1865), 32. Thomas Bangs Thorpe, "The Big Bear of Arkansas," in William T. Porter (ed.), *The Big Bear of Arkansas* (Philadelphia, 1845).

changing mass interests, human gullibility, and the availability of disposable cash money. P. T. Barnum, the apotheosis of this type, remained a moral paradox throughout the era.

The divergence of the northeastern states—including New England and New York, New Jersey, and Pennsylvania, with outposts in Ohio and Maryland—from the rest of the nation becomes increasingly noticeable after 1830. Almanac listings of city populations decade by decade indicate the extent to which the Northeast was urbanized. New York City's population of 200,000 in 1830 had grown to over half a million people by 1850. Baltimore in 1850 achieved a population of 169,000, and the southern port of New Orleans reached 116,000, but the populations of both Boston and Cincinnati also exceeded 100,000, and Philadelphia by 1850 contained 409,000 people. Over 100,000 people lived in Brooklyn, easily overlooked in the shadow of New York City. New York, Brooklyn, and Philadelphia together held over a million people in 1850 when the national population still amounted to less than twenty million. The cities of Richmond and Charleston to the south were exceeded in population by Lowell, Massachusetts, and Newark, New Jersey. Buffalo and Troy, by themselves, had as many people as Richmond, Charleston, and Savannah combined. Density in the North was increasing in both cities and towns. Northern humor, as an adjunct of northern culture, might be expected to show these changes through an expanded interest in political, mercantile, and social concerns, and comic subject matter from northeastern writers does so.

A comparison of state populations is equally instructive in identifying changing northern conditions of life. By 1820 the million mark in population had already been passed by New York, Pennsylvania, and Virginia. By 1850, Ohio and Tennessee had joined this group, but Virginia had added only a modest 200,000. New York, however, had almost tripled in population to 3 million, and Pennsylvania had almost doubled to 2 million. Even compared to the explosive growth of population along newly opened farming frontiers, the changes in Pennsylvania and New York represent a significant watershed in the growth from town to city.[2] New Englanders became capitalists, and the benign Mrs. Partington, invented by B. P. Shillaber in the 1840s, moved from village to city, her benignity her only shield against a world grown incomprehensibly complex.

2. Figures are taken from *The American Almanac and Repository of Useful Knowledge for the Year 1860* (Boston, 1860), 214–16.

By 1836, according to some economic historians, the South's expansion of cotton agriculture had matured to the point where forty cents of every cotton dollar went to northern rather than southern hands for shipping and processing, an indication that the forces of the market economy were coming to dominate social and cultural developments.[3] New York and Philadelphia were becoming world shipping centers for the manufactures of the East as well as the produce of Pennsylvania and New York State. New Orleans enjoyed a similar status for the cotton states, having a large urban population conjoined with some newspaper and publishing facilities, but the southern city seems not to have developed the cultural dominance of its northern sisters. Combined imports for the two largest southern ports, Charleston and New Orleans, were 22 million dollars in 1858; while Philadelphia alone valued imports at 12 million dollars, Boston at 40 million, and New York at 170 million. State accounting methods differed, and the sale of land assets further complicates an understanding of state revenues, but compared to other states, New York and Pennsylvania handled large revenues and maintained large school budgets. Social expenditures, such as those for schools, rapidly became a necessity, and northern philosophers like Horace Mann integrated human needs into their analysis of the commercial needs of the commonwealth. No such phenomenon occurred in the South.

Expansion of the marketplace was one aspect of the growth of Yankee industrialism, which transformed the Northeast and changed the nature of northern towns. Eli Whitney pioneered the mass-production techniques that, with innovations and improvements throughout New England, came to be known as the "American System of Manufacture." He also built an embryo factory village, Whitneyville, just outside of New Haven, Connecticut, before his death in 1825. One version of "Yankee Doodle" chanted:

> We work and sleep and pray in peace—
> By industry we thrive, sir;
> And if a drone won't do his part,
> We'll scout him from the hive, sir.
> . . . .
> We're happy, free, and well to do,
> And cannot want for knowledge;
> For almost every mile or two,
> You find a school or college.

3. See Douglas C. North, *American Economic Development, 1790–1860* (Engle-

East Bridgeport (about 1876), which appeared in Barnum's *Struggles and Triumphs* (1883 edition), showed a harmonious blending of smokestacks and church steeples—an urban pastoral. Mark Twain's Connecticut Yankee, in 1889, queries a knight in armor on first seeing Camelot, "Bridgeport?"

Boston Brahmins projected an idealized factory village system for the mill towns of Lowell and Andover, Massachusetts, and largely succeeded in populating their towns with educated New England farm girls who could assimilate mechanical duties and moral instruction in an industrial setting—at a time when western specialized farm production was already beginning to make the New England farm obsolete.[4]

As William Cox's "Steam," which is reprinted here, suggests, the 1830s were also a time when the railroad began to make its mark on the American countryside. Again, the impact was significantly greater in the North than in the South. Pennsylvania had ninety-six locomo-

---

wood Cliffs, N.J., 1961), and for a slightly more socioeconomic view, Thomas C. Cochran and William Miller, *The Age of Enterprise* (New York, 1953), 1–153.

4. For an arresting description of Yankee commercial and industrial initiative, including commentary on the concept of the New England mill town, see Daniel J. Boorstin, *The National Experience* (New York, 1965), 1–34, Vol. II of Boorstin, *The Americans*, 3 vols.; "For the Fourth of July," in "The Household Songbook," in *War Songs of the Blue and Gray* (New York: n.d.), 19–20.

tives at this time, three times more than any other state in the Union. New York, New Jersey, Virginia, Maryland, and South Carolina each had at least thirty, and Massachusetts had thirty-seven. Even the reclusive Emily Dickinson wrote a satirical poem about a locomotive. Yankee resistance to a device that added little save speed was evident in the slapstick comedy of Cox's steam railroad sketch. Another story, "The First Locomotive," written considerably after the dates of 1801–1810 given in the story, describes Jabez Doolittle's invention of the first on-land, steam-driven locomotive in Wallingford, Connecticut. He achieves immortality when the machine is started up and carries him through the barn wall and into history, "True to his purpose, . . . alternately screwing down the valves, and oiling the piston rod and crank joints, evidently determined that, although he had started off a little unexpectedly, he would redeem the pledge he had given, which was, that when it did go, 'it would go a little slower than chain lightnin', and a darned leetle, too!'" Not too long after Yankeedom provided the railroad with such a compatible myth, the concepts of professionalism and the corporation succeeded as further dominant motifs, merging economics, regional change, and the modern context. One joke collection chronicles a toast given at a railroad dinner, "An honest lawyer, the noblest work of God," to which an old farmer added in a loud voice, "and about the scarcest."[5] Northern social experience incorporated individuals into economic and social relationships that were far more complex than the easy camaraderie of the coon hunt. Even the spiritual excesses shown by Marietta Holley in *Samantha Among the Brethren* are restrained compared to the unfocused ruckus of the camp meeting; religious expression in the Northeast was a far more formalized phenomenon of religious services, congregations, and substantial church buildings.

The literary humor of the Northeast began, much as its southwestern counterpart did, with the recording of oral tales. However, changing social and economic conditions in the North transformed the deadpan Yankee anecdote into a refined literary irony that carried overtones of moral and social commentary. B. A. Botkin's anecdote "The Parsimonious Widower" offers a case in point. A Vermont widower named Henry Pease went courting the widow Perkins, but she

5. "The First Locomotive," in *The Railway Anecdote Book: A Collection of Anecdotes and Incidents of Travel by River and Rail* (New York, 1864), Cox's "Steam" is reprinted; Kempt (comp.), *The American Joe Miller*, 86.

refused him because he had let his farm and house run down into terrible condition. One of the widow's conditions for carrying on the courtship was that Henry mend the old-fashioned stone-lined stove in his kitchen. Since he couldn't bear to get a new lining, he sawed up his wife's slate tombstone and put it in place. When the widow Perkins came to visit Henry and baked him some biscuits in that oven, they came out with the words "Sacred to the memory of my beloved wife Matilda" baked clearly into their bottoms in reversed letters. Mark Twain combined a comparable incident with a comic tall story based on mechanization, and worked it into Jim Blaine's "The Story of the Old Ram" in *Roughing It*. The actual source, fitted to Massachusetts cotton-mill life in the 1840s, has been discovered by Richard Dorson, one of the leading students of the Yankee as a mythical figure, in the *Yankee Blade*:

> "You, I say! She goes pooty, don't she Bos?" said Jonathan enquiringly.
>
> "She don't do anything else," responded the stripper. "But you must be very careful how you move around amongst this *hard ware*. 'Twas only last week, Sir, that a promising young man from Oxford—a student at the academy here—was drawn into that very card, Sir, and before any assistance could reach him, he was run through, and manufactured into No. 16, super extra, cotton warp yarn."
>
> "I s-s-swow! I believe yure joking!" stuttered Jonathan.
>
> "Fact, Sir, and his disconsolate mother came down two days ago, and got five bunches of that same yarn, as melancholy relics."
>
> "By the mighty! That *can't* be true!"
>
> "Fact, Sir, fact! and each of his fellow students purchased a skein apiece, to be set in lockets, and wore in remembrance of departed worth!"

Twain has a man named Wheeler woven into fourteen yards of three-ply carpeting. A modern reader of the story would never suppose that Twain was narrating a Yankee yarn generalized in its presentation to fit into the more cosmopolitan post–Civil War world.[6] The joke is beyond transient changes; the threat of a loss of life and freedom and a submergence in bathos is the source of its ironic power as a "report," which is patently false but fully detailed—the northeastern tall tale.

6. B. A. Botkin, *A Treasury of New England Folklore* (New York, 1964), 112; Richard M. Dorson, *Jonathan Draws the Longbow* (Cambridge, Mass., 1946), 70–71, reprinted this item from *Spirit of the Times*, XVII (October 16, 1847), 396, where it is credited by the *Spirit* to "Gamboge," in the *Yankee Blade*; Samuel L. Clemens [Mark Twain], *Roughing It* (2 vols.; New York, 1913), II, 98–104.

The comic story expresses the peculiar ethos of the universal Yankee nation in contact with the modern world. Individuals have lost control of the forces they have created to improve their world; innocence may be either a blind, a shield, or a useful weapon, and the reader may not always know which one it is.

These tall tales become almost invisible as they blend into the narrative forms of northeastern writers; however, their motive impulses persist. And their anonymity has caused them to remain as unidentified components in the definition of the culture of the Northeast above and beyond the parochial label of "Yankee humor." Dorson has identified the Yankee "greenhorn" as "an ignorant countryman, baffled by urban ways, befuddled by modern machinery, legitimate game for dupes and hoaxes. The industrial age had passed him by; mechanical contrivances caused Jonathan surprises and grief." Yet, the vulgarity of the Bowery vegetable woman, the imagery of the joke, and the comic American exaggeration are in no way chained to the greenhorn concept. As frequently as not, the hoaxer is hoaxed, and even P. T. Barnum himself appears as the dupe of others. Barnum reported that Lewis Gaylord Clark, editor of the *Knickerbocker*, begged to be shown the club that killed Captain Cook and, when Barnum brought out the fraud, thanked the showman by commenting, "I felt quite confident you could accommodate me. I have been in half a dozen smaller museums, and as *they all had it*, I was sure a large establishment like yours would not be without it." Nor is the shrewdness or sternness of the Yankee an impregnable fortress in relation to the seemingly more positive emotions of kindness and love, as in "The Schoolmaster Caught."

A few years ago, when it was the custom for large girls and larger boys to attend district schools, and when flagellations were more common in schools than at the present time, an incident took place in a neighboring town which is worth recording as a reminiscence of school-boy days. One of the largest, plumpest and fairest girls in school happened to violate one of the teacher's rules. The master, a prompt energetic fellow of twenty-five, at once summoned her into the middle of the floor, and, as usual in such cases, the business of the whole school ceased, and the attention of every scholar was directed to the girl, who, it was expected, was to receive a severe punishment. After interrogating the girl a few moments, the master took from his desk a huge ruler, such as we seldom see now-a-days, and commanded the damsel to hold out her hand. She hesitated, when the master, in a blaze of passion, thundered out.—"Will you *give* me your hand?"

"Yes sir, and my *heart* too," promptly replied the girl, at the same time stretching forth her hand to the master and eyeing him with a cunning look. A deathly silence reigned for a moment in the school-room; a moist spot was seen to glisten in the master's eye; the ruler was laid upon the desk and the blushing girl was requested to take her seat, but to *remain after the school was dismissed*!

In three weeks after the school finished, the schoolmaster and the girl were married.[7]

Courtship, marriage, and education provide motifs by which hopes are realized rather than degraded. Whereas southwestern humor battened on the violent incident, the camp meeting gone awry, and the wedding disrupted by disaster, northeastern humor was more subdued. It was consistent with a moral and social milieu derived from Congregationalist humanism, and could easily assimilate sentimental stories as part of its view of humanity. Even in the age of the machine, idealism held a place for family virtues, burlesques by Artemus Ward about his termagant wife Betsy Jane notwithstanding.

The humor of the best authors of the 1830–1890 era is based on the irony arising from the conflict between competitive economics— magnified in northern village and city life—and the simpler virtues of idealistic farmers and federalist political philosophers. The comic writings of Joseph C. Neal, author of *Charcoal Sketches*; Mortimer Thomson, famed as Doesticks; Charles Farrar Browne, the much-emulated Artemus Ward; and Samuel L. Clemens, Mark Twain, captured many of the incongruities of this changing milieu as an "American" experience, and they were followed by a host of lesser writers in the East and, later, Midwest. However, it is easy enough to find materials like those of the northeastern tradition well before this time. Richard Dorson, in *Jonathan Draws the Longbow*, traces one Yankee story back to 1739 and suggests that it may ultimately be a borrowing from an English chapbook. Putting aside the Simple Cobbler of Aggawam, as a colonial anticipator of northeastern humor, "Lord" Timothy Dexter (1743–1806) provides a fascinating study of the early federal mind infused with social irony, well before the literary comedians. His *A Pickle for the Knowing Ones; or, Plain Truth in a Homespun Dress* (1802), in Joycean run-on words and unpunctuated sentences, chided, "I want to know what a sole is I wish to see one not a gizard." Much

7. Dorson, *Jonathan Draws the Longbow*, 70; P. T. Barnum, *Life of P. T. Barnum, Written by Himself* (New York, 1855), 228–29; "The Schoolmaster Caught," *Yankee Notions*, III (July, 1854), 195.

more of his commentary was economic, appropriate to the career of a man who made a fortune selling bed warmers in the West Indies and built a mansion decorated by some fifty-odd wooden statues of the nation's fathers with the intent of supporting American wood-carvers rather than Italian marble masons. To the intense disgust of Rufus W. Griswold, who cited Dexter's postscript in *Curiosities of American Literature* (1843), Dexter went even further in anticipating the literary comedians of the 1860s by adding several hundred assorted punctuation marks at the end of his second edition (1805) so that the "Nowing ones" could "pepper and solt it as they please." [8]

Likewise, the antagonism of the literary comedians to corporations, evident in Artemus Ward's frequent denials that he had ever been a railroad director and Mark Twain's refusal to class the wretched Goshoot Indians with the directors of the Baltimore and Washington Railroad (there being only a plausible resemblance between the tribes), appears very early. The "Speech of David Wood," in *The Spirit of the Farmer's Museum and Lay Preacher's Gazette* (1801), attacked the privileges of wealth. "The 'Squire is a great speculator, he is of the quorum, can sit on the sessions, and fine poor girls for natural misteps; but I am a little rogue, who speculated in only fifty acres of rocks, and must stand here in the pillory." It may be, as Mody Boatright has shrewdly noted in *Folk Laughter on the American Frontier*, that Davy Crockett was well aware, unlike the Supreme Court of the United States, that the Southern Pacific Railroad was not a person. Sir Edward Coke, the English jurist and law-codifier, however, had long before established that corporations have no souls. Lord Edward Thurlow agreed: "You never expected justice from a company, did you? They have neither a soul to lose nor a body to kick." It seems clear in reading Wood's speech and noting the legal precedents that such populist and humanist sentiments are appropriate to any milieu where complex business and commercial interactions invite ethical consideration. [9]

---

8. Dorson, *Jonathan Draws the Longbow*, 20; Samuel L. Knapp, *Life of Lord Timothy Dexter, Etc.* (Boston, 1858), 140. Timothy Dexter's *A Pickle for the Knowing Ones; or, Plain Truth in a Homespun Dress* appears in Knapp, *Life of Dexter*, 123–53. It was originally published in Salem, Mass., in 1802. The "Note to Dexter's Second Edition," containing his comic punctuation, is reprinted with a brief biography in Rufus W. Griswold, *Curiosities of American Literature* (New York [?1843]), 48–49.

9. [Charles F. Browne], *The Complete Works of Artemus Ward* (London, 1922), 254; Ward's character Jim Griggens, in "Soliloquy of a Low Thief" ([Browne], *Complete Works*, 154), follows David Wood's speech very closely, only updating the attack on the squire to suit the emergence of the railroad companies. Clemens, *Roughing It*,

The urbanizing Northeast was an appropriate locus for such a development from the 1830s and even before.

Grim Yankee stories also match the brutality of southwestern humor in a variety of instances, such as the story of a Yankee who slit a hog's mouth from ear to ear in revenge for another practical joke played on himself and claimed that he hadn't actually done anything, that the hog had wandered by and split his own mouth from ear to ear laughing at the earlier joke. On the other hand, more complex stories of social and economic interrelationships point in more sophisticated directions, probing the gamut of social issues. In Philadelphia as early as 1836, Neal's *Gentleman's Vade Mecum* carried a regular feature on stick defense and personal safety from highway robbery in the chatty tone of a guide to manners. Doesticks' piece on garrotting (mugging) was widely circulated in 1857 and reprinted in the New York *Knickerbocker* as a comic social comment. By 1861, *Yankee Notions* offered a silhouette of a man being mugged in the dark with the caption, "Midnight joker—I'm not going to murder you for your money. I just want to give the illustrated newspapers a lift." A change in the texture of northeastern humor might be a predictable outcome of the socializing forces of industrial and urban concentration; "The Story of the Tailor Done Brown," from the first volume of *Yankee Notions* in 1852 shows several changes suggestive of the forming northeastern urban environment with its civic artifacts and economic relationships taking unexpectedly ironic twists.

> Not many years since, there lived in the "moral" city of Boston, two young bucks, rather waggish in their ways, and who were in the habit of patronizing rather extensively, a tailor by the name of Smith. Well, one day, into Smith's shop these young gents strolled. Says one of them— "Smith, we've been making a bet: now we want you to make each of us a suit of clothes—wait till the bet is decided, and then the one who loses will pay the whole." "Certainly, gentlemen; I shall be most happy to serve you," says Smith, and forthwith their measures were taken, and in due course of time the clothes were sent home. A month or two passed

---

I, 133–35; "Speech of David Wood," *The Spirit of The Farmer's Museum* (Walpole, N.H., 1801), 204–206; Mody C. Boatright, *Folk Laughter on the American Frontier* (Gloucester, Mass., 1971), 137. Coke's precedent in the case of Sutton's Hospital, 10 Rep. 39, and Thurlow are cited in Samuel A. Bent (ed.), *Short Sayings of Great Men* (Boston, 1882), 154, under the heading "Corporations Have No Souls." So it seems reasonable to identify their viewpoint as being subject to conscious consideration by northeasterners during this period.

by, and yet our friend, the tailor, saw nothing of his two customers. One day, however, he met them in Washington Street, and thinking it *almost* time the bet was decided, he made up to them, and asked how their clothes fitted.

"Oh! excellently," says one; "by the way, Smith, our bet isn't decided yet."

"Ah!" says Smith, "what is it?"

"Why, I bet that when *Bunker Hill Monument falls it will fall to the south*! Bill here took me up, and when the bet is decided, we'll call and pay that little bill."

Smith's face stretched to double its usual length, but he soon recovered his wonted good humor, and says he—"Boys, *I'm sold*; let's go to Birmingham's and take a '*snifter*,'—and I tell you what, boys, say nothing about it, and I'll send you receipted bills this afternoon.[10]

The commercial side of experience is the center of the comic item. Published in a New York comic magazine, it is not Knickerbocker humor of Washington Irving's sort. Deriving from Boston, it is not a backwoods Yankee comic story of the type of Dan Marble. Containing elements of irony and verbal wit, it is not so completely literary that it can be classed with the literary comedy of the Civil War era. Rather, "The Tailor Done Brown," with other comic pieces from the 1830–1890 era in the Northeast, cuts across accepted demarcations of American humor. The Bunker Hill Monument allows the story to involve a city artifact with its own set of historical and political overtones, vaguely allied to the concept of "morality" introduced at the start of the sketch. The sharp dealing is not the horse swap, but a mercantile agreement on credit and service. Negotiation and verbal cleverness replace violent action. These traits characterize much of the literary humor of the urban Northeast; and Mark Twain, America's most important humorist, invested the personae of his major characters and his own voice with these principles.

The writers in this anthology adhere to a democratic philosophy that is often directly expressed in their political and humanitarian commentary. The Fourth of July was the appropriate time for formal statements of democratic philosophy in the Northeast, and one such statement, made by Mr. Forrest in New York City in 1838, was suffi-

---

10. Dorson, *Jonathan Draws the Longbow*, 92–93; *Gentleman's Vade Mecum*, I (April 16, 1836), 8, *et passim*; *Knickerbocker*, XLIX (April, 1857), 421; *Yankee Notions*, X (January, 1861), 5; and "The Story of the Tailor Done Brown," *Yankee Notions*, I (January, 1852), 9.

ciently concise and patriotically representative to be reprinted in the *New Havener* weekly newspaper on August 4, 1838:

> How grand in their simplicity are the elementary propositions on which our edifice of freedom is erected! a few brief self-evident axioms, furnish the enduring basis of political institutions, which harmoniously accomplish all the legitimate purposes of government to fifteen millions of people. The natural equality of man; the right of a majority to govern, their duty so to govern as to preserve inviolate the sacred obligations of equal and exact justice, with no object in view but the protection of life, property and social order, leaving opinion free as the wind which bloweth where it listeth; these are the plain eternal principles on which our fathers reared that temple of true liberty, beneath whose dome their children congregate this day.[11]

Fixed and immutable laws are seen as bulwarking the rights of the democratic majority. The laws are not actually described as religious, although they are couched in terminology that parallels religious language. Individual responsibility is central; equality and humanity are specified virtues, in keeping with the maintenance of order and the protection of property. The statement is the antithesis of the rough and ready western justice of Judge Lynch and his law, of which Yankee authors speak sarcastically.

Mark Twain, in the suppressed chapter of *Life on the Mississippi*, compared North and South in terms that both confirm and extend Forrest's egalitarian viewpoint. Twain noted that although slavery was gone from the South of the 1870s, uniformity was the rule because whites were not free from a sense of personal danger. Twain commented that in the northern community timid fellows banded together to maintain the law and "secure all citizens from personal danger and from obloquy or social ostracism on account of opinion, political or religious," thus allowing more personal freedom for the individual.[12] Twain, in 1882 when these passages were written, perceived essentially the same federalist spirit in the North that had been its hallmark from the 1830s, and Twain's perception is only one of many indicators of the pervasiveness of the northerner's consciousness of his social cohesion and sense of lawfulness.

In part, the expanded sense of northern involvement in government

---

11. *New Havener*, III (August 4, 1838), 1. "Mr. Forrest" is probably Edwin Forrest, the famed actor.

12. Samuel L. Clemens [Mark Twain], "Suppressed Chapter of *Life on the Mississippi*," *Life on the Mississippi* (New York, 1944), 412–16.

and governance—the pervasive sense of moral responsibility that became so inflamed through Harriet Beecher Stowe's *Uncle Tom's Cabin*
and Doesticks' "The Great Slave Auction of 1859"—was perceived as
a Yankee trait by northerners and southerners alike in the 1830s and
1840s. One "Southron" writing to the *New York Visitor* cited with
fascination the New England barroom as a place for a lesson in American politics: "The ardor of New England politics is extreme. They in-
dulge in a latitude of conversation, and of personal contradiction and
reproach, that in the south would lead to the use of bowie knives and
pistols. . . . it is really amusing to see how learnedly the topers of both
sides talk on this subject, as they stand, tumbler in hand, drinking
each other's health and defeat at the next election!" Nor was the
southerner alone in his opinion, as John Neal's "Alehouse Politicians,"
in *Sartain's Magazine*, confirmed in yet another comic sketch. Neal
tells the story of a Yankee in Montreal who escapes a fight by following a Vermonter's advice to act "like rational critters" and debate the
issue of annexation by a "town-meetin'" style debate, with considerable discussion of social rank, vote selling, crime, and mobocracy. On
the other side was the antagonism of southern conservatives like William Gilmore Simms, whose penchant for treating southerners as gentlemen and depicting his "clowns" as Connecticut men or Long Is-
landers was noted by Griswold. Simms saw in the omnibus—already
coming into prominence in New York City in the 1840s as a means of
public conveyance—a symbol for the leveling aspects of democracy
that he felt vulgarized American experience. He complained in "The
Philosophy of the Omnibus" that northern mass man was "squeezed
out of all shape of humanity, in order that he may get on in the world."
This choice of image is appropriate for a section where New York and
Pennsylvania together boasted 174 steamboats against the 134 distrib-
uted among eight southern states. Simms's target is the leveling "go
ahead" vulgarization of the arts when subjected to "the merchant, the
retailer, the mechanic, the labourer, the lawyer, and the doctor." However, in the Northeast, R. W. Griswold praised the Brahmin historian
George Bancroft for his opposite view that the institutions of democracy were the highest point in human development. Griswold found
this a progressive view of humanity that was "emphatically" American. But Simms's equation of northern urban transportation with the
political and social characteristics of the society he disliked was not
completely inappropriate. By the time Forrest made his Fourth of July
speech in 1838, New York and Ohio agriculture and New York City's

commercial location had already begun the economic and social transformation of the Northeast, and a few northerners like Henry W. Herbert, writing under the suggestive pen name "Frank Forrester," were as antipathetic as Simms to the incursions of modern improvements in the vales and woodlands of New Jersey.[13]

The northern humorists after the Civil War saw the interrelated myths of Jeffersonian democracy, Yankee character, federal idealism, and a manifest destiny of irreversible progress with some of the polish removed, as indeed had James Russell Lowell suggested through Birdofredum Sawin in *The Biglow Papers* in relation to the Mexican-American War in 1845.[14] The retreat into local color and village humor of the crackerbox variety owes more than a little to this revised perspective. Yet even as they backed away from some of the obvious metaphors of physical development, writers like Marietta Holley maintained a sharp and critical eye for the ethical and moral perspective that accepted social responsibility both at home in personal dealings and in national and international life. Such a wide umbrella of ethical perspectives covered a spectrum of writers, from the Knickerbocker anglophobe James K. Paulding to the post-Dickensian political idealist John W. DeForest.

The humor takes every form from brief jokes and newspaper gags and one liners through sketches and stories up to novel length, with varying degrees of consistency in plot, characterization, and related matters. The anecdotal form of northeastern humor lends itself very comfortably to brief dramatizations and set pieces that illustrate not only human foibles but also basic beliefs about life. To translate such idealistic set pieces into dramatic action required some ability to generate a sense of conflict between opposing heroes and villains, but it was by no means necessary that a writer in the Northeast have a narrative ability in order to create comic literature of one sort or another. In fact, in studying the attempts Orpheus C. Kerr (Robert Henry Newell) and Petroleum V. Nasby (David Ross Locke) made at novels after the Civil War, a reader is impressed by their inability to generate humor-

13. A Southron [pseud.], "A Year Among the Yankees," *New York Visitor and Lady's Parlour Magazine*, I (November, 1840), 130–32. John Neal, "Alehouse Politicians," *Sartain's Union Magazine*, VII (March, 1850), 197–204, Rufus W. Griswold, *Prose Writers of America* (Philadelphia, 1847), 19, 30–31. William Gilmore Simms, "The Philosophy of the Omnibus," *Godey's Lady's Book*, XXIII (September, 1841), 104–107; Henry W. Herbert, *The Warwick Woodlands* (Philadelphia, 1850).

14. James Russell Lowell, *The Biglow Papers* (Cambridge, Mass., 1848).

ous contexts to integrate with plot action, which no doubt accounted for their failure to maintain their audiences after the issues surrounding the war receded. Nevertheless, the materials used and the attitudes defined by a variety of writers in the Northeast is sufficient to suggest that a "school" of writers comparable to the southwestern humorists does exist.

The Humorists of the Old Northeast as a School

The controlling interests of the northern school of writers lay in a persistent concern with human values in changing settings. Southern writers did not grapple with comparable issues; for the most part, they observed a class—a lower agrarian class—of frontiersmen in conflict with each other. To the northern writer, the conflicts are far more frequently conflicts of ethics between ideal and real. In many cases, issues are thrown into burlesque, as in the case of the Yankee in the cotton factory who cannot assimilate the pious moralisms of the joking factory hand with his own fear of the machinery and his greenness. The moralistic core of northeastern writings from 1830 to 1890 sustains an important written tradition related to the history of the region and the cities within it. Although New England has a history of social didacticism, it is not correct to see the phenomenon as limited to Boston bluestockings, for the Nova Scotia bluenose Thomas Chandler Haliburton's Sam Slick is moralistic to a fault and the silk-stockinged New Yorker Lewis Gaylord Clark of the *Knickerbocker* cited with highest approval the habits, morals, and income of the Lowell factory workers.[15] The city on a hill merged with the village factory and the neighborhood dry goods store early in the nineteenth century in the Northeast.

Persistently, the didactic tradition in the northern states is blended with humor to make social statements about the relations between individuals. Emphasis is placed on the social aspects of relationships— as in the sympathy and consideration detailed in Seba Smith's "The Pumpkin Freshet," the story of a family's enduring and finding enjoyment even in a cataclysmic floodtime. Relations in war, in politics, and in church revivals are treated similarly, as stories by DeForest, Holley, and a host of other writers suggest. Emphasis is placed not on individ-

15. *Knickerbocker*, XVII (February, 1841), 164.

ual vulgarity but rather on individual dignity, even in DeForest's harshly satiric "An Inspired Lobbyist" (1872) and "The Colored Member" (1872) and in his longer treatment of a similar theme in *Honest John Vane* (1873). DeForest applies bitter irony and hellish imagery to corrupt politicians. He is openly disgusted with heroes who betray elective offices, like John Vane, whose soul is described as being as carnal as a sparerib. Tom Dicker and Ananias Pullwool, the demonic lobbyist, represent this type in "An Inspired Lobbyist." Yet, DeForest openly wonders if it is possible that the "vast, industrious, decent American public" can help "democracy save itself from the corrupting tyranny of capital." [16] Mass urban man is a victim of his brothers' weakness in the face of corrupting wealth and ambition. A failure to live up to personal and group ideals brings about a consequent vulnerability of the political process to fraud and manipulation.

Northeastern writers concentrate less on the stupidity and venality of the upper and refined classes—the comedy of manners of the elevated social orders. More comic to them is the political sophistication of seemingly innocent rustics. The deadpan irony of Artemus Ward, Josh Billings, and Mark Twain has many precedents dating back into the 1830s. James K. Paulding's "Jonathan's Visit to the Celestial Empire" (1830) shows the hero in a variety of complicated political and social interactions that bend the reality of Chinese customs to fit a format that reflects the pragmatic and democratic presumptions of American life, including a delicate set of networks based on trust, law, and social custom—which Jonathan successfully manipulates. Doesticks' *Pluri-bus-tah* (1856), which burlesques the "Young America" movement mercilessly, still manages to describe the gods Jupiter and Venus as Manhattan city dwellers, as vulgarly complacent as any of John Dos Passos' lower classes to follow, but closely involved with the mystique of American national themes. Even Sam Slick, the archetypal Yankee sharper, holds himself responsible for his social relationships in "Female Colleges," a piece which will seem atypical in comparison with Slick pieces before *Nature and Human Nature* (1855). Instead of featuring the "soft soda" peddler as a shrewdly pandering manipulator, the later Sam Slick stories show the clockmaker valuing individual dignity and humility, and the narrator despises himself when he overindulges his ability to scourge the ridiculous. Conservative humanism

16. John W. DeForest, *Honest John Vane* (1873; rpr. State College, Pa., 1960), 223, 230.

provides the real underpinnings for the story. Slick is a reflective man who betrays himself into preying on another person's obvious vanity and regrets his betrayal—a far cry from the commonly accepted view of him as a cynical aphorist who manipulates the country yokels of the northern backwoods.

These traits of northern urban, literary humor identify it as a distinctive school independent of the southwestern tradition. Heretofore, the variety of elements we can subsume under the heading of this school have too frequently been separated unreflectively into such categories as Yankee, Knickerbocker, literary comedian, or nothing at all, since most of the post–Civil War writers in the Northeast do not fit comfortably into any category. The rise of the western humorists and the Chicago School, including George Ade and Finley Peter Dunne (Mr. Dooley), complicates the national picture even more between 1860 and 1900.

I have limited this anthology of northern literary humor to the years 1830–1890 because that seems to be the period when northern writers brought out fresh statements and materials inculcating two or three basic philosophical principles in comic action. They saw masses of men and machines emerging in the context of idealistic American social and political expectations. They recognized increasingly formalized, if not bureaucratized, relationships replacing the rudimentary physical relations of the backwoods. In socioeconomic terms, federalist ideals came into confrontation with the rise of the common man, most visible in Andrew Jackson's election to the presidency in 1828 and the initiation of the political spoils system. Northeastern writers are identifiable by their attempts to grapple with the social and personal consequences of these events, initiating as they do the politics of the American industrial age.

The distinguishing principles of the school seem to be focused around three points. Most obvious is the explicit approval of democratic egalitarianism and the rights of men to participate in self-government, providing that they are educated to the responsibility. A tory like Haliburton and a democrat like Twain or Barnum stand on the same ground on this point. Also of obvious significance are the dislike and rejection of violence in individuals and in social groups and a strong tendency to depict close human relationships as important to the lives of individuals. In burlesque reversal, this second trait is readily combined with the life of the city as seen in the writings of urban humorists like Doesticks. Finally, the writers of the school grapple with problems of social, economic, and moral change in the urbanizing Northeast. From the 1840s, B. P. Shillaber's Mrs. Partington was disgruntled with the Babylonish custom of Christmas, and this sort of restless awareness of change continues to be perceptible in the countrified nostalgia of Seba Smith and Samantha Allen (Marietta Holley's crackerbox narrator) although they are often ambiguous in their implications. Around 1890 the tradition lapses into the Mauve Decade: John S. Draper's Uncle Ben, Ellis P. Butler's Perkins of Portland, and E. N. Westcott's David Harum take over its local color; social and political irony travel westward to become the property of the humorists of the Chicago renaissance. Richard Harding Davis' starched high collar, as captured in Dana's illustrations, would never permit the unbending of language and social formulae marking the best works of the northern tradition; Opie Read and Don Marquis maintained a few of its jokes and idioms but less of the tradition's insistent and uncompromising human demands.

In addition to the explicit concerns of the northern literary humorists in the 1830–1890 era, some specific traits are apparent in the writing, although the more writers that are included in the study, the broader the categories seem to become and the less useful in understanding the motivation of the comedians. The categories also become less useful in understanding a major writer like Mark Twain, whose writings and consciousness fused with and elevated the tradition beyond its regional and even national origins. The writers use jokes as such, in addition to irony and comic episode. Dialectal freedom is the rule, literary puns and colloquial language are evident, and language patterns are relatively free and informal. On this basis, writers like Donald G. Mitchell (Ik. Marvel) or George William Curtis need to be evaluated with some care, for they and several others, although adhering to some points of the tradition, represent an alternative form of comic writing having a much different social orientation from that seen here. The treatment of human rights, slavery, legal and social justice, and urban and village life provides a specific and distinct vocabulary for the writers of the tradition. A sense of commercial enterprise and competition is apparent at a wholly different level from that of the horse swap and with wholly different stakes, even when the story line is oriented, as in Holley's "Jenette Finster's Story," around love rather than economics. Religious belief and moral belief are part of the fund of language that infuses the humor—but as a defining medium for life, not as the butt of jokes from a hostile viewpoint. On this last basis particularly, the southwesterners may be distinguished from the northeasterners in their interests. Even some of the most popular writers, like Frederick S. Cozzens, author of *The Sparrowgrass Papers* (1856), may be distinguished as writing a species of domestic comedy that contributes little to the tradition of political-social comment characteristic of the more important literary humorists of the urban Northeast.

Many of these literary humorists are virtually unknown today, but they form a body of authors writing in a sociopolitical and moral idiom that gives their work the compactness of a school. Some of the authors—Artemus Ward, Josh Billings, Petroleum V. Nasby, and Orpheus C. Kerr, for example—are fortunate in having at least brief samples of their writings reprinted in anthologies. Such is not the fate of Joseph C. Neal, William Cox, James K. Paulding, "Truman Trumbull" (E. J. Gay, whose identity is established by a scant four index cards in the Library of Congress), John W. DeForest, and Marietta Holley. Also, the domestic humorists do not raise social and political questions with the same intensity; where Cozzens and the Danbury News Man (James M. Bailey), and even Eugene Field in Chicago use the same or similar comic items and constructions, they blur the sharp social and political vision evident in the writers chosen for this anthology. Robert J. Burdette was the most heavily represented comic writer in *Mark Twain's Library of Humor* (1888) with the exception of Twain himself, and Thomas Bailey Aldrich's "Ballad of Baby Bell" was one of the most beloved seriocomic pieces of both the New York Bohemians and the western literati for its overblown rhetoric. Yet neither Burdette nor Aldrich seems to have contributed new idioms, ideas, or images, and so they are not presented as central to the school of northeastern humorists, though they would, of course, appear in a more encyclopedic anthology. Here, I have limited the selections to those that clearly show a tradition divergent from the southwestern school, the humorists of which have been so much studied in the past few decades.

The literary comedians also present a special problem. Ward, Nasby, and Kerr in the North, sharing characteristics with their opponent Bill Arp (Charles Henry Smith) in the South, created their most significant writings out of the materials of the Civil War. Artemus Ward's humanist perspective is important because much of his canon and much of his career as a humorous lecturer anticipates Mark Twain. Likewise, B. P. Shillaber of the (Boston) *Carpet-bag*, created an extensive canon and maintained an extensive network of literary contacts that make him more important to the history of American humor than he seems to have received credit for; a survey of the *Carpet-bag* reveals a significant train of social and literary burlesque that looks forward to the writings of Twain, Harte, and the literary comedians in the 1860s and 1870s. However, each of the authors represented by longer selections has contributed something unique and original in his handling of a given phenomenon of the changing Northeast. Selection has ultimately been based on the combination of literary quality, historical interest, and originality in the treatment of the subject. Nor is mere strangeness of subject the criterion for selection, but rather the ability to infuse the subject with significant social viewpoints—the hallmark of the school—that bear on the emerging life of the Northeast. The humor is not folk humor, with one or two possible exceptions. Even Seba Smith, who made his mark as Jack Downing of Portland, Maine, made his way from the backwoods to the literary center of New York, like Twain, as fast as his literary standing allowed. These humorous writings are consciously literary productions, not quasi-folk effusions from the backwoods, even at their most "down home" and folksy.

Even an attempt to fix the geography of the Northeast manufactures difficulties. George W. Kendall, a Vermonter, founded the New Orleans *Picayune*. Mason Locke Weems from the border state of Maryland and James K. Paulding of New York City lead off the selections in Cohen and Dillingham's valuable *Humor of the Old Southwest* (1964) because of their use of southwestern subject matter.[17] Bill Nye headed east as soon as his career permitted, although Mr. Dooley, along with Eugene Field and George Ade, is obviously excluded on the basis of his midwestern location. Mark Twain might also be excluded on the same ground, and yet Twain was clearly immersed in northern literary comedy from his earliest reading. His first publication was in B. P. Shillaber's *Carpet-bag* in 1852, and his literary publications provided him with the money and connections to move to Buffalo and to Hartford and from there to Europe, dividing his time among those centers of civilization for the rest of his life.

Philosophical traits, such as W. D. Howells' allegiance to Boston and the *Atlantic Monthly*, really bind Twain to the humorists of the Northeast. Twain is allied with the Northeast in his consistent fund of political and moral language, his use of urban and vulgar language blending up to the colloquial and informal in much of his own writing in persona, and his explicit defense of the rights of man in the context

17. Hennig Cohen and W. B. Dillingham (eds.), *Humor of the Old Southwest* (Boston, 1964).

of the American vision and its ramifications for the world community. For these reasons, Twain is the apotheosis of the northeastern consciousness of the "Universal Yankee Nation" as it infused the self-concept of those whom Walt Whitman called "Americans of all nations." The relatively early pieces presented here are intended to illustrate his relationship without suggesting that Hannibal, Missouri, is just to the west of Portland, Maine, even though they may be closer in literary geography than they appear on the map. St. Louis, as written about by Mark Twain, has certainly joined urban America, leaving the primitive frontier irretrievably behind.

Representative Authors

As already suggested, the rise of the urban Northeast prior to the Civil War established a new and largely unrecognized comic literary terrain. Much of the terrain was imaginary, that is, literary rather than natural, giving credence to the greatest boast of the northern humorists as it appeared in a statement by Artemus Ward that he was in favor of the Union as it was, and if he couldn't have that, he was in favor of the Union as it wasn't. The important territory was defined by its orientation toward individual ethics as a social problem. Naturally, the best writers in the emerging tradition were individualistic, fiercely democratic and romantic in philosophy—although they would have claimed the contrary—and aware of corporate government and a new urban industrial world. Romantic egalitarianism brought forth comic works that were far more varied than the vernacular humor of the Old Southwest, focused on the plantation and the bear hunt.

Growing towns and cities created previously unknown characters and situations. Jeffersonian assumptions about an educated independent yeomanry underpinning American life were brought into question. Unlike the vernacular humorists of the Southwest, northern writers found a complicated world of business and government where problems of cash and confidence replaced the simple confrontation of the horse swap. In the 1830s Joseph C. Neal's "hard cases" rambled through the pages of Philadelphia's newspapers, dodging the threats of the "Charlies" on night watch, fleeing the Black Maria and the "humane" punishment of Moyomensing Prison—which still fascinated Theodore Dreiser in *The Financier* (1912)—and complaining of their defeats by the city's spoils system. James K. Paulding's Yankee trader traveled as far as the celestial empire to find himself bribing corrupt Chinese judges with ginseng root to escape trumped-up police charges. Wherever the omnibus replaced the blooded quarter horse as a symbol of civilization, new social types and new social relationships came to dominate the landscape. As cities replaced farms, and shop clerks replaced ploughboys, northern humorists grappled with the language and meaning of the changes.

Northern humorists depicted industrial changes—which might also mean social changes—with greater or lesser degrees of awareness. Lewis Gaylord Clark's "A Railroad 'Recussant'" complained that the railroad was able to take one man's upland and cart it into another man's "ma'sh" and sometimes to run over animals "a purpose" without paying for them, because it was a corporation. William Cox in "Steam" (1833), widely reprinted in his era, showed steam men and steam cars taking over a disappearing pastoral landscape, threatening widespread ugliness and death. P. T. Barnum's aggressive response to the transitions from village values to the cash nexus infuriated European critics. With bald-faced assurance, he propounded his enthusiasm for translating the Yankee swap into a commercial program directed at the new mass audience and its ready money; offering as his "sincere prayer" that "I may be reduced to beggary, rather than become a pampered purse-proud aristocrat. . . . I wish *them*, and all the world to know that my father was a *tailor*, and that I am 'a showman' by profession, and all *the gilding* shall make nothing else of me."[18] This democracy bordering on demagoguery, as Mark Twain showed in an 1867 burlesque, was used by Barnum as a license to bring forth fraudulent woolly horses, Washington's nursemaids, and a variety of other spurious attractions that appeared demeaning rather than elevating to aghast foreign critics. Barnum, with characteristic deadpan American affrontery, claimed that the license actually worked the other way around and that the fraudulent attraction was the precondition for real moral education, and Barnum's life gives more than passing support to his contention. In politics he demanded equal rights and education for the African-American as social justice required by the Constitution.

Embodying the democratic stance in a slightly more subtle persona,

---

18. Lewis Gaylord Clark, "A Railroad 'Recusant,' " reprinted in William E. Burton (ed.), *Burton's Cyclopedia of Wit and Humor* (New York, 1875), 359; Barnum, *Life of P. T. Barnum*, 274.

D. C. Johnston's rendition of Ripton Rumsey, calling out for galoshes in the gutter outside a Philadelphia barroom, helps capture Neal's new urban vision: "Every man for himself!"

Mortimer Thomson leaped to fame as Doesticks in the 1850s. His sketches were collected to fill two entire pages of the New York *Tribune* in 1854, and his comic verse and ironic reportage, controlled by his own "voice" represent an important first step toward Mark Twain. Thomson's comedy was also directed at the love of the almighty Yankee dollar in *Pluri-bus-tah* (1856), a verse satire on Longfellow's *Hiawatha* (1855), which portrayed Jupiter as a representative city merchant. But Thomson's moral outrage could outrage the North as well, as it did in the "Great Slave Auction of 1859" reported from Charleston, South Carolina. The *Tribune* issue that carried Thomson's report—a literarily lawless mixture of reportage, sarcasm, irony, melodrama, and sentiment combined with northern humanist idealism characteristic of the tradition—sold out and had to be reprinted in its entirety two days later. The article was printed almost verbatim in the London *Times* and as a tract and was reviewed favorably by the prestigious *Atlantic Monthly*. Such a work demonstrates the strength of the northern literary humorists in combining humor and social ethics in ways that many other localist writers did not attempt.[19]

The clearest sense of the literary innovations that the urban comedians of the Northeast brought about may be obtained by examining the relationships among works by Neal, Thomson, Ward, and Twain. Of the four, only Ward and Neal were raised in an urban environment as such, but all were raised in literary environments of one sort or another. Preeminently, Thomson, Ward, and Neal belong in a class with George H. Derby, to whom Twain often referred as a seminal American humorist. These were literary comedians of flashing colloquial wit, whose irony brought quick-won reputations, linked in each case to a tragically foreshortened career. Both Ward and Doesticks were members of the Bohemian brigade, which manned Pfaff's Cellar on Broadway. All four writers were professional newspapermen who wrote for city dailies at one time or another reporting local items and political news and accustomed to deadlines, white-collar responsibilities in business and social dealings, and the ethical codes of the American press. They are a different breed from many of the correspondents to William Trotter Porter's *Spirit of the Times*, who identified with "the gentlemen of standing, wealth, and intelligence—the very corinthian columns of the community," or were circuit-riding lawyers and doc-

---

19. *Atlantic Monthly*, IV (September, 1859), 386–7. See also David E. E. Sloane, "Mortimer Thomson," in Stanley Tractenberg (ed.), *American Humorists, 1800–1950* (Detroit, 1982), vol. XI of *Dictionary of Literary Biography*.

tors aspiring to that class.[20] Rather, these humorists identify with the young professional class of urban America, with no pretentions to Corinthian columnhood on the one hand or tolerance for the mobocracy at the other extreme.

Joseph C. Neal represents the type. His brief literary career was spent in Philadelphia editing the Democratic daily *Pennsylvanian* and later *Neal's Saturday Gazette*. His stories and sketches appeared in *Godey's*, *Spirit of the Times*, *Graham's*, *Knickerbocker*, and a host of other newspapers and journals through the then-universal "exchanges." In an age of political vituperation, Neal was distinguished for his mildness, courtesy, and urbanity. Yet Neal is unknown at the present time, and his name escapes indexing even in many basic studies of the field. Over a period of ten years, his light sketches of city down-and-outers from the Philadelphia police courts appeared in a number of books grouped together finally as three series of *Charcoal Sketches*, widely admired and imitated. The first series of *Charcoal Sketches* (1838) ran through more than half a dozen editions in two years. They were plagiarized without apology to fill one third of a volume compiled over Charles Dickens' name.[21] However, Neal's name appears penciled only as an afterthought down the side of a list in one of Mark Twain's notebooks on *Mark Twain's Library of Humor*.

Neal's is an urban world full of street slang and worthless "City Worthies," as he headed one set of the sketches in the newspapers. A master of the seemingly inept metaphor, Neal illuminated northern urban life with multiple dimensions that matched the glow over Arkansas created by the big bear. He reasons at one point with mock solemnity, "it therefore flows from this, as water from a hydrant," vulgarizing the tone of an elevated discussion. He adds a political dimension by his description of one character, "Young as he was, his talent for eating was aldermanic." Other imagery is also consistent with a world where, as Neal notes, a man who would in earlier days have been a flower of chivalry is in modern times only "a bird."[22]

20. Norris Yates, *William T. Porter and the "Spirit of the Times"* (Baton Rouge, 1957), 15.

21. *Dictionary of American Biography*, XIII, 399. See David E. E. Sloane, "Joseph C. Neal," in *American Humorists, 1800–1950*. Boz [pseud.] (ed.), *The Pic-nic Papers* (London, 1841), was compiled by Henry Colburn and published to fill out a series in benefit of a fellow printer; nineteen Neal sketches were included, the entire *Charcoal Sketches* as printed. Neal was widely known as the American Dickens, but without any financial advantages from such piratings.

22. Joseph C. Neal, *Charcoal Sketches* (Philadelphia, 1838), 117–18; Joseph C. Neal, *Peter Ploddy, and Other Oddities* (Philadelphia, 1844), 138.

"Orson Dabbs, the Hittite" is one of Neal's most dramatic sketches. In its closing scene, urban life and image are combined with the half-horse, half-alligator boasting associated primarily with the Mississippi backwoods. The dialogue takes place between Dabbs the city bully and the night watchman, an employee of the city corporation:

"Let go, watchy!—let go, my cauliflower! Your cocoa is very near a sledge-hammer. If it isn't hard, it may get cracked."

"Pooh! pooh! don't be onasy, my darlint—my cocoa is a corporation cocoa—it belongs to the city, and they'll get me a new one. Besides, my jewel, there's two cocoas standing here, you know. Don't be onasy—it mayn't be mine that will get cracked."

"I ain't onasy," said Dabbs, bitterly, as he turned fiercely around. "I ain't onasy. I only want to caution you, or I'll upset your apple cart, and spill your peaches."

"I'm not in the wegetable way, my own self, Mr. Horse-radish. You must make less noise."

"Now, look here—look at me well," said Dabbs, striking his fist hard upon his own bosom; "I'm a real nine foot breast of a fellow—stub twisted and made of horse-shoe nails—the rest of me is cast iron with steel springs. I'll stave my fist right through you, and carry you on my elbow, as easily as if you were an empty market basket—I will—bile me up for soap if I don't!"

"Ah, indeed! why, you must be a real Calcutta-from-Canting, warranted not to cut in the eye. Snakes is no touch to you; but I'm sorry to say you must knuckle down close. You must surrender; there's no help for it—none in the world."

"Square yourself then, for I'm coming! Don't you hear the clock-vorks!" exclaimed Dabbs, as he shook off the grip of the officer, and struck an attitude.

He stood beautifully; feet well set; guard well up; admirable science, yet fearful to look upon. Like the Adriatic, Dabbs was "lovelily dreadful" on this exciting occasion. But when "Greek meets Greek," fierce looks and appalling circumstances amount to nothing. The opponent of our hero, after regarding him coolly for a moment, whistled with great contempt, and with provoking composure, beat down his guard with a smart blow from a heavy mace, saying—

" 'Taint no use, no how—you're all used up for bait."

"Ouch!" shrieked Dabbs; "my eye, how it hurts! Don't hit me again. Ah, good man, but you're a bruiser. One, two, three, from you would make a person believe any thing, even if he was sure it wasn't true."

"Very well," remarked the *macerator*, "all I want of you is to behave nice and genteel, and believe you're going to the watch'us, for it's true;

and if you don't believe it yet, why (shaking his mace) I shall feel obligated to conwince you again."[23]

Characteristics of urban life add much to this scene. The watch is a municipal employee, not a ring-tailed roarer, and his function, which he carries out matter-of-factly and even somewhat ruthlessly, is to maintain order. Metaphors are drawn from the neighborhood marketplace, the small manufactory or smithy, and commercial enterprise. The raw power that dominates is not that of the cruel practical joke with its antagonistic motivation; instead, organized city life motivates a force of social intervention; elsewhere the same forces are brought to bear on husbands, political spoilsmen, drunks, poetasters—a wide spectrum of Philadelphia undercrust in the 1830s.

The world of social caste and class is ambiguous in northern humor, where lawful intervention becomes a lively component in the social environment. Sometimes the reader gains this sense through the author's choice of irony or burlesque as his dominant literary format. Elsewhere, however, the changing sense of relationship is overt, as it is in another Neal sketch. Neal's experienced Yankee character advises a passive "Shiverton Shakes" that there are two sets of principles—one to preach and one to practice—and Shakes has got hold of the wrong set, the set invented by "the knowing ones" to check the competition: "Other people is a goose." Timothy Dexter, the shoemaker turned financier, could well have understood this concept, close as it is to the focus of his criticism in *A Pickle for the Knowing Ones*. Assessing a southwestern sketch in Porter's *Spirit of the Times*, Norris Yates comments that its political antibank implications are a bit unusual. The opposite applies for northern urban humor, as in Neal's "The Black Maria." Where Nathaniel Hawthorne might have elevated a natural New England setting to the sublime, Neal's tendency is to draw morals within the context of urban crime. An ex-driver of the Black Maria, "vehicular outcast, hated but yet feared—grand, gloomy, and peculiar," finds himself musing on his riders, "People that are cotch'd, has to ketch it, of course, or else how could the 'fishal folks—me and the judges and the lawyers—yes, and the chaps that make the laws and sell the lawbooks make out to get a living? . . . Being cotch'd makes no great difference, only in the looks of things." Although Jesse Bier has proposed in *The Rise and Fall of American Humor* that the Civil War was instrumental in increasing pessimism in American humor, this

23. Neal, *Charcoal Sketches*, 36–7.

piece, which dates to the 1840s, is by no means the earliest example in its genre. A much earlier analog has already been cited, the "Speech of David Wood" from *The Spirit of the Farmer's Museum*. Neal's piece and the earlier one were virtually recapitulated in Artemus Ward's "Soliloquy of a Low Thief" in the late 1850s. As I suggested earlier, the sentiment is appropriate to any milieu where complex business and commercial interactions invite ethical consideration. It becomes peculiarly American in its emphasis on the disgruntlement of the common man at his exclusion from the privileges of organized society—a burlesque of egalitarian boastfulness.[24] Neal's choice of urban characters and dialect to dramatize these issues sets him apart both from humorists of the Southwest and from the moralists of his day, such as Martin Tupper, Fanny Fern, and his own wife-to-be "Cousin Alice," and makes him of interest in studying the development of comic realism in the Northeast.

Mortimer Thomson, writing as Doesticks, was a dominant figure in American humor from 1854 through 1859, along with John Phoenix and, later, Artemus Ward. Thomson advanced the urban hardcase of Neal by uniting the down-and-outer sentiments with a modestly cultivated colloquial persona that could be at home either in prose or verse, as authorial persona or as omniscient voice. In addition, Thomson was talented in creating burlesque incidents, including his characterizations within a dramatic format, and his sketches therefore have a narrative quality. He managed to merge reportorial duties with comic matter in items for the New York *Tribune*, the short-lived New York *Picayune*, which he edited with William H. Levison for a brief period, and Street and Smith's *New York Weekly*, as well as in a series of comic books extracted from his writing. Thomson's canon is more accurately described as hors d'oeuvre than oeuvre, but his socioallegorical poems *Pluri-bus-tah* and *Nothing to Wear* are notable achieve-

---

24. Neal, *Peter Ploddy*, 114; Yates, *Porter and the "Spirit of the Times,"* 146; Neal, *Peter Ploddy*, 36; "Speech of David Wood," 204–206; [Browne], *Complete Works*, 150. Egalitarianism, treated here as "American," is notably close to the emphasis on the common man and his virtues as expressed in English romanticism from its roots in Goldsmith's "The Deserted Village" and Wordsworth's poems. Dickensian social outrage undoubtedly owes much to this source, and American comic editors and authors were outspoken in their enthusiasm for the poetry of Thomas Hood, particularly his "Song of the Shirt" (reprinted in *Punch* in 1843 after appearing in the *Times*), which displayed in pathetic terms the unhappy plight of the economically depressed seamstresses, creating a demand for reform in their working situation. "Americanism" in social terms, both in its political views and in its "naturalism" has obvious debts to British sources, including Hood, Goldsmith, Barry Cornwall, and others.

ments in American literature in their uniting of literary burlesque, urban slang, and urban imagery with his social and ethical viewpoint.

As a spokesman for the "American" viewpoint of the Northeast, Thomson anticipates the traveler's irony of other American humorists after the Civil War, including Mark Twain, Marietta Holley, and others, even in his lighter pieces such as his most widely famed piece on Niagara Falls. "Niagara; or, Doesticks on a Bender" (1854) predates Mark Twain's "Niagara" by fifteen years. Where Twain cast the experience as a quest for a real Indian souvenir, leading to burlesque violence, Doesticks translates the experience into a vulgarization of "that great aqueous brag of universal Yankeedom." Doesticks reports that he "didn't feel sublime any; tried to, but couldn't; took some beer, and tried again." He keeps taking beer until he is completely drunk, his response to the cupidity of the guides and souvenir sellers. After spending the night in jail, he declares in his own burlesque elevated tone, "Niagara, non est excelsus (ego fui) humbug est! indignus admirationi." Twain's response was similar but was manifested in even more outrageously dramatic action by the narrator's being thrown over the falls by Irish Indians and finally arrested for disturbing the peace with his drowning yells for help. Thomson introduces the traveling naïf of Ward and Twain and, by showing the narrator drunk, establishes a contrast between his "low," or realistic, character and the "ideal," particularly as suggested in his overt references to the genteel "sublimity" that he could not conjure up. The Bohemian reporter thus takes his place as a provisional spokesman for the rising lower middle class, his viewpoint compatible with Twain's slightly more serious comic heroes to come in the novels following the Civil War.[25]

Pluri-bus-tah was published by Thomson in 1856, a burlesque without intended malice toward an author already distinguished as a national landmark, Henry Wadsworth Longfellow, whose *Hiawatha* (1855) provided the poem's motive, motif, and form. *Hiawatha*'s abrupt quasi-mystical trochees produce grotesque comedy when translated from forest imagery comparable to the Finnish epic *Kalevala*, Longfellow's inspiration, to details of lower-caste city neighborhood life. So in the invocation Jupiter is banished to the woodshed, sitting

25. [Mortimer Thomson], *Doesticks, What He Says* (New York, 1855), 27–32, as compared to Samuel L. Clemens [Mark Twain], *Sketches, New and Old* (New York, 1917), 58–67. For more on the relationship between the naïve characters in Artemus Ward and Mark Twain, see David E. E. Sloane, *Mark Twain as a Literary Comedian* (Baton Rouge, 1978).

on the slop pail with legs crossed like Mrs. Bloomer, smoking like the locomotive that deadhead railroad ticket-holders ride to Republican conventions.[26] Even Hiawatha himself, a literary fiction, becomes a character in Doesticks' invocation and takes on the characteristics of a modern politician—as all of the characters, including gods and goddesses, are made into contemporary city types. The literary comedian transforms the ideal into political irony. Jupiter's vulgarization is socialized and politicized by reference to Mrs. Bloomer, and he undergoes further de-idealization as he rises from his slop pail to embrace the approaching "Yankee Goddess America," in the back alley, "trembling lest his wife should see" as she sits in the parlor with her hair in curl papers. The combination of politics, low-class experience, *belles lettres*, and burlesque drama characterizes this as northern urban literary humor. The readiness to translate fictional idealizations from literature into a comic literary work is the hallmark of the northeastern comic tradition and the source of its intellectualism.

Every detail of city life figures in the verse drama and, advancing beyond Neal's use of the unflattering metaphor by itself, contributes to the development of the poem toward a political statement about human rights. At one point, even Barnum's fraudulent Feejee mermaid is described, a symbol of common chicanery in New York City where the children who come to see it "put their skeptic fingers / on their unbelieving noses." Pluri-bus-tah, the Yankee Puritan founding father, takes as his god the "Potent and Almighty Dollar" but places Liberty's picture on the national coinage, as if photographed full-length by Brady, "So that when he kissed his idol, / Liberty felt complimented," though he would have hugged the "Dirty, filthy, greasy, DOLLAR" just as closely "had the female image on it / Been a dog, or been a jackass." Pluri-bus-tah and Liberty are doomed to part, however, over the issue of Negro slavery, as Pluri-bus-tah explains himself to Cuffee in a dramatic monologue that might well be compared to the more belletristic comic dramatic lyrics of Robert Browning:

> "I am white, and I am stronger,
> You are black, and you are weaker,
> And, beside, you have no business,
> And no right to be a nigger."

26. [Mortimer Thomson], *Pluri-bus-tah* (New York, 1856), 30–31. The "Invocation" is reprinted herein.

As much as the tall tale may be claimed to be the mode of the Southwest, the ironic inquiry into the disparity between commercialism and political morality belongs to the Northeast, and Thomson's *Pluri-bus-tah*, before the Civil War, finds both imagery and subject matter in related sociopolitical events. The persistent vulgarization of issues of principle, as a mode of transforming them into imaginative literature and translating their emotional components into dramatic action, is undoubtedly the reason that the Scottish critic John Nichol complained in the 1880s that American humor was so determined not to walk in the footsteps of the British that it went on all fours.[27]

Artemus Ward further condensed Doesticks' urban setting and literary burlesque into his character's personal idiom. Thus, Artemus Ward, the old showman, became a vehicle for stating social ideas without himself depending on false-seeming idealistic abstractions. Ward as narrator is both involved in the action and detached from it. He can make dogmatic speeches, as his speech in defense of the Union against the Copperheads makes clear, but his interactions with others maintain at least a modest sense of dramatic involvement. Ward's "Interview with the Prince Napoleon" is, like most of his sketches, couched in terms of Yankee village mentality. Webster's mantle having fallen into the hands of a dealer in secondhand clothes, Ward himself puts on a clean boiled shirt and starts for Washington to meet "Prints Napoleon":

> "How's Lewis?" I axed, and he sed the Emperor was well. . . . Then I axed him was Lewis a good provider? did he come home arly nites? did he perfoom [Eugené's] bedroom at a onseasonable hour with gin and tanzy? did he go to "the Lodge" on nites when there wasn't any Lodge? . . ."
>
> "I ax these questions, my royal duke and most noble higness and imperials, becaws I'm anxious to know how he stands as a man. I know he's smart. . . . But unless he is *good* he'll come down with a crash one of these days, and the Bonyparts will be Bustid up agin. Bet yer life!"[28]

Ward is a spokesman and actor of American ideals, but he is vulgar in voice and action, like Thomson and Neal, aware of the barroom and bedroom, and like Thomson, speaking in his own voice at that level. He proceeds from the interview to a political ball where he sees the daughter of the corner grocer putting on airs as a "Congressor's wife" and embar-

---

27. [Thomson], *Pluri-bus-tah*, 88–89, 120–21, 128; John Nichol, *American Literature: An Historical Sketch, 1620–1880* (Edinburgh, 1882), 412.
28. [Browne], *Complete Works*, 131.

rasses her for pretending to ignore him. As Ward's intrusively "low demo-crat" personality engulfs national phenomena like the Mormons and the Civil War and international ones like Napoleon, Prince Albert, London, and British history and dignity, American positions are maintained within the selection of idioms and the very vulgarity of attitude that angered crit-ics of literary comedy throughout this period. Yet the pragmatic dignity of the showman's politics is maintained, and his choice of words and images, even in burlesques, approaches universals.

Charles G. Leland amalgamated Charles F. Browne's idealism with his own mild hedonism to create a comparable type in the German immi-grant Hans Breitmann. Leland's first Breitmann ballad appeared in *Graham's Magazine* in 1856, rhymed but set as prose rather than poetry. Leland had already written an Irvingesque metaphysical comedy *Meister Karl's Sketchbook* (1855) without particular success. The Breitmann ballads, however, written in Low Dutch patois, attracted attention as a unique American "macaronic" verse. Leland's German "bummer" was a quasi-mystical beer-drinking refugee from the European revolutions of 1848, materialistic and sentimental. His fictional travels in America took him to Kansas, to the Civil War to find a lost son and lose a best friend in an embattled wood, and into post–Civil War city politics in Philadelphia, approximating Leland's own experiences in many ways and certainly in-culcating his virulent humanism. Leland's most violent statements, how-ever, came in direct opposition to slavery before and during the Civil War. He advocated abolition and, later, emancipation as a war measure and also suggested in one acrid essay that South Carolina be made a black state, anticipating William Melvin Kelley's *A Different Drummer* by a hundred years. All the language conventions opened up by northern ur-ban writers can be found employed for compatible idealistic ends in Le-land's writing, and had he accepted his own figure Breitmann more fully and developed broader capabilities for him, his own reputation would now be higher than it is. Leland scattered his attention between comic Chinese dialect poems, researches into Gypsy language, for which he was internationally acclaimed; work on arts and handcrafts, on which he pub-lished several books; and translations of Heine. In a late volume, *Songs of the Sea and Lays of the Land*, he attempted to return to comic socio-political commentary in verse with modest success, updating the concerns of the late 1860s in fluent colloquial language and placing a few socio-political incidents in comic verse form.

The Aftermath of the War against Slavery

The Civil War cost many of the northern humorists their ability to attack inconsistencies in the national ethos as Doesticks had done in *Pluri-bus-tah*. Physically, many of them were removed from the scene, of course. Joseph C. Neal had died in 1847 at the age of forty. George H. Derby (John Phoenix), associated with the West but born in Dedham, Massachusetts, in 1823, was dead in 1861, leaving behind only *Phoenixiana* (1856) and *The Squibob Papers* (1865). Artemus Ward, just beginning to ripen into a historical visionary, died in 1867 at the age of thirty-four. Charles Graham Halpine (Miles O'Reilly) died shortly after the war, and Doesticks, having lost two wives in the early 1860s in childbed and having been wounded as a noncombatant reporter in war action, seems to have become addicted to opium and alcohol, which he used in an attempt to kill his pain. Mark Twain recorded his admiration for the graceless, petrified power of the alcoholic Nasby's "Cussed be Canaan" lecture four years after the war. It was, he said, composed of "bull's-eye hits, with the slave power and its Northern apologists for target, and his success was due to his matter, not his manner; for his delivery was destitute of art." But Nasby wrote to Twain in July, 1869, that "that lemon, our African brother, juicy as he was in his day, has been squeezed dry. Why howl about his wrongs after said wrongs have been redressed?"[29] B. P. Shillaber's health had been in decline since the 1850s, although the creator of Mrs. Partington worked goutily on at his editing tasks into the 1890s. Cozzens died at his desk one evening in 1869, aged fifty-one.

Only Mark Twain, among all the comedians, transformed the emotional capital of pre–Civil War abolition and early Madisonian federalism into general indictments of inhumanity to man. To do this, he found it necessary to drop back into medieval or local color settings such as those seen in his major novels. Aside from *The Gilded Age* (1873) and *The American Claimant* (1892), only his short stories maintained a contemporary milieu. The items included here show

29. Albert B. Paine (ed.), *Autobiography of Mark Twain* (3 vols.; New York, 1924), I, 147–50. Petroleum V. Nasby to Mark Twain, July 14, 1869, quoted courtesy of Mark Twain Papers, the Bancroft Library, University of California, Berkeley. Nasby noted that the Fifteenth Amendment had busted "Cussed be Canaan" as a lecture. He asked Twain rhetorically why he should screech against the "damnable spirit of cahst [*sic*]" when the victims sit at the first table; when it was a living issue, Nasby went on, he howled feelingly and "felt all that I said and a great deal more. . . . The Reliable Contraband . . . is contraband no more, but a citizen of the United States and I speak of him no more."

Twain at his most adept in transforming social attitudes—such as distrust of corporations and of strident sociopolitical movements, as the women's suffrage movement then seemed to him—into dramatic literature. "Cannibalism in the Cars" is a uniquely Twainian burlesque fiction. It toys with reversals of natural idealism and sublimity and with political idealism and rhetoric, without reference to an overt political event, showing how close seemingly localized items are to the broadest concerns of literary humorists. Even in a variety of ephemera, his attacks on sham moralism elevated him to an international spokesman almost as surely as his major works.

Mark Twain's special power as a fiction writer comes from his ability to invest the techniques of earlier urban humorists in plots that go even further than "Cannibalism in the Cars" in melodramatizing choices between good and evil, between self-interested greed and generous humanity. Twain knew the precedents, and he was far more comprehensive in his knowledge of previous comic writers than has yet been fully documented. All of the humorists mentioned above appear in his notebooks, and he corresponded with Doesticks, Ward, Nasby, and others.[30] Their methods, and the philosophies underlying them, color his works. The picture of corrupted Washington, D.C., in *The Gilded Age* leans heavily on urban details for its irony. Language is exaggerated rather than vulgarized, broadening Twain's power beyond earlier writers as he describes frescoes in the capitol as "the delirium tremens of art" and notes of a statue of Lincoln contemplating an emancipation proclamation that looks like a soiled napkin "that he is finding fault with the washing." Of the unfinished Washington Monument, he wrote, "Still in the distance, but on this side of the water and close to its edge, the monument to the Father of his Country towers out of the mud—sacred soil is the customary term. It has the aspect of a factory chimney with the top broken off. The skeleton of a decaying scaffolding lingers about its summit, and tradition says that the spirit of Washington often comes down and sits on those rafters to enjoy this tribute of respect which the nation has reared as the symbol of its unappeasable gratitude."[31] This narrative voice is much like Doesticks'. Political

---

30. Letters from Ward are reprinted in Albert B. Paine (ed.), *Mark Twain's Letters* (New York, 1917), with some silent bowdlerizations. Doesticks' letters appear in Fred W. Lorch, " 'Doesticks' and *The Innocents Abroad*," *American Literature*, XX (January, 1949), 446–49.

31. Samuel L. Clemens [Mark Twain], *The Gilded Age* (2 vols.; New York, 1915), I, 236–37.

spirits—Washington, Lincoln—are as compromised by tawdry dis-respect as Jupiter and Pluri-bus-tah. As literary comic figures, they even become active, like Hiawatha and his deadhead Indians. One significant alteration in mode is that the narrative voice is not vulgarized, as with Ward or the inebriated Doesticks, but frigidly recites the highest of sublime language against the degraded reality. Twain's power as a social satirist derives from this advance in method, and his burlesques clearly anticipate this development. The rebuttal to Captain Duncan from the New York *World* of 1877 demonstrates how fully Twain had assimilated this methodology into his public voice. His particularization of detail is consistent with the earlier comedians, even in the purposefully maladroit metaphors of Lincoln's napkin and the broken-off factory chimney monument.

The outcome of this development—the highest form to which the tradition might aspire—appears in Twain's investment of the tendencies of northern urban comedy in a figure like Pap Finn in *Adventures of Huckleberry Finn*. Chapter VI of *Huck Finn* centers on Pap Finn's "Call this a govment" speech, and shows how much Twain's writing included elements employed by earlier comedians. The previous chapter treats Pap as an unreformable hardcase who pledges change and nevertheless goes on a bender and destroys the guest room of the town judge. The point of the depiction is not that Pap is a shrewdly conniving Simon Suggs but rather that he is controlled by his own petty vices, and his ability to delude others scarcely benefits himself in any significant way. Huck, on the other hand, has already been seen treating Tom Sawyer's make-believe with scepticism but taking Jim, the slave, rather seriously. Thus, two dramatic figures are ready to come into collision with independent characters established. When Pap kidnaps Huck, he advances the action as plot by bringing his motives and Huck's into a larger setting than their first conflict in Huck's bedroom. Instead of remaining a comic type, Pap takes on increasing seriousness as a character by changing Huck's life, threatening and beating him, and promising to take him farther away to a cabin more remote from town and "stow" him there. Pap manifests aspects of Neal's petty lowlifes and Huck represents the reporter pragmatist. They have opposing objectives, elevated by Twain to the level of continuing plot action—one wants personal freedom, the other wants selfish profit.

When Pap returns to the cabin to deliver his speech, he is Adamic man, "just all mud." In going for the government, Pap introduces social and political overtones into his personal business. "Call this a gov-

ment! why, just look at it and see what it's like. Here's the law a-
standing ready to take a man's son away from him—a man's own son,
which he has had all the trouble and all the anxiety and all the expense
of raising." Note the language of the middle class, including ideas like
anxiety and expense. Pap, continuing, raises a social issue.

> There was a free nigger there from Ohio. . . . He had the whitest shirt
> on you ever see, too, and the shiniest hat [Pap's disreputable hat has just
> been described in detail, creating a dramatic opposition]; and there ain't
> a man in that town that's got as fine clothes as what he had; . . . They
> said he was a p'fessor in a college, and could talk all kinds of languages,
> and knowed everything. . . . It was 'lection day, and I was just about to
> go and vote myself if I warn't too drunk to get there; but when they told
> me there was a state in this country where they'd let that nigger vote, I
> drawed out. . . . I says to the people, why ain't this nigger put up at
> auction and sold?

Even in an isolated cabin three miles out of town in backwoods Mississippi, Twain magnifies Pap's malice by uniting it with politics and
slavery. The reader of Pap's speech responds with the same feeling that
was captured in a story in *The American Joe Miller*, which has an angry squire responding to a wife beater who talks about "getting justice" by insisting that the wife beater cannot get justice here "because
we can't hang you."[32] For Pap, Twain provides immediate burlesque
retribution when Pap kicks the tub and in his pain outswears old Sow-
berry Hagen. Most important, however, is the subordination of the elements of literary comedy to Pap's personality as a whole and to his
violence, which is portrayed much as Neal depicts Orson Dabbs. This
violence continues throughout the chapter and provides Huck with an
even more powerful motivation simply to preserve his life in the face
of Pap's successful defiance of "the law." The political and social implications invested in Pap as a character are subordinated to the paramount action of Huck's search for safety and freedom. Thus, comic
characteristics, rather than being left in isolated short sketches, are integrated into the fabric of the novel.

Throughout the newspapers and periodicals of the North after the
Civil War, bitter article follows bitter article about the boondoggles
and botched campaigns. Failure to follow and destroy retreating Con-
federates was a particularly sore topic among critics of the Union gen-

---

32. Samuel L. Clemens [Mark Twain], *Adventures of Huckleberry Finn* (New York,
1912), 25–41. Kempt (comp.), *The American Joe Miller*, 141.

erals. The horrors of the prison camp also appear as a red thread through retrospectives on the nature of the conflict, and comics like amputee veteran A. F. Hill, who dedicated his anecdotal biography *John Smith's Funny Adventures on a Crutch* (1869) to Artemus Ward, are by no means representative of the undercurrent of anger in northerners' discussions of the battles of the Civil War. Southern poetry about the war is also harsh, but Rollin Osterweis' brilliant examination of *The Myth of the Lost Cause* indicates the extent to which the South philosophically reorganized itself, retreating into moonlight-and-magnolia local color at the very time when the North found itself morally directionless, in the grip of far vaster industrial changes than were dreamed in 1859. Osterweis concludes that the South consciously set out to win the war of ideas, and did so partly through the pages of northern magazines like *Century* and *Lippincott's*, who fell prey to "Southron" Romanticism and the political strategy lying behind it because of their hope of binding the nation's wounds. *Samantha on the Race Problem* (1892) makes stunningly clear, as had DeForest in "The Colored Member" and Albion Tourgee in several lengthy works, what political and social chaos remained after the North capitulated to the southern myth.[33]

The intensity of the emotional demands levied on the North by the Civil War is obvious in Leland's "Bone Ornaments," but it is only in *The New Yankee Doodle* (1868), that the insupportable residual anger burst through the detail of Truman Trumbull's American Aeneid. The song "Yankee Doodle" was pulled toward both sides. A Confederate Yankee Doodle chanted:

> Yankee Doodle said he found
> By all the census figures,
> That he could starve the rebels out,
> If he could steal their niggers.
> Yankee Doodle, doodle doo,
> Yankee Doodle dandy,
> And then he took another drink
> of gunpowder and brandy."[34]

To this, and to the optimism of the historical verse, some answer had to be made. And for E. Jane Gay (Trumbull), the Yankee Doodle for-

33. Rollin G. Osterweis, *The Myth of the Lost Cause, 1865–1900* (Hamden, Conn., 1973); Marietta Holley [Josiah Allen's Wife], *Samantha on the Race Problem* (New York, 1892).

34. "Another Yankee Doodle" in *War Songs of the Blue and Gray*, 66–67.

mat provided an ironic straightjacket for a combination chronicle, history, burlesque, and humanist statement. The agony over the prison camps is strongly expressed, and the portrayal of the conflicting demands on Lincoln as war leader, father of his country, and hero-statesman complements the detailed treatment of southern leaders and daily events. Mundane irony comparable to that employed by Neal and Doesticks is joined with the harshest expressions of political advocacy and outrage. Gay's 341-page epic poem expresses the horror of the North toward the Civil War. The sense of harshness, anger, frustration, and futility in the jerky verse paragraphs with their abrupt "sir" endings is captured by the forced verse contract, a reflected awkwardness that is lost in more polished poems, such as the generally recognized epic treatment *John Brown's Body* by Stephen Vincent Benet. Acrimonious arguments over the mistakes and incapacities of northern leaders may account for Gay's failure to identify herself with her work, but the difficulty of the subject for northern writers seems clear. By 1868, the North had lost Lincoln and was encountering intense resistance to Radical Reconstruction. Northerners had a sense of bankruptcy for a workable solution to the human problems posed by southern politics, and to escape the pain, they retreated into histories—Nicolay and Hay's fifteen volumes on Lincoln, Grant's autobiography as published by Twain's company—and to ephemera such as Doesticks' description of the operation without anesthetic on his war wound or M. Quad's of spying across the lines.[35]

Conclusions

The failure to understand the tradition of comic political criticism, the northern literary idealism, of works like *Pluri-bus-tah* and *The New*

---

35. John G. Nicolay and John Hay, *Abraham Lincoln: A History* (15 vols.; New York, 1890), was serialized in the *Century* between November, 1886, and February, 1890. Grant's *Personal Memoirs of U. S. Grant* (2 vols.; New York, 1885–86) was published by the Charles L. Webster Co. Mortimer Thomson, "Twenty Minutes Under the Knife," *Hours at Home*, X (December, 1869), 118–22, a previously unknown fugitive piece, describes Doesticks' undiagnosed injury, course of suffering, and final operation in graphic detail. M. Quad—"of the Michigan Press," not a northeasterner—offered a story that closely follows the concluding action of *Huck Finn* published a decade later, with a series of spying adventures, narrow escapes, and a black rowing the hero to safety after he is grazed by a shot. M. Quad [pseud.], "Beyond the Picket Lines; or, The Army Reminiscences of Captain Jack," *Ballou's Monthly Magazine*, XXXIX (March, 1874), 260–71.

Yankee Doodle is a remarkable oversight in the study of American literature and American cultural history. Perhaps the problem lies in the dispersion of regional elements in post–Civil War short fiction and humor. Nor does northeastern writing after the Civil War seem to have reclaimed a rationale, as writers from other sections—Robert Burdette of the Burlington, Iowa, *Hawkeye*; "Bitter" Bierce in San Francisco; Bill Nye from Laramie, Wyoming; Mr. Dooley in Chicago—rose to national prominence. The curdled fables of David Ross Locke's *Morals of Abou Ben Adhem* (1875) were hardly the stuff of a renewed vision. Will Carleton made his way from Michigan to New York City with some of the traditional views intact, but his verse, even substituting *City Ballads* (1882) for *Farm Ballads* (1873), was too sentimentalized for Howells to stomach in the *Atlantic*. Only Twain, firmly seated among the Nook Farm bluestockings, translated the tradition of northern literary comedy as a medium of social vision into major fiction.

John W. DeForest and Marietta Holley, in addition to Twain, command attention among the significant northern writers of the post–Civil War era. Both attempted to master colloquial idiom and write from relatively vulgar viewpoints, DeForest from the smoke-filled hotel hallways of New Haven and Washington, D.C., and Holley from the country kitchen of the crackerbox mystic "Josiah Allen's Wife" Samantha. "Jenette Finster's Story" from *Samantha Among the Brethren* (1890) is superficially comparable to Seba Smith's "The Pumpkin Freshet," itself thrown back in time sixty years. Jenette affirms old-fashioned values of loyalty, submission, and love in an environment of cynical self-seeking and disrupted religious beliefs. Jenette is conservative and "Victorian" in her acceptance of woman's position. She makes Joe, who is at least partly a boob, her prize and therefore calls into question her real independence as a person. Thus Holley, ironically but possibly unconsciously, challenges the values she seems to endorse. Much of Holley's argument over equal rights is explicit, but her plot does not support her politics. Perversely independent in her mystical Christianity, reclusiveness, and even the mechanics of collecting literary material, Holley retained no audience when the first scatter shots were fired in the twentieth-century revolt from the village. For both Holley and Smith, personal and family virtues are paramount, but for Holley, who had been a prosuffrage writer almost from her first major publication in 1873, the absence of an urban scene diminishes the force of her message. Her writings may not be urbanized enough, although Samantha in *My Opinions and Betsey Bobbet's* (1873) took to the rails, met President Grant, and lectured Victoria Woodhull on morality in the shadow of the Astor House in New York City. There are also moments in the analysis of Jenette's character when Holley edges, under cover of her countrified dialect, toward the psychological novel. Stressing works as the way to salvation, Samantha's own resolute mysticism about death has at least a minute trace of the later, darker Twain. *Samantha on the Race Problem* (1892), which followed shortly after Holley's inquiry into religion and personal happiness in *Among the Brethren*, is a didactic harangue set in fictional form, most interesting in validating Osterweis' perceptions of the victory of the myth of the lost cause; it also suffers from the lack of a "modern" setting despite its bold attacks on racism.

The literary humorists of the Northeast saw conflicts in terms of individual decency versus an established set of villains—Yankee sharpers, railroad companies, or any almighty company of mean men. Sometimes the villain is even a hero-villain like P. T. Barnum, the world-acknowledged master of fraud who was nonetheless praised in many newspapers. He was a darling of the temperance movement and a firm believer in education of the masses, and he supported the education of blacks and similar social improvements throughout his political career. His program was consistent with that of W. E. B. DuBois, fifty years later.[36] Barnum and Holley agree on issues relating to the Negro. Dichotomies simplify social relations, and for this same reason, Jonathan cheats the celestials and is cheated in return, and the Monopoly and the People's Line are locked in combat. But the thoughtful reader will see in these stories the richer underlayer of complexity—the demand for social justice that complements the needs of the individual. Black men, Chinamen, women, Dutchmen are all on the same footing in this canon. And this seems true despite the occurrence of jarring ethnic or sex-oriented slurs in passing remarks here and there in some of the writers and epidemically in some joke books. Most of these writers believe that man is perfectible, and Mark Twain's despair orig-

---

36. An editorial in the New York *Tribune* (July 14, 1865) on the burning of Barnum's museum, reprinted by Barnum in his *Life of P. T. Barnum*, 244–45, pointed up the paradox of delivering instruction and entertainment to the lower classes and praises Barnum for doing it. See also Neal Harris, *Humbug: The Life of P. T. Barnum* (Boston, 1973). Du Bois' program for Negro education is found in W. E. B. Du Bois, *The Education of Black People*, ed. Herbert Aptheker (Amherst, 1973).

inates in his suppressed Swiftian conviction that they are not, despite his own passionate intellectual adherence to the federalist credo that checks, balances, and ordered political relationships could improve the social welfare of man. The revolt-from-the-village school of writers who achieved prominence in the teens of the following century inculcated this pessimism in the details of the village life accepted so easily by Marietta Holley and romanticized by Twain's tendency to drop into the small-town past of the 1840s for his settings. The modern era, in the person of thinkers like Buckminster Fuller and B. F. Skinner, has abandoned the concept of organized political perfectibility in favor of social engineering—the belief that physical changes in the environment bring about changes in behavior. It is not clear that northern urban writers had a social program that could operate within such a conception of the universe, aside from their specific belief in the importance of education. They wrote from their belief in education and a much more universal belief in the rights and dignity of man.

The question is moot whether humor is the bared fangs of the human race as Thomas Hobbes suggests, the ridiculing leer at the mechanical figure slipping on a banana peel as Henri Bergson suggests, or a social corrective of a lofty sort as perceived by George Meredith. For the American literary humorists of the Northeast, humor serves all of these functions, frequently in the same comic item—which accounts for the English perception of our humor as "lawless extravagance." And it serves yet another function, for it also expresses social idealism and social innocence. The laughter of the northeastern American humorists is psychologically adolescent in a crucial sense. The Deacon who relined his stove with his wife's tombstone; P. T. Barnum, the self-proclaimed master of humbug; and the Mark Twain hero are allied in their egregious and flamboyant revelation of personal constraints and idiosyncrasies. They are masters of the easily discovered secret act; Doesticks drunk in his comic travels and Twain's vandal abroad are drawn on the same model, and a duped farmer who leaps into the air at the supposed moment of revelation, chanting comic verse, as does Jenette Finster's Joe, cannot be far behind. Their real assertion is that innocence is equivalent to harmlessness, one of the longest lasting and most heavily loaded American myths. Barnum's public accepted the Feejee Mermaid, and Marietta Holley never encountered strictures for her writing of travel books without traveling, certainly no more than Paulding was criticized for his blending of American attitudes and

Chinese customs. In fact, it has been suggested that Americans bought Henry Ward Beecher's Civil War novel *Norwood* (1868) because they wanted to hear Beecher's voice, not despite his didacticism.[37] American readers accept these positions because their authors speak for them philosophically.

The world of the northern literary comedians is invested with the American myth of the egalitarian political and social contract, a contract looming more massively over American writers than the shadow of the big bear of Arkansas. An antagonist in *Samantha in Europe* (1895) draws her into a less metaphysical and more social vein. "But he waived off that idee, sayin', as usual, that it wuzn't expected that he wuz a-goin to spend his life and fortune for the sake of the children of the masses, who, two thirds on 'em, wuz better off dead than alive. I *hate* such talk."[38] The constellation of attitudes, difficult to catch in a brief space, is unmistakable in the canon, but it is her social position that is most obvious in this brief incident. Marietta Holley's *My Wayward Pardner* (1880) claims to know even more, enhancing the democratic position with her unabashed liberal Protestant mysticism, frequently leaping completely into otherworldliness in thought and image. The helpless, hopeless entanglement of competing views of capitalist progress and mystical Protestantism frequently seems to render her ineffectual.

The "modern" industrial world of labor conflicts and factory slums preempts the idealized world vision of the literary comedians of the North, and so Ward went abroad, ultimately planning a world tour; Twain drifted here and there in Europe and carried out the world tours that Ward had dreamed of; T. C. Haliburton, anglophile without honor in his own country, stayed long in England; Leland, having devised a crafts-education program for the Philadelphia public schools, quietly pursued Gypsy lore and mended broken pots on the Italian peninsula; Samantha, pretending to go to Europe, remained in quiet isolation, dressed in silks, in her cottage in Watertown, New York. The absolutist limitations of the soulless corporate life were unfitted to the individualized vulgarity that expressed urban rambunctiousness in

37. Henry Nash Smith, "A Textbook of the Genteel Tradition: Henry Ward Beecher's *Norwood*," in Smith, *Democracy and the Novel: Popular Resistance to Classic American Writers* (New York, 1978), 56–74.
38. Marietta Holley [Josiah Allen's Wife], *Samantha in Europe* (New York, 1895), 533–34.

Neal or Thomson's sketches. Will Rogers was the last beneficiary, as midwesterner, of the Indian summer of humor following the advent of the depersonalized and dereligionized corporate world, where the mystique of functional interchangeability replaced the mysticism of equal rights as surely as the methods of Alfred Sloan of General Motors, with his orientation toward corporate development, replaced the individualism of the old-fashioned one-man builder like Harvey Firestone.[39] From the limited, constraining world of Sinclair Lewis, without any mystique of democracy, it is then merely a step to the concentration camp as a model for human control, as displayed in the black humor of Ken Kesey's *One Flew over the Cuckoo's Nest* or Ralph Ellison's *Invisible Man.* Richard Rubenstein has argued brilliantly that the secularization of modern man makes the concentration camp an industrial reality, and it may be that the inability of northern humorists to close with this crucial issue has caused their disappearance as individual writers and has made it difficult to recognize that they form a school with identifiable characteristics, interests, and beliefs allied to the federalist social and political vision.[40]

As Mark Twain matured as a humorist-novelist, he became proficient at developing comic targets into characters embodied in dramatic episodes. His enthusiastic use of burlesque dramatization with value-laden rhetoric shows clearly in the legislative pieces reprinted in this volume. Thus, Miss Watson in *Huck Finn* and the Catholic church in *A Connecticut Yankee* became the embodiments of religious intolerance; Pap and the feuding families and Morgan le Fay and British slave masters became the personalized representatives of political absolutism, just as the railroad symbolized the corporation in Twain's humor. As this maturation took place, Twain's debt to the northeastern tradition became less explicit while his potential as a visionary novelist expanded. Also, his ability to embody positive alternatives in characters

39. Compare Alfred Sloan, *My Years with General Motors* (Garden City, N.Y., 1963), with Harvey Firestone, *Men and Rubber* (Garden City, N.Y., 1926), for an insight into the individualist "old" style and the corporate "new" style, in which responsibilities are assigned to identified groups within the corporate structure, except for ethics, which Sloan feels is everyone's business and therefore has no specific place in his corporate diagram.

40. Richard L. Rubenstein, *The Cunning of History: Mass Death and the American Future* (New York, 1975). See Daniel Boorstin, *The Democratic Experience* (New York, 1974), 3–87, Vol. III of Boorstin, *The Americans*, for an interesting portrait of the go-getter, or "go ahead," spirit.

like Huck Finn, Miles Hendon of *The Prince and the Pauper*, and Pudd'nhead Wilson provided him with a means of dramatizing the best human and intellectual aspects of the professional man—the sort of lawyer-journalist-author who interpreted the egalitarian ethos of the founding fathers for the nineteenth-century inheritors of the democracy. Thus, the individual could overcome the self-protective bureaucracy of established evils of selfish and corrupt capitalism and religion; thus, also, he escaped through extended action the didacticism that makes Marietta Holley's writings appear so outdated. Although other writers in this tradition wrote longer works, Twain alone leaped repeatedly to the level of visionary statement.

Mark Twain's public solution, as distinct from his private sense that the ark would have been improved by having in it an auger and a man boring holes, was to adhere to his temperamentally characteristic vision of a world divided melodramatically between good and bad, flexible and absolutist, professional and corporate, soulful and soulless humanity.[41] He adhered publicly to that model long after it ceased, even to his own mind, to apply to the conditions of American society. His political ideals, based on the tradition, remained his public stance, and he remained a spokesman for highly principled American relationships with the rest of the world, a moral absolutist in the finest democratic tradition and a pragmatic humanitarian in his public face, but largely without a political program for enforcing his beliefs.

Almost all of the comedians of the North used irony and burlesque to display social demands, although DeForest, for one, was willing enough to make flat-footed assertions of his democratic ideals in books like *Honest John Vane*, and Marietta Holley wore her religion on her sleeve. The Appalachian preacher Parson Brownlow promised to fight the "Secesh" until hell froze over, and then go on fighting on the ice.[42] American comic figures make outrageous rejections of an absolute and confining reality in favor of a fantasy of a liberal and permissive society. They do not favor a society without law or rules or manners, but they take a position that accepts individualism. Modern American conservatism has obscured the fine lines of this approach by identify-

---

41. Joseph Twitchell, untitled reminiscences of Mark Twain (MS, n.d., Beinecke Library, Yale University).

42. "American Humour," *Cornhill Magazine*, XIII (January, 1866), 28–43, cites the Brownlow statement as an example of Yankee exaggeration.

ing this stance negatively as a sort of irresponsibility, but the visionary characters of the comedians are quixotically responsible. Their aspirations have a living reality that opposes the slit-eyed cold warrior's alternate vision.

For some reason, writers like Opie Read and Don Marquis, who took over many of the comic mannerisms of the tradition, did not master its political and ethical power. Edgar Fawcett in 1885 depicted a New York merchant in comic blank verse, "Impervious to all else but our own aims / Of self-adornment and superior style," harried by the thought that "Hard is the task to squeeze good gold from pork." But Fawcett's mock drama, clever though it is, fails to achieve mock-epic greatness:

> Mr. Buntling: I did not insult you a bit;
> My motive was proper and fit.
> Your ancestors landed
> With far more expanded
> Ideas than your snobberies hit.[43]

Even a burlesque semichorus and local details in blank verse cannot elevate this to Mortimer Thomson's level of comic discourse. Perhaps their visionary powers were frustrated by the expanded scale of international warfare; perhaps domestic growth even beyond the cityscape of the middle part of the nineteenth century baffled their ability to contrive ironic demands on industry and government for the good of the individual. G. I. Joe, in a Bill Maulden cartoon from World War II, looks down into a fifty-foot shell hole, a raw recruit standing beside him, and mutters one word, "Mice." German intelligence agents, attempting to decipher American psychology, are supposed to have responded, "But it was not mice, it was a *bomb!*" Perhaps this is pitting principles against mortality—and they are not congruent—highlighting the paradox of northern humor, and suggesting the position of later existential black humorists.

A meaningful discussion of northern humor addresses social and political issues in patriotic American terms because such terms are inherent in the comic thought of northern writers in the 1830–1890 period and to a certain extent thereafter, of course. They had idealism, but they lacked a specific political strategy for implementing that ide-

43. [Edgar Fawcett], *The Buntling Ball* (New York, 1885), 7, 10, 130.

alism, and humor was their only tool—in some cases a very effective one as with Ward and Nasby during the Civil War. Paulding's Yankee Jonathan succeeds through personal energy and shrewdness; Haliburton's Sam Slick is seen as failing for the same reason. Seba Smith's family finds strength in its unity; Holley's picture of married life borders on travesty. The on-coming twentieth century may have outrun the ethics of personal responsibility and humanity, and Twain alone escaped to the level of vision that has perpetuated his works as a response to a mercilessly complex civilization.

James K. Paulding

James Kirke Paulding (1778–1860) was a close friend of Washington Irving, with whom he published the *Salmagundi Papers* in 1807 and 1808. His satiric *Diverting History of John Bull and Brother Jonathan* (1812) used a comic localist setting and plot to transform historical events, and his anglophobia and pro-American sentiments appeared in a number of other satires and burlesques. Paulding also created a mythic frontier hero patterned on Daniel Boone in "Nimrod Wildfire," in *The Lion of the West* (1831), and developed a species of romantic realism in *The Dutchman's Fireside* (1831) and other longer fictional works. *The Lay of the Scottish Fiddle* (1818) parodied Sir Walter Scott in verse. In 1824 Paulding was made navy agent for New York, and he became secretary of the navy under Martin Van Buren. During the later years of his life, he wrote practically nothing of significance. Amos L. Herold, *James Kirke Paulding: Versatile American* (New York, 1926), and Evert A. Duyckinck and George L. Duyckinck (eds.), *Cyclopedia of American Literature* (2 vols.; New York, 1855), II, 1–12, provide more detailed information on Paulding's life. See also Ralph M. Aderman, "James Kirke Paulding (1778–1860)," *Antebellum Writers in New York and the South* (Detroit, 1979), 246–48.

"Jonathan's Visit to the Celestial Empire" first appeared in the New York (weekly) *Mirror*, June 18, 1831. The text given here is taken from *The Atlantic Club-Book* (2 vols.; New York, 1834), which was dedicated to Paulding by its editor, George P. Morris, for his services in raising American literature from obscurity. Jonathan, the hero, piloting a sloop manned by a Newfoundland dog, is the maritime counterpart of the midwestern tall-tale hero. However, his milieu is made up of trade, social insight, law, and politics—characteristic interests of the urban and industrial environment. Jonathan's burlesque independence and the free-wheeling translation of Chinese customs into vanities approximating those of the New York *haut monde* are particularly northeastern aspects of Paulding's story. The reader should be aware, as Qui Tran has pointed out to me, that a real Jonathan would have lost all of his money in an hour without any pretense of legality. Furthermore, Chinese national pride in ginseng would have made purchasing it from America unthinkable. Nor would a woman have shown her foot. These features are purposeful intrusions of American life into a Chinese scene to create a comic statement.

Jonathan's Visit to the Celestial Empire

Somewhere about the year 1783, Jonathan, a young fellow who lived away down east, took it into his head to make a voyage to Canton. Accordingly he fitted out his sloop, a tarnation clever vessel of about eighty tons, and taking a crazy old compass for his guide, his two cousins, one a lad about sixteen, and a great Newfoundland dog for his crew, and a couple of rusty revolutionary swords for an armament, he boldly set forth on a voyage to the celestial empire.

Jonathan was a mighty cute lad, and had read a little or so about the great devotion of the Chinese to the herb called ginseng, which every body knows is a remedy for all things. He happened one day to hear an indian doctor give it as his opinion that a certain plant, which grew in the neighborhood of Jonathan's *natale solum*, was very much like the famous Chinese panacea, as he had seen it described. He took a hint from this, and rather guessed he would carry a good parcel along with him on speculation. Accordingly, he gathered a few hundred weight, dried, and stowed it away in one of his lockers, under the cabin floor.

Providence, which seems to take special care of such droll fellows as Jonathan, who calculate pretty considerably on their native energies, blessed him with fair winds and good weather; his old compass behaved to admiration; his ancient chart, which had been torn into fifty thousand pieces and pasted on a bit of tarpaulin, proved a most infallible guide; and some how or other, he would not exactly tell how, he plumped his sloop right into Table Bay, just as if the old fellow had been there a hundred times before.

The dutch harbor-master was sitting under his hat on his piazza, when he beheld, through the smoke of his pipe, his strange apparition of a vessel, scudding like a bird into the bay. He took it for the famous

Flying Dutchman, and such was his trepidation, that he stuck his pipe into his button-hole without knocking out the ashes, whereby he burnt a hole in his waistcoat. When Jonathan rounded to, and came to anchor, the harbor-master ventured to go on board to get information concerning this strange little barque. He could talk English, Dutch fashion, for indeed he had been promoted to the office on account of his skill in languages.

"Whence came you, Mynheer?" quoth he.

"Right off the reel from old Salem, I guess," replied Jonathan.

"Old Salem—whereabouts is dat den? I tont know any sich place about here."

"I guess not. What's your name, squire?"

"Hans Ollenbockenoffenhaffengraphensteiner ish my name."

"Whew! why it's as long as a pumpkin vine—now aint it?"

"But whereabouts ish dish blashe you speague of?" reiterated the harbor-master.

"O, it's some way off—about six or eight thousand miles down west there."

"Six tousand duyvels!" muttered Hans with the long name. "Do you tink I vill pelieve such a cog and pullsh tory as dat, Mynheer?"

"If you don't believe me, ask my two cousins there—and if you don't believe them, ask my dog. I tell you I come right straight from old Salem, in the United States of Amerrykey."

"United Sthaites of vat? I never heard of any United Sthaites but de Sthaites of Hollant."

"Ah—I suppose not—they've jist been christened I 'spose now, likely you've never heard of the new world neither, have you mister—what's your name?"

"Hans Ollenbockenoffenhaffengraphensteiner—I told you zo pefore."

"Maybe you'll have to tell me again before I know it by heart, I calculate. But did you never hear of the new world, squire?"

"Not I—ant if I hat, I vould'nt hafe pelieved it. Tare ish no new vorlt zinze de tiscovery of de Cape of Good Hoop dat I know. Put, gome along, you must co vid me to de gubernador."

Jonathan puzzled the governor about as much as he had done the harbor-master. But his papers were all fair and above board, and the governor had not only heard of the new world, but of the United States of Amerrykey, as Jonathan called them. Accordingly he was permitted to enjoy all the privileges of the port.

Nothing could exceed the wonder and curiosity excited by the vessel among the people at the Cape. That he should have made a voyage of so many thousand miles, with such a crew and such an outfit, was, in their opinion, little less than miraculous; and the worthy governor could only account for it by the aid of witchcraft, which, he had somewhere been told, abounded in the new world. Jonathan was the greatest man, and his dog the greatest dog at the Cape. He dined with the governor and burgomasters; cracked his jokes with their wives and daughters, danced with the Hottentots, and might have married a rich Dutch damsel of five hundred weight, and five thousand ducats a year, provided he would have given up old Salem forever.

After partaking of the hospitalities of the Cape a few days, Jonathan began to be in a hurry to prosecute his voyage. He knew the value of time as well as money. On the sixth day he accordingly set sail amid the acclamations of the inhabitants, taking with him a hippopotamus, an ourangoutang, and six ring-tailed monkeys, all of which he had bought on speculation. One of his cousins had, however, been so smitten with the country about the Cape, or with the charms of a little Dutch maiden, that he determined to stay behind, marry, and improve the inhabitants—on speculation. A Dutch sailor offered to supply his place, but Jonathan declined, saying he guessed his other cousin and the Newfoundland dog, who was a pretty particular cute kritter, could sail his sloop quite round the world and back again.

Not much of interest occurred during the voyage until he arrived at Macao, where he excited the same astonishment, underwent the same scrutiny, returned the same satisfactory answers, and came off as triumphantly as he did at the Cape of Good Hope. While here, he saw every thing, inquired about every thing, and went every where. Among other adventures, he one day accompanied his cousin in a fishing-boat, to see if they fished as the people did on the banks of Newfoundland. Unfortunately a violent storm came on; some of the boats were lost, and their crews drowned. The survivors went and offered up some of their paddles at the great temple of Neang-ma-ko. Those that were able added some matches and gilt paper. Jonathan's other cousin here determined to stay behind at Macao. It occurred to him he might make a speculation by curing the fish after the manner of mackerel. Jonathan did not much like this, but he said "never mind, I partly guess I can do without him."

Jonathan had now no one but his Newfoundland dog to assist in the navigation of his sloop. But he thought to himself, his voyage was almost at an end, and, at all events, if he hired any of the Macao people, they would be offering up matches and gilt paper to Neang-ma-ko, instead of minding their business. So he set sail for Canton, the Chinese prognosticating he would go to the bottom, because he did not make an offering to Neang-ma-ko, and the Portuguese that he would go to the devil, because he did not pay his devoirs to the virgin.

At Lin-Tin he was taken for a smuggler of opium by some, and for a magician by others, when they saw his vessel, heard where he hailed from, and became convinced that his whole crew consisted of a New-foundland dog. The commander of the fleet of ships of war stationed at Lin-Tin, to prevent the smuggling of opium into the celestial empire, seized the sloop, and devoted its brave commander to the indignation of the mighty emperor, who is brother to the sun and moon. Hereupon Jonathan bethought himself of a piece of the herb he had brought with him and had in his pocket. "It is a mighty good chance," thought he, "to try if it's the identical thing." Accordingly he took a convenient opportunity of presenting to the valiant commander a bit about as big as his finger. The admiral, whose name was Tizzy-Wizzy-Twang-Lang, stared at him at first with astonishment, then at the present with almost dismay, and thrusting it into his pocket, immediately caused it to be proclaimed that the "foreign barbarian" was innocent of the crime, or the intention of smuggling opium, and might go any where he pleased. Tizzy-Wizzy-Twang-Lang then sat down and wrote a despatch to the governor of Canton, stating that he had routed the "foreign barbarians," destroyed their fleet, and thrown all their opium overboard. After which he shut himself up in his cabin and took a morsel of the treasure Jonathan had presented him, about as large as the head of a pin. It is astonishing how much better he felt afterwards.

In the mean while Jonathan had set sail, and was ploughing his way towards Canton, with a fair wind and a good prospect of making a great speculation, for he had ascertained to a certainty that the article he had brought with him was the real ginseng, which was worth five times its weight in gold. He went ashore at the village of Ho-tun, where he saw the people catching wild ducks and geese, which they fatten by feeding in the dark. "That's a good hint," said Jonathan, shutting one eye, "and I'll tell the folks at old Salem." While he was walking about, seeing into every thing, he was unexpectedly saluted by a shower of stones from a parcel of children, with their hair sticking up behind like two horns. Jonathan thought this tarnation ungenteel; but he prudently suppressed his anger, considering he was in a strange country, and was come to try his fortune.

"May I be buttered," quoth Jonathan, as he approached Canton, and saw the countless boats moored in streets on the river, or flitting about in every direction—"may I be buttered, if here isn't a city all afloat. This beats all nater!"

And sure enough, here was a scene that might have made one of our Indians wonder. The whole world seemed on the water. Junks, with two eyes staring at the bows—canal-boats, flower-boats, pleasure-boats, and boats of all sizes and descriptions, filled with all sorts of people, lay moored in regular streets, or were moving about to and fro in every direction, painted in all the colors of the rainbow, and ornamented with gold leaf and grinning monsters having no prototypes in nature, or any where else but in the grotesque imagination of the artists of the celestial empire.

The busy activity of some of these boats was singularly contrasted with the luxurious ease of others, in which might be seen a couple of Chinese dandies reclining on mats and resting their heads on bamboo pillows, with pipes in their mouths, either listlessly contemplating the scene before them, or gazing with lack-lustre eye on the picture of some favorite beauty with penciled eyebrows, nails like a tiger, and feet almost invisible. Others were performing the ceremony of chin-chin-jos, which consists in throwing bits of burning paper into the water, while the din of innumerable gongs contributed a species of music to the scene that made honest Jonathan stop his ears in reverential dismay.

When our adventurer moored his sloop at Whampoa, in the midst of a fleet of vast ships, of almost all the nations of Europe, they did not know what to make of her. All he could say failed in convincing them that he had come from such a long distance, in such a vessel, navigated by such a crew. Besides, what could have brought him to Canton? He had neither money to purchase, nor cargo to exchange for Chinese commodities, except it might be his river horse, his ourang-outang, and his monkeys.

Jonathan kept his own secret. He had heard that the Chinese were as sharp as the "leetle end of nothing whittled down," and determined to be as sharp as the best of them. Accordingly nothing could be got out of him, except, that he had come on his own bottom, and meant to turn a penny some how or other. He said nothing about his ginseng, which he had, as I before stated, stowed away in a secret locker.

The story of the strange man and the strange vessel that had been navigated from the new world by a man and a dog, made a great noise, and thousands flocked to see them. The gentleman who officiated as American consul, without, however, having a regular appointment, behaved in the most kind and friendly manner to Jonathan, and introduced him to a hong, or as our hero called him, a *hung*-merchant, who undertook to do his business for him, that is, if he had any to do, which seemed rather doubtful.

"I chin-chin you," said Fat-qua, the hongman.

"You don't now, do you?" quoth Jonathan. "Well then, I chin-chin you, and so we are even, I guess."

Fat-qua was very anxious to know all about Jonathan's business; but the Chinese were such plaguy slippery fellows, he was afraid to trust them with his secret. He therefore, very gravely, and with infinite simplicity, commended to him his cargo of live stock, begged he would dispose of them to the best advantage, and invest the proceeds in a cargo of notions. Fat-qua did not know whether to laugh or be angry—however, he concluded by laughing, and promising to do his best.

The trifle which Jonathan brought with him had been all expended in maintaining himself and his dog, and Fat-qua did not feel inclined to advance any on the security of his live stock. This being the case, Jonathan one day brought a pound or two of his ginseng, and asked him carelessly what it might be likely worth in these parts?

"Hi yah!" exclaimed the hong-merchant in astonishment. "No, have got some more of he—hi yah?"

"Some small matter—not much," said Jonathan, who was of opinion if he displayed the whole parcel at once, it might lower the price and injure his speculation.

Fat-qua disposed of the two pounds of ginseng for a thumping sum, which Jonathan pocketed in less than no time, and chuckled in his sleeve, as he thought of the means to get rid of the whole at the same rate. A day or two after, he delivered the hong-merchant a few pounds more, which he said he had accidentally found in a place where he had stowed away and forgot it.

"Hi yah! Missee Joe Notting, I chin-chin you." And he began to have a great respect for Missee Joe Notting.

In this way, by slow degrees, did friend Jonathan bring forth his hoard of hidden treasures, till it was all disposed of, and he found himself in possession of almost half a million of dollars; for, it is to be recollected, this happened long before the value of ginseng was brought down to almost nothing by the large quantities carried to China, in consequence of the successful speculation of Jonathan.

Every time he produced a new lot, he declared it was all he had left, and consequently, to the last moment the price was kept up. Fat-qua began to believe that Joe Notting had discovered some hidden place where it grew, in the neighborhood of Canton, or that he dealt with the prince of darkness. He accordingly caused him to be watched, but our hero was too wide awake for the hong-merchant.

"Hi yah! Missee Joe Notting—some yet more—when you shall tink shall you no more have—hey? Every day here come you—say the last is he—hi yah! I tink no last come forever."

"I han't another stick to save my gizzard," said Jonathan, and this time, he spoke like a man of honor. He had at last sold out his hoard, with the exception of a small parcel for presents, and to use on an emergency.

Jonathan was now thinking he would gather himself together, and point his bowsprit strut towards home. But first he determined to see about him, for he expected to be asked a heap of questions when he got amongst his old neighbors; and not to be able to tell them all about the celestial empire, would be to show he had little or no gumption.

He accordingly visited the famous flower garden of Fa-Tee, where he saw a vast collection of the most beautiful flowers, and roses of all colors. Returning, he passed through the suburb of Ho-Nam, where he was called Fan-kwei, which means "foreign devil," and pelted handsomely with stones, according to the hospitable custom of the inhabitants.

Jonathan was now so rich, that he felt himself a different man from what he was when the boys pelted him at the village of Ho-tun. He had moreover seen the bamboo so liberally employed on the backs of the Chinese by their own officers and magistrates, that he thought he might make use himself of this universal panacea for all offences in the celestial empire. Accordingly, he sailed forth among those inhospitable rogues, and plied his stick so vigorously that the rabble fled before him, crying out "Fan-kwei!" and making motions significant of cutting off the head, as much as to say that would be his end at last. The reader must know that beheading is considered the most disgraceful of all punishments in the celestial empire, where they do everything differently from the rest of the world.

A formal complaint was laid before the Gan-chat-sze, a minister of justice at Canton, against the Fan-kwei, who had feloniously bam-booed the mob of Ho-Nam. Fat-qua, one of our hero's securities, was taken into custody till his forthcoming, and an express sent off to Pe-kin to announce the intelligence to the brother of the sun and moon, that a Fan-kwei had beaten at least two hundred of his valiant and in-vincible subjects, who could not bring themselves to soil their fingers by touching even the clothes of a foreign barbarian.

Jonathan was soon arrested, and being carried before the illustrious Gan-chat-sze, was astonished at seeing the infinite mischief he had done. There was one poor man who had his eye put out; another his head fractured; a third his arm broken; and what was worse than all this, three children were so disabled that they could not stand, all by Jonathan's bamboo, which was about as thick as your finger.

This was a serious business for a Fan-kwei. But his friend Fat-qua whispered in his ear—

"Hi yah—Missee Joe Notting—you some more have got of that grand—Hi yah! You stand under me—hey?"

Jonathan tipped him a knowing wink, and Fat-qua then crept close to the ear of the incorruptible Gan-chat-sze, and whispered him in like manner; but what he said being only intended for the ear of justice, must not be disclosed. The effect, however was miraculous, the Gan-chat-sze forthwith started up in a mighty passion, and, seizing his bamboo, attacked the complainants in the suit with such wonderful vigor, that he actually performed a miracle, and restored every one of them to the use of their limbs. After this, he discharged the offender with a caution, which Fat-qua translated into excellent English, and the next day Jonathan sent him by the hands of the same discreet friend a pound of ginseng.

"Hi yah! Missee Joe—more some yet, hey! Believe him make him as him go along—Hi yah! Chin-chin you, Missee Joe Notting."

Fat-qua was determined to signalize this triumph of Chinese justice over prejudice against foreigners, by a great feast of bears-claws, birds-nests, and all the delicacies of the east. He, therefore, invited a number of the Fan-kweis about the factory, to meet Jonathan at his country-seat, near the gardens of Fa-Te, and they had a jolly time of it. Our hero was complimented with a pair of chop-sticks of the most elegant construction and materials, which he managed with such skill, that, by the time the dinner was over, he was well nigh starved to death.

The hong-merchant, Fat-qua, was a jolly little fellow, "about knee-high to a toad," as Jonathan used to say, and fond of a good glass of wine. He plied his guests pretty neatly, until they began to feel a little top-heavy, and sailed away one by one under rather high steam, leaving Jonathan and his friend alone together, the latter fast asleep. Jonathan was by this time in high feather, and thought this would be a good time to take a peep at the establishment of his friend, that he might know something of these matters when he got home.

He arose without disturbing the little fat gentleman, and proceeded to penetrate into the interior of the house, until he came to the female apartments, in one of which he saw a young lady smoking, to whom he paid his compliments with a low bow. Her pipe was formed of slender pieces of bamboo, highly polished, with a bowl of silver and a mouthpiece of amber. Her hair was beautifully long, and tastefully dressed with flowers and gold and silver bodkins, and the whole atmosphere of the room was perfumed with jasmine and other odoriferous plants and shrubs. By her side lay a guitar, on which she seemed to have been playing.

The entrance of Jonathan threw her into great confusion, and she uttered several violent screams, which however brought no one to her assistance. The illustrious Fat-qua was still sleeping in his seat, and the servants making merry as usual with the remains of the feast. Jonathan attempted an apology for his intrusion, but the more he apologized the louder the young lady screamed. Jonathan wondered what could be the matter with her.

"Well, I never saw any thing like this growing among corn—what's come over the gal? May I be chiselled if I don't think she's afeared I'll eat her. But why the dickens, if she's frightened, don't she scamper off, that being the most nat'ral way of getting out of danger." Jonathan did not know the feet of the poor young damsel were not more than two inches and a half long, and that she could no more run than fly. They were what the Chinese poets call a couple of "golden lilies."

Encouraged by this notion, that her pretending to be frightened was all sheer affectation, he approached her still nearer, took up the guitar, and begged her to play him a tune, such as "Yankee Doodle," or any thing of that sort that was pretty easily managed, for he did not much admire any of your fine fashionable gimcracks. Jonathan was a plaguy neat kind of a chap—as handsome a lad as might be seen; tall and straight; with blue eyes, white forehead, and red cheeks, a little rusted to be sure with the voyage.

The pretty creature with the little feet, whose name was Shangtshee, ventured at last to look at this impudent intruder, and, sooth to say, he did not appear so terrible at the second glance as at the first. She smiled, and put out her small foot for Jonathan to admire. She then took her guitar and played him a tune—it was not "Yankee Doodle" to be sure, but it rather pleased Jonathan, for he declared it beat all, he'd be switched if it didn't. Shangtshee seemed to understand the compliment, for she smiled and put out her other golden lily, I suppose to show Jonathan she had a pair of them. Jonathan admired the pipe; she handed it to him, he put it to his lips, and giving it back again, she put it to her lips, which our hero finally concluded came as near to kissing as twopence to a groat.

"How the kritter blushes," thought Jonathan. He did not know she was painted half an inch thick after the fashion of the Chinese ladies. As they sat thus exchanging little pleasant civilities, which, innocent as they were, endangered both their lives, they were alarmed, at least the lady—for Jonathan had never particularly studied Chinese customs—by the sound of a guitar, at some short distance, in the garden. It approached nearer, and, in a few minutes, seemed directly under the window of the apartment. Shangtshee appeared greatly agitated, and begged Jonathan by signs to depart the way he came. But Jonathan had no notion of being scared by a tune, and declined to budge an inch. It was a nice tune, and he didn't much mind if he heard another just like it.

Presently the music ceased, and all at once the young Shangtshee screamed a scream almost as loud as the former ones. "What can have got into the curious varmint now, I wonder?" quoth Jonathan. He little suspected she had caught a glimpse of the face of her lover through the blinds. This young man was called Yu-min-hoo, which signifies feathered, because he was a great poet, and took such high flights that his meaning was sometimes quite out of sight. He always carried an ink-bottle suspended to his button, a bamboo pen stuck behind his ear, and a book under his arm, in which he wrote down his thoughts that none might escape him. He made verses upon Shangtshee, in which he compared her to a dish of bear's claws, since her nails were at least six inches long, and she was a delicacy which the epicure might admire every day in the year. It was this sentiment which he had set to music and sung on this eventful evening under the window of his mistress.

Yu-min-hoo was petrified when he saw his Shangtshee sitting so cosily by the side of a Fan-kwei, which, as I said before, means foreign devil. His indignation was terrible and his jealousy prodigious. He had thoughts of sitting down by the light of the moon and writing a furious ode, consigning the Fan-kwei to all the Chinese devils, which are the ugliest in the world. Even their gods are monsters, what then must the others be? On second thoughts, however, Yu-min-hoo restrained his muse, and in a moment or two they heard the clatter of his wooden shoes gradually receding. Shangtshee again entreated with her eyes, her hands, nay, her very feet, that Jonathan would make himself scarce. The tears ran down her cheeks, and like torrents of rain wore deep channels in them that almost spoiled their beauty.

Jonathan tried all he could to comfort her, when what was his surprise and indignation at her base ingratitude, he was saluted with a scratch of those long nails that constitute the most unequivocal claim of a Chinese lady to rank. It was a scratch so emphatic and well-directed, that every nail, and most especially the little finger nail, left its mark on his cheek, and it was preceded and followed by a scream of the highest pretensions.

Our hero was astounded at this salutation. He had heard of love taps, but never of such as these. But he soon understood the whole squinting of the business as slick as a whistle, when he saw little Fat-qua standing before him breathing fire and looking fury from his dark sharp-cornered eyes.

"Hi yah!—Missee Joe Notting—spose tink you daughter my one flower-woman—hey?"

Jonathan endeavoured to convince Fat-qua that there was not the least harm in sitting by the side of a young woman in a civil way—that it was done in his country every day in the year, particularly on Sundays—and that the women there were quite as good as the Chinese, though they did not wear wooden shoes, and nails six inches long.

Fat-qua was wroth at this indecorous comparison of the Fan-kwei ladies with those of the celestial empire; he ordered his servants to seize Jonathan as a violator of Chinese etiquette, and a calumniator of wooden shoes and long nails. He determined in the bitterness of his heart to have him immediately before the worshipful Gan-chat-sze, who would not fail to squeeze some of his dollars out of him.

But further reflection induced him to abandon this course. He recollected, when the fumes of the wine were somewhat dissipated, that both himself and his daughter would be disgraced and dishonored if it were publicly known that she had been in company with a Fan-kwei, a stain of the deepest dye according to the statutes of the celestial empire, in any but common women. The only way, therefore, was to make the best of a bad business. Accordingly he bribed his servants to secrecy—married his daughter to the poet—and swore never to invite another Missee Joe Notting to dine with him so long as there was a woman in his house. He had never, he said, met with a fellow of this *chop* before.

Various were the other adventures of our hero, which are forever incorporated in the annals of the celestial empire, where he figures as the "Great Fan-kwei, Joe Notting." My limits will not suffice to particularize them all, else would I record how he was fined a thousand dollars by his old friend, Gan-chat-sze, for bambooing a valiant sentinel who refused to let him enter the gates of Canton without a bribe; how his river-horse, being tired of confinement, took an opportunity to jump overboard, whereby he upset a boat and came nigh drowning the passengers. This cost him three thousand dollars more. His next adventure was picking up the body of a drowned man in the river one evening, in passing between his sloop and the shore, whose murder he was found guilty of before Gan-chat-sze, who kindly let him off for ten thousand dollars; advising him at the same time through the hong-merchant, Fat-qua, to take the earliest opportunity of making himself invisible within the precincts of the celestial empire.

"I partly guess I'll take his advice, and pull up stakes," said Jonathan. "I never saw such a tarnal place. It beats everything, I swow. Why, squire Fat-qua, I'll tell you what—if you'll only come to our parts, you may go jist where you please—do jist as you please—and talk to the gals as much as you please. I'll be choked if it isn't true, by the living hokey."

"Hi yah! Missee Joe Notting," replied Fat-qua, "she must be some very fine place, dat Merrykey."

"There you are right, squire. But, good by; I finally conclude it's best to cut stick. They're plaguy slippery fellows here; if they aint, may I be licked by a chap under size."

Jonathan received the remainder of his money, which he was then earnestly advised to invest in bills, and at the same time to sell his vessel, and embark for home in a safer conveyance.

"D'ye think I'm a fellow of no more gumption than that?" said he. "I'll be darned if there's a tighter safer thing than my old sloop ever sailed across the salt sea; and as for your paper money, I've had enough of that in my own country in my time."

He declined shipping a crew, for he said he must trust, in that case, to strangers; and he thought to himself that he could easily induce his two cousins to go home with him now he was so rich. It happened as he had anticipated; both gladly rejoined him again, each having failed in his speculation. The Dutchmen at the Cape forbade the one using a machine he had invented for saving labor, lest it might lower the price of their negroes; and the Portuguese and Chinese refused to eat the fish of the other, because he neither crossed himself before the picture of the virgin, nor burnt gilt paper to the image of Neang-ma-ko.

A prosperous voyage ended in Jonathan's happy return to Salem, where he became a great man, even to the extent of being yclept honorable. He lived long and happily, and his chief boast to the end of his life was, that he had been the first of his countrymen to visit the celestial empire, and the only man that navigated with a Newfoundland dog for an officer.

৯৯ William Cox ৫৬

William Cox (?–1851?) was born in England about the turn of the century and became an active literary and theater critic in New York City in the 1820s, contributing regularly to the New York *Mirror*. He burlesqued contemporary literary fashions in "The Man of the Flymarket Ferry" and "Oysters," both much-admired pieces in the 1830s. Cox advocated the dramatic principle in writing, thus advancing short fiction over the Addisonian essay form. In the 1830s he returned to England, corresponding regularly with the *Mirror* on literary and theatrical matters. A volume of his essays, *Crayon Sketches* (New York, 1833) by "An Amateur," included "Steam" among other comic and serious matter. The text here is from *The Atlantic Club-Book* (2 vols.; New York, 1834). A brief biography of Cox appears in Evert A. Duyckinck and George L. Duyckinck (eds.), *Cyclopedia of American Literature* (2 vols.; New York, 1855), II, 243–44.

Steam

I had a dream, which was not all a dream.
　　—Byron

Modern philosophy, anon,
Will, at the rate she's rushing on,
Yoke lightning to her railroad car,
And, posting like a shooting star,
Swift as a solar radiation
Ride the grand circuit of creation.
　　—Anon.

I have a bilious friend, who is a great admirer and imitator of Lord Byron; that is, he affects misanthropy, masticates tobacco, has his shirts made without collars, calls himself a miserable man, and writes poetry with a glass of gin-and-water before him. His gin, though far from first-rate, is better than his poetry; the latter, indeed, being worse than that of many authors of the present day, and scarcely fit for an album; however, he does not think so, and makes a great quantity. At his lodgings, a few evenings ago, among other morbid productions, he read me one entitled "Steam," written in very blank verse, and evidently modelled after the noble poet's "Darkness," in which he takes a bird's eye view of the world two or three centuries hence, describes things in general, and comes to a conclusion with, "Steam was the universe!" Whether it was the fumes arising from this piece of solemn bombast, or whether I had unconsciously imbibed more hollands than my temperate habits allow of, I cannot say, but I certainly retired to bed like Othello, "perplexed in the extreme." There was no "dreamless sleep" for me that night, and Queen Mab drove full gallop through every nook and cranny of my brain. Strange and fantastical visions floated before me, till at length came one with all the force and clearness of reality.

I thought I stood upon a gentle swell of ground, and looked down upon the scene beneath me. It was a pleasant sight, and yet a stranger might have passed it by unheeded; but to me it was as the green spot in the desert, for there I recognised the haunt of my boyhood. There was the wild common on which I had so often scampered "frae mornin' sun till dine," skirted by the old wood, through which the burn stole tinkling to the neighboring river. There was the little ivy-covered church with its modest spire and immovable weathercock, and clustering around lay the village that I knew contained so many kind and loving hearts. All looked just as it did on the summer morning when I left it, and went a wandering over this weary world. To me the very trees possessed an individuality; the branches of the old oak (there was but one) seemed to nod familiarly towards me, the music of the rippling water fell pleasantly on my ear, and the passing breeze murmured of "home, sweet home." The balmy air was laden with the hum of unseen insects, and filled with the fragrance of a thousand common herbs and flowers; and to my eyes the place looked prettier and pleasanter than any they have since rested on. As I gazed, the "womanish moisture" made dim my sight, and I felt that yearning of the heart which every man who has a soul feels—let him go where he will, or reason how he will—on once more beholding the spot where the only pure, unsullied part of his existence passed away.—Suddenly the scene changed. The quiet, smiling village vanished, and a busy, crowded city occupied its place. The wood was gone, the brook dried up, and the common cut to pieces and covered with a kind of iron gangways. I looked upon the surrounding country, if country it could be called, where vegetable nature had ceased to exist. The neat, trim gardens, the verdant lawns and swelling uplands, the sweet-scented meadows and waving cornfields, were all swept away, and fruit, and flowers, and herbage, appeared to be things uncared for and unknown. Houses and factories, and turnpikes and railroads, were scattered all around; and along the latter, as if propelled by some unseen infernal power, monstrous machines flew with inconceivable swiftness. People were crowding and jostling each other on all sides. I mingled with them, but they were not like those I had formerly known—they walked, talked, and transacted business of all kinds with astonishing celerity. Every thing was done in a hurry; they ate, drank, and slept in a hurry; they danced, sung, and made love in a hurry; they married, died, and were buried in a hurry, and resurrection-men had them out of their graves before they well knew they were in them. Whatever was done, was done upon the high-pressure principle. No person stopped to speak to another in the street; but as they moved rapidly on their way, the men talked faster than women do now, and the women talked twice as fast as ever. Many were bald; and on asking the reason, I was given to understand that they had been great travellers, and that the rapidity of modern conveyances literally scalped those who journeyed much in them, sweeping whiskers, eyebrows, eye-lashes, in fact, every thing in any way movable, from their faces. Animal life appeared to be extinct; carts and carriages came rattling down the highways, horseless and driverless, and wheelbarrows trundled along without any visible agency. Nature was out of fashion, and the world seemed to get along tolerably well without her.

At the foot of the street my attention was attracted by a house which they were building, of prodigious dimensions, being not less than seventeen stories high. On the top of it several men were at work, when, dreadful to relate, the foot of one of them slipped, and he was precipitated to the earth with a fearful crash. Judge of my horror and indignation on observing the crowd pass unheeding by, scarcely deigning to cast a look on their fellow-creature, who doubtless lay weltering in his blood; and the rest of the workmen went on with their several avocations without a moment's pause in consequence of the accident. On approaching the spot, I heard several in passing murmur the most incomprehensible observations. "Only a steam-man," said one. "Won't cost much," said another. "His boiler overcharged, I suppose," cried a third; "the way in which all these accidents happen!" And true enough, there lay a man of tin and sheet-iron, weltering in hot water. The superintendent of the concern, who was not a steam-man, but made of the present materials, gave it as his opinion that the springs were damaged, and the steam-vessels a little ruptured, but not much harm done; and straightway sent the corpse to the blacksmith's (who was a flesh-and-blood man) to be repaired. Here was then at once a new version of the old Greek fable, and modern Prometheuses were actually as "plentiful as blackberries." In fact, I found upon inquiry, that society was now divided into two great classes, living and "locomotive" men, the latter being much the better and honester people of the two; and a fashionable political economist of the name of Malthus, a lineal descendant of an ancient, and it appears, rather inconsistent system-monger, had just published an elaborate pamphlet, showing the manifold advantages of propagating those no-provender-consuming individuals in preference to any other. So that it appeared, that any industrious mechanic might in three months have a full-grown family about him, with the full and comfortable assurance that, as the man says in Chrononhotonthologos, "they were all his own and none of his neighbors."

These things astonished, but they also perplexed and wearied me. My spirit grew sick, and I longed for the old world again, and its quiet and peaceable modes of enjoyment. I had no fellowship with the two new races of beings around me, and nature and her charms were no more. All things seemed forced, unnatural, unreal—indeed, little better than bare-faced impositions. I sought the banks of my native river; it alone remained unchanged. The noble stream flowed gently and tranquilly as of yore, but even here impertinent man had been at work, and pernicious railroads were formed to its very verge. I incautiously crossed one of them, trusting to my preconceived notions of time and space, the abhorred engine being about three-quarters of a mile from me; but scarcely had I stepped over, when it flew whizzing past the spot I had just quitted, and catching me in its eddy, spun me around like a top under the lash. It was laden with passengers, and went with headlong fury straight toward the river. Its fate seemed inevitable—another instant and it would be immersed in the waves; when lo! it suddenly sunk into the bosom of the earth, and in three seconds was ascending a perpendicular hill on the opposite bank of the river. I was petrified, and gazed around with an air of helpless bewilderment, when a gentleman, who was doubtless astonished at my astonishment,

The narrator in William Cox's "Steam" (1833) is astounded by a fallen steam-man in a dream-vision of the new industrial world. This illustration accompanied the story in William E. Burton's *Cyclopedia of Wit and Humor* (1858).

shouted in passing, "What's the fellow staring at?" and another asked "if I had never seen a tunnel before?"

Like Lear, "my wits began to turn." I wished for some place where I might hide myself from all around and turned instinctively to the spot where the village ale-house used to stand. But where, alas! was the neat thatched cottage that was wont so often to

> "impart
> An hour's importance to the poor man's heart?"

Gone! and in its place stood a huge fabric, labelled "Grand Union Railroad Hotel." But here also it was steam, steam, nothing but steam! The rooms were heated by steam, the beds were made and aired by steam, and instead of a pretty, red-lipped, rosy-cheeked chambermaid, there was an accursed machine-man smoothing down the pillows and bolsters with mathematical precision; the victuals were cooked by steam, yea, even the meat roasted by steam. Instead of the clean-swept hearth

> "With aspen boughs, and flowers, and fennel sweet,"

there was a patent steam-stove, and the place was altogether hotter than any decent man would ever expect to have any thing to do with. Books and papers lay scattered on a table. I took up one of the former; it was filled with strange new phrases, all more or less relating to steam, of which I knew nothing, but as far as I could make out the English of the several items, they ran somewhat thus:

"*Another shocking catastrophe.*—As the warranted-safe locomotive smoke-consuming, fuel-providing steam-carriage Lightning, was this morning proceeding at its usual three-quarter speed of one hundred and twenty-seven miles an hour, at the junction of the Hannington and Slipsby railroads, it unfortunately came in contact with the steam-carriage Snail, going about one hundred and five miles per hour. Of course, both vehicles with their passengers were instantaneously reduced to an impalpable powder. The friends of the deceased have the consolation of knowing that no blame can possibly attach to the intelligent proprietors of the Lightning, it having been clearly ascertained that those of the Snail started their carriage full two seconds before the time agreed on, in order to obviate in some degree, the delay to which passengers were unavoidably subjected by the clumsy construction and tedious pace of their vehicle."

"*Melancholy accident.*—As a beautiful and accomplished young lady of the name of Jimps, a passenger in the Swift-as-thought-locomotive, was endeavoring to catch a flying glimpse of the new Steam University, her breathing apparatus unfortunately slipped from her mouth, and she was a corpse in three-quarters of a second. A young gentleman who had been tenderly attached to her for several days, in the agony of his feelings withdrew his air-tube and called for help; he of course shared a similar fate. Too much praise cannot be given to the rest of the passengers, who, with inimitable presence of mind, prudently held their breathing-bladders to their mouths during the whole of this trying scene," &c. &c.

A Liverpool paper stated that "The stock for the grand Liverpool and Dublin tunnel under the Irish channel, is nearly filled up." And a Glasgow one advocated the necessity of a floating wooden railroad between Scotland and the Isle of Man, in order to do away with the tiresome steamboat navigation. I took up a volume of poems, but the similes and metaphors were all steam; all their ideas of strength, and power, and swiftness, referred to steam only, and a sluggish man was compared to a greyhound. I looked into a modern dictionary for some light on these subjects, but got none, except finding hundreds of curious definitions, such as these:

"*Horse, s.* an animal of which but little is now known. Old writers affirm that there were at one time several thousands in this country."

"*Tree, s.* vegetable production; once plentiful in these parts, and still to be found in remote districts."

"*Tranquillity, s.* obsolete; an unnatural state of existence, to which the ancients were very partial. The word is to be met with in several old authors," &c. &c.

In despair I threw down the book, and rushed out of the house. It was mid-day, but a large theatre was open, and the people were pouring in. I entered with the rest, and found that whatever changes had taken place, money was still money. They were playing Hamlet by steam, and this was better than any other purpose to which I had seen it applied. The automata really got along wonderfully well, their speaking faculties being arranged upon the barrel-organ principle, greatly improved, and they roared, and bellowed, and strutted, and swung their arms to and fro as sensibly as many admired actors. Unfortunately in the grave scene, owing to some mechanical misconstruction, Hamlet exploded, and in doing so, entirely demolished one of the gravediggers, carried away a great part of Laertes, and so injured the rest of the dramatis personnae that they went off one after the other like so many crackers, filling the house with heated vapor. I made my escape; but on reaching the street things were ten times worse than ever. It was the hour for stopping and starting the several carriages, and no language can describe the state of the atmosphere. Steam was generating and evaporating on all sides—the bright sun was obscured—the people looked parboiled, and the neighboring fisherman's lobsters changed color on the instant; even the steam inhabitants appeared uncomfortably hot. I could scarcely breathe—there was a blowing, a roaring, a hissing, a fizzing, a whizzing going on all around—fires were blazing, water was bubbling, boilers were bursting—when lo! I suddenly awoke and found myself in a state of profuse perspiration. I started up, ran to the window, and saw several milk-men and bakers' carts, with horses in them, trotting merrily along. I was a thankful man. I put on my clothes, and while doing so, made up my mind to read no more manuscript poems, and eschew gin and water for the time to come.

❧ Joseph C. Neal ❧

Joseph C. Neal (1807–1847) was raised in genteel poverty in Philadelphia. He was educated in his mother's bookstore and lending library and left Philadelphia only briefly in 1829 to gather journeyman experience in the "flush times" coalfields of Pottstown, Pennsylvania. He was editor of the Philadelphia daily *Pennsylvanian* from 1831 through 1844, with breaks to recoup his always-fragile health. With Louis Godey he founded the *Philadelphia Saturday News* and went on to found *Neal's Saturday Gazette*, one of the most intelligently literate weeklies of the 1840s. He encouraged comic writers like John S. Robb and Frances M. Berry Whitcher (Widow Bedott) and was known himself as the "American Boz" for his Dickensian sketches of urban down-and-outers, published first in his weeklies and then as "City Worthies" in the *Pennsylvanian*.

The two sketches reprinted here express Neal's credo of urban northeastern life, restrained and philosophical, yet aware of politics and crime, pragmatic in viewpoint. "Peter Brush" first appeared in the *Gentleman's Vade Mecum* and then in the *Pennsylvanian* in 1835, where Peter confronts a gentleman and asks for a "circular recommend" to any spoils job. The version reprinted here, which appeared only in the Philadelphia *Saturday News and Literary Gazette* (August 13, 1836), shows a night watchman who speaks, like Peter, in low dialect, making clear Neal's intention that Peter be seen as a "cowboy" following only his own interests, not a burlesque character identified with one political party or the other. "The News-boy," from the *United States Magazine and Democratic Review* (July, 1843), was written to accompany a Hogarthian sketch by F. O. C. Darley; it was published in book form in 1843 and in 1844 and collected in *Neal's Charcoal Sketches: Three Books Complete in One* (Philadelphia, 1865), the source of this text.

Peter Brush; or, The Great Used Up

It was November; soon after election time, when a considerable portion of the political world are apt to be despondent, and external things appear to do their utmost to keep them so. November, the season of dejection, when pride itself loses its imperious port; when ambition gives place to melancholy; when beauty hardly takes the trouble to look in the glass; and when existence doffs its rainbow hues, and wears an aspect of such dull, commonplace reality, that hope leaves the world for a temporary excursion, and those who cannot do without her inspiring presence, borrow the aid of pistols, cords, and chemicals, and send themselves on a longer journey, expecting to find her by the way:—a season, when the hair will not stay in curl; when the walls weep dewy drops, to the great detriment of paper-hangings, and of every species of colouring with which they are adorned; when the banisters distil liquids, any thing but beneficial to white gloves; when nature fills the ponds, and when window-washing is the only species of amusement at all popular among housekeepers.

It was on the worst of nights in that worst of seasons. The atmosphere was in a condition of which it is difficult to speak with respect, much as we may be disposed to applaud the doings of nature. It was damp, foggy, and drizzling; to sum up its imperfections in a sonorous and descriptive epithet, it was "orrid muggy weather." The air hung about the wayfarer in warm, unhealthy folds, and extracted the starch from his shirt collar and from the bosom of his dickey, with as much rapidity as it robbed his spirits of their elasticity, and melted the sugar of self-complacency from his mind. The street lamps emitted a ghastly white glare, and were so hemmed in with vapory wreaths, that their best efforts could not project a ray of light three feet from the burner. Gloom was universal, and any change, even to the heat of Africa, or to the frosts of the arctic circle, would, in comparison, have been delightful. The pigs' tails no longer waved in graceful sinuosities; while the tail of each night-roving, hectoring bull-dog ceased flaunting toward the clouds, a banner of wrath and defiance to punier creatures, and hung down drooping and dejected, an emblem of a heart little disposed to quarrel and offence. The ornamentals of the brute creation being thus below par, it was not surprising that men, with cares on their shoulders and raggedness in their trousers, should likewise be more melancholy than on occasions of a brighter character. Every one at all subject to the "skiey influences," who has had trouble enough to tear his clothes, and to teach him that the staple of this mundane existence is not exclusively made up of fun, has felt that philosophy is but a barometrical affair, and that he who is proof against sorrow when the air is clear and bracing, may be a very miserable wretch, with no greater cause, when the wind sits in another quarter.

Peter Brush is a man of this susceptible class. His nervous system is of the most delicate organization, and responds to the changes of the weather, as an Eolian harp sings to the fitful swellings of the breeze. Peter was abroad on the night of which we speak; either because, unlike the younger Brutus, he had no Portia near to tell him that such exposure was "not physical," and that it was the part of prudence to go to bed, or that, although aware of the dangers of miasma to a man of his constitution, he did not happen at that precise moment to have access to either house or bed; in his opinion, two essential pre-requisites to couching himself, as he regarded taking it *al fresco*, on a cellar door, not likely to answer any sanitary purpose. We incline ourselves to the opinion that he was in the dilemma last mentioned, as it had previously been the fate of other great men. But be that as it may, Mr. Peter Brush was in the street, as melancholy as an unbraced drum, "a gib-ed cat, or a lugged bear."

Seated upon the curb, with his feet across the gutter, he placed his elbow on a stepping-stone, and like Juliet on the balcony, leaned his head upon his hand—a hand that would perhaps have been the better of a covering, though none would have been rash enough to volunteer to be a glove upon it. He was in a dilapidated condition—out at elbows, out at knees, out of pocket, out of office, out of spirits, and out in the street—an "out and outer" in every respect, and as *outré* a mortal as ever the eye of man did rest upon. For some time, Mr. Brush's reflections had been silent. Following Hamlet's advice, he "gave them an understanding, but no tongue;" and he relieved himself at intervals by spitting forlornly into the kennel. At length, suffering his locked hands to fall between his knees, and heaving a deep sigh, he spoke:—

"A long time ago, my ma used to put on her specs and say, 'Peter, my son, put not your trust in princes;' and from that day to this I haven't done any thing of the kind, because none on 'em ever wanted to borry nothing of me; and I never see a prince or a king,—but one or two, and they had been rotated out of office,—to borry nothing of them. Princes! pooh!—Put not your trust in politicianers—them's my sentiments. You might jist as well try to hold an eel by the tail. I don't care which side they're on, for I've tried both, and I know. Put not your trust in politicianers, or you'll get a hyst.

"Ten years ago it came into my head that things weren't going on right; so I pretty nearly gave myself up tee-totally to the good of the republic, and left the shop to look out for itself. I was brimfull of patriotism, and so uneasy in my mind for the salvation of freedom, I couldn't work. I tried to guess which side was going to win, and I stuck to it like wax;—sometimes I was a-one side, sometimes I was a t'other, and sometimes I straddled till the election was over, and came up jist in time to jine the hurrah. It was good I was after; and what good could I do if I wasn't on the 'lected side? But, after all, it was never a bit of use. Whenever the battle was over, no matter what side was sharing out the loaves and the fishes, and I stepped up, I'll be hanged if they didn't cram all they could into their own mouths, put their arms over some, and grab at all the rest with their paws, and say, 'Go away, white man, you ain't capable.'—Capable! what's the reason I ain't capable? I've got as extensive a throat as any of 'em, and I could swallow the loaves and fishes without choking, if each loaf was as big as a grindstone and each fish as big as a sturgeon. Give Peter a chance, and leave him alone for that. Then, another time when I called—'I want some spoils,' says I; 'a small bucket full of spoils. Whichever side gets in, shares the spoils, don't they?' So they first grinned, and then they ups and tells me that virtue like mine was its own reward, and that spoils might spoil me. But it was *no* spoils that spoilt me, and *no* loaf and fish that starved me—I'm spoilt because I couldn't get either. Put not your trust in politicianers—I say it agin. Both sides used me jist alike. Here I've been serving my country, more or less, these ten years, like a patriot—going to town meetings, hurraing my daylights out, and getting as blue as blazes—blocking the windows, getting licked fifty times, and having more black eyes and bloody noses than you could shake a stick at, all for the common good, and for the purity of our illegal rights—and all for what? Why, for nix. If any good has come of it, the country has put it into her own pocket, and swindled me out of my arnings. I can't get no office! Republics is ungrateful! It wasn't reward I was after. I scorns the base insinivation. I only wanted to be took care of, and have nothing to do but to take care of the public, and I've only got half—nothing to do! Being took care of was the main thing. Republics *is* ungrateful; I'm swaggered if they ain't. This is the way old sojers is served."

Brush, having thus unpacked his heart, heaved a deep sigh or two, and laid his head upon the stone, for the purpose of considering his condition more at his ease; but soon unwittingly—for well he knew the consequences—fell into a troubled, murmuring sleep, in which his words were mere repetitions of what he had said before, the general scope of the argument being to prove the received axiom of former times, that republics do not distribute their favours in proportion to services rendered, and that, in the speaker's opinion, they are not, in this respect, much better than the princes against whom his mother cautioned him. Such, at least, was the conviction of Mr. Brush; at which he had arrived, not by theory and distant observation, but by his own personal experience.

It is a long lane which has no turning, and it is a long sleep, especially in the open air, which is not interrupted by those in authority. Peter Brush found it so in this instance, as he had, indeed, more than once before. His agitated slumbers were soon disturbed by the relentless paw of an officer of the night.

"Get up, Commodore," said he of the mace and badge. "Your ma will be waiting for you, and your pappy, the major will be apt to hide you."

"Don't be official and trouble yourself about other people's business," remarked Brush, trying to open his eyes. "Don't be official; it isn't the genteel thing."

"Not official!—What do you mean by that? Do you want me to neglect my business? I'm official, by being appinted a watchman, and it's my duty to meddle with other people's business, and to have a finger in every pie what's baking. Don't give me none of your slack," continued the Charley, expanding with the pride of office, and shaking his mace, "or I'll give you some of my tight."

"Oh, very well—be as sassy as you please—you've got an office— you've got one of the fishes, though it is but a minny, and I ain't; but if I had, I'd show you a thing or two. Be sassy, be official, be anything, Mr. Noodle-soup. It isn't saying much for the corporation that they chose you, when Peter Brush was on the list for promotion, that's all; though you are so stiff, and think yourself pretty to look at. But them that's pretty to look at, ain't good 'uns to go, or you wouldn't be poking here.—Be off—there's no more business afore this 'ere meeting, and you may adjourn."

"What's all that? Why, you're so corned as to come under the act agin tipsy people, as well as the act supplementary to an act, entitled an act for the suppression of loafing. Where did you get the liquor?—

As "Charlies" of the night watch sleep in the corners, one of Joseph C. Neal's "city worthies" contemplates his down-and-out status in D. C. Johnston's title page to Neal's *Charcoal Sketches* (1838). Johnston and F. O. C. Darley both worked in conjunction with Neal in the 1830s and 1840s.

how did you come so very how comed you so [*sic*] ? Fie! you a gentleman's son!"

"Watchy, its owing to the weather—part to the weather, and part
because republics is ungrateful—that's considerable the biggest part.
Either part is excuse enough, and both together makes it a credit.
When it's such weather as this, it takes the electerising fluid; and if you
want to feel something like—do you know what something like is?—
it's cat-bird, jam up—if you want to feel so, you must pour a little of
the electerising fluid into you.—In this kind of weather you must tune
yourself up, and get rosumed, or you ain't good for much—tuned up
to concert pitch—but all that's a trifle. Put not your trust in politicianers."

"And why not, Mr. Rosum?"

"Why not? Help us up—there—steady she goes—hold on—why
not? Look at me; that's why—I'm a riglar patriot—look at my coat—
I'm all for the public good—twig the holes in my trousers. I'm steady
in my course, and upright in my conduct—don't let me fall down—
I've tried all parties, year in and year out, just by way of making myself popular and agreeable; and I've tried to be on both sides at once,"
roared Brush, with great emphasis, as he slipped into the gutter; "and
this is the end of it."

This striking illustration of the results of the political course he pursued, and of the danger of being on two sides at once, being achieved,
Brush, by the aid of his good natured auditor, scrawbled ashore, where
he sat, the picture of the shipwrecked mariner.

"Now, you must come along with me," said the Charley, helping
him along; "I'll take care of you. But what made you a politicianer—
ain't you good for nothing else—haven't you got a trade?"

"Trade! yes," replied Brush, contemptuously; "but what's a trade,
when a feller's got a soul? I love my country, and I want an office—I
don't care what, so it's fat and easy. I've a genius for governing; for
telling people what to do, and look at 'em do it. I want to take care of
my country, and I want my country to take care of me. Head work is
the trade I'm made for—talking; that's my line. Talking in the streets,
talking in the bar rooms, talking in the oyster cellers. Talking is the
grease for the wagon wheels of the body politic and the body corpu-
lent; and nothing will go on well till I've got my say in the matter: for I
can talk all day, and most of the night, only stopping to wet my whistle. But parties is all alike—all ungrateful; no respect for genus; no
respect for me. I've tried both sides, got nothing, and I've a great mind

to knock off, and call it half a day. I would, if my genus didn't make me talk, and think, and sleep so much, I can't find time to work."

"Yes, but Mr. Rosum, you must go before the Mayor first, Mr. Rosum."

"No, I'd rather not. Stop—now I think of it, I've asked him before, but perhaps if you'd speak a good word, he'd give me the first vacancy. Introduce me properly, and say I want something to do shocking—no, not something to do—I want something to get; my genus won't let me work. I'd like to have a fat salary and to be general superintendent of things in general, and nothing in particular, so I could walk about the streets, and see what is going on. Now, put my best leg foremost—say how I can make speeches, and how I can hurra at elections."

"No, I won't; you're a candidate for thirty days, and we'll have you examined in the morning. Every man for himself."

That Brush's qualifications were found sufficient there can be no doubt, and it is to be supposed, therefore, that, by virtue of an instrument, entitled [an act for the suppression of loafing, Peter was duly transmitted to Moyomensing Prison.]

The News-boy

Arms have had their day. The age of steel is past. The thunders of Mont St. Jean formed the grand finale to the melodrama of military exploit, and the curtain fell, never to rise again, upon the last scene of martial greatness, when the laurelled warriors of France cast aside the baton of command to have recourse to their spurs. Bellona then went to boarding-school, and learned to comb her refractory locks into the pliant graces of the toilet, while Mars obtained a situation in a counting-house, and seated upon a three-legged stool, still nibs his pen to gain a livelihood. Romance expired at Waterloo. Chivalry expended itself when Ney was foiled; and the Belgian peasant unconsciously depicts the moral of the fall of the empire when he boils potatoes in the helmet of the knight, and cooks his mutton in a breastplate of the "Guard." The world is tired of slaughter—the poetry of the shambles is exhausted. We live as long as we can now, and find existence none the worse for having a full supply of arms and legs. A body like a cullender is not essential to reputation, and death has become so unpopular that it is only by special favour that ambition can get itself hanged.

New elements produce new combinations. When the musket rusts in a garret, and glory puzzles over the multiplication table and retails brown sugar, the restless impulses of humanity seek excitements before unknown. Strategy exhibits itself in the marts of trade. Napoleons are financiers. The sun of Austerlitz bursts through the clouds which overhang the stock exchange. Bulls and bears constitute the contending hosts of modern times, and there is no analogy to the "maraud," unless we find it in embezzlement and defalcation. We are "smart" now—exceeding smart, and pugnacity is thrown to the dogs. Learning, too, leaves its solidity in the cloister, and, no longer frighted by trumpets and sulphurous vapors, spreads itself thinly abroad. Being in haste, the world reads as it runs, so that heavy books, like heavy artillery, remain in the arsenals. Man, commercial man, speculating man, financial man—man, heedless of gory greatness, but eager for cash, must know all that is in agitation. Having ceased to kill his neighbour, he is anxious to ascertain what his neighbour is about, that he may turn him and his doings to profitable account; and hence, in the place of those gaudy banners which used to flout the sky, instead of the oriflamme of nations, which once rallied their battalia, we gather round the newspaper, not with sword, and shield, and casque, but with ink-stained jacket and with pen in ear. Our clarion now, more potent than the Fontarabian horn, is the shrill voice of the news-boy, that modern Minerva, who leaped full blown from the o'erfraught head of journalism; and, as the news-boy is in some respects the type of the time—an incarnation of the spirit of the day,—a few words devoted to his consideration may not be deemed amiss.

As the true Corinthian metal was formed from the meltings of the devoted city, thus the news-boy is the product of the exigencies of the era. The requirements of the age always bring forth that which is wanted. The dragon teeth of tyranny have often caused the earth to crop with armed men, and the nineteenth century, thirsting for information and excitement, finds its Ganymede in the news-boy. He is its walking idea, its symbol, its personification. Humanity, in its new shape, is yet young and full of undefined energies, and so is he. The first generation of his race not having outgrown their business, the important part which youth thus trained, is destined to play in human affairs, is as yet too imperfectly developed even for the meditations of the most speculative philosopher that ever extracted glowing sunbeams from the refreshing cucumber; but, as nature does nothing in vain, it is fair to infer that the news-boy is destined, in one way or another, to fix the period which gave him birth, in the niche of history. Too many powerful elements combine in him not to be productive of grand results. What is the news-boy—what is necessary to his original constitution—what faculties are involved, cherished, strengthened and made, as it were, the preponderating forces of his character, by the calling to which he is devoted? Survey the news-boy—extract him from the buzzing crowd and place him on a pedestal, while you analyze his character in its psychological and physical details, estimating, at the same time, the past and future operation of circumstances in educating him for mature effort in the contentions of men. Anatomize him, and "see what breeds about his heart." A rough study, truly— soiled garments and patches. The youth is not precisely fitted for presentation in the drawing-room, evident though it be that his self-possession would not desert him in the presence of an empress. Valets and body servants do not trouble themselves about him. Father and mother, brother and sister, if such there be, have enough to do in struggling for their own existence, without attending to the details of his costume, and many a repair is the result of his own handiwork in hours stolen from needful rest. That battered hat, grown foxy by exposure, is picturesque in its proportions, not so much from careless usage as from hard service, and those oxhide boots, embrowned and cracked, have shamed the feats of plank-walking pedestrians. Sooth to say, our hero is somewhat uncouth in his externals. That fair damsel there would scarcely covet him for a parlour pet. He would not shine amid carpet knights, nor would Titania weary Oberon with prayers to have him for her henchman. The news-boy would not weep either, if he were to know that perfumed pride and silken delicacy thus curl the nose at him; for he would be lost and wearied in such preferment. Observe his frame, so light, yet so strong;—so pliant, wiry and enduring. No "debile wretch" enters the ranks of these juvenile Praetorians; or, if he should venture on services so far beyond his capacity, exhaustion soon removes him. Glance at the expression of that weather-beaten face, prematurely channelled into line and hardened into muscle. Care, courage and resolution are in every curve of those compacted lips. The soft roundness of childhood has departed long since. That mouth knows more of the strong word, the keen retort, the well-weighed phrases of the bargainer, of cunning solicitation, and of the fierce wrangle, than of the endearing kisses of affection. It brings no memory of rosebuds. It is no poetic feature for romance to dwell upon, but a mouth of plain reality—of confirmed utilitarianism. It wreathes itself more readily into the mould of worldly intrepidity, than into the gentle dimples of early life. It is, in the news-boy, as in all mankind beside, a key to the individual mysteries of our nature. The impulses, the ruling trait, are here developed, and the news-boy offers no exception to the rule. The glance of his eye is as cold, but as bright, as the beaming sun of a frosty morning, which sparkles on the ice, but melts it not. Still, though self-interest and sordid calculation dwell in its depths, we find a laughing devil there, which feasts on satire and sports like the chevaliers of old, à l'outrance. Its jokes bite shrewdly, and the lance of its wit displays the point "unbated," though not "envenomed." When the news-boy turns awhile from business to the pleasures of companionship, he asks no quiet recreation. His raillery and his pleasant tricks both deal in heavy blows and rude interchanges. Your nice, nervous sensibility finds no quarter from one whose very existence in all its phases is roughness. Should he hereafter learn to woo, it will be "as the lion *woos* his bride."

Such is the *physique* of the news-boy, and it contains many of the constituent points of greatness. Tossed early into the world, the impediments which cause other men to fail, are soon surmounted in his path. He has no kindly arm to lean upon, and, through mistaken tenderness, to make his steps unsteady. He is his own staff—his own protector. Of diffidence, he never heard the name—he does not know its nature. Imaginary barriers cannot interpose between him and his object; for he recognises none as worthier than he, and self-distrust plays no fantastic tricks to defeat the consummation of what he may resolve. He lives in deeds, and not in dreamy speculation—he is an actor, not a looker on, and practice has given him that estimate of his own powers which rarely falls below the mark, and which, best of all, surrounds disappointment with no unreal terrors. When he falls, he falls but to rise again with renewed strength, like the fabled Antaeus. And while continued collision with the world thus hardens his intellectual being, his muscular energies, which sustain the spirit, receive a training of proportionate severity. He has no tender years. Let wealthy youth be housed in luxury, and guarded from the storm. Soft couches and protracted slumbers do not enervate the news-boy. Compared to him, the sun itself is a sluggard. No morning ray finds him in bed; the moon and stars witness his uprisings, and he travels forth in darkness to commence his daily toil. Let the rain fall in torrents—the lightning flash—the thunders roar, the news-boy laughs at the elemental strife. Heat and cold are alike indifferent to one who has such duties to perform. It is on him that society waits for its mental aliment, and can he falter—can he shrink before winds and showers, before frosts and heats, who, more truly than any human being, is the "schoolmaster abroad?" No—others may crouch around the fire, or shrink beneath their blankets, at the sound of winter's threatening blasts; but the news-boy springs up, whistling cheerily, to encounter any hardship that may oppose him.

Now, it is contended that whole masses and classes of youth, thus educated, thus trained—who live, as it were, by their wits—by their boldness, their address, their perseverance—whose faculties are always literally at the grindstone—who daily practise endurance, fortitude, self-restraint, abstinence, and many other virtues; who are preeminently frugal and industrious; who learn to understand men and boys, dandies and dandizettes, and are schooled to emulation and competition—must of necessity produce something—not a little of roguery, mayhap, which is often the fungous growth, the untrimmed shoot, of a certain grade of cleverness. But we look for more than this—if genius is ever latent, the life of the news-boy must bring it forth. The blows which fall on him, would elicit sparks from the flint. In the school which boasts of such a pupil, society is the book, adversity the teacher, and harsh circumstance plays the part of rod and ferula. He is scourged into wisdom, almost before others can walk alone.

In what peculiar way, Tom Tibbs, whose admirable portrait graces our present number, is likely to distinguish himself, remains to be seen. His faculties are expansive—roaming like summer bees. The moment of concentration, when genius, rallying upon its focus, burns its way through all impediments, has not yet come to him. But Tibbs is one of whom expectation may be entertained. In fact, he has long been spoken of as a "hopeful youth," by many of those who know him; and though the phrase may often be applied derisively, as a sort of *lucus a non lucendo*, still this is but the vulgar error, which cannot comprehend the kittenhood of lionism—the unappreciated infancy of power. No one ever achieved distinction who did not begin by being a nuisance, just as greatness in a single walk, of necessity constitutes a bore; and it may be so with Tibbs. He has already learned the one great lesson of success. He looks upon the community as a collective trout—a universal fish, which must nibble at his bait, lie in his basket, and fill his frying-pan. On this maxim, heroes have overrun the world. It has been the foundation, not only of fortunes, but of empires. Why should it not elevate Tibbs? Especially as his soul has not been whittled down to a single point, by the process of acquiring the knowledge to which we refer. Tibbs has the affections, the sympathies, the twining tendrils of the heart, in as great perfection as can be expected in one who has been taught to look upon downright fact as the great purpose of existence. The pennies, however, do not engross him utterly; but when he is in pursuit of the pennies, that pursuit is made paramount. He takes his business as Falstaff did his sack, "simple, of itself;" and his pleasures are imbibed "neat," never spoiling both by an infusion and admixture of either. That soldier is a poor sentinel who nods upon his post, and would both watch and wink upon a tour of duty. The winkings of Tibbs are wisely condensed into a continuous slumber; and when he watches, it is generally found that his eyes are quite as widely open as the eyes of other people.

Tom Tibbs had a father, a necessity from which it is believed the greatest are not exempt, and in Tom's case, as indeed in many others, it was a hard necessity, from which it would have pleased him to be excused. Tom's father was a disciplinarian—that is, he compounded for his own delinquencies by a compensatory severity upon the delinquencies of others. When he had made a fool of himself abroad, he balanced the account and atoned for the folly, by chastising Tom at home, and thus went to bed with a cleared conscience and a weary arm. When he had spent more money upon a recreation than precisely suited his circumstances, the family were put upon short commons, and Tom's contingent of shoes and jackets, as well as those of his brothers and sisters—for he is not the only scion of Tibbsism—was economically retrenched. The elder Tibbs piqued himself much upon his paternal kindness in teaching prudence to his offspring. "You'll bless me for it," said he, with tears in his eyes, as he prepared to hammer them all round, after having been fined for wheeling his barrow upon the pavement, "you'll bless me for it the longest day you have to live." The elder Tibbs was patriarchal—he made the law as the necessity arose, carrying it into effect himself, and its adaptation to circumstances was wonderful. Any trouble in solving the equity of the case was instantly obviated by flogging Tom, and then old Tibbs would exclaim, "My conscience is easy—I do my best towards these naughty children—my duty is fulfilled—if they come to bad ends, they can't blame me for it. I have spared no pains to bring 'em up properly," and he had not been sparing, so far as the strap was concerned.

Fillin' Woman's Speah Under Difficulties mocks the idealization of "woman's sphere" by conservatives like Samantha Allen's friend Betsey Bobbet in *My Opinions and Betsey Bobbet's* (1873). Barnum's "Happy Family"—a cage of lions and other assorted animals supposed to live in perfect harmony—is pictured on the wall.

Mrs. Tibbs was a tender-hearted woman, who did not exactly understand parental duties as they were received by her husband; yet, being somewhat overcrowed by the commanding spirit of her mate, she sometimes almost began to think that Tom must indeed be rather a bad boy to require the neat's leather so often. But Mrs. Tibbs loved her children, and did her best to console them, thus preserving a verdant spot in Tom's otherwise arid heart; for, as his cuticle was hardened, his spirit also grew callous.

The pressure of the times, however, at last compelled the Tibbs family to migrate westward; and the father, when two days out from the city, having become warm with his own eloquence upon the difficulties of making a living, called Tom to his side and diverged into a personal episode and an individual apostrophe:

"It's so hard now to get along in the world, that I shouldn't wonder, if any thing happened to me, if these children were to starve. Tom, Tom, how often have I told you that you'd never come to good! Tom, Tom! you'll break my heart! Where's that strap? I don't want to do it, but I must!"

Tom, however, could not be prevailed upon to "stay to supper," and escaped, retracing his steps to the city, and dissolving all connection with the strap. He thought that he had received quite as much "bringing up," in that respect, as was necessary.

Tom felt his destiny strong within him. He threw himself into the bosom of the news-boys, and through their kindness, for they are a kindly race when properly approached, soon became one of the most distinguished of the corps. No one can sell more adroitly than he; his perseverance is mingled with tact, and his verbal embellishments as to the peculiar interest of the number of the journal he has to sell, are founded on fact. He never announces the steamer to be in before she is telegraphed, nor indulges in the false pretences which so often derogate from the dignity of the profession. He estimates its importance, and proceeds upon principle. The traveller who trades with Tibbs, at the cars, or on board the steamboat, may safely buy under the ringing of the last bell, without finding too late that his pennies have been exchanged for newspapers stale as an addled egg, and freshly pumped on, to give them an appearance of juvenility. Nor does Tom ever avail himself of hasty departures, to be oblivious in the matter of returning change. He does not, under such circumstances, "as some ungracious pastors do," put your quarter in one pocket and fumble for sixpences in the other, until the train darts away; nor would he, if tempted to the performance of this unworthy feat, add insult to injury, by holding up the cash when distance had made its reception impossible, or by assuming that burlesque expression of hypocritical astonishment with which some paper-venders, in a similar catastrophe, outrage your feelings besides wronging your purse. As Tom often justly remarks to such of his colleagues as are habituated to these practices, "This 'ere chiselling system won't do. Nobody likes to be chiselled, and when you have chiselled everybody, why then they'll get a law passed, and chisel us all to chips. A joke to-day is often a licking to-morrow, mind I tell you."

Tom's philosophy was, at once, Franklinian and indisputable. He felt the necessity of obviating all danger of a war of races. He knew that nothing but mischief was to be anticipated, if all the rest of the human family were to be "chiselled" into a hostility against the news-boys; for the minority always stand in the predicament of being presented and suppressed as a nuisance, whenever the stronger party think fit to exercise the power of numbers; and, as a natural consequence, Tom was opposed to the practice of clustering about a corner and selling newspapers in a flock. "A sprinkling of news-boys, one or two in every square," thought he, "is well enough. It's good for trade, and makes things lively; but to be cutting up, so fashion, all in a jam, why people go on t'other side of the way, and retailing's done for. I vote for scatteration. Folks hate being obligated to fight their way through the literary circles."

But Tibbs, with all his good sense, has a weakness. There is a forte and a foible to every blade, and even such a blade as a news-boy cannot escape the common lot of humanity. Sound upon the general principle of not annoying others, yet, in the indulgence of his humour, he sometimes makes an exception. He especially dislikes Mr. Sappington Sapid, a starched gentleman of the old school, who never reads a journal, cares nothing for the current of events, and entertains a perfect horror of the modern style of newspapers and of all concerned in their distribution. In fact, he attributes much of the evils of the time to cheap journalism, and he has not been sparing of an expression of his views on the subject, whenever the opportunity was afforded. On some one of these occasions, it was his luck to wound the feelings of Thomas Tibbs, and Tibbs accordingly marked him for a sufferer.

Incessantly was Mr. Sappington Sapid assailed. Not a news-boy passed his door without ringing the bell to ascertain whether a paper was not required—he never walked the streets without perpetual and ridiculous solicitations. When he appeared, all customers were left for his special annoyance, and, in consequence of failing in the attaint one day, when he directed an indignant kick at the provoking Tibbs— unpractised individuals should never essay the rapid and extemporaneous application of the foot—Mr. Sappington Sapid sat suddenly and unexpectedly down in a puddle of water, in full sight of a legion of his tormentors, who never forgot the incident, but would rehearse it, to the delight of their fellows, whenever the unfortunate man happened to present himself, and Tibbs was especially dexterous in giving the broadest effect to the incident.

What a vitality there is in our worst mishaps! It would be nothing, comparatively, if disaster were circumscribed by its immediate consequences, and it would have made but little figure in Mr. Sapid's memoirs had he only caught cold by the operation referred to; but when a personal sorrow is transmuted into a general joke, it becomes, *ipso facto*, a living piece of attendant biography, a walking companionship, which even smiles over a man's last resting-place. Death itself affords no refuge to the hero of a "ridicule." "Poor fellow!" say his dearest friends, "perhaps it's wrong to mention it now, but, by-the-way, did you ever hear how,—ha! ha! ho!—how he made such a fool of himself at Mrs. Dunover's pic-nic? Ho! ho! ha! Poor soul!!"

Rob a church, or lay logs on the rail-road, and there is a chance that the last may be heard of it; but if a drollery, no matter how sad in its essence, be created at any one's expense, he and it are so far married that they cling together through life, while the jest is a "relict," to move *post mortem* mirth, autopsical grins and necrological merriment. A dear departed is much more likely to be resurrectionised by a surviving joke, than by the most intrepid of body-snatchers, and the best of portraits is not so good a memento as being implicated in an anecdote which is sure to create laughter. Under an inkling of this truth, Mr. Sapid always denies that he is the person who "shook his foot" at the news-boys.

But there are bounds to patience. A man is but a bottle before the fire of mischance, and when the heat becomes insupportable, he must of necessity explode, no matter how tightly corked by fortitude, or wired down by philosophy. "The grief that will not speak," is a deadly inward fermentation. They who survive sorrow, are those who "exteriorize" sorrow, and give sorrow a free channel. To scold is the vital principle of practical hygiene for the ladies, and grumbling humanity rarely needs the doctor. The inference therefore is, that the average of existence would be at a higher rate, if the admirable counter-irritant of round swearing were not proscribed in refined society, thus killing people by the suppressed perspiration of an indignant spirit.

Sapid, however, was none of these. Patience might sit upon a monument, if she liked; but there was nothing of the marble-mason in his composition, nor did he at all affect the "statuesque," when vexation chafed his heart. If preyed upon in this way, though he never indulged in Commodore Trunnion's expletives, nor "shotted his discourse" like that worthy commander, yet he did not, by any means, pray in return, as Dinah had often reason to acknowledge, when the chamber pitcher was left vacant of water, or when forgetful Boots failed in the performance of his resplendent office. No! Sappington Sapid makes people hear of it when he is offended, justly thinking it better that their ears should be annoyed, than that he should pine away of an unexpressed inflammation.

It was a bright forenoon, such as elicits snakes in the country, and evolves the fashionable in cities, when Mr. Sappington Sapid walked firmly along the street, filled with a settled purpose. His coat was buttoned up to the chin, to prevent the evaporation of his stern resolve;

his lips were drawn together, as if to obviate all danger of evasion by word of mouth; his hat had settled martially down almost to the bridge of his nose, while his heels saluted mother earth so determinedly, that his whole frame-work jarred at the shock. If ever a man displayed outward symptoms of having his mind made up into the most compact kind of a parcel, it was Sappington Sapid, on this memorable occasion. No beggar would have dared to ask charity from him, under such an aspect. He was safe from being solicited to take a cab. They who met him, made way instinctively. "Under him, their genius was rebuked; as, it is said, Mark Antony's was by Caesar;" a psychological phenomenon often manifest, when, by the force of an emergency, even inferior men are screwed up to the sublime,—just as valour's self shrinks abashed from the angry presence of a cornered cat.

But whither wandered Sapid? No one knew. He had taken breakfast without a word, and had wandered forth in equal silence. Counsel he sought not—sympathy he did not require. When we are girded up, of our own impulse, to pull the trigger of a catastrophe, advice is felt to be an impertinence, and no spur is needed to prick the sides of our intent. We are a sufficiency unto ourselves. Legions could not make us stronger, and, therefore, Sapid disdained companionship or an interchange of thought. He, Sapid, was enough to fill the canvas for the contemplated picture. He was the tableau, all alone, so far as his share in the incident was to be concerned.

Some clue to his state of mind may be afforded, when it is known that he was visited by a night-mare, a journalistic incubus, on the previous night. An immense Tom Tibbs sat upon his breast, and tried to feed him with penny papers. His head seemed to grow to the size of a huge type-foundery, and each of his ears roared like a power press. Then again, he was flattened into an immense sheet, and they printed him as a "Double Brother Jonathan," with pictorial embellishments. He was expanded into whole acres of reading for the people, and did not awake until he was folded, pasted up, and thrust into the mail-bag; when, protesting against the ignominy of being charged "at the usual rate of newspaper postage," he sprang up convulsively, and found that his night-cap had got over his nose.

"Is this the office of the 'National Pop-gun and Universal Valve Trumpet?' " inquired Sapid, in sepulchral tones.

"Hey—what? Oh!—yes," gruffly replied the clerk, as he scrutinized the applicant.

"It is, is it?" was the response.

"H-umpse;" being a porcine affirmative, much in use in the city of brotherly love.

"I am here to see the editor, on business of importance," slowly and solemnly articulated Sapid.

There must have been something professionally alarming in this announcement, if an opinion may be formed from the effect it produced.

"Editor's not come down yet, is he, Spry?" inquired the clerk, with a cautionary wink at the paste-boy.

"Guess he ain't more nor up yet," said Spry; "the mails was late, last night."

"I'll take a seat till he does come," observed Sapid, gloomily.

Spry and the clerk laid their heads together, in the most distant corner of the little office.

"Has he got a stick?" whispered one.

"No, and he isn't remarkable big, nuther."

"Any bit of paper in his hand—does he look like State House and a libel suit? It's a'most time—not had a new suit for a week."

"Not much; and, as we didn't have any scrouger in the 'Gun' yesterday, perhaps he wants to have somebody tickled up himself. Send him in."

St. Sebastian Sockdolager, Esq., the editor of "The National Popgun and Universal Valve Trumpet," sat at a green table, elucidating an idea by the aid of a steel pen and whitey-brown paper, and, therefore, St. Sebastian Sockdolager did not look up when Mr. Sapid entered the sanctum. The abstraction may, perhaps, have been a sample of literary stage effect; but it is certain that the pen pursued the idea with the speed and directness of a steeplechase, straight across the paper, and direful was the scratching thereof. The luckless idea being at last fairly run down and its brush cut off, Mr. Sockdolager threw himself back in his chair, with a smile of triumph.

"Tickletoby!" said he, rumpling his hair into heroic expansiveness.

"What?" exclaimed Sapid, rather nervously.

"My dear sir, I didn't see you—a thousand pardons! Pray, what can be done for you in our line?"

"Sir, there is a nuisance—"

"Glad of it, sir; the 'Gun' is death on a nuisance. We circulate ten thousand deaths to any sort of a nuisance every day, besides the weekly and the country edition. We are a regular smash-pipes in that line—surgical, surgical to this community—we are at once the knife and the sarsaparilla to human ills, whether financial, political or social."

"Sir, the nuisance I complain of, lies in the circulation—in its mode and manner."

"Bless me!" said Sockdolager, with a look of suspicion; "you are too literal in your interpretations. If your circulation is deranged, you had better try Brandreth, or the Fluid Extract of Quizembob."

"It is not my circulation, but yours, which makes all the trouble. I never circulate,—I can't without being insulted."

"Really, mister, I can't say that this is clearly comprehensible to perception. Not circulate! Are you below par in the 'money article,' or in what particular do you find yourself in the condition of being 'no go'? Excuse my facetiae and be brief, for thought comes tumbling, bumping, booming"—and Sockdolager dipped his pen in the ink.

Mr. Sappington Sapid unravelled the web of his miseries. "I wish you, sir, to control your boys—to dismiss the saucy, and to write an article which shall make 'em ashamed of themselves. I shall call on every editor in the city, sir, and ask the same—a combined expression for the suppression of iniquity. We must be emancipated from this new and growing evil, or our liberties become a farce, and we are squushed and crushed in a way worse than fifty tea-taxes."

"Pardon me, Mr. Whatcheecallem; it can't be done—it would be suicidal, with the sharpest kind of a knife. Whatcheecallem, you don't understand the grand movement of the nineteenth century—you are not up to snuff as to the vital principle of human progression—the propulsive force has not yet been demonstrated to your benighted optics. The sun is up, sir; the hill-tops of intellect glow with its brightness, and even the level plain of the world's collective mediocrity is gilded by its beams; but you, sir, are yet in the foggy valley of exploded prejudice, poking along with a tuppenny-ha'penny candle—a mere dip. Suppress sauciness! Why, my dear bungletonian, sauciness is the discovery of the age—the secret of advancement! We are saucy now, sir, not by the accident of constitution—temperament has nothing to do with it. We are saucy by calculation, by intention, by design. It is cultivated, like our whiskers, as a super-added energy to our other gifts. Without sauciness, what is a news-boy? what is an editor? what are revolutions? what are people? Sauce is power, sauce is spirit, independence, victory, every thing. It is, in fact,—this sauce, or 'sass,' as the vulgar have it—steam to the great locomotive of affairs. Suppress, indeed! No, sir; you should regard it as part of your duty as a philanthropist and as a patriot, to encourage this essence of superiority in all your countrymen; and I've a great mind to write you an article on that subject, instead of the other, for this conversation has warmed up my ideas so completely, that justice will not be done to the community till they, like you, are enlightened on this important point."

St. Sebastian Sockdolager, now having a leading article for "The National Pop-gun and Universal Valve Trumpet," clearly in his mind, was not a creature to be trifled with. An editor in this paroxysm, however gentle in his less inspired moments, cannot safely be crossed, or even spoken to. It is not wise to call him to dinner, except through the keyhole, and to ask for "more copy," in general a privileged demand, is a risk too fearful to be encountered. St. Sebastian's eye became fixed, his brow corrugated, his mouth intellectually ajar.

"But, sir, the nuisance"—said Sappington.

"Don't bother!" was the impatient reply, and the brow of St. Sebastian Sockdolager grew black as his own ink.

"The boys, sir, the boys!—am I to be worried out of my life and soul?"

The right hand of St. Sebastian Sockdolager fell heavily upon the huge pewter inkstand—the concatenation of his ideas had been broken—he half raised himself from his chair and glanced significantly from his visiter to the door.

"Mizzle!" said he, in a hoarse, suppressed whisper.

The language itself was unintelligible—the word might have been Chaldaic, for all that Sapid knew to the contrary; but there are situations in which an interpreter is not needed, and this appeared to be one of them. Sapid never before made a movement so swiftly extemporaneous.

He intends shortly to try whether the Grand Jury is a convert to the new doctrine of sauciness.

Tibbs, in the meantime, grows in means and expands in ambition. Progress is in his soul, like a reel in a bottle. He aspires already to a "literary agency," and often feels as if he were destined to publish more magazines at a single swoop than there are now in existence, each of which shall have upon its cover, a picture of "The News-Boy," while the same device shall gleam upon the panels of his coach.

❧ George P. Morris ❧

George P. Morris (1802–1864) spread popular literature and song across the Northeast through the pages of the New York *Mirror*, which he edited with N. P. Willis from 1822 through 1837, and later the *New Mirror, Evening Mirror, Mirror Library* (reprinting popular literary pieces from the weekly and daily *Mirror* and low-priced editions of contemporary British poets), and from 1846 the *Home Journal*. After Joseph Dennie, he became the field marshal of the movement for a national literature, which he served, as Willis wrote in *Graham's Magazine* (April, 1845), by becoming "the best-known poet of the country by acclamation, not by criticism . . . breast-high in the common stream of sympathy." Morris's most widely acclaimed poem was "Woodsman Spare That Tree"; others covered subjects as diverse as navy life and the western frontier. Working life was celebrated in "Song of the Sewing Machine" and the City Corporation of New York requested "Croton Ode" to commemorate the completion of the city's major aquaduct.

" 'The Monopoly' and 'The People's Line' " was published in *The Little Frenchman and His Water Lots* (Philadelphia, 1839), where it stands out among a number of more rambling pieces as Morris' most contained and well-plotted story. A lengthy introductory paragraph on competition was added to the story when it was printed in the short-lived *New Mirror* ("Extra" edition, 1844) as "The Stage Competitors: A Tale of the Road," and it is this version that is reprinted here. Aside from Willis' biography in *Graham's*, which became the basis of a lengthy "Memoir" in *The Poems of George P. Morris* (3rd ed.; New York, 1860), 13–48, essays praising Morris include Poe's "George P. Morris" as a "Minor Contemporary" in *The Works of Edgar Allan Poe* (10 vols.; Chicago, 1895), VIII, 272–76, and George W. Bungay's "George P. Morris and N. P. Willis," in *Off-hand Takings; or, Crayon Sketches* (New York, 1854), 43–51.

The Stage Competitors: A Tale of the Road

He hears
On all sides, from innumerable tongues,
A dismal universal hiss, the sound
Of public scorn.
　—Milton

Applause
Waits on success; the fickle multitude,
Like the light straw that floats along the stream,
Glide with the current.
　—Franklin

Two of a trade can never agree.
　—Proverb

The proprietors of steamboats, railroads, and stagecoaches, not unfrequently carry the spirit of competition to a ruinous and ridiculous extent. A few years ago, we went to Albany and were "found" for half a dollar! and it is within the recollection of everybody that Gibbons, for a long period, run his boats from New-York to New-Brunswick for twelve-and-a-half cents! More recently, Mr. Vanderbilt, a large capitalist, and doubtless an enterprising man, with a view of breaking down what was denominated the "odious eastern monopoly," placed several swift and commodious steamers on the Boston line, and you would take a trip from New-York to Providence for the trifling consideration of half a dollar, lawful currency! Whether the public—the misused, flattered, cajoled, long-suffering and indulgent public—is ultimately benefited by these reductions of the fare to an inadequate price, or otherwise, is not for us to determine; and we, therefore, leave the investigation of the subject, now and for ever, to those more skilled and curious in such matters. Yet we have a right to an opinion; and, as this is certainly a free country, we presume no one will quarrel with us—if we keep it entirely to ourselves. In a crowded steamer, however, whose deck and cabin are thronged with what the great bard calls "all sorts of people," there is but little comfort. Still we would not be understood as raising our feeble voice in defence of any monopoly under the sun; but more especially that of steamboats. Far be it from us. We are patriots; but, what is a greater evidence of our honesty and disinterestedness, we have no stock in them whatever; and, as we are nothing but a "waif upon the world's wide common," we never expect to have any; unless we should draw a prize in the lottery, or some unknown or unheard-of rich relation should die, and unexpectedly shower his bounties upon us; or any other unimaginable, improbable, and impossible thing should occur, of which we have not the remotest conception at the present moment. We therefore, of course, prefer a spirited and liberally-managed opposition in all cases, whenever the number of travellers will warrant such an arrangement, and when mere angry feelings, jealousy, hatred, and all uncharitableness, are not the governing motive and groundwork of the competition. But we have often noted, that the great contending parties have generally some concealed motive, some private end in view, and, that, while they are endeavouring, like the Hibernian cats, to eat each other up—"all up!"—they profess the most profound respect and regard for that public, which, in the main, they are constantly striving to overreach. The public, however, like a *re*-public, is proverbially ungrateful; and, seeing the pains that people take to impose upon each other, it does not hesitate, in its turn, to impose upon everybody. Our reminiscences furnish us with a case in point.

Not many years ago, there lived on Long-Island a jolly, well-to-do, honest old Dutchman, who drove a stage from Brooklyn to Jamaica for two dollars a passenger. This had been the charge since Adam was a "little peevish boy," or since the time whereof the memory of man "runneth not to the contrary." It was sanctioned by immemorial usage, and had all the crust of antiquity about it. Nobody thought of disputing the matter. It was settled, like the legal codes of old, and was a thing not to be sacrilegiously meddled with, or altered on any account whatever. The proprietor's great-grandfather had driven the same route, and so had all his other ancestors, and none of them had managed to realize more than enough to make both ends meet when Christmas came round. But it was left for these Mesmeric days, and for modern innovators, to work wonderful changes in the destinies of Jamaica, which was then a mere dot on the unexplored map of Long-Island. You might have held it in the hollow of your hand, or Major Noah could have put it into his breeches pocket. It has assumed vast consequence since that period—which was before the discovery of lithography, unquestionably the most magnificent and imposing art of modern times—and is an incorporated city—in embryo!—with its mayor and its aldermen—its commodious edifices—its steeples, domes, and courthouses—its spacious taverns and its heaven-aspiring liberty-rods, and all the other requisites of a thriving American metropolis! If the future greatness of Jamaica may be gathered from the thousands of building-lots that have been laid out and disposed of for notes of hand that were never redeemed, and if one may at all rely upon the prophecies of the eloquent and disinterested quondam speculators of Wall-street, "who looked into the seeds of time, and said which *place* would grow and which would not," then is Jamaica, without the shadow of a doubt, predestined to become the capital of the world!

Oh, Lithography! let me apostrophize thee! Thou art indeed a mighty wizard—and hast performed more miracles in our day and generation than all the soothsayers, seers, and necromancers of the olden time! There is no obstacle that thou canst not overcome—no difficulty that thou canst not surmount! Does a mountain oppose thy onward march—one wave of thy wand, and it hides its diminished head and disappears for ever! Is a valley too deep and broad for thy lofty purposes—another flourish of thy potent staff, and lo! it is as level as the plain! Is a river inconvenient to ford, and does it endeavour to frustrate thy plans, thou hast but to will it—and, presto! its waters recede, and the warm and genial earth, beautifully checkered, and converted into streets, avenues, spacious squares and sumptuous building-lots, remains in its stead! Thou canst people the wilderness—for the woods, like those of Birnam, will "unfix their earthbound roots," and move before thee—and thou canst command the "desert to bud and blossom like the rose," and it is even so! Thou canst found settlements, villages, towns, and cities wherever thou listest—in the interior, by the running river, the quiet lake, or on the more boisterous borders of the ocean! 'Tis all the same to thee, Lithography. Thou canst do anything—everything—all things—*on paper!*

But I am wandering from my subject; and must take care that, in my admiration for the most sublime of all modern inventions—always save and excepting the "noble science of money-making"—I do not lose the reader as well as myself in the labyrinths of imagination and metaphor.

In the course of time, travelling increased on the Jamaica turnpike; the Dutchman had his stage full every trip, and began to thrive. But the star of his good fortune, although it had risen clear and unclouded, was not long in the ascendant; for, one fine morning, there came another stage driver, the owner of a new turn-out, as fine as a fiddle, who put in his claims for patronage.

He was a full-grown stripling, of little credit, but some ready money,

The competitive spirit of the North is evident in this comic illustration of Francis Durivage's "The Fastest Funeral on Record," from Burton's *Cyclopedia of Wit and Humor* (1858). Durivage's story surpasses the cartoon, for he describes the president of Harvard College, waving his "tile" and yelling, "Go it, boots!"

and he secretly resolved upon bearing off the palm from the quiet, but covetous Dutchman. At first he demanded the usual rates, and divided the business with his old-established rival; but finding that he had less custom, that he was looked upon as an interloper, and that all faces were set against him, he resolved to cut down the fare to a single dollar—and he did so, greatly to the satisfaction of the applauding multitude.

This was a sad blow to the prospects of the poor old Dutchman, whose carriage was instantly deserted; all the fickle populace instinctively flocking to the glossy vehicle of his adversary, who cracked his whip in high glee as he dashed along the dusty and unpaved streets of Brooklyn. At first Mynheer did not know what to make of the matter, so he lighted his pipe and looked to St. Nicholas for the solution of a mystery, altogether too profound for his comprehension. One day, however, a friend unravelled it to him, and suggested the propriety of a reduction also in his price; whereupon the whole truth flashed upon him in the twinkling of an eye, and he instantly resolved, in defiance of the good examples of his forefathers, to humble himself to the insignificant fare of his pestilent competitor. Now all was right again, and things went on as swimmingly as before, until the new-comer again lowered the fare—called his omnibus the "People's Line," and branded his opponent's "The Monopoly;" upon which the Dutchman flew into a violent passion, broke his pipe into a thousand pieces, and swore by all the saints in the calendar, that he would thereafter carry his passengers for nothing! And so strange was his demeanour, flying hither and yonder in a hurricane of hot haste and hotter disdain that all his neighbours stigmatized him as the "Flying Dutchman;" a name which to this very hour is still fresh in the memory of that mysterious personage the "oldest inhabitant."

The "People's Line," not in the least disconcerted by this unexpected calamity, also came down to *nothing!* and painted on the panels of the carriage the figure of a fiery old man addressing a multitude, and begging them to ride in his carriage gratis, with the motto,

"Nothing can come of nothing; *try* again."

This was evidently intended as a hit at the "Flying Dutchman," who retorted by staining the "Interloper," as he always persisted in designating the "People's Line," with certain Dutch epithets, which respect for our readers prevents us from translating into veritable English. Fierce were the animosities—bitter the feuds—and arduous the struggles that ensued between the belligerents. Long they lasted, and fatal promised to be the consequences to both. Every expedient was resorted to; but as neither would yield an inch of ground to the other, they both went on, season after season, running the stages at their own expense, and annoying everybody who would listen to them, with a full and particular recital of their wrongs, their wrath, and their wranglings. At last, the owner of the "People's Line," fairly wearied out by the obstinacy and perseverance of the redoubtable Dutchman, caused a mammoth handbill to be struck off and posted from the East River to the Atlantic Ocean, in which he stated, in ponderous capital letters, that he would not only carry his passengers "for nothing," but that he would actually pay each and every one the sum of twenty-five cents for going? To the unhappy Dutchman this was the drop too much; and it effectually did the business for his now unpopular and detested "Monopoly," which was denounced at every tavern by the roadside as a paltry, mean, and "unconstitutional" concern, while the "People's

Line" was lauded to the third heaven for its liberality and public spirit. The Flying Dutchman flew no more. His spirit was evidently broken as well as his prospects, and his horses crawled daily to and from Jamaica at a snail's pace, equally unmindful of whip or rein—evidently sympathizing in their master's disappointment and discomfiture. Yet go the Dutchman would—he had become accustomed to the occupation—it was second nature to him; and as he could not easily overcome the force of habit; he preferred working for nothing and finding himself, to relinquishing the road entirely to his indefatigable annoyer. "His shirtless Majesty!" as some audacious poet has impertinently called the sovereign people! however, generally gave its countenance and support to its own line, which still kept its speed and its reputation. It speaks volumes—volumes, did I say? it speaks ten thousand bookstores—for the intelligence and good feeling of our locomotive countrymen, and, as faithful chroniclers, we are bound to record the fact, that not a single individual ever applied for the two shillings, that had been so generously and disinterestedly tendered, every one being actually contented with going the whole distance gratis, and with being thanked into the bargain!

One day, however, a long, thin, lank-sided, mahogany-faced downeaster chanced to read the mammoth handbill with the ponderous capitals; and without a moment's hesitation, he decided upon bestowing his corporeal substance snugly in the backseat of the "People's Line;" and it so fell out that he was the only passenger.

The down-easter was a talkative, prying, speculative, crinkum-crankum, jimcrack sort of a fellow, who propounded more questions in a single minute than one could answer in a whole hour; and, in less time than you could say Jack Robinson, he was at the bottom of all the difficulty, and in possession of every particular respecting the rival lines. He was "free of speech and merry;" joked with the proprietor; ridiculed the flying Dutchman, called him an old cockalorum, and finally denounced him as an inflated, overgrown, purse-proud capitalist, who advocated a system of exclusive privileges contrary to the spirit of our glorious institutions, and dangerous to the liberties of the country!—and he even went so far as to recommend that a town meeting should be immediately called to put the old blockhead down, and banish him from the sunshine of the public favour for ever!

"I *will* put him down!" said the driver.

"And he shall stay *put*, when he *is* down!" replied Jonathan, with an approving nod of the head.

At the various stopping-places, Jonathan—who was not a member of any of the temperance societies, for those institutions were not founded at the time of which we are writing—to show his good-fellowship, but with no other motive, did not scruple to drink sundry villanous bar-room compounds, at the expense of his new acquaintance, who that day was so overjoyed to find that the stage of the "Monopoly" was compelled to go the whole route entirely empty, that his hilarity and flow of boisterous humour knew no bounds, and he snapped his fingers, and said he did not care a fig for the expense—not he?

"Here's to the People's Line!" drank Jonathan.

"The People's Line for ever!" shouted the driver.

"And confusion to the Monopoly!" rejoined the down-easter.

"With all my heart!" echoed the friend of the people.

"The Flying Dutchman is deficient in public spirit!" said the landlord, a warlike little fellow, who was a major in the militia.

"Behind the age we live in!" remarked a justice of the peace.

"And he deserves to run the gauntlet from Brooklyn to Jamaica for violating the constitution!" responded all the patriots of the bar-room.

"I say, mister! you're a fine specimen of a liberal fellow," said Jonathan, as his companion paid the reckoning, resumed the ribands, and touched the leaders gayly. "You deserve encouragement, and you shall have it. I promise it to you, my lad," continued he, as he slapped the "People's Line" on the shoulder like an old and familiar friend, "and that's enough. The Flying Dutchman, forsooth! why he's a hundred years behind the grand march of improvement, and as he will never be able to overtake it, I shall henceforward look upon him as a mere abstract circumstance, unworthy of the least regard or notice."

Jonathan weighed every word of the last sentence before he pronounced it, for he was, upon the whole, rather a cute chap, and had no notion of letting his friendship for the one party involve him in a lawsuit for a libel on the other.

The overjoyed proprietor thanked him heartily for his good wishes, and for the expression of his contempt for the old "Monopoly," and the lumbering vehicle thundered on toward Jamaica.

Arrived, at last, at the termination of the journey, the driver unharnessed the horses, watered them, and put them up for the night. When he turned to take his own departure, however, he observed that Jonathan, who, after all said and done, candour compels us to acknowledge had rather a hang-dog sort of look, seemed fidgety and discontented, that he lingered about the stable, and followed him like a shadow wherever he bent his steps.

"Do you stop in this town, or do you go further?" asked the driver.

"I shall go further, when you settle the trifle you owe me," replied Jonathan, with a peculiar, knowing, but serious expression.

"That *I* owe *you?*"

"Yes—is there not *something* between us?"

"Not that I know of."

"Why, mister, what a short memory you've got—you should study mnemonics, to put you in mind of your engagements."

"What do you mean? There must be some mistake!"

"Oh! but there's no mistake at all," said Jonathan, as he pulled a handbill from his pocket, unfolded it with care, and smoothed it out upon the table. It was the identical mammoth handbill with the ponderous capitals.

"That's what I mean. Look there, Mr. People's Line. There I have you, large as life—and no mistake whatever. That's your note of hand—it's a fair business transaction—and I will trouble you for the twenty-five cents, in less than no time; so shell it out, you 'tarnal critter."

"My Christian friend, allow me to explain, if you please. I confess that it's in the bill; but, bless your simple soul, nobody ever thinks of asking me for it."

"Did you ever!" ejaculated Jonathan. "Now, that's what I call cutting it a leetle too fat! but it's nothing to me. I attend to nobody's affairs but my own; and if other people are such ninnyhammers as to forgive you the debt, that's no reason why I should follow their example. Here are your conditions, and I want the mopuses. A pretty piece of business, truly, to endeavour to do your customers out of their just and legal demands in this manner. But I can't afford to lose the amount, and I won't—What! haven't I freely given you my patronage—liberally bestowed upon you the pleasure of my company, and, consequently, afforded you a triumph over that narrow-contracted 'Monopoly?' and now you refuse to comply with your terms of travel, and pay me my money, you ungrateful varmint, you! Come, mister, it's no use putting words together in this way. I'll expose you to 'old Monopoly' and everybody else, if you don't book-up like an honest fellow; and I won't leave the town until I am satisfied."

"You won't?"

"No."

"Are you serious?"

"Guess you'll find I am."

"And you *will* have the money?"

"As sure as you stand there."

"What! the twenty-five cents?"

"Every fraction of it."

"And you won't go away without it?"

"Not if I stay here till doomsday; and you know the consequence of detaining me against my will."

"What is it?"

"I'll swinge you, you *pyson sarpent*, you!"

"You'll what?"

"I'll sue you for damages."

"You will?"

"Yes; I'll law you to death, sooner than be defrauded out of my property in this manner; so, down with the dust, and no more nonsense about it."

The bewildered and crest-fallen proprietor, perceiving, from Jonathan's tone and manner, that all remonstrance would be in vain, and that he was irrevocably fixed in his determination to extract twenty-five cents from his already exhausted coffers, at length slowly and reluctantly put into his hand the bit of silver coin representing that amount of the circulating medium.

Jonathan, we blush to say, took the money, and what is more, he put it into his pocket; and what is moreover, he positively buttoned it up, as if to "make assurance doubly sure," and to guard it against the possibility of escape.

"Mister," said he, after he had gone coolly through the ceremony, looking all the while as innocently as a man who had just performed a virtuous action; "mister, I say, you must not think that I set any more value on the insignificant trifle you have paid me, than any other gentleman: a twenty-five cent piece, after all, is hardly worth disputing about—it's only a quarter of a dollar—which any industrious person may earn in a little while, if he chooses—the merest trifle in the world—a poor little scroundrel of a coin, that I would not, under other circumstances, touch with a pair of tongs—and which I would scorn to take even now—*if it were not for the principle of the thing!* To show you, however, that I entertain a high respect for the "People's Line," that I wish old cockalorum to the devil, and that I do not harbour the slightest ill-will toward you for so unjustifiably withholding my legal demands, the next time that I come this way, I will unquestionably give your stage the preference—unless the "Flying Dutchman" holds out greater inducements than you do, *in which case, I rather calculate, I shall feel myself in duty bound to encourage him!"*

Since the veritable circumstances here related, the Jamaica railroad has entirely superseded the necessity of both the "Monopoly" and the "People's Line" of stages, and their public-spirited proprietors, after making a prodigious noise in the world, have retired under the shade of their laurels, deep into the recesses of private life. There we shall leave them to enjoy whatever satisfaction may be gathered from the proud consolation of having expended every farthing they were worth in the world, for the gratification of a public that cares no more about them than the man in the moon.

❧ Thomas C. Haliburton ❧

Thomas C. Haliburton (1796–1865), Canadian Tory humorist without honor in his own country, established his reputation in North America and England as the father of Sam Slick, a shrewd yankee clock peddler who used "soft sawder" to open tightly held New England purses, commenting all the while on human nature. From the first *Clockmaker* printing in 1836 through *The Attaché, The Letter Bag of the Great Western, The Old Judge,* two volumes of collected American comic stories, *Sam Slick's Wise Saws and Modern Instances,* and *Nature and Human Nature,* Haliburton showed a broad range of abilities in burlesque, local color narrative, dialect humor, and satire—indicating that his reputation as "Sam Slick" only reflects a portion of his real achievement.

Nature and Human Nature (London, 1855) shows Sam Slick in a reflective mood, conversing with Dr. Cutler about politics and individual responsibility, observing the Negro servant Sorrow, convincing the beautiful half-caste Jessie that miscegenation may not be the crime she suspects, and reasoning aphoristically on the lot of political and social man. "Female Colleges," from this volume, attacks the fashionable finishing school—and with it enslavement to fashion rather than humane common sense—in burlesque, but also shows an alternative, and humbling, weakness in Slick; the sketch thus provides insight into the well-rounded conservatism of its author. V. L. O. Chittick, *Thomas Chandler Haliburton ("Sam Slick"): A Study in Provincial Toryism* (New York, 1924) justly remains the standard work on Haliburton.

Female Colleges

After Sorrow had retired, we lighted our cigars, and turned to for a chat, if chat it can be called one, where I did most of the talking myself.

"Doctor," said I, "I wish I had had more time to have examined your collection of minerals. I had no idea Nova Scotia could boast of such an infinite variety of them. You could have taught me more in conversation in five minutes than I could have learned by books in a month. You are a mineralogist, and I am sorry to say I aint, though every boarding-school miss, now-a-days, in our country consaits she is. They are up to *trap* at any rate, if nothing else, you may depend," and I gave him a wink.

"Now don't, Slick," said he, "now don't set me off, that's a good fellow."

"'Mr. Slick,' said a young lady of about twelve years of age, to me wunst, 'do you know what gray wackey is? for I do.'

"'Don't I,' sais I; 'I know it to my cost. Lord! how my old master used to lay it on!'

"'Lay it on!' she said, 'I thought it reposed on a primitive bed.'

"'No it don't,' said I. 'And if anybody knows what gray wackey is, I ought; but I don't find it so easy to repose after it as you may. *Gray* means the gray birch rod, dear, and *wackey* means layin it on. We always called it gray whackey in school, when a feller was catching particular Moses.'

"'Why how ignorant you are!' said she. 'Do you know what them mining tarms, *clinch*, *parting*, and *black bat* means?'

"'Why, in course I do!' sais I; 'clinch is *marrying*, parting is getting *divorced*, and black bat is where a fellow *beats* his wife black and blue.'

"'Pooh!' said she, 'you don't know nothing.'

"'Well,' sais I, 'what do you know?'

"'Why,' said she, 'I know Spanish and mathematics, ichthiology and conchology, astronomy and dancing, mineralogy and animal magnetism, and German and chemistry, and French and botany. Yes, and the use of the globes too. Can you tell me what attraction and repulsion is?'

"'To be sure I can,' said I, and I drew her on my knee, and kissed her. 'That's attraction, dear.' And when she kicked and screamed as cross as two cats, 'that, my pretty one,' I said, 'is repulsion.

Now I know a great many things you don't. Can you hem a pocket-handkerchief?'

" 'No.'

" 'Nor make a pudding?'

" 'No.'

" 'Nor make Kentucky batter?'

" 'No.'

" 'Well, do you know any useful thing in life?'

" 'Yes, I do; I can sing, and play on the piano, and write valentines,' sais she, 'so get out.' And she walked away, quite dignified, muttering to herself, 'Make a pudding, eh! well, I *want to know!*'

"Thinks I to myself, my pretty little mayflower, in this everlastin' progressive nation of ourn, where the wheel of fortune never stops turning day or night, and them that's at the top one minute are down in the dirt the next, you may say 'I *want* to know' before you die, and be very glad to change your tune, and say, 'Thank heaven I *do* know!' "

"Is that a joke of yours," said the doctor, "about the young girl's geology, or is it really a fact?"

"Fact, I assure you," said I. "And to prove it I'll tell you a story about a Female College that will shew you what pains we take to spoil our young ladies to home. Miss Liddy Adams, who was proprietor and 'dentess (presidentess) of a Female College to Onionville, was a relation of mother's, and I knew her when she was quite a young shoat of a thing to Slickville. I shall never forget a flight into Egypt I caused once in her establishment. When I returned from the embassy, I stopped a day in Onionville, near her university—for that was the name she gave hern; and thinks I, I will just call and look in on Lid for old acquaintance sake, and see how she is figuring it out in life. Well, I raps away with the knocker, as loud as possible, as much as to say, make haste, for there is somebody here, when a tall spare gall with a vinegar face, opened the door just wide enough to show her profile, and hide her back gear, and stood to hear what I had to say. I never see so spare a gall since I was raised. Pharaoh's lean kine warn't the smallest part of a circumstance to her. She was so thin, she actilly seemed as if she would have to lean agin the wall to support herself when she scolded, and I had to look twice at her before I could see her at all, for I warn't sure *she warn't her own shadow.*"

"Good gracious!" said the Doctor, "what a description! but go on."

" 'Is the mistress to home?' said I.

" 'I have no mistress,' said she.

" 'I didn't say you had,' sais I, 'for I knew you hadn't afore you spoke.'

" 'How did you know that?' said she.

" 'Because,' sais I, 'seein so handsome a lady as you, I thought you was one of the professors; and then I thought you must be the mistress herself, and was a thinking how likely she had grow'd since I seed her last. Are you one of the class-teachers?'

"It bothered her; she didn't know whether it was impudence or admiration; *but when a woman arbitrates on a case she is interested in, she always gives an award in her own favour.*

" 'Walk in, Sir,' said she, 'and I will see,' and she backed and backed before me, not out of deference to me, but to the hooks of her gown, and threw a door open. On the opposite side was a large room filled with galls, peeping and looking over each other's shoulders at me, for it was intermission.

" 'Are these your pupils?' sais I; and before she could speak, I went right past into the midst of em. Oh, what a scuddin' and screamin' there was among them! A rocket explodin' there couldn't a done more mischief. They tumbled over chairs, upsot tables, and went head and heels over each other like anything, shouting out, 'A man! a man!'

" 'Where—where?' sais I, a chasin' of them 'show him to me, and I'll soon clear him out. What is he doing of?'

"It was the greatest fun you ever see. Out they flew through the door at the other eend of the room, some up and some down-stairs, singing out, 'A man! a man!' till I thought they would have hallooed their daylights out. Away I flew after them, calling out, 'Where is he? show him to me, and I'll soon pitch into him!' when who should I see but Miss Liddy in the entry, as stiff and as starch as a stand-up shirt collar of a frosty day. She looked like a large pale icicle, standing up on its broad end, and cold enough to give you the ague to look at her.

" 'Mr. Slick,' said she, 'may I ask what is the meaning of all this unseemly behavior in the presence of young ladies of the first families in the State?'

"Says I, '*Miss* Adam,' for as she used the word *Mr.* as a handle to me, I thought I'de take a pull at the *Miss*, 'some robber or housebreaker has got in I rather think, and scared the young feme*nine* gender students, for they seemed to be running after somebody, and I thought I would assist them.'

" 'May I ask, Sir,' a drawin' of herself up to her full height, as

Sam Slick disrupts the overly sheltered young ladies of Liddy Adams' female academy. This portrait appeared as the frontispiece to *Nature and Human Nature* (1855).

straight and as prim as a Lombardy poplar, or rather, a bull-rush, for that's all one size. 'May I ask, Sir, what is the object of your visit here—at a place where no gentlemen are received but the parents or guardians of some of the children.'

"I was as mad as a hatter; I felt a little bit vain of the embassy to London, and my Paris dress, particularly my boots and gloves, and all that, and I will admit, there is no use talkin, I rather kinder sorter thought she would be proud of the connection. I am a good-natured man in a general way, when I am pleased, but it ain't safe to ryle me, I tell you. When I am spotty on the back, I am dangerous. I bit in my breath, and tried to look cool, for I was determined to take revenge out of her.

" 'Allow me to say, Sir,' said she, a perkin up her mouth like the end of a silk purse, 'that I think your intrusion is as unwelcome as it is unpardonable. May I ask the favour of you to withdraw? if not, I must introduce you to the watchman.'

" 'I came,' sais I, 'Miss Adam, having heard of your distinguished college in the saloons of Paris and London, to make a proposal to you; but, like a bull—

" 'Oh dear!' said she, 'to think I should have lived to hear such a horrid word, in this abode of learning!'

" 'But,' I went on, without stopping, 'like a bull in a chiny-shop, I see I have got into the wrong pew; so nothin' remains for me but to beg pardon, keep my proposal for where it will be civilly received, at least, and back out.'

"She was as puzzled as the maid. But women ain't throwed off their guard easily. If they are in a dark place, they can feel their way out, if they can't see it. So says she, dubious like:

" 'About a child, I suppose?'

" 'It is customary in Europe,' sais I, 'I believe, to talk about the marriage first, isn't it? but I have been so much abroad, I am not certified as to usages here.'

"Oh, warn't she brought to a hack! She had a great mind to order me out, but then that word 'proposal' was one she had only seen in a dictionary—she had never heard it; and it is such a pretty one, and sounded so nice to the ear; and then that word 'marriage' was used also, so it carried the day.

" 'This is not a place, Mr. Slick, for foundlings, I'de have you to know,' said she, with an air of disgust, 'but children whose parents are of the first class of society. If,' and she paused and looked at me scrutinisin, 'if your proposals are of *that* nature, walk in here, Sir, if you please, where our conversation will not be overheard. Pray be seated. May I ask, what is the nature of the proposition with which you design to honour me?' and she gave me a smile that would pass for one of graciousness and sweet temper, or of encouragement. It hadn't a decided character, and was a non-committal one. She was doin' quite the lady, but I consaited her ear was itching to hear what I had to say, for she put a finger up, with a beautiful diamond ring on it, and brushed a fly off with it; but, after all, perhaps it was only to show her lily-white hand, which merely wanted a run at grass on the after-feed to fatten it up, and make it look quite beautiful.

" 'Certainly,' sais I, 'you may ask any question of the kind you like.'

"It took her aback, for she requested leave to ask, and I granted it; but she meant it different.

"Thinks I, 'My pretty grammarian, there is a little grain of difference between, "May I ask," and, "I must ask." Try it again.'

"She didn't speak for a minute; so to relieve her, sais I:

" 'When I look round here, and see how charmingly you are located, and what your occupation is, I hardly think you would feel disposed to leave it; so perhaps I may as well forbear the proposal, as it isn't pleasant to be refused.'

" 'It depends,' she said, 'upon what the nature of those proposals are, Mr. Slick, and who makes them' and this time she did give a look of great complacency and kindness. 'Do put down your hat, Sir. I have read your Clockmaker,' she continued; 'I really feel quite proud of the relationship; but I hope you will excuse me for asking, why did you put your own name to it, and call it "Sam Slick the Clockmaker," now that you are a distinguished diplomatist, and a member of our embassy at the court of Victoria the First? It's not an elegant appellation that, of Clockmaker,' sais she, 'is it?' (She had found her tongue now). 'Sam Slick the Clockmaker, a factorist of wooden clocks especially, sounds trady, and will impede the rise of a colossal reputation, which has already one foot in the St. Lawrence, and the other in the Mississippi.'

" 'And sneezes in the Chesapeake,' sais I.

" 'Oh,' said she, in the blandest manner, 'how like you, Mr. Slick! you don't spare a joke, even on yourself. You see fun in everything.'

" 'Better,' sais I, 'than seeing harm in everything, as them galls—'

" 'Young ladies,' said she.

" 'Well, young ladies, who saw harm in me because I was a man.

What harm is there in their in seeing a man? You ain't frightened at one, are you, Liddy?'

"She evaded that with a smile, as much as to say, 'Well, I ain't much skeered, that's a fact.'

" 'Mr. Slick, it is a subject not worth while pursuing,' she replied. 'You know the sensit*ive*ness, nervous delicacy, and scrupulous innocence of the fair sex in this country, and I may speak plainly to you as a man of the world. You must perceive how destructive of all modesty in their juvenile minds, when impressions are so easily made, it would be to familiarise their youthful eyes to the larger limbs of gentlemen enveloped in pantaloons. To speak plainly, I am sure I needn't tell you it ain't decent.'

" 'Well,' sais I, 'it wouldn't be decent if they wern't enveloped in them.'

"She looked down to blush, but it didn't come natural, so she looked up and smiled, (as much as to say, do get out you impudent critter. I know its bunkum as well as you do, but don't bother me. I have a part to play.) Then she rose and looked at her watch, and said the lecture hour for botany has come.

" 'Well,' sais I, a taking up my hat, 'that's a charming study, the loves of the plants, for young ladies, ain't it? they begin with natur, you see, and—' (well, she couldn't help laughing). 'But I see you are engaged.'

" 'Me,' said she, 'I assure, Sir, I know people used to say so, afore General Peleg Smith went to Texas.'

" 'What that scallawag,' said I. 'Why, that fellow ought to be kicked out of all refined society. How could you associate with a man who had no more decency, than to expect folks to call him by name!'

" 'How?' said she.

" 'Why,' sais I, 'what delicate-minded woman could ever bring herself to say Pe-*leg*. If he had called himself Hujacious Smith, or Largerlimb Smith, or something of that kind, it would have done, but Pe*leg* is downright ondecent. I had to leave Boston wunst a whole winter, for making a mistake of that kind. I met Miss Sperm one day from Nantucket, and says I, 'Did you see me yesterday, with those two elegant galls from Albany?'

" 'No,' said she, 'I didn't.'

" 'Strange, too,' said I, 'for I was most sure I caught a glimpse of you, on the other side of the street, and I wanted to introduce you to them, but warn't quite sartain it was you. My,' sais I, 'didn't you see a very *unfashionable* dressed man,' (and I looked down at my Paris boots, as if I was doing modest), 'with two angeliferous females. Why, I had a *leg* on each arm.'

" 'She fairly screamed out at that expression, rushed into a milliner's shop, and cried like a gardner's watering-pot. The names she called me ain't no matter. They were the two Miss Legge's of Albany, and cut a tall swarth, I tell you, for they say they are descended from a governor of Nova Scotia, when good men, according to their tell, could be found for governors, and that their relations in England are some pumpkins, too. I was as innocent as a child, Letty.'

" 'Well,' said she, 'you are the most difficult man to understand, I ever see—there is no telling whether you are in fun or in earnest. But as I was a saying, there was some such talk afore General Smith went to Texas; but that story was raised by the Pawtaxet College folks, to injure this institution. They did all they could to tear my reputation to chitlins. Me engaged, I should like to see the man that—'

" 'Well, you seemed plaguey scared at one just now,' sais I. 'I am sure it was a strange way to show you would like to see a man.'

" 'I didn't say that,' she replied, 'but you take one up so quick.'

" 'It's a way I have,' said I, 'and always had, since you and I was to singing-school together, and larnt sharps, flats, and naturals. It was a crochet of mine,' and I just whipped my arm round her waist, took her up and kissed her, afore she knowed where she was. Oh Lordy! Out came her comb, and down fell her hair to her waist, like a mill-dam broke loose; and two false curls and a braid fell on the floor, and her frill took to dancin' round, and got wrong side afore, and one of her shoes slipt off, and she really looked as if she had been in an indgian-scrimmage, and was ready for scalpin'.

" 'Then you ain't engaged, Liddy,' sais I; 'how glad I am to hear that, it makes my heart jump, and cherries is ripe now, and I will help you up into the tree, as I used to did when you and I was boy and gall together. It does seem so nateral, Liddy, to have a game of romps with you again; it makes me feel as young as a two-year-old. How beautiful you do look, too! My, what a pity you is shut up here, with these young galls all day, talking by the yard about the corrallas, calyxes, and staminas of flowers, while you

> " 'Are doomed to blush unseen,
> And waste your sweetness on the desert air.'

" 'Oh,' said she, 'Sam, I must cut and run, and "blush unseen," that's a fact, or I'm ruinated,' and she up curls, comb, braid, and shoe, and off like a shot into a bed-room that adjoined the parlour, and bolted the door, and double-locked it, as if she was afraid an attachment was to be levied on her and her chattels, by the sheriff, and I was a bumbailiff.

"Thinks I, old gall, I'll pay you off for treating me the way you did just now, as sure as the world. 'May I ask, Mr. Slick, what is the object of this visit?' A pretty way to receive a cousin that you haven't seen so long, ain't it? and though I say it, that shouldn't say it, that cousin, too, Sam Slick, the attaché to our embassy to the Court of Victoria, Buckingham Palace. You couldn't a treated me wuss, if I had been one of the liveried, powdered, bedizened, be-bloated footmen from 't'other big house there of Aunt Harriette's.' I'll make you come down from your stilts, and walk naterel, I know, see if I don't.

"Presently she returned, all set to rights, and a little righter, too, for she had put a touch of rouge on to make the blush stick better, and her hair was slicked up snugger than before, and looked as if it had growed like anything. She had also slipped a handsome habit-shirt on, and she looked, take her altogether, as if, though she warn't engaged, she ought to have been afore the last five hot summers came, and the general thaw had commenced in the spring, and she had got thin, and out of condition. She put her hand on her heart, and said, 'I am so skared, Sam, I feel all over of a twitteration. The way you act is horrid.'

" 'So do I,' sais I, 'Liddy, it's so long since you and I used to—'

" 'You ain't altered a bit, Sam,' said she, for the starch was coming out, 'from what you was, only you are more forrider. Our young men, when they go abroad, come back and talk so free and easy, and take such liberties, and say it's the fashion in Paris, it's quite scandalous. Now, if you dare to do the like again, I'll never speak to you the longest day I ever live, I'll go right off and leave, see if I don't.'

" 'Oh, I see, I have offended you,' sais I, 'you are not in a humour to consent now, so I will call again some other time.'

" 'This lecture on botany must now be postponed,' she said, 'for the hour is out some time ago. If you will be seated, I will set the young students at embroidery, instead, and return for a short time, for it does seem so nateral to see you, Sam, you saucy boy,' and she pinched my ear, 'it reminds one, don't it, of by-gones?' and she hung her head a-one side, and looked sentimental.

" 'Of by-gone larks,' said I.

" 'Hush, Sam,' she said 'don't talk so loud, that's a dear soul. Oh, if anybody had come in just then, and caught *us*.'

("*Us*," thinks I to myself, "I thought you had no objection to it, and only struggled enough for modesty-like; and I did think you would have said, caught *you*.")

" 'I would have been ruinated for ever and ever, and amen, and the college broke up, and my position in the literary, scientific, and intellectual world scorched, withered, and blasted for ever. Ain't my cheek all burning, Sam? it feels as if it was all a-fire;' and she put it near enough for me to see, and feel tempted beyond my strength. 'Don't it look horrid inflamed, dear?' And she danced out of the room, as if she was skipping a rope.

"Well, well," sais I, when she took herself off. "What a world this is. This is evangelical learning; girls are taught in one room to faint or scream if they see a man, as if he was an incarnation of sin; and yet they are all educated and trained to think the sole object of life is to win, not convert, but win one of these sinners. In the next room propriety, dignity, and decorum, romp with a man in a way to make even his sallow face blush. Teach a child there is harm in everything, however innocent, and so soon as it discovers the cheat, it won't see no sin in anything. That's the reason deacons' sons seldom turn out well, and preachers' daughters are married through a window. Innocence is the sweetest thing in the world, and there is more of it, than folks generally imagine. If you want some to transplant, don't seek it in the inclosures of cant, for it has only conterfeit ones, but go to the gardens of truth and of sense. Coerced innocence is like an imprisoned lark, open the door and it's off for ever. The bird that roams through the sky and the groves unrestrained knows how to dodge the hawk and protect itself, but the caged one the moment it leaves its bars and bolts behind, is pounced upon by the fowler or the vulture.

"Puritans whether in or out of the church (for there is a whole squad of 'em in it, like rats in a house who eat up its bread and undermine its walls,) make more sinners than they save by a long chalk. They ain't content with real sin, the pattern ain't sufficient for a cloak, so they sew on several breadths of artificial offences, and that makes one big enough to wrap round them, and cover their own deformity. It enlarges the margin, and the book, and gives more texts.

"Their eyes are like the great magnifier at the Polytechnic, that shows you many-headed, many-armed, many-footed, and many-tailed awful monsters in a drop of water, which were never intended for us to see, or Providence would have made our eyes like Lord Rosse's telescope, (which discloses the secrets of the moon,) and given us springs that had none of these canables in 'em. Water is our drink, and it was made for us to take when we were dry and be thankful. After I first saw one of these drops, like an old cheese chock full of livin things, I couldn't drink nothing but pure gin or brandy for a week. I was scared to death. I consaited when I went to bed I could audibly feel these critters fightin like Turks and minin my inerds, and I got narvous lest my stomach like a citadel might be blowed up and the works destroyed. It was frightful.

"At last I sot up and said Sam, where is all your common sense gone. You used to have a considerable sized phial of it, I hope you ain't lost the cork and let it all run out. So I put myself in the witness-stand and asked myself a few questions.

" 'Water was made to drink, warn't it?'

" 'That's a fact.'

" 'You can't see them critters in it with your naked eye?'

" 'I can't see them at all, neither naked or dressed.'

" 'Then it warn't intended you should?'

" 'Seems as if it wasn't,' sais I.

" 'Then drink, and don't be skeered.'

" 'I'll be darned if I don't, for who knows them wee-monstrosities don't help digestion, or feed on human pyson. They warn't put into Adam's ale for nothin, that's a fact.'

" 'It seems as if they warn't,' sais I. 'So now I'll go to sleep.'

"Well, puritans' eyes are like them magnifiers; they see the devil in everything but themselves, where he is plaguy apt to be found by them that want him; for he feels at home in their company. One time they vow he is a dancin master, and moves his feet so quick folks can't see they are cloven, another time a music master, and teaches children to open their mouths and not their nostrils in singing. Now he is a tailor or miliner, and makes fashionable garments, and then a manager of a theatre, which is the most awful place in the world; it is a reflex of life, and the reflection is always worse than the original, as a man's shadow is more dangerous than he is. But worst of all, they solemnly affirm, for they don't swear, he comes sometimes in lawn sleeves, and looks like a bishop, which is popery, or in the garb of high churchmen, who are all Jesuits. Is it any wonder these cantin fellows pervert the understanding, sap the principles, corrupt the heart, and destroy the happiness of so many? Poor dear old Minister used to say, 'Sam, you must instruct your conscience, for an ignorant or superstitious conscience is a snare to the unwary. If you think a thing is wrong that is not, and do it, then you sin, because you are doing what you believe in your heart to be wicked. It is the intention that constitutes the crime.' Those sour crouts, therefore, by creating artificial and imitation sin in such abundance, make real sin of no sort of consequence, and the world is so chock full of it, a fellow gets careless at last and wont get out of its way, it's so much trouble to pick his steps.

"Well, I was off in a brown study so deep about artificial sins, I didn't hear Liddy come in, she shut the door so softly and trod on tiptoes so light on the carpet. The first thing I knew was I felt her hands on my head, as she stood behind me, a dividin of my hair with her fingers.

" 'Why, Sam,' said she, 'as I'm a livin' sinner if you aint got some white hairs in your head, and there is a little bald patch here right on the crown. How strange it is! It only seems like yesterday you was a curly-headed boy.'

" 'Yes,' sais I, and I hove a sigh so loud it made the window jar; 'but I have seen a great deal of trouble since then. I lost two wives in Europe.'

" 'Now do tell,' said she. 'Why you don't!—oh, jimminy criminy! two wives! How was it, poor Sam?' and she kissed the bald spot on my pate, and took a rockin-chair and sat opposite to me, and began rockin backwards and forwards like a fellow sawin wood. 'How was it, Sam, dear?'

" 'Why,' sais I, 'first and foremost, Liddy, I married a fashionable lady to London. Well, bein out night arter night at balls and operas, and what not, she got kinder used up and beat out, and unbeknownst to me used to take opium. Well, one night she took too much, and in the morning she was as dead as a herring.'

" 'Did she make a pretty corpse?' said Lid, lookin very sanctimonious. 'Did she lay out handsum? They say prussic acid makes lovely corpses; it keeps the eyes from fallin in. Next to dyin happy, the greatest thing is to die pretty. Ugly corpses frighten sinners, but elegant ones win them.'

" 'The most lovely subject you ever beheld,' said I. 'She looked as if she was only asleep; she didn't stiffen at all, but was as limber as ever you see. Her hair fell over her neck and shoulders in beautiful curls just like yourn; and she had on her fingers the splendid diamond rings I gave her; she was too fatigued to take 'em off when she retired the night afore. I felt proud of her even in death, I do assure you. She was handsome enough to eat. I went to ambassador's to consult him about the funeral, whether it should be a state affair, with all the whole diplomatic corps of the court to attend it, or a private one. But he advised a private one; he said it best comported with our dignified simplicity as republicans, and, although cost was no object, still it was satisfactory to know it was far less expense. When I came back she was gone.'

" 'Gone!' said Liddy, 'gone where?'

" 'Gone to the devil, dear, I suppose.'

" 'Oh my!' said she. 'Well, I never, in all my born days! Oh, Sam, is that the way to talk of the dead!'

" 'In the dusk of the evening,' sais I, 'a carriage, they said, drove to the door, and a coffin was carried up-stairs; but the undertaker said it wouldn't fit, and it was taken back again for a larger one. Just afore I went to bed, I went to the room to have another look at her, and she was gone, and there was a letter on the table for me; it contained a few words only. 'Dear Sam, my first husband is come to life, and so have I. Good-bye, love.' '

" 'Well, what did you do?'

" 'Gave it out,' said I, 'she died of the cholera, and had to be buried quick and private, and no one never knew to the contrary.'

" 'Didn't it almost break your heart, Sammy?'

" 'No,' sais I. 'In her hurry, she took my dressing-case instead of her own, in which was all her own jewels, besides those I gave her, and all our ready-money. So I tried to resign myself to my loss, for it might have been worse, you know,' and I looked as good as pie.

" 'Well, if that don't beat all, I declare!' said she.

" 'Liddy,' sais I, with a mock solemcoly air, 'every bane has its antidote, and every misfortin its peculiar consolation.'

" 'Oh, Sam, that showed the want of a high moral intellectual education, didn't it?' said she. 'And yet you had the courage to marry again?'

" 'Well, I married,' sais I, 'next year in France a lady who had refused one of Louis Philip's sons. Oh, what a splendid gall she was, Liddy! she was the star of Paris. Poor thing! I lost her in six weeks.'

" 'Six weeks! Oh, Solomon!' said she, 'in six weeks!'

" 'Yes,' sais I, 'in six short weeks.'

" 'How was it, Sam? do tell me all about it; it's quite romantic. I vow, it's like the Arabian Nights' Entertainment. You are so unlucky, I swow I should be skeered—'

" 'At what?' sais I.

" 'Why, at—'

"She was caught there; she was a goin to say, 'At marryin you,' but as she was a leadin of me on, that wouldn't do. Doctor, you may catch a gall sometimes, but if she has a mind to, she can escape if she chooses, for they are as slippery as eels. So she pretended to hesitate on, till I asked her again.

" 'Why,' sais she, a looking down, 'at sleeping alone tonight, after hearing of these dreadful catastrophes.'

" 'Oh,' sais I, 'is that all?'

" 'But how did you lose her?' said she.

" 'Why, she raced off,' said I, 'with the Turkish ambassador, and if I had a got hold of him, I'de a lammed him wuss than the devil beatin tan-bark, I know. I'de a had his melt, if there was a bowie-knife out of Kentucky.'

" 'Did you go after her?'

" 'Yes; but she cotched it afore I cotched her.'

" 'How was that, Sam?'

" 'Why, she wanted to sarve him the same way, with an officer of the Russian Guards, and Mahomet caught her, sewed her up in a sack, and throwed her neck and crop into the Bosphorus, to fatten eels for the Greek ladies to keep Lent with.'

" 'Why, how could you be so unfortunate?' said she.

" 'That's a question I have often axed myself, Liddy,' sais I; 'but I have come to this conclusion: London and Paris ain't no place for galls to be trained in.'

" 'So I have always said, and always will maintain to my dying day,' she said, rising with great animation and pride. 'What do they teach there but music, dancing, and drawing? The deuce a thing else; but here is Spanish, French, German, Italian, botany, geology, mineralogy, icthiology, conchology, theology—'

" 'Do you teach angeolology and doxyology?' sais I.

" 'Yes, angeolology and doxyology,' she said, not knowing what she was a talking about.

" 'And occult sciences?' sais I.

" 'Yes, all the sciences. London and Paris, eh! Ask a lady from either place if she knows the electric battery from the magnetic—'

" 'Or a *needle* from a *pole*,' sais I.

" 'Yes, sais she, without listening, 'or any such question, and see if she can answer it.'

"She resumed her seat.

" 'Forgive my enthusiasm,' she said, 'Sam, you know I always had a great deal of that.'

" 'I know,' said I, 'you had the smallest foot and ankle of anybody in our country. My! what fine-spun glass heels you had! Where in the world have you stowed them to?' pretendin to look down for them.

" 'Kept them to kick you with,' she said, 'if you are sassy.'

"Thinks I to myself; what next as the woman said to the man who kissed her in the tunnel. You are coming out, Liddy.

" 'Kick,' said I, 'oh, you wouldn't try that, I am sure, let me do what I would.'

" 'Why not.' said she.

" 'Why,' sais I, 'if you did you would have to kick so high, you would expose one of the larger limbs.'

" 'Mr. Slick,' said she, 'I trust you will not so far forget what is due to a lady, as to talk of showing her larger limbs, it's not decent.'

" 'Well, I know it ain't decent,' said I, 'but you said you would do it, and I just remonstrated a little, that's all.'

" 'You was saying about London and Paris,' said she, 'being no place for educating young ladies in.'

" 'Yes,' sais I, 'that painful story of my two poor dear wives, (which is 'all in my eye,' as plain as it was then) illustrates my theory of education in those two capitals. In London, females who are a great deal in society in the season, like a man who drinks, can't stop, they are at it all the time, and like him, sometimes forget the way home again. In Paris, galls are kept so much at home before marriage, when they once get out, they don't want to enter the cage again. They are the two extremes. If ever I marry, I'll tell you how I will lay down the law. Pleasure shall be the recreation and not the business of life with her. Home the rule—parties the exception. Duty first, amusement second. Her head-quarters shall always be in her own house, but the outposts will never be neglected.'

" 'Nothin like an American woman for an American man, is there?' said she, and she drew nearer, lookin up in my face to read the answer, and didn't rock so hard.

" 'It depends upon how they are brought up,' said I, looking wise. 'But Liddy,' sais I, 'without joking, what an amazin small foot that is of yours. It always was, and wunst when it slipt through a branch of the cherry-tree, do you recollect my saying, well I vow that calf was suckled by two cows? now don't you Liddy?'

" 'No, Sir,' said she, 'I don't, though children may say many things that when they grow up, they are ashamed to repeat; but I recollect now, wunst when you and I went through the long grass to the cherry-tree, your mother said, 'Liddy, beware you are not bit by a garter-snake, and I never knew her meanin till now,' and she rose up and said, 'Mr. Slick, I must bid you good morning.'

" 'Liddy,' sais I, 'don't be so pesky starch, I'll be dod fetched if I meant any harm, but you beat me all holler. I only spoke of the calf, and you went a streak higher and talked of the garter.'

" 'Sam,' said she, 'you was always the most impedent, forredest, and pertest boy that ever was, and travellin hain't improved you one mite or morsel.'

" 'I am sorry I have offended you Liddy,' sais I, 'but really now how do you manage to teach all them things with hard names, for we never even heard of them at Slickville. Have you any masters?'

" 'Masters,' said she, 'the first one that entered this college, would ruin it for ever. What, a man in this college! where the juvenile pupils belong to the first families—I guess not. I hire a young lady to teach rudiments.'

" 'So I should think,' sais I, 'from the specimen I saw at your door, she was rude enough in all conscience.'

" 'Pooh,' said she, 'well, I have a Swiss lady that teaches French, German, Spanish, and Italian, and an English one that instructs in music and drawing, and I teach history, geography, botany, and the sciences, and so on.'

" 'How on earth did you learn them all?' said I, 'for it puzzles me.'

" 'Between you and me, Sam,' said she, 'for you know my brought-ens up, and it's no use to pretend—primary books does it all, there is question and answer. I read the question, and they learn the answer. It's the easiest thing in the world to teach now a days.'

" 'But suppose you get beyond the rudiments?'

" 'Oh, they never remain long enough to do that. They are brought out before then. They go to Saratoga first in summer, and then to Washington in winter, and are married right off after that. The domestic, seclusive, and exclusive system, is found most conducive to a high state of refinement and delicacy. I am doing well, Sam,' said she, drawing nearer, and looking confidential in my face. 'I own all this college, and all the lands about, and have laid up forty thousand dollars besides;' and she nodded her head at me, and looked earnest, as much to say, 'that is a fact, ain't it grand?'

" 'The devil you have,' said I, as if I had taken the bait. 'I had a proposal to make.'

" 'Oh,' said she, and she coloured up all over, and got up and said,

'Sam, won't you have a glass of wine, dear?' She intended it to give me courage to speak out, and she went to a closet, and brought out a tray with a decanter, and two or three glasses on it, and some frosted plumb-cake. 'Try that cake, dear,' she said, 'I made it myself, and your dear old mother taught me how to do it;' and then she laid back her head, and larfed like anything. 'Sam,' said she, 'what a memory you have; I had forgot all about the cherry-tree, I don't recollect a word of it.'

" 'And the calf,' said I.

" 'Get along,' said she, 'do get out;' and she took up some crumbs of the cake, and made em into a ball as big as a cherry, and fired it at me, and struck me in the eye with it, and nearly put it out. She jumped up in a minit: 'Did she hurt her own poor cossy's eye?' she said, 'and put it een amost out,' and she kissed it. 'It didn't hurt his little peeper much, did it?'

"Hullo, sais I to myself, she's coming it too *pee*owerful strong altogether. The sooner I dig out the better for my wholesomes. However, let her went, she is wrathy. 'I came to propose to you—'

" 'Dear me,' said she, 'I feel dreadful, I warn't prepared for this; it's very unexpected. What is it, Sam? I am all over of a twiteration.'

" 'I know you will refuse me,' sais I, 'when I look round and see how comfortable and how happy you are, even if you ain't engaged.'

" 'Sam, I told you I weren't engaged.' she said; 'that story of General Smith is all a fabrication, therefore, don't mention that again.'

" 'I feel,' said I, 'it's no use. I know what you will say, you can't quit.'

" 'You have a strange way,' said she, rather tart, 'for you ask questions, and then answer them yourself. What *do* you mean?'

" 'Well,' sais I, 'I'll tell you Liddy,'

" 'Do, dear,' said she, and she put her hand over her *eyes*, as if to stop her from *hearing* distinctly. 'I came to propose to you—'

" 'Oh, Sam,' said she, 'to think of that!'

" 'To take a seat in my buggy,' sais I, 'and come and spend a month with sister Sally and me, at the old location.'

"Poor thing, I pitied her; she had one knee over the other, and, as I said, one hand over her eyes, and there she sot, and the way the upper foot went bobbin up and down was like the palsy, only a little quicker. She never said another word, nor sighed, nor groaned, nor anything, only her head hung lower. Well, I felt streaked, Doctor, I tell *you*. I felt like a man who had stabbed another, and knew he ought to be hanged for it; and I looked at her as such a critter would, if he had to look on, and see his enemy bleed to death. I knew I had done wrong—I had acted spider-like to her—got her into the web—tied her hand and foot, and tantalized her. I am given to brag, I know, Doctor, when I am in the saddle, and up in the stirrups, and leavin all others behind; but when a beast is choked, and down in the dirt, no man ever heard me brag I had rode the critter to death.

"No, I did wrong, she was a woman, and I was a man, and if she did act a part, why, I ought to have known the game she had to play, and made allowances for it. I dropt the trump card under the table that time, and though I got the odd trick, she had the honours. It warn't manly in me, that's a fact; but confound her, why the plague did she call me 'Mr.,' and act formal, and give me the bag to hold, when she knew me of old, and minded the cherry-tree, and all that. Still she was a woman, and a defenceless one, too, and I didn't do the pretty. But if she was a woman, Doctor, she had more clear grit than most men have. After a while, she took her hand off her eyes, and rubbed them, and she opened her mouth and yawned so, you could see down to her garters amost.

" 'Dear me!' said she, trying to smile; but, oh me! how she looked! Her eyes had no more expression than a China aster, and her face was so deadly pale it made the rouge she had put on look like the hectic of a dying consumption. Her ugly was out in full bloom, I tell *you*. 'Dear cousin Sam,' said she, 'I am so fatigued with my labours as president-ess of this institution, that I can hardly keep my peepers open. I think, if I recollect—for I am ashamed to say I was a noddin—that you *proposed* (that word lit her eyes up) that I should go with you to visit dear Sally, Oh, Sam!' said she, (how she bit in her temper that hitch, didn't she?) 'you see, and you saw it at first, I can't leave on so short a notice; but if my sweet Sally would come and visit me, how delighted I should be! Sam, I must join my class now. How happy it has made me to see you again after so many years! Kiss me, dear; good bye—God bless you!' and she yawned again till she nearly dislocated her jaw. 'Go on and write books, Sam, for no man is better skilled in human natur and *spares it less* than yourself.' What a reproachful look she gave me then! 'Good bye, dear!'

"Well, when I closed the door, and was opening of the outer one, I heard a crash. I paused a moment, for I knew what it was. She had fainted, and fell into a conniption fit.

" 'Sam,' sais I to myself, 'shall I go back?'

" 'No,' sais I, 'if you return there will be a scene; and if you don't, if she can't account naterally for it, the devil can't, that's all.'

"Doctor, I felt guilty, I tell you. I had taken a great many rises out of folks in my time, but that's the only one I repent of. Tell you what, Doctor, folks may talk about their southern gentlemen, their New York prince-merchants, and so on, but the clear grit, bottom and game is New England (Yankee-doodle-dum). Male or female, young or old, I'll back 'em agin all creation."

Squire show this chapter to Lord Tandembery, if you know him; and if you don't, Uncle Tom Lavender will give you a letter of introduction to him; and then ask him if ever he has suffered half so much as Sam Slick has in the cause of edication.

〜 Seba Smith and Elizabeth Oakes Smith 〜 (Mrs. Seba Smith)

Seba Smith (1792–1868) and Elizabeth Oakes Smith (1806–1893) were married in 1823, sharing from that time on a peculiarly balanced family relationship and independent careers. Seba Smith's Major Jack Downing of Portland, Maine, came to prominence in the Portland *Courier* in 1830 as a practical backwoodsman criticising Portland social life—Portland being a major American seaport at that time—and the Maine legislature. Jack Downing became a popular commentator but Seba Smith's career remained modest, even after he moved to New York City in 1839; in addition to the various series of Downing letters, he published a wide variety of material including metrical romances, urban humor, a textbook on geometry, and the warmly nostalgic recollections of country kinsmanship shown in "The Pumpkin Freshet" and related stories from *'Way Down East; or, Portraitures of Yankee Life* (Philadelphia, 1854).

Elizabeth Oakes Smith was more widely popular than her husband for her sentimental romances based on American themes, which gained Poe's and R. W. Griswold's approval. "How to Tell a Story," reproduced from *Graham's Magazine*, XXII (January, 1843), 33–35, is rather unrepresentative of her usual tone as a genteel essayist. Because the piece foreshadows the methods of Artemus Ward and Mark Twain as humorous lecturers, however, it is of considerable interest as an illustration of the mixture of sophisticated technique with local details of modern life and backwoods materials. Particularly useful critical studies of the Smiths include Milton Rickels and Patricia Rickels, *Seba Smith* (Boston, 1977), and Alice Wyman, *Two American Pioneers: Seba Smith and Elizabeth Oakes Smith* (New York, 1927).

The Pumpkin Freshet

Aunt Patty Stow is sixty-seven years old; not quite as spry as a girl of sixteen, but a great deal tougher—she has seen tough times in her day. She can do as good a day's work as any woman within twenty miles of her, and as for walking, she can beat a regiment. General Taylor's army on the march moved about fifteen miles a day, but Aunt Patty, on a pinch, could walk twenty. She has been spending the summer with her niece in New York; for Aunt Patty has nieces, abundance of them, though she has no children; she never had any. Aunt Patty never was married, and, for the last thirty years, whenever the question has been asked her, why she did not get married, her invariable reply has been, "she would not have the best man that ever trod shoe-leather." Aunt Patty has been spending the summer in New York, but she does n't *live* there; not she! she would as soon live on the top of the Rocky Mountains. If you ask her where she does *live*, she always answers,

"On Susquehanna's side, fair Wyoming."

This, to be sure, is a poetical license, and before you get the sober prose answer to your question, Aunt Patty will tell you that she is "a great hand for poetry," though the line above is the only one she has ever been known to quote, even by the oldest inhabitant. When you get at the truth of the matter, you find she does live "on Susquehanna's side," but a good ways from "fair Wyoming," that being in Pennsylvania, while her residence, for fifty-eight years has been in the old Indian valley of Oquago, now Windsor, in Broome county, New York. There, in that beautiful bend of the Susquehanna, some miles before it receives the waters of the Chenango, Aunt Patty has been "a fixture" ever since the white inhabitants first penetrated that part of the wilderness, and sat down by the side of the red man. There, when a child, she wandered over the meadows and by the brook-side to catch trout, and clambered up the mountains to gather blueberries, and down into the valleys for wild lillies.

This valley of Oquago, before the revolutionary war, was the favorite residence of an Indian tribe, and a sort of half-way ground, a resting-place for the "six nations" at the north, and the tribes of Wyoming at the south, in visiting each other. It was to the Indians in Oquago valley, that the celebrated Dr. Edwards, while a minister in Stockbridge, Mass., sent the Rev. Mr. Hawley as a missionary; and also sent with him his little son, nine years old, to learn the Indian language, with a view of preparing him for an Indian missionary. And when the French war broke out, a faithful and friendly Indian took charge of the lad, and conveyed him home to his father, carrying him a good part of the way on his back. But all this happened before Aunt Patty's time, and before any white family, except the missionary's, resided within a long distance of Oquago.

About the year of 1788, some families came in from Connecticut, and settled in the valley, and Aunt Patty's father and mother were the first. Thus brought up to experience the hardships and privations of a pioneer life in the wilderness, no wonder Aunt Patty should be much struck on viewing for the first time the profusion and luxury and mode of life in a city. The servant girl was sent out for some bread, and in five minutes she returned with a basket of wheat loaves, fresh biscuit and French rolls. Aunt Patty rolled up her eyes and lifted up both hands.

"Dear me!" says she, "do you call that bread? And where, for massy sake, did it come from so quick now? Does bread rain down from heaven here in New York, jest as the manna in the Bible did to the children of Israel?"

"Oh, no, Aunt Patty, there's a baker only a few steps off, just round the next corner, who bakes more than a hundred bushels a day; so that we can always have hot bread and hot cakes there, half a dozen times a day if we want it."

"A hundred bushels a day!" screamed Aunt Patty, at the top of her voice; "the massy preserve us! Well, if you had only been at Oquago at the time of the great punkin freshet, you would think a good deal of having bread so handy, I can tell you."

Aunt Patty's niece took her with her to the Washington Market of a Saturday evening, and showed her the profusion of fruits and vegetables and meats, that covered an area of two or three acres.

"The Lord be praised!" said Aunt Patty, "why, here is victuals enough to feed a whole nation. Who would have thought that I should a-lived through the punkin freshet to come to see such a sight as this before I die?"

At the tea table, Mrs. Jones, for that was the name of Aunt Patty's niece, had many apologies to make about the food; the bread was too hard and the butter was too salt, and the fruit was too stale, and something else was too something or other. At the expression of each apology, Aunt Patty looked up with wonderment; she knew not how to understand Mrs. Jones; for, to her view, a most grand and rich and dainty feast was spread before her. But when Mrs. Jones summed up the whole by declaring to Aunt Patty she was afraid she would not be able to make out a supper of their poor fare, Aunt Patty laid down her knife, and sat back in her chair, and looked up at Mrs. Jones with perfect astonishment.

"Why, Sally Jones!" said she, "are you making fun of me all this time, or what is it you mean!"

"No, indeed, Aunt Patty, I only meant just what I said; we have rather a poor table to night, and I was afraid you would hardly make a comfortable tea."

Aunt Patty looked at Mrs. Jones about a minute without saying a word. At last she said, with most decided emphasis, "Well, Sally Jones, I can't tell how it is some folks get such strange notions in their heads but I can tell you, if you had seed what I seed, and gone through what I have gone through, in the punkin freshet, when I was a child, and afterwards come to set down to sich a table as this, you'd think you was in heaven."

Here Mr. Jones burst out into a broad laugh. "Well done, Aunt Patty!" said he, shoving back his cup and shaking his sides; "the history of that *pumpkin freshet* we must have; you have excited my curiosity about it to the highest pitch. Let us have the whole story now, by way of seasoning for our poor supper. What was the pumpkin freshet? and when was it, and where was it, and what did you have to do with it? Let us have the whole story from first to last, will you?"

"Well, Mr. Jones, you ask me a great question," said Aunt Patty, "but if I can't answer it, I don't know who can—for I seed the punkin freshet with my own eyes, and lived on the punkins that we pulled out of the river for two months afterwards. Let me see—it was in the year 1794; that makes it sixty years ago. Bless me, how the time slips away. I was only about seven years old then. It was a woodsy place, Oquago Valley was. There was only six families in our neighborhood then, though there was some more settled away further up the river. Major Stow, my uncle, was the head man of the neighborhood. He had the best farm, and was the smartest hand to work, and was the stoutest and toughest man there was in them parts. Major Buck was the minister. They always called him Major Buck, because he'd been a major in the revolutionary war, and when the war was over he took to preaching, and come and lived in Oquago. He was a nice man; everybody sot store by Major Buck."

"Oh, well, I don't care about Major Buck, nor Major Stow," said Mr. Jones, "I want to hear about the pumpkin freshet. What was it that made the pumpkin freshet?"

"Why, the rain, I suppose," said Aunt Patty, looking up very quietly.

"The rain?" said Mr. Jones; "did it rain pumpkins in your younger days, in the Oquago Valley!"

"I guess you'd a-thought so," said Aunt Patty "if you had seen the punkins come floating down the river, and rolling along the shore, and over the meadows. It had been a great year for punkins that year. All the corn-fields and potato-fields up and down the river was spotted all over with 'em, as yellow as goold. The corn was jest beginning to turn hard, and the potatoes was ripe enough to pull. And then, one day, it begun to rain, kind of easy at first; we thought it was only going to be a shower; but it did n't hold up all day, and in the night it kept raining harder and harder, and in the morning it come down with a power. Well, it rained steady all that day. Nobody went out into the fields to work, but all staid in the house and looked out to see if it would n't hold up. When it come night, it was dark as Egypt, and the rain still poured down. Father took down the Bible and read the account about the flood, and then we went to bed. In the morning, a little after daylight, Uncle Major Stow come to the window and hollowed to us, and says he, turn out all hands, or ye'll all be in the river in a heap.

"I guess we was out of bed about the quickest. There was father, and mother, and John, and Jacob, and Hannah, and Suzy, and Mike, and me, and Sally, and Jim, and Rachel, all running to the door as hard as we could pull. We didn't stand much about clothes. When father un-barred the door and opened it—'oh,' says Uncle Major, says he, 'you may go back and dress yourselves, you'll have time enough for that; but there's no knowing how long you'll be safe, for the Susquehanna has got her head up, and is running like a race-horse. Your hen-house has gone now. At that Hannah fetched a scream that you might a heard her half a mile, for half the chickens was her'n. As soon as we got our clothes on, we all run out, and there we see a sight. It still rained a little, but not very hard. The river, that used to be away down in the holler, ten rods from the house, had now filled the holler full, and was up within two rods of our door. The chicken-house was gone, and all the hens and chickens with it, and we never seed nor heard nothin' of it afterwards.

"While we stood there talking and mourning about the loss of the chickens, father he looked off upon the river, for it begun to be so light that we could see across it now, and father spoke, and says he, 'what upon airth is all them yellow spots floating along down the river?'

"At that we all turned round and looked, and Uncle Major, says he, 'by King George, them's punkins! If the Susquehanna hasn't been robbing the punkin fields in the upper neighborhood, there's no snakes in Oquago.'

"And sure enough, they was punkins; and they kept coming along thicker and thicker, spreading away across the river, and up and down as far as we could see. And bime-by Mr. Williams, from the upper neighborhood, come riding down a horseback as hard as he could ride, to tell us to look out, for the river was coming down like a roaring lion, seeking whom he may devour. He said it had run over the meadows and the low grounds, and swept off the corn-fields, and washed out the potatoes, and was carrying off acres and acres of punkins on its back. The whole river, he said, was turned into a great punkin-field. He advised father to move out what he could out of the house, for he thought the water would come into it, if it did n't carry the house away. So we all went to work as tight as we could spring, and Uncle Major he put to and helped us, and we carried out what things we could, and carried them back a little ways, where the ground was so high we thought the river could n't reach 'em. And then we went home with Uncle Major Stow, and got some breakfast. Uncle Major's house was on higher ground, and we felt safe there.

"After breakfast, father went down to the house again, to see how it looked, and presently he come running back, and said the water was up to the doorsill. Then they began to think the house would go, and we all went down as quick as we could, to watch it. When we got there, the water was running into the door, and was all the time rising. 'That house is a gone goose,' says Uncle Major, says he, 'it's got to take a journey down the river to look after the hens and chickens.'

"At that, mother begun to cry, and took on about it as though her heart would break. But father, says he, 'la, Patty,' mother's name was Patty, and I was named after her; father, says he, 'la, Patty, it's no use crying for spilt milk, so you may as well wipe up your tears. The house aint gone yet, and if it should go, there's logs enough all handy here, and we can build another as good as that in a week.'

" 'Yes,' says Uncle Major, says he, 'if the house goes down stream, we'll all turn to and knock another one together in short order.' So mother begun to be pacified. Father went and got a couple of bedcords and hitched on to one corner of the house, and tied it to a stump; for, he said, if the water come up only jest high enough to start the house, maybe the cords would keep it from going. The water kept a-rising, and in a little more than an hour after we got back from uncle's, it was two foot deep on the floor.

" 'One foot more,' says Uncle Major, says he, 'will take the house off its legs.'

"But, as good luck would have it, one foot more didn't come. We watched and watched an hour longer, and the water kept rising a little, but not so fast as it did, and at last we could n't see as it ris any more. And, as it had done raining, after we found it didn't rise any for an hour, Uncle Major he pronounced his opinion that the house would stand it. Then did n't we feel glad enough? Before noon the water begun to settle away a little, and before night it was clear out of the house. But Uncle Major said it was so wet, it would never do for us to stay in it that night, without we wanted to ketch our death a-cold. So we all went up to his house, and made a great camp bed on the floor, and there we all staid till morning. That day we got our things back into the house again, and the river kept going down a little all day.

"But oh, such a melancholy sight as it was to see the fields, you don't know. All the low grounds had been washed over by the river, and everything that was growing had been washed away and carried down stream, or else covered up with sand and mud. Then in a few weeks after that, come on the starving time. Most all the crops was cut off by the freshet; and there we was in the wilderness, as it were, forty miles from any place where we could get any help, and no road only a blind footpath through the woods. Well, provisions began to grow short. We had a good many punkins that the boys pulled out of the river as they floated along the bank. And it was boiled punkins in the morning, and boiled punkins at night. But that was n't very solid food, and we hankered for something else. We had some meat, though not very plenty, and we got some roots and berries in the woods. But as for bread, we did n't see any from one week's end to another.

"There was but very little corn or grain in the neighborhood, and what little there was could n't be ground, for the hand-mill had been carried away by the freshet. At last, when we had toughed it out five or six weeks, one day Uncle Major Stow, says he, 'well, I aint a-going to stand this starving operation any longer. I am going to have some bread and flour cake, let it cost what 'twill.'

"We all stared and wondered what he meant.

" 'I tell ye,' says he, 'I'm a-going to have some bread and flour cake before the week's out, or else there's no snakes in Oquago.'

" 'Well, I should like to know how you are a-going to get it,' says father, says he.

" 'I'm a-going to mill,' says Uncle Major, says he. 'I've got a half bushel of wheat thrashed out, and if any of the neighbors will put in enough to make up another half bushel, I'll shoulder it and carry it down to Wattle's ferry to mill, and we'll have one feast before we starve to death. It's only about forty miles, and I can go and get back in three or four days.'

"They tried to persuade him off the notion of it, 'twould be such a long tiresome journey; but he said it was no use; his half bushel of wheat had got to go, and he could as well carry a bushel as a half bushel, for it would only jest make a clever weight to balance him. So Major Buck and three other neighbors, who had a little wheat, put in half a peck apiece, and that made up the bushel. And the next morning at daylight, Uncle Major shouldered the bushel of wheat, and started for Wattle's ferry, forty miles, to mill.

"Every night and morning while he was gone, Major Buck used to mention him in his prayers, and pray for his safe return. The fourth day, about noon, we see Uncle Major coming out of the woods with a bag on his shoulder; and then, if there was n't a jumping and running all over the neighborhood, I won't guess again. They all sot out and run for Uncle Major's house, as tight as they could leg it, and the whole neighborhood got there about as soon as he did. In come Uncle Major, all of a puff, and rolled the bag off his shoulder on to the bench.

" 'There, Molly,' says he; that was his wife, his wife's name was Molly; 'there, Molly, is as good a bushel of flour meal as you ever put your hands into. Now go to work and try your skill at a short cake. If we don't have a regular feast this afternoon, there's no snakes in Oquago. Bake two milk-pans full, so as to have enough for the whole neighborhood.'

" 'A short cake, Mr. Stow,' says Aunt Molly, says she, 'why what are you thinking about? Don't you know we haven't got a bit of shortnin' in the house; not a mite of butter, nor hog's fat, nor nothin'? How can we make a short cake?'

" 'Well, maybe some of the neighbors has got some,' says Uncle Major, says he.

" 'No,' says Aunt Molly, 'I don't believe there's a bit in the neighborhood.'

"Then they asked Major Buck, and father, and all round, and there wasn't one that had a bit of butter or hog's fat.

" 'So your short cake is all dough again,' says Aunt Molly, says she.

" 'No taint, nother,' says Uncle Major, 'I never got agin a stump yet, but what I got round it some way or other. There's some of that bear's grease left yet, and there's no better shortnin' in the world. Do let us have the short cake as soon as you can make it. Come, boys, stir round and have a good fire ready to bake it.'

"Then Aunt Molly stripped up her sleeves, and went at it, and the boys knocked round and made up a fire, and there was a brisk business carried on there for awhile, I can tell you. While Aunt was going on with the short cakes, Uncle Major was uncommon lively. He went along and whispered to Major Buck, and Major Buck looked up at him with a wild kind of a stare, and says he, 'you don't say so!'

"Then Uncle Major whispered to mother, and mother says she, 'why, Brother Stow, I don't believe you.'

" 'You may believe it or not,' says Uncle Major, says he, 'but 'tis true as Major Buck's preachin'.'

"Then Uncle Major walked up and down the room, whistlin' and snappin' his fingers, and sometimes strikin' up into Yankee Doodle.

"Aunt Molly she dropped her work, and took her hands out of the dough, and says she, 'Mr. Stow, I wonder what's got into you; it must be something more than the short cakes I'm sure, that's put such life into you.'

" 'To be sure, 'tis,' says Uncle, 'for the short cakes hain't got into me yet.' And then he turned round and give a wink to mother and Major Buck.

" 'Well, there now,' says Aunt Molly, says she, 'I know you've got some kind of a secret that you've been telling these folks here, and I declare I won't touch the short cakes again till I know what 'tis.'

"When Aunt Molly put her foot down, there 'twas, and nobody could move her. So Uncle Major knew he might as well come to it first as last; and says he, 'well, Molly, it's no use keeping a secret from you; but I've got something will make you stare worse than the short cakes.'

" 'Well, what is it, Mr. Stow?' says Aunt Molly, 'out with it, and let us know the worst of it.'

" 'Here,' says Uncle Major, says he, pulling out a little paper bundle out of his pocket, and holding it up to Aunt Molly's face; 'here, smell of that,' says he.

"As soon as Aunt Molly smelt of it, she jumped right up and kissed Uncle Major right before the whole company, and says she, 'it's tea! as true as I'm alive, it's the real bohea. I haven't smelt any before for three years, but I knew it in a moment.'

" 'Yes,' says Uncle Major, 'it's tea; there's a quarter of a pound of the real stuff. While my grist was grinding, I went into the store, and there I found they had some tea; and, thinks I, we'll have one dish for all hands, to go with the short cakes, if it takes the last copper I've got. So I knocked up a bargain with the man, and bought a quarter of a pound; and here 'tis. Now, Molly, set your wits to work, and give us a good dish of tea with the short cakes, and we'll have a real thanksgiving; we'll make it seem like old Connecticut times again.'

" 'Well, now, Mr. Stow, what shall we do?' says Aunt Molly, 'for there isn't a tea-kettle, nor a tea-pot, nor no cups and sarcers in the neighborhood.'

"And that was true enough; they had n't had any tea since they moved from Connecticut, so they had n't got any tea-dishes.

" 'Well, I don't care,' says Uncle Major, says he, 'we'll have the tea, any how. There's the dish-kettle, you can boil the water in that, and you can steep the tea in the same, and when it's done I guess we'll contrive some way or other to drink it.'

"So Aunt Molly dashed round and drove on with the work, and got the short-cakes made, and the boys got the fire made, and they got the cakes down to baking, and about four quarts of water hung on in the dish-kettle to boil for tea, and when it began to boil, the whole quarter of a pound of tea was put into it to steep. Bime-by they had the table set out, and a long bench on one side, and chairs on the other side, and there was two milk-pans set on the table filled up heaping full of short-cakes, and the old folks all sot down, and fell to eating, and we children stood behind them with our hands full, eating tu. And oh, them short-cakes seems to me, I never shall forget how good they tasted the longest day I live.

"After they eat a little while, Uncle Major called for the tea; and what do you think they did for tea-cups? Why, they took a two quart wooden bowl, and turned off tea enough to fill it, and sot it on to the table. They handed it up to Major Buck first, as he was the minister, and sot to the head of the table, and he took a drink, and handed it to Uncle Major Stow, and he took a drink, and then they passed it all round the table, from one to t'other, and they all took a drink; and when that was gone, they turned out the rest of the tea, and filled the bowl up, and drinked round again. Then they poured some more water into the dish-kettle, and steeped the tea over again a few minutes, and turned out a bowlful, and passed it round for us children to taste of. But if it want for the name of tea, we had a good deal rather have water, for it was such bitter, miserable stuff, it spoilt the taste of the short-cakes. But the old folks said if we didn't love it, we needn't drink it; so they took it and drinkt up the rest of it.

"And there they sot all the afternoon, eating short-cakes, and drinking tea, and telling stories, and having a merry thanksgiving of it. And that's the way we lived at the time of the punkin freshet in the valley of Oquago."

Note—The main incidents in this sketch, in relation to the early settlement of Oquago Valley, the "pumpkin freshet," Major Stow's pedestrian journey of forty miles to mill, the bushel of wheat, the short-cakes and the tea, are all historically true.

How to Tell a Story

No character is more genial to a child than a good story-teller—one that with a serene fullness pours out incident and narrative, peril and "hair-breadth 'scape," tale of enormous serpent or deadly beast, of wild or chivalric adventure, till the old clock behind the door is heard to tick with a solemn loudness, and the elders begin to yawn and stir the ashes in token of weariness. Most heartily do I pity either man or woman who has no such delicious reminiscence. It was my good fortune when a child to pass much of my time at an old country farmhouse, where the many retainers, the primitive and exact ordering of the household had in it much of the baronial style of which we read amongst our Saxon ancestors. The principal apartment for ordinary occasions was a long hall, or dining-room, in the centre of which was spread a table capable of holding the whole family—from the head down to the youngest servant. Our New England gentry are exact observers of precedence, and in the old families where any degree of state is observed, a single glance at the ordering of the table betrays the relative position of each member. At the head sit the master and mistress, then occasional visiters, next the children ranged according to the age of each, and then came the upper domestics, as they might be termed, old, respectable retainers, who sometimes join a few words in the conversation at the head of the table; but always in a subdued and respectful voice—followed next by the younger servants, "to the manor born" as it were, but as yet too young to share in its dignities.

After the morning and evening meal, which is announced by the blowing of a horn, each member places his chair to the wall, and the patriarch of the family reads a portion of scripture from the "big ha'bible, once his father's pride," and then,

"The saint, the husband, and the father prays."

At night, when the household arrangements were completed, this long room with its dim recesses, its antique furniture and quaint ornaments, was the place to give impressiveness to a story. Here might one shudder at the supernatural, stare at the marvelous, and thrill at the bold and magnanimous. Here was the place, too, to bemoan the cruelty of "Queen Eleanor" to "Fair Rosamond," to weep for the lover by "Yarrow flowing," and to rejoice in the retribution of the proud and "cruel Barbara Allen." These and many other ballads, such as the "Milk White Doe," "Fair Margaret and Sweet William," "Lord James and Fair Eleanor," were preserved in rude manuscript and learned orally, and most have been in this way preserved by tradition and brought over to this country by the first settlers; the writer having never seen them in print till he found them in Perry's reliques and long after she had been familiar with them as chanted in the old farmhouse.

The city is no place for story-telling—nothing is in harmony. A story to go well must be either in a rich antique room, or old-fashioned farm-house, where things have an air of quaintness and permanency; in our rough cottage with smoky rafters; or, better still, in some rude cabin upon the wild frontier. In such places we abandon ourselves to any fantastic illusion, and are not ashamed to yield faith, nor to be swayed by the emotions of the tale. A sea story need be told by some weather-beaten tar by the sea shore, or by a dim wood fire with a fierce tempest raging without; unless you have the good fortune to hear it by the forecastle itself. A good story-teller should be exceedingly careful never to mis-time, nor mis-place his narrative. If his miserable fortune afford him nothing better than a carpeted room, with sofas and chandeliers, be sure to make the light dim; let it come from behind some piece of statuary, or heavy-stuffed chair, a rose bush, or large geranium, that outline and faint shadows be cast—then if he have a quiet voice, and not too much of the detail, a very good illusion may be produced.

Children, in whom the love of the marvelous is alway predominant, and who never weary at the twice-told tale, will adopt all sorts of expedients to hear one. They may be found in the garret turning over musty relics and old records, in the desire for suggestion; and they drag forth triumphantly a rusty sword, a cocked hat, a worm-eaten log book, or time hallowed garment, any one of which may afford material for a story. The boy sits on the steps of the grocer, lolls upon the pump at the corner, or leans over the tafferel of the ship, and he is listening to some history of stirring adventure. Do not call him away, he is building up the materials for a man—a man firm, enterprising, and self-sustained—the only wealth, the only true dignity.

A story-teller should never hurry, least of all be interrupted—as for himself he should think for the time being only of his story; give himself up and become a part of what he relates. Nothing mars a story like pre-occupation. I believe all I am writing was suggested to me when about eight years old, from the fact of having unfortunately asked Mrs. Smith, a respectable country woman, rejoicing in that rarest of names, to tell me the story of a Catamount. Her husband was also happy in the name of John, but as these two favorite names happened to conjoin in union as well as many of his neighbors, it was not always easy to determine the individual specified. In a transition state of society, a man frequently receives a soubriquet, indicating some quality of mind, person or achievement, by which he is distinguished from those about him. It is an ancient practice sanctioned by history, and one mode by which names were created. The aborigines in this way named their chiefs and warriors. Mr. John Smith, of the country town of which I am speaking, was hence called Catamount Smith.

Great was my curiosity to learn why. I questioned every one. Why is Mr. Smith called Catamount John?

"Why? Because he killed the Catamount."

There was the fact; but I wanted the story—all the details—the enormous size of the animal, his growl, his tremendous leap, the fierce contest, the peril, and finally to be in at the death. Once seduced by the good-natured face of Catamount John, I ventured to crave the story, blushing up to the eyes while I did so.

"Mr. Smith, will you tell me how you killed the Catamount?"

He turned his bland face full upon mine, placed his rough, broad palm upon my head and answered,

"My dear, I shot him."

"But how, Mr. Smith, how?"

"I took my gun and pointed, so—'suiting the action to the word,' and shot him through the—." I ran out of the room to hide my vexation.

At this moment, Mrs. Catamount Smith passed by me, bearing an enormous pan of butter, fresh from the churn. Now Mrs. Smith would never have deluded anything but a child into a belief that she could tell a story. She was entirely deficient in that quality of repose, so essential to the thing. She was a little, plump, bustling dame, forever on the alert to see that all was neat and tidy. Her sleeves were always up at the elbow, her apron white as snow, and the frill of her cap blowing back with her quick tread. Short people never stoop, and Mrs. Smith being very short and very round, tipped somewhat backward when she walked.

That night, when all the family were in bed, except a faithful domestic named Polly, I seated myself beside the good old lady, to hear the story of the Catamount. The reader must bear with me while I relate the thing just as it transpired.

Mrs. Smith gave one keen look about the apartment, to convince herself that all was right, and then stuck her needle into a sheath affixed to her belt, and commenced knitting and talking at the same moment.

"John and I began house-keeping in the log house down by the pond, about a mile from the place where the meeting-house now—(la, Polly, there's Jacob's buskins on the back of your chair, and they must be bound round to-night; do go right to work on them)—where did I leave off?—where the meeting-house now stands. 'Twas another thing to be fixed out then, to what it is now-a-days. I was considered very well off—my father gave me a cow and a pig—and I had spun and wove sheets and kiverlids, besides airning enough to buy a chist of draws, and a couple of chairs. Then my mother launched out a nice bed, a wheel, and some kettles. We hadn't much company in them times, our nighest neighbor was over the mountain, five mile off—(now did you ever—I liked to forgot them are trousis of Ephraim's—he's tied his handkercher round his knee all day, to kiver up the hole—Polly, get my wax and thimble, and the patches, and I'll go right to work). Well, what was I sayin'? Oh, we hadn't much company, and my old man made a settle, with a high back, and bought chairs two at a time, as our family grew larger."

"But, my dear ma'am, you promised to tell me about the Catamount."

"Yes, yes, I'm comin along to it. Well, John had got together a yoke of oxen, some sheep, and other cattle, and we began to be pretty considerable forehanded. He was a nice, smart man, and nobody should say he had a lazy wife. (Polly, just sweep the hearth up.)

We had no machines then to card our wool, and I had to card it all myself—for I never hired *help* till after our Jacob was—"

"Dear Mrs. Smith, the Catamount!"

"Yes, child, I'm eeny most to it. Let me see—till after Jacob was born—then I hired Lydia Keene, as smart a girl she was, as ever wore shoe leather. By this time we had eighteen or twenty sheep, and John used to drive them into the pen and count them every night, to be sure that the wolves or panthers hadn't got any of 'em; for the beasts were pretty thick about the mountain, and many a time I've stood to the door, and heard them howl and cry, to say nothing of the foxes and screech owls that kept up a rumpus all night long. (Dear me, this snappy wood now has burnt a hole in my apron—it looks jist like a pipe hole—I do so hate to see it. I'll mend it now, and then 'twill be done with. I never put off any thing till to-morrow, that can be done to-day—that's the way to—) Now do n't fidget, child, you see I'm almost to it; that's the way to get fore-handed, as I was saying. Well, one morning John went out, and found the sheep all huddled together into a corner, trembling pitifully. He counted them, and one was missing. This was a loss, for I needed the wool for winter kiverlids. (There, Polly, you've forgot the apples you're a goin to pare for the pan-dowdy, now the buskins is done, you better get them under way.)

"Well, the next night John took Rover—now Rover was the largest dog I ever see, near about as large as a heifer, and the knowingest critter I ever laid eyes on. Well, John took him out to the pen, and told him to watch the sheep. John'll never forget how that critter looked up in his face, and licked his hand when he left him, just as if he knew what would come of it, and wanted to say good bye; nor how he crouched down before the bars, and laid his nose upon his paws, and looked after him solemn-like. Poor Rover! The next morning John was up airly, for he felt kind a worried. He went out to the sheep pen, and sure enough the first thing he see, was—(Polly, you've just cut a worm-hole into your apples)—the first thing he see, was poor Rover dead by the bars, his head torn right open, and another sheep gone. John's dander was fairly up—he took down the gun, there it hangs on the hooks, took his powder-horn and bullets, and started off. I tried to coax him to set a trap, or to watch by the sheep-pen. But John always had a will of his own, and was the courageousest man in the town, and he declared he'd have nothing to do with any such cowardly tricks. He'd kill the critter in broad day-light, if 'twas only to revenge poor Rover. So he started off. He tracked the critter about a mile round by the mountain, which in them days was covered with trees to the very top. (Polly, jist take them are trousis, and lay them down by Ephraim's chamber door; he'll want them in the morning.)

Well, John now missed Rover dreadfully, to scent out the beast—he moved along carefully, searching into the trees—expectin he might be down upon him every minit. All at once he heard the bark ripped up from a tree almost over his head, and then a low, quick growl, and there was the Catamount jist ready for his spring—(my conscience, Polly, there's that new soap all running out o' the barrel into the cellar, I saw it had sprung a leak about supper time, and then I forgot all about it again.")

The word "spring" had been the unlucky association, and away she darted to the cellar, followed by the faithful Polly.

"Mrs. Smith, Mrs. Smith, do finish the story!"

"La! child—John shot him!" she screamed from the foot of the stairs.

P. T. Barnum

Phineas T. Barnum (1810–1891) shocked Europeans with the Yankee chicanery and "go ahead" spirit of his *Life of P. T. Barnum* (New York, 1855), revised into *Struggles and Triumphs; or, Forty Years' Recollections of P. T. Barnum* in 1866 and periodically updated and republished until Barnum's death. The 1871 edition is the source of the items reprinted here. Apotheosis of the Yankee sharper in the new industrial world, Barnum, as myth, claims principles subservient to money-getting. However, his uncompromising stands on human rights and temperance won him many friends among conservatives in America. In addition to the excerpts from his autobiography, which illustrate Barnum's moral and social position, two stories about him from *Yankee Notions*, I (1852), are included to give an indication of the humor generated by Barnum as a figure—a figure that gave Artemus Ward his character in the hands of Charles F. Browne and so interested Mark Twain that Barnum's traits appear in many of Twain's hero-showmen such as Hank Morgan in *A Connecticut Yankee in King Arthur's Court* (1889).

Barnum was himself interested in humor. He unsuccessfully wooed Mark Twain to enter joint ventures, sending him batches of newspaper clippings in the 1870s. As early as 1853, he had helped Charles G. Leland edit a column of comic copy for the New York *Illustrated News*, and he published his own collection, *Funny Stories* (New York & London, 1890). As the two stories from *Yankee Notions* suggest, a mythology rapidly gathered around Barnum as a social phenomenon. Many of his scandalous frauds, such as the attempt to buy Shakespeare's home, were conscious transformations of naïve reverence into the entrepreneurial spirit. Neil Harris' *Humbug: The Art of P. T. Barnum* (Boston, 1973) is an outstanding study of the complex background and career of P. T. Barnum with implications for American culture beyond its immediate subject; it supersedes M. R. Werner,

Barnum (New York, 1923) and Joel Benton, *Life of Hon. Phineas T. Barnum* (n.p., 1891). The angriest response to Barnum's amorality is found in "Revelations of a Showman," *Blackwood's Magazine,* LXXVII (February, 1855), 187–201.

From *Struggles and Triumphs; or, Forty Years' Recollections of P. T. Barnum*

Leaving nothing undone that would bring Barnum and his Museum before the public, I often engaged some exhibition, knowing that it would directly bring no extra dollars to the treasury, but hoping that it would incite a newspaper paragraph which would float through the columns of the American press and be copied, perhaps, abroad, and my hopes in this respect were often gratified.

I confess that I liked the Museum mainly for the opportunities it afforded for rapidly making money. Before I bought it, I weighed the matter well in my mind, and was convinced that I could present to the American public such a variety, quantity and quality of amusement, blended with instruction, "all for twenty-five cents, children half price," that my attractions would be irresistible, and my fortune certain. I myself relished a higher grade of amusement, and I was a frequent attendant at the opera, first-class concerts, lectures, and the like; but I worked for the million, and I knew the only way to make a million from my patrons was to give them abundant and wholesome attractions for a small sum of money.

About the first of July, 1842, I began to make arrangements for extra novelties, additional performances, a large amount of extra advertising, and an outdoor display for the "Glorious Fourth." Large particolored bills were ordered, transparencies were prepared, the free band of music was augmented by a trumpeter, and columns of advertisements, headed with large capitals, were written and put on file.

I wanted to run out a string of American flags across the street on that day, for I knew there would be thousands of people passing the Museum with leisure and pocket-money, and I felt confident that an unusual display of national flags would arrest their patriotic attention, and bring many of them within my walls. Unfortunately for my purpose, St. Paul's Church stood directly opposite, and there was nothing to which I could attach my flag-rope, unless it might be one of the trees in the church-yard. I went to the vestrymen for permission to so attach my flag rope on the Fourth of July, and they were indignant at what they called my "insulting proposition"; such a concession would be "sacrilege." I plied them with arguments, and appealed to their patriotism, but in vain.

Returning to the Museum I gave orders to have the string of flags made ready, with directions at daylight on the Fourth of July to attach one end of the rope to one of the third story windows of the Museum, and the other end to a tree in St. Paul's churchyard. The great day arrived, and my orders were strictly followed. The flags attracted great attention, and before nine o'clock I have no doubt that hundreds of additional visitors were drawn by this display into the Museum. By half-past nine Broadway was thronged, and about that time two gentlemen in a high state of excitement rushed into my office, announcing themselves as injured and insulted vestrymen of St. Paul's Church.

"Keep cool, gentlemen," said I; "I guess it is all right."

"Right!" indignantly exclaimed one of them, "do you think it is right to attach your Museum to our Church? We will show you what is 'right' and what is law, if we live till to-morrow; those flags must come down instantly."

"Thank you," I said, "but let us not be in a hurry. I will go out with you and look at them, and I guess we can make it all right."

Going into the street I remarked: "Really, gentlemen, these flags look very beautiful; they do not injure your tree; I always stop my balcony music for your accommodation whenever you hold week-day services, and it is but fair that you should return the favor."

"We could indict your 'music,' as you call it, as a nuisance, if we chose," answered one vestryman, "and now I tell you that if these flags are not taken down in ten minutes, *I* will cut them down."

His indignation was at the boiling point. The crowd in the street was dense, and the angry gesticulation of the vestryman attracted their attention. I saw there was no use in trying to parley with him or coax him, and so, assuming an angry air, I rolled up my sleeves, and exclaimed, in a loud tone,—

"Well, Mister, I should just like to see you dare to cut down the American flag on the Fourth of July; you must be a 'Britisher' to make such a threat as that; but I'll show you a thousand pairs of Yankee hands in two minutes, if you dare to attempt to take down the stars and stripes on this great birth-day of American freedom!"

"What's that John Bull a-saying," asked a brawny fellow, placing

P. T. Barnum's museum sported portraits of his curiosities on the walls of his building and flags and banners strung across Broadway in profusion. In the lower corner of this illustration, the showman outfoxes the furious vestrymen who protest the use of church property to anchor his display.

himself in front of the irate vestryman; "Look here, old fellow," he continued, "if you want to save a whole bone in your body, you had better slope, and never dare to talk again about hauling down the American flag in the city of New York."

Throngs of excited, exasperated men crowded around, and the vestryman, seeing the effect of my ruse, smiled faintly and said, "Oh, of course it is all right," and he and his companion quietly edged out of the crowd. The flags remained up all day and all night. The next morning I sought the vanquished vestrymen and obtained formal permission to make this use of the tree on following holidays, in consideration of my willingness to arrest the doleful strains of my discordant balcony band whenever services were held on week days in the church.

On that Fourth of July, at one o'clock, P.M., my Museum was so densely crowded that we could admit no more visitors, and we were compelled to stop the sale of tickets. I pushed through the throng until I reached the roof of the building, hoping to find room for a few more, but it was in vain. Looking down into the street it was a sad sight to see the thousands of people who stood ready with their money to enter the Museum, but who were actually turned away. It was exceedingly harrowing to my feelings. Rushing down stairs, I told my carpenter and his assistants to cut through the partition and floor in the rear and to put in a temporary flight of stairs so as to let out people by that egress into Ann Street. By three o'clock the egress was opened and a few people were passed down the new stairs, while a corresponding number came in at the front. But I lost a large amount of money that day by not having sufficiently estimated the value of my own advertising, and consequently not having provided for the thousands who had read my announcements and seen my outside show, and had taken the first leisure day to visit the Museum. I had learned one lesson, however, and that was to have the egress ready on future holidays.

Early in the following March, I received notice from some of the Irish population that they meant to visit me in great numbers on "St. Patrick's day in the morning." "All right," said I to my carpenter, "get your egress ready for March 17"; and I added, to my assistant manager: "If there is much of a crowd, don't let a single person pass out at the front, even if it were St. Patrick himself; put every man out through the egress in the rear." The day came, and before noon we were caught in the same dilemma as we were on the Fourth of July; the Museum was jammed and the sale of tickets was stopped. I went to the egress and asked the sentinel how many hundreds had passed out?

"Hundreds," he replied, "why only three persons have gone out by this way and they came back, saying that it was a mistake and begging to be let in again."

"What does this mean?" I inquired; "surely thousands of people have been all over the Museum since they came in."

"Certainly," was the reply, "but after they have gone from one saloon to another and have been on every floor, even to the roof, they come down and travel the same route over again."

At this time, I espied a tall Irish woman with two good-sized children whom I had happened to notice when they came in early in the morning.

"Step this way, madam," said I politely, "you will never be able to get into the street by the front door without crushing these dear children. We have opened a large egress here and you can pass by these rear stairs into Ann Street and thus avoid all danger."

"Sure," replied the woman, indignantly, "an' I'm not going out at all, nor the children aither, for we've brought our dinners and we are going to stay all day."

Further investigation showed that pretty much all of my visitors had brought their dinners with the evident intention of literally "making a day of it." No one expected to go home till night; the building was overcrowded, and meanwhile hundreds were waiting at the front entrance to get in when they could. In despair I sauntered upon the stage behind the scenes, biting my lips with vexation, when I happened to see the scene-painter at work and a happy thought struck me: "Here," I exclaimed, "take a piece of canvas four feet square, and paint on it, as soon as you can, in large letters—

☞ TO THE EGRESS."

Seizing his brush he finished the sign in fifteen minutes, and I directed the carpenter to nail it over the door leading to the back stairs. He did so, and as the crowd, after making the entire tour of the establishment, came pouring down the main stairs from the third story, they stopped and looked at the new sign, while some of them read audibly: "To the Aigress,"

"The Aigress," said others, "sure that's an animal we haven't seen," and the throng began to pour down the back stairs only to find that the "Aigress" was the elephant, and that the elephant was all out o'doors, or so much of it as began with Ann Street. Meanwhile, I began to accommodate those who had long been waiting with their money at the Broadway entrance.

Notwithstanding my continual outlays for additional novelties and attractions, or rather I might say, because of these outlays, money poured in upon me so rapidly that I was sometimes actually embarrassed to devise means to carry out my original plan for laying out the entire profits of the first year in advertising. I meant to sow first and reap afterwards. I finally hit upon a plan which cost a large sum, and that was to prepare large oval oil paintings to be placed between the windows of the entire building, representing nearly every important animal known in zoology. These paintings were put on the building in a single night, and so complete a transformation in the appearance of an edifice is seldom witnessed. When the living stream rolled down Broadway the next morning and reached the Astor House corner, opposite the Museum, it seemed to meet with a sudden check. I never before saw so many open mouths and astonished eyes. Some people were puzzled to know what it all meant; some looked as if they thought it was an enchanted palace that had suddenly sprung up; others exclaimed, "Well, the animals all seem to have 'broken out' last night," and hundreds came in to see how the establishment survived the sudden eruption. At all events, from that morning the Museum receipts took a jump forward of nearly a hundred dollars a day, and they never fell back again. Strangers would look at this great pictorial magazine and argue that an establishment with so many animals on the outside must have something on the inside, and in they would go to see. Inside, I took particular pains to please and astonish these strangers, and when they went back to the country, they carried plenty of pictorial bills and lithographs, which I always lavishly furnished, and thus the fame of Barnum's Museum became so widespread, that people scarcely thought of visiting the city without going to my establishment.

In fact, the Museum had become an established institution in the land. Now and then some one would cry out "humbug" and "charlatan," but so much the better for me. It helped to advertise me, and I was willing to bear the reputation—and I engaged queer curiosities, and even monstrosities, simply to add to the notoriety of the Museum.

Dr. Valentine will be remembered by many as a man who gave imitations and delineations of eccentric characters. He was quite a card at the Museum when I first purchased that establishment, and before I introduced dramatic representations into the "Lecture Room." His representations were usually given as follows: A small table was placed in about the centre of the stage; a curtain reaching to the floor covered the front and two ends of the table; under this table, on little shelves and hooks, were placed caps, hats, coats, wigs, moustaches, curls, cravats, and shirt collars, and all sorts of gear for changing the appearance of the upper portion of the person. Dr. Valentine would seat himself in a chair behind the table, and addressing his audience, would state his intention to represent different peculiar characters, male and female, including the Yankee tin peddler; "Tabitha Twist," a maiden lady; "Sam Slick, Jr.," the precocious author; "Solomon Jenkins," a crusty old bachelor, with a song; the down-east school-teacher with his refractory pupils, with many other characters; and he simply asked the indulgence of the audience for a few seconds between each imitation, to enable him to stoop down behind the table and "dress" each character appropriately.

The Doctor himself was a most eccentric character. He was very nervous, and was always fretting lest his audience should be composed of persons who would not appreciate his "imitations." During one of his engagements the Lecture Room performances consisted of negro minstrelsy and Dr. Valentine's imitations. As the minstrels gave the entire first half of the entertainment, the Doctor would post himself at the entrance to the Museum to study the character of the visitors from their appearance. He fancied that he was a great reader of character in this way, and as most of my visitors were from the country, the Doctor, after closely perusing their faces, would decide that they were not the kind of persons who would appreciate his efforts, and this made him extremely nervous. When this idea was once in his head, it took complete possession of the poor Doctor, and worked him up into a nervous excitement which it was often painful to behold. Every country-looking face was a dagger to the Doctor, for he had a perfect horror of exhibiting to an unappreciative audience. When so much excited that he could stand at the door no longer, the disgusted Doctor would come into my office and pour out his lamentations in this wise:

"There, Barnum, I never saw such a stupid lot of country bumpkins in my life. I shan't be able to get a smile out of them. I had rather be horse-whipped than attempt to satisfy an audience who have not got the brains to appreciate me. Sir, mine is a highly intellectual entertainment, and none but refined and educated persons can comprehend it."

"Oh, I think you will make them laugh some, Doctor," I replied.

"Laugh, sir, laugh! why, sir, they have no laugh in them, sir; and if they had, your devilish nigger minstrels would get it all out of them before I commenced."

"Do n't get excited, Doctor," I said; "you will please the people."

"Impossible, sir! I was a fool to ever permit my entertainment to be mixed up with that of nigger singers."

"But you could not give an entire entertainment satisfactorily to the public; they want more variety."

"Then you should have got something more refined, sir. Why, one of those cursed nigger breakdowns excites your audience so they do n't want to hear a word from me. At all events, I ought to commence the entertainment and let the niggers finish up. I tell you, Mr. Barnum, I won't stand it! I would rather go to the poor-house. I won't stay here over a fortnight longer! It is killing me!"

In this excited state the Doctor would go upon the stage, dressed very neatly in a suit of black. Addressing a few pleasant words to the audience, he would then take a seat behind his little table, and with a broad smile covering his countenance would ask the audience to excuse him a few seconds, and he would appear as "Tabitha Twist," a literary spinster of fifty-five. On these occasions I was usually behind the scenes, standing at one of the wings opposite the Doctor's table, where I could see and hear all that occurred "behind the curtain." The moment the Doctor was down behind the table, a wonderful change came over that smiling countenance.

"Blast this infernal, stupid audience! they would not laugh to save the city of New York!" said the Doctor, while he rapidly slipped on a lady's cap and a pair of long curls. Then, while arranging a lace handkerchief around his shoulders, he would grate his teeth and curse the Museum, its manager, the audience and everybody else. The instant the handkerchief was pinned, the broad smile would come upon his face, and up would go his head and shoulders showing to the audience a rollicking specimen of a good-natured old maid.

"How do you do, ladies and gentlemen? You all know me. Tabitha Twist, the happiest maiden in the village; always laughing. Now, I'll sing you one of my prettiest songs."

The mock maiden would then sing a lively, funny ditty, followed by faint applause, and down would bob the head behind the table to prepare for a presentation of "Sam Slick, junior."

"Curse such a set of fools" (off goes the cap, followed by the curls). "They think it's a country Sunday school" (taking off the lace handkerchief). "I expect they will hiss me next, the donkeys" (on goes a light wig of long, flowing hair). "I wish the old Museum was sunk in the Atlantic" (puts on a Yankee round-jacket, and broadbrimmed hat). "I never will be caught in this infernal place, curse it;" up jump head and shoulders of the Yankee, and Sam Slick junior, sings out a merry—

"Ha! ha! why, folks, how de dew. Darn glad to see you, by hokey; I came down here to have lots of fun, for you know I always believe we must laugh and grow fat."

After five minutes of similar rollicking nonsense, down would bob the head again, and the cursing, swearing, tearing, and teeth-grating would commence, and continue till the next character appeared to the audience, bedecked with smiles and good-humor.

. . . .

In June 1843, a herd of yearling buffaloes was on exhibition in Boston. I bought the lot, brought them to New Jersey, hired the race course at Hoboken, chartered the ferry-boats for one day, and advertised that a hunter had arrived with a herd of buffaloes—I was careful not to state their age—and that August 31st there would be a "Grand Buffalo Hunt" on the Hoboken race course—all persons to be admitted free of charge.

The appointed day was warm and delightful, and no less than twenty-four thousand people crossed the North River in the ferryboats to enjoy the cooling breeze and to see the "Grand Buffalo Hunt." The hunter was dressed as an Indian, and mounted on horseback; he proceeded to show how the wild buffalo is captured with a lasso, but unfortunately the yearlings would not run till the crowd gave a great shout, expressive at once of derision and delight at the harmless humbug. This shout started the young animals into a weak gallop and the lasso was duly thrown over the head of the largest calf. The crowd roared with laughter, listened to my balcony band, which I also furnished "free," and then started for New York; little dreaming who was the author of this sensation, or what was its object.

Mr. N. P. Willis, then editor of the *Home Journal*, wrote an article illustrating the perfect good nature with which the American public submit to a clever humbug. He said that he went to Hoboken to witness the Buffalo Hunt. It was nearly four o'clock when the boat left the foot of Barclay Street, and it was so densely crowded that many persons were obliged to stand on the railings and hold on to the awning posts. When they reached the Hoboken side a boat equally crowded was coming out of the slip. The passengers just arriving cried out to those who were coming away, "Is the Buffalo Hunt over?" To which came the reply, "Yes, and it was the biggest humbug you ever heard of!" Willis added that passengers on the boat with him instantly gave three cheers for the author of the humbug, whoever he might be.

After the public had enjoyed a laugh for several days over the Hoboken "Free Grand Buffalo Hunt," I permitted it to be announced that the proprietor of the American Museum was responsible for the joke, thus using the buffalo hunt as a sky-rocket to attract public attention to my Museum. The object was accomplished and although some people cried out "humbug," I had added to the notoriety which I so much wanted and I was satisfied. As for the cry of "humbug," it never harmed me, and I was in the position of the actor who had much rather be roundly abused than not to be noticed at all. I ought to add, that the forty-eight thousand sixpences—the usual fee—received for ferry fares, less what I paid for the charter of the boats on that one day, more than remunerated me for the cost of the buffaloes and the expenses of the "hunt," and the enormous gratuitous advertising of the Museum must also be placed to my credit.

. . . .

Barnum's Speech to the Connecticut Legislature on Equal Rights

Let the educated free negro feel that he is a man; let him be trained in New England churches, schools and workshops; let him support himself, pay his taxes, and cast his vote, like other men, and he will put to everlasting shame the champions of modern democracy, by the overwhelming evidence he will give in his own person of the great Scripture truth, that "God has made of one blood all the nations of men." A human soul, "that God has created and Christ died for," is not to be trifled with. It may tenant the body of a Chinaman, a Turk, an Arab or a Hottentot—it is still an immortal spirit; and amid all assumptions of caste, it will in due time vindicate the great fact that, without regard to color or condition, all men are equally children of the common Father.

. . . .

The State of Connecticut, like New Jersey, is a border State of New York. New York has a great commercial city, where Aldermen rob by the tens of thousands, and where principal is studied much more than principle. I can readily understand how the negro has come to be debased at the North as well as at the South. The interests of the two sections in the product of negro labor were nearly identical. The North wanted Southern cotton and the South was ready in turn to buy from the North whatever was needed in the way of Northern supplies and manufactures. This community of commercial interests led to an identity in political principles especially in matters pertaining to the negro race—the working race of the South—which produced the cotton and consumed so much of what Northern merchants and manufacturers sold for plantation use. The Southern planters were good customers and were worth conciliating. So when Connecticut proposed in 1818 to continue to admit colored men to the franchise, the South protested against thus elevating the negroes, and Connecticut succumbed. No other New England State has ever so disgraced herself; and now Connecticut democrats are asked to permit the white citizens of this State to express their opinion in regard to re-instating the colored man where our Revolutionary sires placed him under the Constitution. Now, gentlemen, "democrats" as you call yourselves, you who speak so flippantly of your "loyalty," your "love for the Union" and your "love for the people;" you who are generally talking right and voting wrong, we ask you to come forward and act "democratically," by letting your masters, the people, speak.

The word "white" in the Constitution cannot be strictly and literally construed. The opposition express great love for white blood. Will they let a mulatto vote half the time, a quadroon three-fourths, and an octoroon seven-eighths of the time? If not, why not? Will they enslave seven-eighths of a white man because one-eighth is not Caucasian? Is this democratic? Shall not the majority seven control the minority one? Out on such "democracy."

But a Democratic minority committee (of two) seem to have done something besides study ethnology. They have also paid great attention to fine arts, and are particularly anxious that all voters shall have a "genius for the arts." I would like to ask them if it has always been political practice to insist that every voter in the great "unwashed" and "unterrified" of any party should become a member of the Academy of Arts before he votes the "regular" ticket? I thought he was received into the full fellowship of a political party if he could exhibit sufficient "inventive faculties and genius for the arts," to enable him to paint a black eye. Can a man whose "genius for the arts" enables him to strike from the shoulder scientifically, be admitted to full fellowship in a political party? Is it evident that the political artist has studied the old masters, if he exhibits his genius by tapping an opponent's head with a shillelagh? The oldest master in this school of art was Cain; and so canes have been made to play their part in politics, at the polls and even in the United States Senate Chamber.

"Is genius for the arts and those occupations requiring intellect and wisdom" sufficiently exemplified in adroitly stuffing ballot boxes, forging soldiers' votes, and copying a directory, as has been done, as the return list of votes? Is the "inventive faculty" of "voting early and often," a passport to political brotherhood? Is it satisfactory evidence of "artistic" genius, to head a mob? and a mob which is led and guided by political passion, as numerous instances in our history prove, is the worst of mobs. Is it evidence of "high art" to lynch a man by hanging him to the nearest tree or lamp post? Is a "whiskey scrimmage" one of the lost arts restored? We all know how the "artists" of both political parties are prone to embellish elections and to enhance the excitements of political campaigns by inciting riots, and the frequency with which these disgraceful outbreaks have occurred of late, especially in some of the populous cities, is cause for just alarm. It is dangerous "art."

. . . .

But some persons have this color prejudice simply by the force of education, and they say, "Well, a nigger is a nigger, and he can't be anything else. I hate niggers, anyhow." Twenty years ago I crossed the Atlantic, and among our passengers was an Irish judge, who was coming out to Newfoundland as chief justice. He was an exceedingly intelligent and polished gentleman, and extremely witty. The passengers from the New England States and those from the South got into a discussion on the subject of slavery, which lasted three days. The Southerners were finally worsted, and when their arguments were exhausted, they fell back on the old story, by saying: "Oh! curse a nigger, he ain't half human anyhow; he had no business to be a nigger, etc." One of the gentlemen then turned to the Irish judge, and asked his opinion of the merits of the controversy. The judge replied:

"Gentlemen, I have listened with much edification to your arguments pro and con during three days. I was quite inclined to think the anti-slavery gentlemen had justice and right on their side, but the last argument from the South has changed my mind. I say a 'nigger has no business to be a nigger,' and we should kick him out of society and trample him under foot—always provided, gentlemen, you prove he was born black at his own particular request. If he had no word to say in the matter of course he is blameless for his color, and is entitled to the same respect that other men are who properly behave themselves!"

Mr. Speaker: I am no politician, I came to this legislature simply because I wished to have the honor of voting for the two constitutional amendments—one for driving slavery entirely out of our country; the other to allow men of education and good moral character to vote, regardless of the color of their skins. To give my voice for these two philanthropic, just, and Christian measures is all the glory I ask legislativewise. I care nothing whatever for any sect or party under heaven, as such. I have no axes to grind, no logs to roll, no favors to ask. All I desire is to do what is right, and prevent what is wrong. I believe in no "expediency" that is not predicated of justice, for in all things—politics, as well as everything else—"I know that honesty is the best policy." A retributive Providence will unerringly and speedily search out all wrong doing; hence, right is always the best in the long run. Certainly, in the light of the great American spirit of liberty and equal rights which is sweeping over this country, and making the thrones of tyrants totter in the old world, no party can afford to carry slavery, either of body or of mind. Knock off your manacles and let the man go free. Take down the blinds from his intellect, and let in the light of education and Christian culture. When this is done you have developed a man. Give him the responsibility of a man and the self-respect of a man, by granting him the right of suffrage. Let universal education, and the universal franchise be the motto of free America, and the toiling millions of Europe, who are watching you with such intense interest, will hail us as their saviors. Let us loyally sink "party" on this question, and go for "God and our Country." Let no man attach an eternal stigma to his name by shutting his eyes to the great lesson of the hour, and voting against permitting the people to express their opinion on this important subject. Let us unanimously grant this truly democratic boon. Then, when our laws of franchise are settled on a just basis, let future parties divide where they honestly differ on State or national questions which do not trench upon the claims of manhood or American citizenship.

Barnum and the Barber

Anonymous

Barnum is undeniably a genius in his way, and withal a fellow of infinite humor, having a heart as open as day to melting charity. A faithful biography of the man would be one of the most amusing books in our language.

We happened to be a passenger on the steamer "E. W. Stevens," coming up the Ohio last spring, and Jenny Lind and her troupe, accompanied by P. T. Barnum, were on board.

Evidently to beguile the tedium of this sort of still-life, Barnum, in little groups of his friends and his "body-guard," exhibited several feats of sleight-of-hand, which would have done honor to the renowned "Wizard of the North." In one of these, a quarter of a dollar disappeared so magically, that for the life of us, we could not guess what had become of it.

The barber, a colored man, owned by the captain, had been looking on, as it were, by stealth, and his superstitious notion immediately invested the traveller with the powers of a league with the Devil.

The next morning, the wonder worker seated himself for the operation of shaving, and the colored gentleman ventured to dip into the mystery.

"Beg pardon, Mr. Barnum, but I have heard a great deal about you, and I saw more than I wanted to see, last night. Is it true that you have sold yourself to the Devil, so that you can do what you've a mind to?"

"Oh, yes, that was the bargain between us," was the reply.

"How long did you agree for?" he asked.

"Only nine years," replied Barnum; "I have had three of them already. Before the other six are out, I shall find a way to nonplus the old gentleman—and I have told him so to his face."

At this avowal, a larger space of white than usual was seen in the darkey's eyes, and he inquired—

"Is it not by this bargain that you are enabled to get so much money?"

"Certainly," replied Barnum, "no matter *who* has money, nor where he keeps it—in his box or till—or anywhere about him, I have only just to speak the words, and it is certain to come."

The shaving was completed in silence, but the thoughts had been busy in the barber's mind, and he embraced the speediest opportunity to transfer his bag of coin to the Iron Safe in the charge of the clerk of the boat.

The movement did not escape the lynx eyes of the magician, and immediately a joke was on foot.

"And now hand me a cent," said Barnum; "I will send it to his Infernal Majesty, and bring it back forthwith."

A cent was handed to him—it was tossed into the air, and disappeared.

"Where will you have it appear?"

"Under this plate," was the answer.

The plate was turned—and lo! the cent was there. The barber lifted it from the table, and instantly dropped it. It was scorching hot!

"And now," continued Barnum, "I will turn you into a cat, and change you back directly."

"You can't do *that*," said the barber, but evidently with some suspicion of his own judgment.

"You shall see," said the magician, solemnly. "You run only one risk; if anything happens to me, by losing remembrance of his Majesty's pass-word, or anything of the kind, you will remain a black tom forever. Are you ready for the operation?"

The barber fled in consternation, and was so seriously troubled, that Captain Brown feared he would jump overboard. On being informed of the extremity of the joke, Barnum kindly explained the whole thing to the subject of his fun—including even (as we were informed) the tricks of the mysterious quarter and the red-hot cent.

"By golly!" said the barber, in the exultation characteristic of his race, "I'll come Barnum over the colored people anyhow—ha! ha! ha!"

The Man That Got Humbugged

Anonymous

The stage in which I was a passenger had stopped to change horses, and "feed" the passengers, at a small town in Vermont, and dinner over, we were awaiting the arrival of the stage upon an intersecting route, to proceed upon our journey. Segars had been lighted, and by way of passing our time, we had commenced a critical examination of the mammoth pictorial posters of Barnum's Menagerie, which covered the walls of the spacious barroom. Barnum's name opened a fruitful topic of conversation; every one present seemed stored with anecdotes of the "Napoleon of Showmen," and the Woolly Horse, the Feejee Mermaid, and Joice Heth, were not forgotten in the discussion which followed.

Suddenly, a long, slabsided individual, with an owl-like expression of wisdom and dignity, who had been listening to our remarks with an evident desire to take a hand, broke out—

"I spose you think that's an all-fired big consarn? Anybody would that hadn't seen it."

"Then I suppose you have seen it," said my friend.

"Yaas, I seen it at Springfield," was the reply; "it's a *darn'd humbug!*"

"Is it possible?" said the Major, seeing a prospect of fun. "Couldn't you oblige us with a description of the institution?"

"Certainly," said the Yankee; "here's the stage, and as soon as we get started, I'll give you all the items. They can't humbug me very often, and when they do, I calklate to advertise for 'em till I git square."

In a few minutes we were under headway, and our verdant friend commenced unbosoming himself.

"Yer see, Barnum was going to show his caravan down to Springfield, Fourth of July, and I thought there would be a good chance to see the elephant and celebrate the day, both at onc't. What I wanted to see more than all the rest was the Car of Jugglenot, drawn by a string of elephants."

"Did it meet your expectations?"

"I never seen one sight of it. Before I got in town, they'd got all through paradin,' the elephants was unharnessed, and the Car of Jugglenot was backed into a woodshed. I made up my mind right off, then, that the hull consarn was a humbug."

"Was Barnum aware that you were to be in town?"

"Not as I know on."

"If he had known it, he would doubtless have waited. But you visited the exhibition, I suppose."

"Of course; I was bound to do that, if it bust me. That was a bigger humbug than all the rest."

"How so?"

"Why, in the first place I expected to see Jenny Lind."

"Was she announced in the bills?"

"I don't know; I didn't read 'em, but I axed the man that stuck up the picters if she would be there, and he said 'yes,' and that she'd sing the bird song standing on the top of a cage of cockatoos and parrots. She wan't there, and I never seen one sight of her—and then I knowed the whole consarn was a darned humbug.

"Well, then, I went round and took a look at the elephants—had hard work to get round teu; there was more than a hundred thousand people in the tent. I got where they was, and the folks was all feedin 'em with apples, and cakes and things. I had some doughnuts in my hat, so I held it out to one of the darned things, to see if he'd take one."

"Did he take one?"

"He took 'em all, *and the hat teu, darn him*, and stuck 'em into his nasty, peaked mouth, and begun ter chaw. I hollered to the keeper and told him it was a bran new hat. He said never mind, he'd git it agin."

"Did he get it?"

"Yes, he got it, but a hat an't much account after an elephant's *chawed* it. *Then*, I'd a sworn the hull consarn was a humbug.

"Well, I took a look at Tom Thumb, and the Ceylong Chief, and the man that fiddled with his toes, and the feller that went in with the lions. The wild animals was well enough, but I didn't see as they looked any different from anybody else's. I *expected* Barnum's lions would be twice as big as any others. There was one thing, though, that was fust rate, that was the wax statuatary—especially the 'intemperance family.' I told the man that tuk care of it, I wished every body that ever drinked a drop of sperrits had to stand and look at that about a week—they'd never want to drink agin. He said he wished so teu.

"Take it all round, though, I was mad; I didn't see what I expected, and I didn't like the idee of bein humbugged, so I inquired of one of the men that was stirrin' up the monkeys, where Barnum was, and he pointed him out to me, selling lemonade, out of a wagon. I went up to him, thinking I'd give him a piece of my mind. Sez I—

"Mr. Barnum—"

"Sixpence a glass," sez he.

"I looked at his lemonade; there was jest one lone, solitary, second-handed slice of lemon in a whole wash-tub full of it, and he peddlin it out at sixpence a glass. That made me madder than all the rest, so sez I, loud and auditably—

"Mr. Barnum, I think your show is a darned humbug."

"Young man," sez he, "I spose you paid to come in?"

"Sposin I did?" sez I.

"Well, sposin you hev," sez he; "you've paid your quarter, and you've a perfect right to think just what you d——n please."

"Why did you not demand your money back?" asked the Major, after the sensation caused by this recital had somewhat subsided. "You certainly could have compelled them to refund your quarter."

"You see, the truth is," replied the Yankee, scratching his head, "I didn't pay no quarter—*I crawled in under the canvas!*"

❧ Mortimer N. Thomson ❧ (Q. K. Philander Doesticks, P.B.)

Mortimer N. Thomson (1831–1875), known as "Q. K. Philander Doesticks" as he rose to fame in the middle 1850s, exemplified the idealism of the New York Bohemians. In a series of comic sketches, compiled in *Doesticks: What He Says* (1855), Doesticks captured in burlesque the social customs of the rising classes of the city. In *Pluri-bus-tah: A Song That's by No Author* (1856) and *Nothing to Say* (1857), literary burlesques of Longfellow's *Hiawatha* and William Allen Butler's *Nothing to Wear*, he applied rhyme and contemporary language, with a dash of popular slang and political jargon, to point up contemporary topics of national greed, slavery, and the morality of wealth and mobocracy. Excerpts of *Pluri-bus-tah* (New York, 1856) are reprinted here. As a reporter for the antislavery New York *Tribune*, Thomson disguised himself and attended one of the most notorious slave auctions of the era. The *Tribune* published his account of it on March 9, 1859, and it was reprinted almost verbatim in the London *Times*. Later, it was republished as a tract, and the *Atlantic Monthly* praised it highly. The suggestion that it set the North aflame with its mixture of sarcasm and melodrama may well be true. The text given here was taken from the original *Tribune* article.

During the Civil War, Thomson lost two young wives in childbed and was himself seriously wounded as a noncombatant reporter for the *Tribune*. He was credited with a number of heroic deeds. Although he continued to produce comic columns, "A Great Slave Auction" was his last important work. Fletcher D. Slater's thesis, "The Life and Letters of Mortimer Thomson" (Northwestern University, 1931), is the only extended treatment Doesticks has received beyond one or two brief articles and standard biographical entries. My critical essay on Doesticks appears in *American Humorists, 1800–1950* (Detroit, 1982).

From *Pluri-bus-tah*

Introduction

Don't you ask me, whence this burlesque;
Whence this captious fabrication,
With its huge attempt at satire,
With its effort to be funny,
With its pride in Yankee spirit,
With its love of Yankee firmness,
With its flings at Yankee fashions,
With its slaps at Yankee humbug,
With its hits at Yankee follies,
And its scoffs at Yankee bragging,
With its praise of all that's manly,
All that's honest, all that's noble,
With its bitter hate of meanness,
Hate of pride and affectation.
With its scorn of slavish fawning,
Scorn of snobs, and scorn of flunkies,
Scorn of all who cringe before the
Dirty but "almighty dollar?"
　　Don't you ask—for I shan't tell you,
Lest you, too, should be a Yankee
And should turn and sue for libel,
Claiming damage—God knows how much.

Here the faint-hearted author vanishes in a tremulous flourish of coat-tails, and "Doesticks," appearing, learnedly discourses as follows:

Should you ask *me* where *I* found it?
Found this song, perhaps so stupid,
Found this most abusive epic?
I should answer, I should tell you
That "I found it at my Uncle's,"
"Number one, around the corner,"
In a paper, in a pocket,
In a coat, within a bundle,

Tied up, ticketed and labelled,
Labeled by my careful "Uncle;"
Placed within a cozy recess,
On a shelf behind a curtain.
Here I found this frantic poem;
And "my Uncle," kind old "Uncle,"
Told me that the hard-up author,
One day borrowed two and sixpence
On this coat, and on this bundle.
Months had flown, and still the author
Hadn't yet redeemed his pledges,
Hadn't paid the two and sixpence.
So "my Uncle," *dear* old "Uncle,"
Kind, accommodating "Uncle,"
Sold to me this precious bundle,
And this poem lay within it.

This is where I got this epic,
Epic pawned for two and sixpence.
But, where is the hard-up author?
Whether writing, whether starving,
Whether dead, or in the almshouse,
I don't care—nor does the public.

If, still further, you should ask me,
"Who is this dear noble 'Uncle?'
Tell us of this kind old 'Uncle;' "
I should answer your inquiries
Straightway, in such words as follow:
"In the Bowery and in Broome street,
Neighbor to the fragrant gin-shop;
In a dark and lonesome cellar
Dwells the Hebrew—dwells 'my Uncle.'
You can tell his habitation
By the golden balls before it.

"Here 'my Uncle,' kind old 'Uncle,'
Dear, disinterested 'Uncle,'
Sits and sings his 'song of sixpence.'
'Sixpence here for every farthing,
Every farthing that I lend you
You shall soon return me sixpence:
And, that by the risk I lose not,

Ere I lend you dimes or dollars,
You shall leave a hundred values
Of the money which you borrow;
Which, if you don't pay my sixpence,
Shall be forfeit then forever.
Sixpence here for every farthing,
Every farthing pays me sixpence.'
   "Here the painters bring their pictures,
Precious, beautiful creations;
Bring them to my kind old 'Uncle.'
He to cherish native talent,
And encourage home-bred genius,
Gives the artist, on his pictures,
Half the first cost of the canvas.
And the author takes his poem,
Which has cost him months of labor;
On which he has poured his life* out—
Takes it to my kind old 'Uncle,'
Who, to cherish native talent,
Gives him what the ink has cost him,
What the ink with which he wrote it.
   "But the poet and the painter
Are Americans, and natives
Of the land which leaves them beggars.
That's the reason why they're starving—
Why they need 'my Uncle's' sixpence.**
This is how this naughty poem
Once was 'up a spout' in Broome Street—
This is all about 'my Uncle'—
Good-by, 'Uncle'—go to thunder."
   Ye, who love to scold your neighbors,
Love to magnify their follies,
Love to swell their faults and errors,

---

*By "*life*" the author does not mean autobiography.
**The *native* poet and the *native* painter are a couple of native jackasses. If Muggins's poem won't sell, let him Frenchify himself, and become "Chevalier Muggins" or "Monsieur de Mogyns;" and if Dobbs can't find a market for his picture, let him transmogrify himself into an Italian, and call himself "Signor Doboni," and both will find customers enough. If Miss Donovan, the Irish songstress, can't make her music pay expenses, she adds an "i" to her Celtic cognomen, and straightway as "Signorina Donovani," she creates a sensation. *Vide Hist. Ital. Opera, every volume within the memory of man.*

Love to laugh at other's dullness,
Making sport of other's failings—
Buy this modern Yankee fable;
Buy this song that's by no author.
   Ye, who love to laugh at nonsense,
Love the stilted lines of burlesque,
Want to read a song historic,
Want to read a song prophetic,
Want to read a mixed-up story
Full of facts and real transactions,
Which you know are true and life-like—
Also full of lies and fictions,
Full of characters of fancy
And imaginary people,
Buy this home-made Yankee fable;
Buy this song that's by no author.
   Ye, who want to see policemen,
Roman heroes, modern Bloomers,
Heathen gods of every gender,
News-boys, generals, apple-peddlers,
Modern ghosts of ancient worthies,
Editors, and Congress members
With their bowie-knives and horsewhips,
Saints and scoundrels, Jews and Gentiles,
Honest men of ancient fable,
With historic modern villains,
Jumbled up in dire confusion,
Dovetailed in, at once regardless
Of all place or date or country;
Making such a curious legend
As the world has never read of;
Headless, tailless, soulless, senseless,
Even authorless and foundling—
Buy this modern Yankee fable,
Buy this song that's by no author.
   Ye, who sometimes in your rambles
Through the alleys of the city,
Where the smell of gas escaping,
And the odors of the gutters,
And the perfume of the garbage,

The frontispiece of Doesticks' *Pluri-bus-tah* (1856) shows the allegorized national spirit of the Yankee Puritan, warts and all.

And the fragrance of the mud-carts
Don't remind you of the country,
Or the redolence of roses;
Pause by some neglected book-stall,
For awhile to muse and ponder
On the second-hand collection:
If you find among the volumes,
Disregarded, shabby volumes,
One which answers to *our* title,
Buy it here and read hereafter—
Buy this modern Yankee fable,
Buy this song that's by no author.

I. The Pipe, and Who Smoked It; with All the Particulars

In the ancient heathen heaven,
On a side hill called Olympus,
Mister Jupiter, the mighty,
With his wife and all his children,
With his Juno and the babies,
Sat one morning eating breakfast.
On his feet he had his slippers,
On his lap he laid his napkin,
In his hand he held the paper,
Looking at the "City Items;"
To his lips he raised the buckwheat
Pancakes, dripping with molasses—
To his lips he raised the coffee,
Throwing back his head celestial,
Opening wide his jawbones godlike,
Showed the winding pathway for it,
Saying to it—"Run down this way."
    From a shelf within a closet,
Taking down his pipe of comfort,
With its bowl of yellow meerschaum,
With its stem of india-rubber,
And its mouth-piece made of ivory;
Filled the bowl with best tobacco,
Breathed upon a lump of charcoal,

Till, in flames, it burst and kindled—
Then, in meek obedience to that
Superstition of the ladies,
That tobacco scents the curtains,
Mister Jupiter, the mighty,
As a signal to the kitchen
That he had devoured his breakfast,
And they might wash up the dishes,
Walked out doors into the woodshed,
There to smoke his pipe of comfort.
  In the woodshed, on the slop-pail,
In his slippers and his shirt-sleeves;
With one leg across the other
In the style of Mrs. Bloomer,
At the Woman's Rights Convention,
Mister Jupiter sat smoking:
And the smoke rose fast and faster,
As he sat there puffing, puffing,
Like a furious locomotive—
A celestial locomotive.
First a single line of darkness,
Then a denser, bluer vapor,
Ever rising, rising, rising
Till it touched the roof above him,
And rolled outward through the chink-holes.
  But the nations didn't see it,
And the Indians couldn't see it,
Or the warriors wouldn't see it,
If they did, they didn't mind it,
They had other things to look to.
For the Delewares and Mohawks,
All the Shoshonies and Blackfeet,
All the Pawnees and Omawhaws,
With their squaws and their pappooses,
Had their hunting grounds deserted,
To attend a grand convention,
Red republican mass-meeting,
Which you'll find, described in detail,
In the "Song of Hiawatha."
Hiawatha gave them tickets

Over all the lakes and rivers,
So they all went free, as deadheads.
   Through the window of the woodshed,
Through the smoke so thick and solid,
Through his spectacles so clouded,
Through his little kitchen-garden,
Through the shadows of the beanpoles,
Mister Jupiter, the mighty,
Saw a maiden coming toward him.
   To his feet, at once, he started—
Threw the slop-pail in a corner,
Threw his spectacles far from him,
Threw his pipe into the ashes,
Threw his slippers through the window—
Through the smoke, and through the doorway,
Through the alley, through the garden,
He went rushing forth, to meet her.
   Then and there he met and kissed her,
Then and there he long embraced her,
Looking backward toward the kitchen,
Trembling lest his wife should see him.
Little fear of that, however,
For his spouse was in the parlor,
With her hair put up in papers,
With her feet in ragged slippers,
With a torn and dirty dress on,
Studying the latest fashions.
   Who then, was this stranger maiden?
Who was this pedestrian female?
   Hear ye! hear ye! patient reader:
This fair lady was a goddess,
Dressed in deerskin shoes and leggins,
Dressed in wampum, beads, and feathers—
Quite a quisby looking goddess,
Still a goddess without question.
Miss America her name was,
And she used to live in heaven,
In the ancient, heathen heaven,
Till she had a "muss" one evening,

Had a little row with Juno,
And was forced to leave those "diggins."
   Jupiter on earth had placed her—
Made her ruler of the nations,
Made her mistress of the redskins,
Queen of all the tribes of warriors:
Made her queen of all the country,
All the continent so mighty,
Which was named for her cognomen,
Named America, the glorious.*
   For awhile her reign went smoothly,
And her amiable subjects
Shot, and killed, and scalped each other,
Roasted, broiled and stewed each other
With most excellent good-nature,
To her utmost satisfaction:
Then she liked their sports and pastimes,
Much enjoyed her situation.
But she now returned to heaven,
Seeking Jupiter, the mighty.
What she came there to complain of,
What she said, and what she wanted,
You shall hear if you'll be patient.
   Mister Jupiter, the mighty,
Quick returning to the woodshed,
On his lap took up the lady,
Bade her tell him all her story.
Thus she spake, with tears, and sobbing,
"All the Indians whom you gave me,
Have cleared out and left the country.
When the poet, Henry Wadsworth,
Wrote the song of Hiawatha,
He took all my Indian subjects,
All my pretty, playful warriors,
With their toys, the knife and war-club,
With their pretty games of scalping,

*There is a ridiculous story that this country was called America from one Americus Vespucius, a foreigner, and a papist. The friends of "Sam" will, undoubtedly, feel much obliged to the author for his vindication of the fair name of the continent.

And their pleasant sports of roasting,
And their other torture-pastimes,
Took them all to make a book of.
All the Indians have departed,
All the land is now deserted;
In it there is not a warrior,
Not a squaw, pappoose, or puppy;
Nothing left—save Indian summer—
He's got all my Indians somewhere."
   Speaking thus, she put her finger
In her mouth, as little children
Always do when grieved and troubled,
Then began to sob and blubber.
   Mister Jupiter, the mighty,
In his arms then took the maiden,
Talked to her in tones endearing,
Talked to her in tender accents,
Talked to her as human mothers
Do to peevish human babies.
"Don't it cry, the darling Ducky,
Henry Wadsworth *sha'n't* abuse it:
It *shall* have some pretty playthings.
Let the naughty Henry Wadsworth
Have the ugly, nasty Indians,
For his song of Hiawatha,
You shall have some handsome white men,
From across the boundless ocean,
Who shall be your pets and playthings.
Dry its eyes now, Ducky dearest,
Kiss papa, and then run homeward."
   Then the maiden stopped her crying,
Wiped her nose upon her apron,
On her spotted doeskin apron;
Kissed old Jupiter, the mighty,
Slyly, so his wife, so jealous,
Shouldn't find it out and scratch him—
Then ran back to earth to wait for
The fulfillment of the promise.
And old Jupiter, the mighty,
As he sat upon the slop-pail,

Looking through the unwashed window,
Saw her vanish through the garden,
Through the shadows of the bean-poles,
Through the clouds of smoke, ascending,
Rising from his pipe of comfort.
. . . .

X. What the Hero Worshiped

As the money poured upon him,
In a golden stream upon him,
Pluri-bus-tah came to love it,
Better, every day, and better.
As the pile kept on increasing,
So his love grew stronger with it.
And he loved his shining money,
Better, every day, and better:
Better, soon, than truth or honor.
But he built his costly churches,
Chapels, altars, meeting-houses,
Through his land, in every hamlet,
Through his land, on every hill-side.
    And in these he worshiped heaven,
Blacked with care his boots each Sunday,
Changed his shirt and put his coat on,
Shirt and piety together;
Keeping bright his Christian armor,
In the closet with his broadcloth,
With his Sunday boots and broadcloth.
    And on each lamented Sunday,
Would put on both suits together.
With his boots, put on his bounty,
With his shirt, his zeal and fervor,
With his vest, his orthodoxy,
With his pants, pull on religion,
Tie his creed up in his neckcloth.
Thus would go to Christian service,
Sleeping through the prayers and sermon.
Yet at night he'd take his suit off,

Take his broadcloth Sunday suit off;
With it take his Christian zeal off,
Roll them carefully together,
Lock them in a drawer together,
Never wearing suit of broadcloth,
Never putting on religion,
Save before the pious people,
For a dozen hours on Sunday.
    Yet he worshiped truly, fondly,
With the most intense devotion,
Tireless, weariless devotion.
But the idol that he worshiped
Did not dwell with priests or pastors,
Seldom lived in Christian churches.
It was one that he had whittled
From a block of shining metal;
Which he ever had about him,
In the bottom of his pocket,
Bottom of his deepest pocket.
    And he bowed and knelt before it,
Not one day in seven only,
But each morning's early sunlight
Brought the thoughts of this his idol.
And each night's uneasy slumber
Brought the dreams of this his idol.
And he bowed and knelt before it,
Daily, hourly, without ceasing—
As attentive to his idol
As are Branch and Briggs to Matsell.
    In the street and in the market,
And in sanctimonious Wall-street,
On the wharves beside the sea-shore,
In the mud beside the sea-shore,
Here he knelt, and cringed, and groveled,
To the deity he worshiped.
    Should you ask me, "What this idol?
What this god that Pluri-bus-tah
Knelt before, and bowed and prayed to,
Prayed to with such zeal and fervor

That he cut his pantaloons through—
Cut his knees upon the gravel?"
This should be my instant answer:
"Money, money, money, money!"
Coppers, fips, and dimes, and quarters,
All received some veneration,
Some respect and veneration.
But the god he wildly worshiped,
Traded off his heart and soul for,
(As of old did Doctor Faustus,
Swapping jackknives with the Devil),
Was the king of dimes and quarters,
Was the god of Pluri-bus-tah.
And the prayers which he, on Sunday,
Offered to the King of Heaven,
To 'Our Father,' King of Heaven,
From his lips fell strange and coldly.
But the week-day prayer he uttered,
Daily, hourly prayer he uttered,
From his heart came hot and earnest,
And the language run this wise:
'Potent, and ALMIGHTY DOLLAR!'
　　On the face of this his idol,
He had placed the graven image,
Image and the superscription,
Of his wife, his Free-Love partner,
Liberty, in scarlet-night-cap,
As, if living now, she might be
Photographed, full length, by Brady,
Graced the side of every dollar;
So that when he kissed his idol,
Liberty felt complimented,
Thinking it was her dear picture
Pluri-bus-tah loved so fondly.
　　Never maiden more mistaken,
Pluri-bus-tah loved the *dollar*,
Potent and "ALMIGHTY DOLLAR,"
Dirty, filthy, greasy, DOLLAR!
And he would have loved as truly,

Hugged as closely, kissed as fondly,
Had the female image on it
Been a dog, or been a jackass.

XI. Fight Number Three, with Variations

Well, their honeymoon had lasted
Longer than had been expected.
Fifty years had passed, and left them
Better, firmer friends than ever.
But there came a fearful quarrel;
Pluri-bus-tah, on one morning,
Straying through his southern rice-fields,
Through his sugar-cane plantation,
Through the fields of snowy cotton,
Through his acres of tobacco,
Thought how many dimes they brought him.
But the thought of what they cost him,
What he paid for work and labor
Was a saddening reflection;
And he turned the matter over,
Thought how he could be more saving,
Save the sum his broad plantations,
Yearly cost for work and labor.
 As he cast his eye about him,
Sable Cuffee met his vision.
Cuffee was a powerful darkey,
Rich in muscle and in sinew,
Strong and vigorous and active;
And his skull, like boiler iron,
And his hands, like legs of mutton,
And his feet, like small portmanteaus,
And his back, so broad and brawny,
Made him just the very person
To do Pluri-bus-tah's toiling,
In his Southern rice plantations.
 Pluri-bus-tah pondered on it,
Pondered long upon the question;
But, at last, he made his mind up,

And resolved to conquer Cuffee,
Make him work and do his drudging.
But he didn't mean to pay him,
Pay him for his toiling labor,
That would be no speculation,
For he loved his darling dollars;
And his thought was how to save them,
Keep them in his breeches pocket.
He resolved to conquer Cuffee,
Make him work for him for nothing,
Make him work, or else he'd lick him.
   Pluri-bus-tah then got ready;
For the battle then made ready;
First took off his coat and jacket,
Put his boots on, rolled his sleeves up;
Then he took a horn of whisky,
Old Monongahela whisky,
Whisky made of Indian corn-juice,
Of the juice of the Mondainin,
Treated of in Hiawatha;
Drank about a half a gallon,
Then went out to fight with Cuffee.
   Pretty soon he met with Cuffee,
Said, "Good morning to you, Cuffee;
How are all the babies, Cuffee?
How is pretty Mistress Cuffee?"
For a while he talked with Cuffee;
Then he made a face at Cuffee;
Then, at once, squared off at Cuffee,
Instantly "sailed into" Cuffee;
And he whaled away at Cuffee,
Injured and astonished Cuffee!
Cuffee's shins were bruised and battered;
Cuffee's ribs were sore and aching;
Cuffee's wool was torn and tangled;
Cuffee's head was mauled and pummeled
Till his eyes stuck out like onions,
And his nose looked like a sausage,
Juicy sausage, damaged sausage.
And each lip looked like an oyster,

Like a huge, disfigured oyster;
Like an oyster with the shell off.
Cuffee yelled and begged for mercy,
Cuffee yielded and was conquered.
    Then the victor, Pluri-bus-tah,
Fastened Cuffee's hands behind him,
Tied his huge feet close together,
Put him in a top-sail schooner,
"Toted" him "way down the river,"
Put him on his rice plantations,
Made him hoe, and dig, and grub there;
Told him if he didn't do it,
He'd come every day and thrash him,
Every morning after breakfast.
    Should you ask me "What's the reason?"
I should answer, I should tell you,
In the words of Pluri-bus-tah,
In the words he spoke to Cuffee,
"I am white, and I am stronger,
You are black, and you are weaker,
And, beside, you have no business,
And no right to be a nigger."
    After this triumphant battle
Pluri-bus-tah started homeward,
Thrust his hands into his pockets,
And went whistling on his journey.
But the wonder in his mind was,
What would Liberty, his partner,
Say about this new achievement?
Truly, he was slightly fearful
That she might rebel against it,
Make a row and scratch his eyes out.

From "American Civilization Illustrated: A Great Slave Auction"

The largest sale of human chattels that has been made in Star-Spangled
America for several years took place on Wednesday and Thursday of

last week, at the Race Course near the City of Savannah, Georgia. The lot consisted of four hundred and thirty-six men, women, children and infants, being that half of the negro stock remaining on the old Major Butler plantation which fell to one of the two heirs to that estate. Major Butler dying, left a property valued at more than a million of dollars, the major part of which was invested in rice and cotton plantations, and the slaves thereon, all of which immense fortune descended to two heirs, his sons, Mr. John A. Butler, sometime deceased, and Mr. Pierce M. Butler, still living, and resident in the City of Philadelphia, in the free State of Pennsylvania. Losses in the grand crash of 1857–8, and other exigencies of business, have impelled the latter gentleman to realize on his Southern investments, that he may satisfy sundry pressing creditors, and be enabled to resume business with the surplus, if any. This necessity led to a partition of the negro stock on the Georgia plantations, between himself and the representative of the other heir, the widow of the late John A. Butler, and the negroes that were brought to the hammer last week were the property of Mr. Pierce M. Butler of Philadelphia, and were in fact sold to pay Mr. Pierce M. Butler's debts. The creditors were represented by Gen. Cadwallader, while Mr. Butler was present in person, attended by his business agent, to attend to his own interests.

The sale had been advertised largely for many weeks, and as the negroes were known to be a choice lot and very desirable property, the attendance of buyers was large. The breaking up of an old family estate is so uncommon an occurrence that the affair was regarded with unusual interest throughout the South. For several days before the sale every hotel in Savannah was crowded with negro speculators from North and South Carolina, Virginia, Georgia, Alabama and Louisiana, who had been attracted hither by the prospects of making good bargains. Nothing was heard for days, in the barrooms and public rooms but talk of the great sale, criticisms of the business affairs of Mr. Butler, and speculations as to the probable prices the stock would bring. The office of Joseph Bryan the negro broker who had the management of the sale, was thronged every day by eager inquirers in search of information, and by some who were anxious to buy, but were uncertain as to whether their securities would prove acceptable. Little parties were made up from the various hotels every day to visit the Racecourse, distant some three miles from the city, to look over the chattels, discuss their points, and make memoranda for guidance on the day of sale. The buyers were generally of a rough breed, slangy, profane and bearish, being for the most part, from the back river and swamp plantations, where the elegancies of polite life are not perhaps developed to their fullest extent. In fact the humanities are sadly neglected by the petty tyrants of the rice fields that border the great Dismal Swamp, their knowledge of the luxuries of our best society comprehending only revolvers and kindred delicacies.

. . . .

How They Were Treated in Savannah

The negroes were brought to Savannah in small lots, as many at a time as could be conveniently taken care of, the last of them reaching the city the Friday before the sale. They were consigned to the care of Mr. J. Bryan, Auctioneer and Negro Broker, who was to feed and keep them in condition until disposed of. Immediately on their arrival they were taken to the Race Course, and there quartered in the sheds erected for the accommodation of the horses and carriages of gentlemen attending the races. Into these sheds they were huddled pell-mell, without any more attention to their comfort than was necessary to prevent their becoming ill and unsalable. Each "family" had one or more boxes or bundles, in which were stowed such scanty articles of their clothing as were not brought into immediate requisition, and their tin dishes and gourds for their food and drink.

It is, perhaps, a fit tribute to large-handed munificence to say that, when the negro man was sold, there was no extra charge for the negro man's clothes; they went with the man, and were not charged in the bill. Nor is this altogether a contemptible idea, for many of them had worldly wealth, in the shape of clothing and other valuables, to the extent of perhaps four or five dollars; and had all these been taken strictly into the account, the sum total of the sale would have been increased, possibly, a thousand dollars. In the North, we do not necessarily sell the harness with the horse; why, in the South, should the clothes go with the negro?

In these sheds were the chattels huddled together on the floor, there being no sign of bench or table. They eat and slept on the bare boards, their food being rice and beans, with occasionally a bit of bacon and corn bread. Their huge bundles were scattered over the floor, and thereon the slaves sat or reclined, when not restlessly moving about, or gathered into sorrowful groups, discussing the chances of their future fate. On the faces of all was an expression of heavy grief; some appeared to be resigned to the hard stroke of Fortune that had torn them from their homes, and were sadly trying to make the best of it; some sat brooding moodily over their sorrows, their chins resting on their hands, their eyes staring vacantly, and their bodies rocking too and fro, with a restless motion that was never stilled; few wept, the place was too public and the drivers too near, though some occasionally turned aside to give way to a few quiet tears. They were dressed in every possible variety of uncouth and fantastic garb, in every style and of every imaginable color; the texture of the garments was in all cases coarse, most of the men being clothed in the rough cloth that is made expressly for the slaves. The dresses assumed by the negro minstrels when they give imitations of plantation character, are by no means exaggerated; they are instead, weak and unable to come up to the original. There was every variety of hat, with every imaginable slouch; and there was every cut and style of coat and pantaloons, made with every conceivable ingenuity of misfit, and tossed on with a general appearance of perfect looseness that is perfectly indescribable except to say that a Southern negro always looks as if he could shake his clothes off without taking his hands out of his pockets. The women, true to the feminine instinct, had made, in almost every case, some attempt at finery. All wore gorgeous turbans, generally manufactured in an instant out of a gay-colored handkerchief by a sudden and graceful twist of the fingers; though there was occasionally a more elaborate turban, a turban complex and mysterious, got up with care and ornamented with a few beads or bright bits of ribbon. Their dresses were mostly coarse stuff, though there were some of gaudy calicoes; a few had earrings, and one possessed the treasure of a string of yellow and blue beads. The little children were always better and more carefully dressed than the older ones, the parental pride coming out in the shape of a yellow cap pointed like a miter, or a jacket with a strip of red broadcloth round the bottom.

· ·

At about 11 o'clock the business men took their places, and announced that the sale would begin. Mr. Bryan, the negro-broker, is a dapper little man, wearing spectacles, and a yachting hat, sharp and sudden in his movements, and perhaps the least bit in the world officious—as earnest in his language as he could be without actual swearing, though acting much as if he would like to swear a little at the critical moments; in fact, conducting himself very much like a member of the Young Men's Christian Association. Mr. Bryan did not sell the goods, he merely superintended the operation, and saw that the entry clerks did their duty properly. The auctioneer proper was a Mr. Walsh, who deserves a word of description. In personal appearance he is the very opposite of Mr. Bryan, being careless in his dress instead of scrupulous, a large man instead of a little one, a fat man instead of a lean one, and a good-natured man instead of a fierce one. He is a rollicking old boy, with an eye ever on the lookout, and that never lets a bidding nod escape him; a hearty word for every bidder who cares for it, and a plenty of jokes to let off when the business gets a little slack. Mr. Walsh has a florid complexion, not more so perhaps than is becoming, and possibly not more so than is natural in a whisky country. Not only is his face red, but some cause has blistered off the skin in spots, giving him a peely look—taking his face all in all, the peeliness and the redness combined make him look much as if he had been boiled in the same pot with a red cabbage.

Mr. Walsh mounted the stand and announced the terms of the sale, "one-third cash, the remainder payable in two equal annual installments, bearing interest from the day of sale, to be secured by approved mortgage and personal security, or approved acceptances on Savannah, Ga., or Charleston, S.C. Purchasers to pay for papers." The buyers, who were present to the number of about two hundred, clustered around the platform; while the negroes, who were not likely to be immediately wanted, gathered into sad groups in the background to watch the progress of the selling in which they were so sorrowfully interested. The wind howled outside, and through the open side of the building the driving rain came pouring in; the bar down stairs ceased for a short time its brisk trade; the buyers lit fresh cigars, got ready their catalogues and pencils, and the first lot of human chattels are led upon the stand, not by a white man, but by a sleek mulatto, himself a slave, and who seems to regard the selling of his brethren, in which he so glibly assists, as a capital joke. It had been announced that the negroes would be sold in "families," that is to say, a man would not be parted from his wife, or a mother from a very young child. There is perhaps as much policy as humanity in this arrangement, for thereby many aged and unserviceable people are disposed of, who otherwise would not find a ready sale.

The first family brought out were announced on the catalogue as

Name	Age	Remarks
George	27	Prime Cotton Planter
Sue	26	Prime Rice Planter.
George	6	Boy Child
Harry	2	Boy Child

The manner of buying was announced to be, bidding a certain price apiece for the whole lot. Thus George and his family were started at $300, and were finally sold at $600 each, being $2,400 for the four. To get an idea of the relative value of each one, we must suppose George worth $1,200, Sue worth $900, Little George worth $200, and Harry worth $100. Owing, however, to some misapprehension on the part of the buyer as to the manner of bidding, he did not take the family at this figure, and they were put up and sold again, on the second day, when they brought $620 each, or $2,480 for the whole—an advance of $80 over the first sale.

It seems as if every shade of character capable of being implicated in the sale of human flesh and blood, was represented among the buyers. The Georgia fast young man, with his pantaloons tucked into his boots, his velvet cap jauntily dragged over to one side, his cheek full of tobacco, which he bites from a huge plug, which resembles more than anything else, an old bit of a rusty wagon tire, and who is altogether an animal of quite a different breed from your New York fast man, was there. His ready revolver or his convenient knife, were ready for instant use in case of a heated argument. White neck-clothed, gold-spectacled, and silver-haired old men were there, resembling in appearance that noxious breed of sanctimonious deacons we have at the North, who are perpetually leaving documents at your door that you never read, and the business of whose mendicant life it is to eternally solicit subscriptions for charitable associations, of which they are treasurers. These gentry, with quiet step and subdued voice, moved carefully about among the live stock, ignoring, as a general rule, the men, but tormenting the women with questions which, when accidentally overheard by the disinterested spectator, bred in that spectator's mind an almost irresistible desire to knock somebody down. And then, all imaginable varieties of rough backwoods rowdies, who began the day in a dispirited manner, but who, as its hours progressed, and their practices at the bar became more prolific in results, waxed louder and talkier and more violent, were present, and added a characteristic feature to the assemblage. Those of your readers who have read "Uncle Tom"—and who has not?—will remember, with peculiar feelings, Legree, the slave-driver and woman-whipper. That that character is not over-drawn or too highly colored, there is abundant testimony. Witness the subjoined dialogue: A party of men were conversing on the fruitful subject of managing refractory "niggers;" some were for severe whipping, some recommending branding, one or two advocated other modes of torture, but one huge brute of a man, who had not taken an active part in the discussion, save to assent with approving nod to any unusually barbarous proposition, at last broke his silence by saying, in an oracular way, "You may say what you like about managing niggers; I'm a driver myself, and I've had some experience, and I ought to know. You can manage ordinary niggers by lickin' 'em and givin' 'em a taste of the hot iron once in a while when they're extra ugly; but if a nigger really sets himself up against me, I can't never have any patience with him. I just get my pistol and shoot him right down; and that's the best way."

. . . .

The Love Story of Jeffrey and Dorcas

Jeffrey, chattel No. 319, marked as a "prime cotton hand," aged 23 years, was put up. Jeffrey being a likely lad, the competition was high. The first bid was $1,100, and he was finally sold for $1,310. Jeffrey was sold alone; he had no incumbrance in the shape of an aged father or mother, who must necessarily be sold with him; nor had he any children, for Jeffrey was not married. But Jeffrey, chattel No. 319, being human in his affections, had dared to cherish a love for Dorcas, chattel No. 278; and Dorcas, not having the fear of her master before her eyes, had given her heart to Jeffrey. Whether what followed was a just retribution on Jeffrey and Dorcas, for daring to take such liberties with their master's property as to exchange hearts, or whether it only goes to prove that with black as with white the saying holds, that "the course of true love never did run smooth," cannot now be told. Certain it is that these two lovers were not to realize the consummation of their hopes in happy wedlock. Jeffrey and Dorcas had told their loves, had exchanged their simple vows, and were betrothed, each to the other as dear, and each by the other as fondly bowed, as though their skins had been of fairer color. And who shall say that in the sight of Heaven and all holy angels, these two humble hearts were not as closely wedded as any two of the prouder race that call them slaves?

Be that as it may, Jeffrey was sold. He finds out his new master; and, hat in hand, the big tears standing in his eyes, and his voice trembling with emotion, he stands before that master and tells his simple story, praying that his betrothed may be bought with him. Though his voice trembles, there is no embarrassment in his manner; his fears have killed all the bashfulness that would naturally attend such a recital to a stranger, and before unsympathizing witnesses; he feels that he is pleading for the happiness of her he loves, as well as for his own, and his tale is told in a frank and manly way.

"I loves Dorcas, young mas'r, I loves her well an' true; she says she loves me, and I know she does; de good Lord knows I loves her better than I loves any one in de wide world—never can love another woman half so well. Please buy Dorcas, mas'r. We're be good sarvants to you long as we live. We're be married right soon, young mas'r, and de chillun will be healthy and strong, mas'r, and dey'll be good sarvants, too. Please buy Dorcas, young mas'r. We loves each other a heap—do, really, true, mas'r."

Jeffrey then remembers that no loves and hopes of his are to enter into the bargain at all, but in the earnestness of his love he has forgotten to base his plea on other grounds till now, when he bethinks him and continues, with his voice not trembling now, save with eagerness to prove how worthy of many dollars is the maiden of his heart:

"Young mas'r, Dorcas prime woman—A 1 woman, Sa. Tall gal, Sir; long arms, strong, healthy, and can do a heap of work in a day. She is one of de best rice hands on de whole plantation; worth $1,200 easy, mas'r, an' fus'-rate bargain at that."

The man seems touched by Jeffrey's last remarks, and bids him fetch out his "gal, and let's see what she looks like."

Jeffrey goes into the long room and presently returns with Dorcas, looking very sad and self possessed, without a particle of embarrassment at the trying position in which she is placed. She makes the accustomed courtesy, and stands meekly with her hands clasped across her bosom, waiting the result. The buyer regards her with a critical eye, and growls in a low voice that the "gal has good p'ints." Then he goes on to a more minute and careful examination of her working abilities. He turns her round, makes her stoop, and walk; and then he takes off her turban to look at her head that no wound or disease be concealed by the gay handkerchief; he looks at her teeth, and feels of her arms, and at last announces himself pleased with the result of his observations, whereat Jeffrey, who has stood near, trembling with eager hope, is overjoyed, and he smiles for the first time. The buyer then crowns Jeffrey's happiness by making a promise that he will buy her, if the price isn't run up too high. And the two lovers step aside and congratulate each other on their good fortune. But Dorcas is not to be sold till the next day, and there are twenty-four long hours of feverish expectation.

Early next morning is Jeffrey alert, and hat in hand, encouraged to unusual freedom by the greatness of the stake for which he plays, he addresses every buyer, and of all who will listen he begs the boon of a word to be spoken to his new master to encourage him to buy Dorcas. And all the long morning he speaks in his homely way with all who know him that they will intercede to save his sweetheart from being sold away from him forever. No one has the heart to deny a word of promise and encouragement to the poor fellow, and, joyous with so much kindness, his hopes and spirits gradually rise until he feels almost certain that the wish of his heart will be accomplished, and Dorcas too is smiling, for is not Jeffrey's happiness her own!

At last comes the trying moment, and Dorcas steps up on the stand.

But now a most unexpected feature in the drama is for the first time unmasked; Dorcas is not to be sold alone, but with a family of four others. Full of dismay, Jeffrey looks at his master, who shakes his head, for, although he might be induced to buy Dorcas alone, he has no use for the rest of the family. Jeffrey reads his doom in his master's look, and turns away, the tears streaming down his honest face.

So Dorcas is sold, and her toiling life is to be spent in the cotton fields of South Carolina, while Jeffrey goes to the rice plantation of the Great Swamp.

And tomorrow, Jeffrey and Dorcas are to say their tearful farewell, and go their separate ways in life to meet no more as mortal beings.

But didn't Mr. Pierce Butler give them a silver dollar apiece? Who shall say there is no magnanimity in slaveowners?

In another hour I see Dorcas in the long room, sitting motionless as a statue, with her head covered with a shawl. And I see Jeffrey, who goes to his new master, pulls off his hat and says, "I'm very much obliged, Mas'r, to you for tryin' to help me. I knows you would have done it if you could—thank you, Mas'r—thank you—but—

its—berry—hard"—and here the poor fellow breaks down entirely and walks away, covering his face with his battered hat, and sobbing like a very child.

He is soon surrounded by a group of his colored friends, who with an instinctive delicacy most unlooked for, stand quiet, and with un- covered heads about him.

· ·

Mr. Pierce Butler Gives His People a Dollar a Piece

Leaving the Race buildings, where the scenes we have described took place, a crowd of negroes were seen gathered eagerly about a man in their midst. That man was Mr. Pierce M. Butler of the free city of Philadelphia, who was solacing the wounded hearts of the people he had sold from their firesides and their homes, by doling out to them small change at the rate of a dollar a head. To every negro he had sold, who presented his claim for the paltry pittance, he gave the munificent stipend of one whole dollar, in specie; he being provided with two can- vas bags of 25 cent pieces, fresh from the mint, to give an additional glitter to his munificent generosity.

As the last family stepped down from the block, for the first time in four days, the rain ceased, the clouds broke away, and the soft sunlight fell on the scene. The unhappy slaves had many of them been already removed, and others were now departing with their new masters.

That night, not a steamer left that Southern port, not a train of cars sped away from that cruel city, that did not bear each its own sad bur- den of those unhappy ones, whose only crime is that they are not strong and wise. Some of them maimed and wounded, some scarred and gashed by accident, or by the hands of ruthless drivers—all sad and sorrowful as human hearts can be.

But the stars shone out as brightly as if such things had never been, the blushing fruit trees poured their fragrance on the evening air, and the scene was as calmly sweet and quiet as if Man had never marred the glorious beauty of Earth by deeds of cruelty and wrong. All nature was as wondrously beautiful and glorious as in that earlier day when "All the men of God shouted for joy, and the morning stars sang together," and the burden of that celestial song was Freedom to Mankind.

E. Jane Gay (Truman Trumbull, A.M.)

E. Jane Gay (1830–1919) never publicly admitted her authorship of *The New Yankee Doodle* (New York, 1868), a scathingly sarcastic verse history of the Civil War so detailed that the book reached 341 pages. Dedicated to those who fought the monster treason "in order that the Union might be perpetual, and freedom made universal wherever the national emblem floats in the sunshine of heaven," this Union *Aenead*, constricted by the "Yankee Doodle" verse format, reached into the emotional, political, and historical aspects of the war and captured them in the copious details of daily war events. Gay was born in New Hampshire and lived the last thirteen years of her life in England, but nothing is known of the rest of her life, and she is not listed in any American literary histories. As reticent as Widow Bedott and Josiah Allen's Wife among northeastern female humorists, Gay shrank from public acknowledgment of her work perhaps because of the acidity of her portraits and the horror of some of her narrative details. A second amended edition of *A New Yankee Doodle* was prepared but never printed. Gay's identity is established only by four index cards in the Library of Congress, remains of notes obtained from her niece in 1951.

From *The New Yankee Doodle*

Chapter IX

When first the rebs began to shoot
At Yankee Doodle Dandy,
They counted Sambo in "to boot,"

They said "He'd work in handy."
While master led the chivalry
  At home *he'd* keep the pot on,
Would cure the bacon, grind the corn,
  And cultivate the cotton.

"The *mud-sills*, on the other hand,
  Unless ubiquitous, sir,
Would have no tillers of the land;
  The Yanks iniquitous, sir,
Would reap destruction close at home,
  The while they sowed abroad—
Supported by no Patriarch's rule,
  And governed by no God.

"The servile race was trained so well,
  In case of a disaster
Why, Sam would hasten to the field,
  And *battle* for his master."
Well, Sambo toiled and Sambo dreamed,
  And nothing Sambo spoke, sir,
Till Yankee guns and bay'nets gleamed,
  And sleeping Sambo woke, sir.

"Ole Missus," rising in the morn,
  And very much belated,
Declared the house felt all forlorn—
  And strange! no breakfast waited.
For Sambo Cook the night before,
  All suddenly inspired,
Had closed outside his cabin door,—
  In Sunday clothes attired—

With Dinah and the little ones,
  Had taken, in the damp,
And cold, and dark, the road that runs
  Into the Yankee camp.
Abe's generals saw the tide set in,
  It wasn't to their notion;
Some did with their small brooms begin
  To sweep back, sir, the ocean.

Said they, "Our well digested plan,
  Our *duty* strict defines,

These *fugitives*, sirs, never can,
    Come thus within our lines." [1]
Ben Butler down in Fort Monroe
    Held Sambo out his hand, sir,
Said he, "You're *free* to come or go,
    My worthy *Contraband*," sir.

And some cried out that Mac [2] was right,
    And some hurrahed for Ben, sir,
Some said that Sambo was a *fright*,
    That black folks were not men, sir,
But beasts of burden; (it was clear
    As any point in law, sir,)
That Sambo shortly would appear
    The chief man in the war, sir.

Some didn't fight for Sambo's cause,
    But just to save the nation;
The Constitution and the laws
    Had well defined *his* station.
Old Hunter swore the slaves had souls,
    And perfect right to freedom,
Were stretching out towards this goal,
    Would fight, and he would *lead them*.

And Lincoln, in a groping way,
    Surmised 'twould trouble save, sir,
If Congress would the rebels pay
    To liberate the slaves, [3] sir.
Then sent a Governor Stanley down
    The stubborn rebs to rule, sir,
Who ordered straight in Newbern town,
    To close the colored schools, sir. [4]

---

1. See General Order No. 33, Department of Washington, July 17, 1861. Halleck's proclamation of February 23, 1862. General Buell's letter of March 6th, 1862, to Hon. J. R. Underwood. General Hooker's letter, March 26, 1862. General McClellan's letter to President Lincoln, July 7th, 1862.

2. Extract from General McClellan's letter to President Lincoln, July 7th, 1862, Camp near Harrison's Landing: "Neither confiscation of property, political executions of persons, territorial organization of states, nor forcible abolition of slavery, should be contemplated for a moment."

3. See message of 6th March, 1862.

4. 28th May, 1862.

Old Jonathan pricked up his ear,
   Said he, "What is this clatter,
About the black man that I hear?
   It is a serious matter.

  . . . .

And British sympathizers were
   All barking in accord, sir;[5]
For in perverted garbled guise
   The news had gone abroad, sir;
And hints that looked like threats came back
   Across the briny water,
That Johnny Bull his brains did rack
   To "stop the horrid slaughter."

And Jonathan had some bad boys,
   Unfriendly to the cause, sir;
They rallied now, and raised a cry
   Of "Union as it was," sir.[6]
They said the war perverted was
   If Sambo lost his collar;
They wouldn't "give another man,
   And not another dollar."

Said Jonathan, "My lads, look here,
   You set of wretched shirks!
Your miserable rebel souls
   You'd bolster with such quirks.
'Tis such as you more mischief do
   Than Stonewall on the border.
To block your, game, you coward crew,
   A speedy *draft* I'll order."

Then Congress, just to show the rebs
   This spunky Yankee nation
Ain't scared at trifles, made by law
   An Act of Confiscation.[7]

---

5. 9th July, 1862. Public meetings in England called on the Government to mediate, and, if necessary, to acknowledge the independence of the South.

6. At New York a meeting was held at Cooper Institute, responsive to a call addressed to those who desired the *Union as it was*. Speeches by J. Brooks, Fernando Wood, Wickliff, of Ky., and others.

7. Passed the Senate 12th July, 1862.

The very day the Bill was passed,
  (I don't know that he waited,)
Three thousand slaves, at Vicksburg held,
  Ben Butler confiscated.[8]

And volunteers sprang into life,
  The quota far above, sir;
Said Jonathan, "We'll end this strife
  If Abe takes off his gloves, sir."
He sent a message then to Abe,
  That *all means* coming handy
To throttle treason, must be used
  By Yankee Doodle Dandy.

So Abraham sits down and dreams—
  Said he, "Thus far I *can* go—
When Jonathan tells me of means,
  He must refer to Sambo.
Well, if my generals like the plan,
  One thing is pretty clear, sir,
If Sambo *wants* to be a man
  I shall not interfere, sir.

"With what I want, and what I feel,
  I must not hold communion,
The object paramount to me,
  Is to restore the Union.[9]
If I can compass best the end
  By freeing all the slaves, sir,
I'll free them *all*; if slavery
  Will help the cause to save, sir,

"I'll save the cause *with* slavery;
  Of if by war's coercion
A *part* to be freed, and Union saved,
  Why, then, I'll free a portion.
Poor Sambo's fate doth trouble me,
  It's heavy on my soul, sir,
But just as far as I can see,
  It's out of *my* control, sir."

. . . .

8. General Butler confiscated 3,000 slaves employed on the Vicksburg Canal.
9. See President Lincoln's reply to Horace Greeley, August 22, 1861.

"Now who will cross that stream of death,
   The rifle-pits to try, sir?"
Cried Hendershott, the drummer-boy,
   "*I'm ready*, though I die, sir."
Then leaped into a boat.—"My lad,
   Give way to older hands, sir."
The boy hung on behind the boat,
   And was the *first* to land, sir.

   . . . .

Slow, dreadful work; at last the stream
   Is crossed,[10] the foe in sight, sir,
Secure beyond the sullen town,[11]
   Entrenched upon the heights, sir.
Now, up the slopes, where cannon deal
   Out canister and grape,
Good heavens! from such a storm of fire
   Can anything escape?

They stagger back, they charge again,
   They waver, reel and fall—
Recharge, until the carnage might
   The stoutest heart appall.
All day they press, as if their death
   Were emulous to meet;
But never foe at Malvern Hill
   Won such a dread defeat.

Night fell, the battered army lay,
   Some sunk in dreamless sleep;
But eyes there were that o'er that day
   Hot bitter tears did weep.
Twelve thousand men, who in the morn,
   Were glad in buoyant life,
Now "missing"—lying mangled—torn,
   Or martyred in the strife.

How sped the hours on yonder slopes?
   Did any dream of home,
To flickering, fluttering, fainting hearts,
   Did any succor come?

10. Union troops crossed the river 11th of December, 1862.
11. Fredericksburg, Va.

Drop down the curtain, let our gaze
  Be clouded by the night;
Ah me! but there are those who live
  Who saw and bore the sight.

The army lay two days in camp
  Expecting General Lee, sir;
Lee didn't come, he was content
  With Fabian policy, sir.
Then Burnside wrote to Abraham,
  "We couldn't stand the fire
Lee won't come out and fight us fair,
  And—so—we must retire."

Abe read the note, and with a groan,
  He handed it to Chase.[12]
Said he, "This will not help your *Loan*,"
  Then—tried the worst to face;
And wondered how Old Jonathan
  Would bear the chilling news;
"If *I* were gone," thought he, "they might
  A better leader choose.

"But then things do not go by chance
  In this strange world of ours;
And Right will not be crushed by Wrong—
  There *is* a Ruling Power.
I'm but a way through which to work
  God's plan: I cannot alter;
I can be patient. He is wise,
  His purpose will not falter."

But Abram's Cabinet declared
  They felt aggrieved; in fine,
Old Jonathan was finding fault,
  They'd better all resign;[13]
Things didn't please *him*—as for that
  Nobody *could* be pleased, sir;
The odium would fall on *them*,
  They'd like to be released, sir.

12. Chase, Secretary of the Treasury.
13. Secretaries Seward and Chase tendered their resignations December 18th, in

"Why, as to *blame*," said honest Abe,
    "*That* isn't hard to bear, sir;
Old Jonathan *is* bowed to earth
    With sorrow and with care, sir.
If he can have the heart to blame,
    Perhaps 'twill do him good, sir;
And I don't mind, it's all the same,
    He'll quickly change his mood, sir."

Just here a note from Jonathan
    Was put in Abram's hand:
"I write in haste, dear Abe," it ran,
    "That you may understand
A Nor'-west storm is setting in,
    You may rough weather find, sir;
But just stand steady at the helm,
    And scud before the wind, sir.

"Nail to the mast the starry flag,
    Look out each rotten plank, sir;
Don't touch at any foreign port,
    And never drop an anchor.
Don't swerve a hair's breadth from your course,
    Whatever blasts may come, sir;
You've got the *chart* now safe aboard,
    Let drive the vessel home, sir."

"Ah! that reminds me now," said Abe,
    "Here, Seward, take a chair, sir;
Pull out that lower table-drawer,
    The chart is lying there, sir."
Abe tried his hand (he was to do
    What never could be altered)—
"It must not tremble," Abram said,
    "Or men may say I faltered.

"They had fair warning I would strike,
    The *rebs would have it so*, sir;
Now come what will, I keep my word
    Alike with friend and foe, sir.

---

consequence of the action of some Republican senator concerning the fight on the Rappahannock. They were subsequently withdrawn.

The Union Ball and *The Secession Ball* appeared in *Yankee Notions*, XI (April, 1862), 112–13. The two, though crudely drawn, accurately summarize the attitudes of the North during the Civil War. A few years later, agricul-

Because the South *wants* to be blind,
   Shall we hold back the sun?"
Abe took his pen, sat down and signed
   His Order No. One.[14]
. . . .
Dupont was worsted and the rebs
   Thereby were so elated

14. Emancipation Proclamation, issued January 1, 1863, in the form of Order No. 1.

ture as practiced on small family farms probably would have received a less prominent treatment, for the North was industrializing rapidly.

> They would have burst, but they were used
>   To being so inflated.
> But while they crowed in ecstacy,
>   Bold Grierson hot haste made, sir,[15]
> And swept clean through their Dixie Land
>   Upon his famous raid, sir.
>
> And Morgan's troopers rob and slay
>   Like other chivalrie, sir,

15. Left La Grange April 17, 1863.

While Jeff sends up his imps to play
  In Eastern Tennessee, sir.
They pinch the children—fathers kill,
  And flog the grey-haired mother,
And loose their hounds among the hills,
  To hunt the fleeing brother.

Theft, murder, aye, and crimes too foul
  To breathe in mortal ear
They perpetrate, and Jeff will howl
  In agony of fear,
When in the retribution land,
  He hears the devil say, sir,
"Here comes the prince of our brave band
  Of chivalry in grey, sir."

Chapter XXIV

In Richmond one bright April day
  Jeff gave a dinner party
To Orr and Wigfall, Foote and Clay,
  And Pryor (just as hearty
As when he went with flag of truce
  And drank the Major's brandy[16]
Way down in Sumter, to the tune
  Of Yankee Doodle Dandy.)
And Stephens came, but couldn't stay
  He said he felt quite sick, sir.
At sight of food, his liver lay
  As heavy as a brick, sir.
He took his hat, and went away
  With a decided shiver,
He didn't know, I'm free to say,
  His conscience from his liver.

16. Pryor acting on the staff of Beauregard, went to propose conditions to Major Anderson. During the interview Pryor helped himself to a glass of *something* which he mistook for brandy. The doctor and a dose of ipecac (and some say a stomach pump,) were summoned to enable Pryor to survive the effects of the dram, which the doctor pronounced poison."—*See Tribune, April 19, 1861.*

"Now, gentlemen," said Jeff, "you'll find
   This is a splendid roast
Of Yankee beef, caught on a raid,
   Let's give old Jeb a toast;
Says Wigfall, "This is better fare,
   Than dining on mule meat, sirs,
They say Port Hudson garrison,
   Think mice and rats a treat, sirs."

"Ah, well!" said Jeff, "our soldiers dine
   On glory every day,
But taste this sparkling champagne wine,"—
   "Oh! yes," said Clement Clay;
"This wine has run Old Abe's blockade."
   "Not so," said Jeff, "it came, sir,
From *New York friends*, a present made,
   By—well! we'll call no names, sir.

"They wish us well, and by the by,
   Peace movements are begun;
Our friends have found their voice at last,
   And Abram's course is run.
The mighty rabble of New York,
   Has caught the infectious cry, sir,
Raised by the Hoosiers of the West,
   Ere long they will *defy*, sir,

"The dungeons which had been their doom
   But one short year ago;
Vallandigham in Congress *now*,
   The white flag dares to show.
This party now will not consent
   The South to subjugate, sir,
We've but in one more shock of arms,
   Our course to vindicate, sir."

Said Mr. Foote, "I'll introduce[17]
   In Congress resolutions,

17. On January 28, 1863, Henry S. Foote introduced resolutions, offering an alliance offensive and defensive with such of the Northwest States as would lay down their arms, etc., etc.

That this confederation deems,
  It would be no intrusion
If these *North Western States* lay down
  Their arms, and ask admission,
We'd grant them Mississippi trade,
  On only one condition.

"That they unite with us in war,
  In fierce undying hate, sir,
Of everything, that ever saw
  The curs'd New England States, sir."
"I'd die in peace," said Jeff, "if I
  Could only once behold,
The South and West in one firm tie,
  The North 'out in the cold.' "

"Our organ, Jeff," said Mr. Orr,
  "I mean the *Daily News*,
Is coming out a *little strong*,
  I'm fearful we shall lose
What we have gained, if Jonathan
  Our intercourse should guess, sir;
He's fit for any deed; he might
  The *Daily News* suppress, sir."

"No fears," said Jeff, "Old Jonathan
  Is busy with the negroes,
Fernando Wood's a Union man,
  For anything that *he* knows;
He has enough to do, to feed
  His mercenary Hessians,
And furnish powder to his Grant,
  At least that's *my* impression."
. . . .

And while he crossed—a little feint
  By Sherman's wise direction,
Was carried out at Haynes' Bluff
  For Pemberton's inspection.
With transports, iron-clads and boats,
  Up the Yazoo he lay,
At evening disembarked, as if
  He came this time to stay.

The rebels gathered for a fight,
   Their strength began to vaunt, sir,
But Sherman starts late in the night,
   And steams away to Grant, sir.
Meanwhile McClernand gains the height,
   With Logan strikes a blow,
That takes Port Gibson from the rebs,[18]
   And does quite plainly show

To Pemberton—"The bull-dog's" teeth,
   He feels the grinders craunch, sir,
He squirms away, and General Grant
   At Grand Gulf takes his lunch, sir;
And Pemberton, who wants more men,
   Sends off to General Jo,
Who gives this very good advice—
   "*Unite, and beat the foe.*"

Jeff Davis said, the while he smiled,
   "Vicksburg could not be shaken,
That Grant, old Jonathan beguiled,
   It *never would* be taken."
Some weak-kneed rebs began to wince
   And breathe a little hard,
And said, Jeff should the Yanks convince
   By sending Beauregard.

Grant paused a moment, should he go,
   Thought he, to General Banks,
And take Port Hudson, Bank's troops
   Would reinforce his ranks.
The Mississippi governor howled,
   And wrote a proclamation,
Which like a blister on the rebs,
   Drew out an inflammation.

Said Grant, "I can't afford to *wait*,
   The case is very clear,
I must make haste and operate
   On Vicksburg in the rear."

18. Battle of Port Gibson, May 1, 1863.

He draws his plans. His corps go out,
   McPherson finds the foe, sir,
At Raymond[19]—makes him face about,
   Which so distresses Jo, sir.

He sallies out from Jackson—*he*[20]
   Will meet Grant's bold advance,
His military eye takes in
   McPherson at a glance;
He squints at Sherman, who sends out
   To spy the ground in front, sir;
Then pushes up—Jo doesn't wait
   To bear the battle's brunt, sir.

He takes a northward flight, nor stops
   Till some time after dark,
Then Grant he faces to the rear,
   With Vicksburg for his mark;
. . . .

Be patient, man, and speak out plain
   Your anger does not good, sir."

"It *does* do good," roared Jonathan;
   "I mustn't make a noise?
God help us! Abraham," he groaned,
   "They're *murdering* our boys!"
"Too many, sir," said Abraham,
   "Are counted with the slain."
"It isn't *that*. They're *starving* them
   In Southern jails," said Jane.

"We're just up from Annapolis,[21]
   We've seen such dreadful woe,
I'm fearful I should speak amiss
   If I should try to show,
What I have seen, as to and fro
   The hospitals I've walked, sir."[22]

19. Battle of Raymond, May 12, 1863.
20. May 14th, Battle of Jackson.
   21. In the late (May, 1864,) temporary resumption of the cartel, boat loads of half-naked living skeletons, foul with filth and covered with vermin, were landed at Annapolis.
   22. See Report of Commission of Inquiry, appointed by Sanitary Commission. Published by Littell, Boston.

"What do they say?" said Abraham:
   Said Betsey Jane, "I've talked, sir,

"To these poor living skeletons,
   Of friends—of going home, sir,
But on their pinched and pallid face
   A *smile* has never come, sir.[23]
Our words of kindness—all too late,
   Are powerless to save,
For food alone—crushed, desolate,
   They still have strength to crave.

"From bed to bed, from ward to ward,[24]
   The same sad sight," said Jane,
"Blank, bony faces, staring out
   Above the counterpane;
Beneath the sheet—oh, misery!
   Shrivelled to skin and bone,
Our boys—alive—some famine-wild,
   Some idiotic grown.

"The sunken eye, the blighted skin—
   Sand-bruised, and dead, and rough,
The bones protruding—sockets dry—
   Oh! Abe, it is enough
To break one's heart to contemplate
   Such agony unspoken,"
"Hush! hush!" said Jonathan, "there—wait—
   For Abe's is being broken."

Old Abe had sunk down in his chair,
   His head upon his breast,
His hands were clenched and Betsey heard
   A groan but half repressed,
She opened up her reticule,
   "Here is a photograph, sir,
I've brought to show you—it is *one*,
   There's many more than half, sir,

"Of our exchanged, resembling it,
   For one may stand for all."

23. "As if they had passed through a period of physical and mental agony, which had driven the smile from their faces forever."—*Page 5 of Report.*
24. See *Report,* as above.

"Do they all *die?*" said Abraham,
 "This *dead* form doth appall!"
"That is a *living* skeleton—
 My boy. John was his name, sir;
His grandsire, Jonathan and I
 Just from his bedside came, sir.

"He doesn't know us, sir, as yet,
 He wails at every breath
For food; we dole it out, for food
 Is agony and death
To those so long kept starving, Abe,
 And Jonathan and I,
Have smothered grief as day by day
 We've listened to that cry,

"Till Jonathan has grown quite faint,
 And sick with indignation,
And I have come to ask you if
 The honor of the nation,
Must be maintained at *such* a price?
 If rebels, loathsome, vile,
Must hold our soldiers till they rot
 In Libby and Belle Isle?"

"Ask Jonathan," said Abraham,
 "Whate'er *he says is law.*"
"I'm thinking of Fort Pillow, Abe,[25]
 And slaves they took in war;
We *must* be just. This foul abuse
 Is with a purpose done, sir,
It had its origin, Old Abe,
 When strife was first begun, sir."

"They say it's dire necessity;
 They haven't food to spare."
"Good heavens, Abe!" said Jonathan,
 "Their *cattle* better fare.
Besides, they were not forced by want,
 When they their prisons made, sir,

25. April 12, 1864, Fort Pillow was captured, and the garrison murdered after surrender.

To choose a pestilential swamp
   The site for their stockade, sir."

"It didn't add to their supplies
   To mark out a *dead line*, sir;
And water's free—and yet our men
   For *water* pant and pine, sir;
The country's full of forests, Abe,
   They grudge our boys the logs,
And fireless, and shelterless,
   They've grovelled like the hogs.[26]

"No, Abraham, it's done to *kill*!
   Old Winder's foul stockade
Has slain more men for Jefferson
   Than all Lee's cannonade;
The only way that I can see
   This horror to abate,
Is to make Grant the remedy
   You can't retaliate."

"Well, Jonathan," said Betsey Jane,
   "While Satan, sir, is stalking
All through the land, 'tis very plain
   I have no time for *talking*.
I'll go back to the soldier's bed,
   You'll find out, I dare say, sirs,
Some plan to save them—*when they're dead*,
   That's *not* a woman's way, sirs."

"What would *you* do?" said Abraham;
   Said Betsey Jane, in answer,
"I would not waste most precious time
   In poulticing a cancer.
You *threatened* to retaliate,
   And won our grateful thanks, sir,
But after the report we found
   Your cartridges were blanks, sir.

"I wouldn't be surprised at all,
   Were Jeff now safe in jail,

26. "They lay in the ditch, as the most protected place, heaped upon one another and lying close together, as one of them expressed it, like hogs in winter, taking turns as

You two would talk, and talk, and call
  A court, and give him bail."
Here Abram smiled. "Yes, sir," said Jane,
  "You *men*, with all your reason,
Are fit to twist and turn out Jeff
  As *innocent of Treason.*"

Old Jonathan uneasily,
  Was pacing to and fro
Across the floor. "Come, Betsey Jane,"
  Said he, "it's time to go.
You'd better speak to Stanton, Abe,
  These cruelties *must* cease, sir,
Our starving soldiers *must* obtain,
  Some way, a quick release, sir."

Then Abe called Stanton, who declared,
  Whatever folks might say,
That he, for one, would *not* consent,
  To give Jeff his own way;
"We've thirty thousand stalwart rebs,
  Jeff wants them now at home—
For them he'll fill our hospitals."
  Said Abe, "The boys *must come.*

"It's no use, Stanton, we must fight
  The rebels at their *strongest*—
Give Jeff his reinforcements; if
  The right way *is* the longest,
It will not matter in the end,
  So History may tell,
Not that our work was *quickly* done,
  But that we *did it well!*"

Thus "man for man," the cartel ran,
  And sorrowful to know,
That never Charon o'er the Styx
  Steered such a load of woe,
As down the James to Jonathan,
  And Betsey Jane, who waited,

to who should have the outside of the road. In the morning, the row of the previous
night was marked by the motionless forms of those who were sleeping on in their last
sleep—frozen to death."—*Sanitary Commission Report, page 11.*

The truce-boat steamed, with nameless grief,
  And misery deep freighted.
. . . .

(Just here, Old Jonathan, distressed
  At news from New Orleans;[27]
Asks Abraham if *he* can tell
  What *that* confusion means?
That Abe has quite too many schemes
  He has some strong suspicions;
Too many irons in the fire,
  Too many expeditions.)

He says to Grant, "You'd better spy
  The nature of the ground, sir;
I think you'll need right now to tie
  The loose strings lying round, sir,
In all directions. There's a snarl
  Down on Red River floating,
Where Porter doth amuse the rebs
  With his new style of boating."

So Grant drew out his telescope,
  And pointed it southwest,
"All right," said he to Jonathan,
  "Just set your mind at rest,
Your Porter won't be drowned this time,
  He's resting on the *Banks*, sir;
There is a chap named Bailey[28] there,
  Who well deserves your thanks, sir.

"He saved your fleet by building dams,
  It's done in splendid shape, sir;
Your army's safe, let Banks alone
  For getting out of scrapes, sir;
You just keep quiet, Jonathan,
  The signs are looking well,
I'll fight it out upon this line
  Though it should take a spell."

27. Red River Expedition.
28. Lieutenant-Colonel Bailey, Fourth Wisconsin Volunteers, who constructed a
dam to raise the river and liberate the fleet. The passage of the boats was completed on
the 15th of May, 1864.

Charles G. Leland

Charles G. Leland (1824–1903), best known for his low-German "bummer" Hans Breitmann, had the most varied career of any American humorist, actively publishing for fifty years or more in comic dialect verse. His works included *Hans Breitmann's Ballads* (1868), *Pidgeon English Sing-Song* (1876), *Songs of the Sea and Lays of the Land* (1895), political polemics, and editorial columns. Leland also edited the New York *Illustrated News* (1853), *Graham's Magazine* (1856–1857), the New York *Knickerbocker* (1857–1859), *Vanity Fair* (1860), and the *Continental Monthly* (1860–1862). His aesthetic treatise *Sunshine in Thought* (1862) made one of the earliest serious arguments for literary realism as an optimistic component of the "steam-engine whirling realism" of the new industrial age. Leland published craft instruction books, folk tale collections, travel humor (*The Egyptian Sketch-Book* [1874]), burlesque philosophical disquisitions (*Meister Karl's Sketch-Book* [1855]), and his own *Memoirs* (1903). In the field of linguistics he was credited with discovering the Shelta Gypsy dialect. The Hans Breitmann poems originated in a dialect prose-poem Leland tossed offhandedly into a *Graham's Magazine* editorial column in May, 1857, over a decade before John Hay and Bret Harte began producing comic poems in Pike County dialect.

Leland's *Memoirs* offer an arresting description of the transition from the Federal to the Victorian era in America. *Meister Karl* evidenced the metaphysical bent of Melvillian prose, but the onset of the Civil War brought forth bitter propaganda, of which "Bone Ornaments," from the *Continental Monthly*, II (July, 1862), 5, is reprinted here. It is a ringing example of the comedian turned war hawk. Leland and his brother Henry, also a talented comic writer, served in the war; and Henry received the wound that caused his premature death. The Breitmann ballads reprinted here—"Breitmann in Battle," "Ballad,"

"A Ballad Apout de Rowdies," and "Breitmann in Politics"—are from *Hans Breitmann's Ballads* (Philadelphia, 1869). They show the emergence of post–Civil War politics in the North, but also capture the intellectual nostalgia of Hans as a representation of the German intellectual commoner after the 1848 Revolution. "The Rise and Fall of Gloryville," "Zion Jersey Boggs," and "The Story of Mr. Scroper, Architect," taken from *Songs of the Sea and Lays of the Land* (London, 1895), provide verse equivalents of Twain's and DeForest's fictionalizations of Gilded Age corruption. My essay on Leland appears in *American Humorists, 1800–1950* (Detroit, 1982). Leland's *Memoirs* are supplemented by Elizabeth R. Pennell, *Charles G. Leland: A Biography* (Boston, 1906).

Bone Ornaments

Silent the lady sat alone:
In her ears were rings of dead men's bone;
The brooch on her breast shone white and fine,
'Twas the polished joint of a Yankee's spine;
And the well-carved handle of her fan,
Was the finger-bone of a Lincoln man.
She turned aside a flower to cull,
From a vase which was made of a human skull;
For to make her forget the loss of her slaves,
Her lovers had rifled dead men's graves.
Do you think I'm describing a witch or ghoul?
There are no such things—and I'm not a fool;
Nor did she reside in Ashantee;
No—the lady fair was an F.F.V.

Breitmann in Battle

*Tunc tapfre ausfuhrere Streitum et
Rittris dignum potuere erjagere lobum.*

Der Fader und der Son

I dinks I'll go a fitin—outspoke der Breitemann,
"It's eighdeen hoonderd fordy eight since I kits swordt in hand;
Dese fourdeen years mit Hecker all roostin I haf been,
Boot now I kicks der Teufel oop and goes for sailin in."

"If you go land out-ridin," said Caspar Pickletongue,
"Foost ding you knows you cooms across some repels prave and
    young,
Away down Sout' in Tixey, dey'll split you like a clam"—
"For dat," spoke out der Breitmann, "I doos not gare one tam!"

Who der Teufel pe's de repels und vhere dey kits deir sass,
If dey make a run on Breitmann he'll soon let out de gas;
I'll split dem like kartoffels: I'll slog em on de kop;
I'll set de plackguarts roonin so dey don't know vhere to shtop."

Und den outshpoke der Breitmann, mit his schlaeger py his side:
"Forvarts, my pully landsmen! it's dime to run and ride;
Will riden, will fighten—der Copitain I'll pe,
It's sporn und horn und saddle now—all in de Cavallrie!"

Und ash dey rode troo Winchester, so herrlich to pe seen,
Dere coomed some repel cavallrie a riden on de creen;
Mit a sassy repel Dootchman—an colonel in gommand:
Says he, "Vot Teufel makes you here in dis mein Faderland?

"You're dressed oop like a shentleman mit your plackguard Yankee
    crew,
You mudsills and meganics! Der Teufel put you troo!
Old Yank you ought to shtay at home und dake your liddle horn,
Mit some oldt voomans for a noorse"—der Breitmann laugh mit
    shkorn.

Und should I trink mein lager-bier und roost mine self to home?
Ife got too many dings like you to mash beneat' my thoom:
In many a fray und fierce foray dis Deutschman will be feared
Pefore he stops dis vightin trade—'twas dere he greyed his peard."

"I pools dat peard out by de roots—I gifes him sooch a dwist
Dill all de plood roons out, you tamned old Apolitionist!
Your creenpacks mit your swordt und watch right ofer you moost
    shell,
Und den you goes to Libby straight—und after dat to h—ll!"

German immigrants land at New Orleans, establishing the conditions for Leland's Hans Breitmann to appear on the American scene, from Burton's *Cyclopedia of Wit and Humor.*

"Mein creenpacks und mein schlaeger, I kits 'em in New York,
To gife dem up to creenhorns, young man, is not de talk;"
De heroes shtopped deir sassin' here und grossed deir sabres dwice,
Und de vay dese Deutschers vent to vork vos von pig ding on ice.

Der younger fetch de older such a gottallmachty smack
Der Breitmann dinks he really hears his skool go shplit und crack;
Der repel choomps dwelfe paces back, und so he safe his life:
Der Breitmann says: "I guess dem choomps you learns dem of your
    vife."

"If I should learn of vomans I dinks it vere a shame,
Bei Gott I am a shentleman, aristograt, and game.
My fader vos anoder—I lose him fery young—
Ter teufel take your soul! Coom on! I'll split your waggin' tongue!"

A Yankee drick der Breitmann dried—dat oldt gray-pearded man—
For ash the repel raised his swordt, beneat' dat swordt he ran.
All roundt der shlim yoong repel's waist his arms oldt Breitmann
    pound,
Und shlinged him down oopon his pack und laidt him on der
    ground.

"Who rubs against olt kittle-pots may keep vite—if he can.

Say vot you dinks of vightin now mit dis old shentleman?
Your dime is oop; you got to die, und I your breest vill pe;
Peliev'st dou in Morál Ideas? If so I lets you free."

"I don't know nix apout Ideas—no more dan pout Saint Paul,
Since I peen down in Tixey I kits no books at all;
I'm greener ash de clofer-grass; I'm shtupid as a shpoon;
I'm ignoranter ash de nigs—for dey takes de *Tribune*.

"Mein fader's name vas Breitmann, I heard mein mutter say,
She read de bapers dat he died after she rooned afay;
Dey say he leaf some broperty—berhaps 'twas all a sell—
If I could lay mein hands on it I likes it mighty well."

"Und vas dy fader Breitmann? *Bist du* his kit und kin?
Denn know dat *ich* der Breitmann dein lieber Vater bin?"
Der Breitmann poolled his hand-shoe off und shooked him
    py de hand;
"Ve'll hafe some trinks on strengt of dis—or else may I pe tam'd!"

"Oh! fader, how I shlog your kop," der younger Breitmann said;
"I'd den dimes sooner had it coom right down on mine own headt!"
"Oh, never mind—dat soon dry oop—I shticks him mit a blaster;
If I had shplit you like a fish, dat vere an vorse tisasder."

Dis fight did last all afternoon—*wohl* to de fesper tide,
Und droo de streeds of Vinchesder, der Breitmann he did ride.
Vot vears der Breitmann on his hat? De ploom of fictory!
Who's dat a ridin' py his side? "Dis here's mein son," says he.

How stately rode der Breitmann oop!—how lordly he kit down?
How glorious from de great *pokal* he drink de bier so prown!
But der Yunger bick de parrel oop und schwig him all at one.
"Bei Gott! dat settles all dis dings—I *know* dou art mein son!"

Der one has got a fader; de oder found a child.
Bote ride oopon one war-path now in pattle fierce und wild.
It makes so glad our hearts to hear dat dey did so succeed—
Und damit hat sein' Ende DES JUNGEN BREITMANN'S LIED.

Ballad

Der noble Ritter Hugo
  Von Schwillensaufenstein,
    Rode out mit shpeer and helmet,
Und he coom to de panks of de Rhine.

Und oop dere rose a meer maid,
  Vot hadn't got nodings on,
Und she say, "Oh, Ritter Hugo,
    Vhere you goes mit yourself alone?"

And he says, "I rides in de creenwood
  Mit helmet und mit shpeer,
Till I cooms into em Gasthaus,
    Und dere I trinks some beer."

Und den outshpoke de maiden
  Vot hadn't got nodings on:
"I tont dink mooch of beoplesh
    Dat goes mit demselfs alone.

"You'd petter coom down in de wasser,
  Vere deres heaps of dings to see,
Und hafe a shplendid tinner
    Und drafel along mit me.

"Dere you see de fisch a schwimmin,
  Und you catches dem efery one:"—
So sang dis wasser maiden
    Vot hadn't got nodings on.

"Dere ish drunks all full mit money
  In ships dat vent down of old;
Und you helpsh yourself, by dunder!
    To shimmerin crowns of gold.

"Shoost look at dese shpoons und vatches!
  Shoost see dese diamant rings!
Coom down und full your bockets,
    Und I'll giss you like avery dings.

"Vot you vantsh mit your schnapps und lager?
  Coom down into der Rhine!
Der ish pottles der Kaiser Charlemagne
    Vonce filled mit gold-red wine!"

Dat fetched him—he shtood all shpell pound;
   She pooled his coat-tails down,
She drawed him oonder der wasser,
   De maidens mit nodings on.

A Ballad Apout de Rowdies

De moon shines ofer de cloudlens,
   Und de cloudts plow ofer de sea,
Und I vent to Coney Island,
   Und I took mein Schatz mit me.
Mine Schatz, Katrina Bauer,
   I gife her mein heart und vordt;
Boot ve tidn't know vot beoples
   De Dampsschiff hafe cot on poard.

De preeze plowed cool und bleasant,
   We looket at de town
Mit sonn-light on de shdeebles,
   Und wetter fanes doornin round.
Ve sat on de deck in a gorner
   Und dropled nopody dere,
Ven all aroundt oos de rowdies
   Peginned to plackguard und schvear!

A voman mit a papy
   Vas sittin in de blace;
Von tooket a chew tobacco
   Und trowed it indo her vace.
De voman got coonvulshons,
   De papy pegin to gry;
Und de rowdies shkreemed out a laffin,
   Und saidt dat de fun vas "high."

Pimepy ve become some hoonger
   Katrina Baur und I,
I openet de lit of mine pasket,
   Und pringed out a cherry bie.
A cherry kooken mit pretzels,
   "How goot!" Katrina said,

Ven a rowdy snatched it from her,
    Und preaked it ofer mine het.

I dells him he pe a plackguart
    I gifed him a biece my mind,
I vouldt saidt it pefore a tousand,
    Mit der teufel himself pehind.
Den he knocks me down mit a sloong-shot,
    Und peats me plack und plue;
Und all de plackguards kick me,
    Dill I vainted, und dat ish drue.

De rich American beoples
    Don't know how de rowdies shtrike
Der poor hardt-workin Sherman,
    He knows it more ash he like.
If de Deutsche speakers und bapers
    Are sometimes too hard on dis land,
Shoost dink how de Deutsch kit driven
    Along by de rowdy's hand!

From "Breitmann in Politics"

I. The Nomination

When ash de var vas ober,
    Und Beace her shnow-wice vings,
Vas vafin o'er de coondry
(In shpods) like afery dings;
Und heroes vere revardtet,
    De beople all pegan
To say 'tvas shame dat nodings
    Vas done for Breitemann.

No man wised how id vas shtartet,
    Or where der fore shlog came,
Boot dey shveared it was a cinder,
    Dereto a purnin shame:

"Dere is Schnitzerl in de Gustom-House—
 Potzblitz! can dis dings pe?—
Und Breitmann he hafe nodings:
 Vot sights is dis to see!

"Nod de virst ret cendt for Breitmann!
 Ish *dis* do pe de gry
On de man dat sacked de repels
 Und trinked dem high and dry?
By meine Seel' I shvears id,
 Und vot's more I deglares id's drue,
He vonce gleaned out a down in half an oor,
 Und shtripped id strumpf und shoe.

"He was shoost like Koenig Etzel,
 Of whom de shdory dell,
Der Hun who go for de Romans
 Und gife dem shinin hell,
Only dis dat dey say no grass vouldt crow
 Vhere Etzel's horse had trot,
Und I really peliefe vere Breitmann go
 De hops shpring oop, bei Gott!"

If once you tie a dog loose,
 Dere ish more soon gets arount,
Und wenn dis vas shtartedt on Breitmann
 It was rings aroom be-foundt;
Dough *vhy* he *moost* hafe somedings
 Vas not by no mean glear,
Nor tid it, like Paulus' confersion,
 On de snap to all abbear!

Und, in facdt, Balthazar Bumchen
 Saidt he couldtent nicht blainly see
Vy a veller for gadderin riches
 Shood dus revartedt pe:
Der Breitmann own drei Houser,
 Mit a wein-handle in a stohr,
Dazu ein Lager-Wirthschaft,
 Und sonst was—somedings more.

Dis plasted plackguard none-sense
 Ve couldn't no means shtand,

From a narrow-mineted shvine's kopf,
   Of our nople captain grand:
Soosh low, goarse, betty *bornirtheit*
   A shentleman deplores;
So ve called him *verfluchter Hundsfott*
   Und shmysed him out of toors.

So ve all dissolfed dat Breitmann
   Shouldt hafe a nomination
To go to de Legisladoor,
   To make some dings off de nation;
Mit de helb of a Connedigut man,
   In whom ve hafe great hobes,
Who had shange his boledics fivdeen dimes,
   Und derefore knew de robes.
. . . .

III. Mr. Twine Explains Being "Sound upon the Goose"

Dere in his crate corved oaken shtuhl
   Der Breitmann sot he:
He lookt shoost like de shiant
   In de Kinder hishdorie;
Und pefore him, on de tische,
   Vas—vhere man alfays foundt it—
Dwelf inches of goot lager,
   Mit a Boemisch glass aroundt it.

De foorst vordt dat der Breitmann spoke
   He maked no sbeech or sign:
De next remark vas, "*Zapfet aus!*"—
   De dird vas, "*Schenket ein!*"
Vhen in coomed liddle Gottlieb
   Und Trina mit a shtock
Of Allerbest Markgraefler wein—
   Dazu dwelf glaeser Bock.

Denn Misder Twine deglare dat he
   Vas happy to denounce

Dat as Copdain Breitmann suited oos
  Egsockdly do an ounce,
He vas ged de nomination,
  And need nod more eckshblain:
Der Breitmann dink in silence,
  And denn roar aloudt, CHAMPAGNE!

Den Mishder Twine, while trinken wein,
  Mitwhiles vent on do say,
Dat long insdruckdions in dis age
  Vere nod de dime of tay;
Und de only ding der Breitmann need
  To pe of any use
Vas shoost to dell to afery mans
  He's *soundt oopon der coose.*

Und ash dis little frase berhops
  Vas nod do oos bekannt,
He dakes de liberdy do make
  Dat ve shall oondershtand,
And vouldt tell a liddle shdory
  Vitch dook blace pefore de wars:
Here der Breitmann not to Trina,
  Und she bass aroundt cigars.

"Id ish a longe dime, now here,
  In Bennsylvanien's Shtate,
All in der down of Horrisburg
  Dere rosed a vierce depate,
'Tween vamilies mit cooses,
  Und dose vhere none vere foundt—
If cooses might, by common law,
  Go squanderin aroundt?

"Dose who vere nod pe-gifted
  Mit gooses, und vere poor,
All shvear de law forbid dis crime,
  Py shings and cerdain sure;
But de coose-holders teklare a coose
  Greadt liberty tid need,
And to pen dem oop vas gruel,
  Und a mosdt oon-Christian teed.

"Und denn anoder party
    Idself tid soon refeal,
Of arisdograts who kepd no coose,
    Pecause 'twas not shendeel:
Tey tid not vish de splodderin geese
    Shouldt on deir pafemends bass,
So dey shoined de anti-coosers,
    Or de oonder lower glass!"

Here Breitmann led his shdeam out:
    "Dis shdory goes to show
Dat in poledicks, ash lager,
    Virtus in medio.
De drecks ish ad de pottom—
    De skoom floads high inteed;
Boot das bier ish in de mittle,
    Says an goot old Sherman lied.

"Und shoost apout elegdion-dimes
    De scoom und drecks, ve see,
Have a pully Wahl-verwandtschaft,
    Or election-sympathie."
"Dis is very vine," says Misder Twine,
    "Vot here you indroduce:
Mit your bermission, I'll grack on
    Mit my shdory of de coose.

"A gandertate for sheriff
    De coose-beholders run,
Who shvear de coose de noblest dings
    Vot valk peneat de sun;
For de cooses safe de Capidol
    In Rome long dimes ago,
Und Horrisburg need safin
    Mighty pad, ash all do know.

"Acainsd dis mighdy Goose-man
    Anoder veller rose,
Who keepedt himself ungommon shtill
    Ven oders came to plows;
Und if any ask how 'twas he shtoodt,
    His vriends wouldt vink so loose,

This illustration from Cornelius Mathews' "The Great Charter Contest in Gotham" (1838) is taken from Burton's *Cyclopedia of Wit and Humor*. It illustrates the battle for the votes of ignorant Irish and German immigrants as the spirit of Jacksonian reform became increasingly prominent.

Und visper ash dey dapped deir nose:
   'He's soundt oopon de coose!

" 'He's O.K. oopon de soobject;
   Shoost pet your pile on dat;
On dis bartik'ler quesdion
   He intends to coot it fat.'
So de veller cot elegded
   Pefore de beople foundt
On *vitch* side of der coose it vas
   He shtick so awful soundt.

"Dis shdory's all I hafe to dell,"
   Says Misder Hiram Twine;
"Und I advise Herr Breitmann
   Shoost to vight id on dis line."
De volk who of dese boledics
   Would oder shapters read,
Moost waiten for de segondt pardt
   Of dis here Breitmann's Lied.

The Rise and Fall of Gloryville

Where the rockiest Rocky Mountains interview the scornful skies,
And the sager kinds of sage-bush in the middle distance rise,
There the cultured eye descending from the dreamlike azure hill,
Lights in an aesthetic foreground on the town of Gloryville.

It was in the Middle Ages—'bout the end of Sixty-eight,
So I found the hoary legend written on an ancient slate—
That one Ezry Jenks prospecting, when he reached this blooming
   spot,
Thus uplifted to his pardner: "Glory! Moses, let us squat!"

Thus rebounded Moses Adams: "Glory was the foremost word
Which in the untrammelled silence of this wilderness was heard,
And I answer, dimly feelin' like a prophet, grand and slow,
'Glory kinder sounds like Money—up to glory let her go.' "

And this casual conversation in the year of Sixty-eight,
As if by an inspiration he recorded on a slate,

Which 'twas said in later ages—six weeks after—used to hang
As a curiositary in the principal shebang.

On the spot that very evening they perceived a beauteous gleam
From a grain of shining metal in a wild auriferous stream:
As their eyes remarked the symptom thus their tongues responsive
    spoke:
"In this undiscovered section there *is* pay-dirt, sure as smoke!"

Little boots or little shoes it to inform you how, like crows
To a carcase, folks came flying, and the town of Glory rose;
As in country schools the urchins cast each one a spittle-ball,
Till at last a monstrous paper fungus gathers on the wall.

'Long the road they built their cabins, in a vis-a-visual way,
As if each man to his neighbor kind of wished to have his say;
But 'twas also said that like two rows of teeth the houses grew,
Threatening uncommon danger to the stranger passing through.

Yes, for like the note of freedom sounded on Hibernia's harp,
Every person in the party was a most uncommon sharp;
And it got to be a saying that from such an ornery cuss
As a regular Gloryvillin—oh, good Law deliver us!

First of all the pay-dirt vanished or became uncommon rare,
Then they wandered more than ever to the Cross and from the
    Square,
For when all resources failed them nary copper did they mind,
For they had fine-answering Genius, which is never left behind.

So they got incopperated as a city fair and grand,
Spreading memoirs of their splendour over many a distant land,
Mind I say in *distant* places—people near them knew
Into what unearthly beauty the great town of Glory grew.

Then they sent an ex-tra Governor over seas and far beyond,
Even unto distant Holland, loaded up with many a bond,
Splendidly engraved in London, having just the proper touch
Quite imposing—rather—for they did impose upon the Dutch.

And with every bond the Governor had a picture to bestow
Of the town of Gloryville a-bathing in the sunset's glow;
This they had performed in Paris by an artist full of cheek,
Who was told to draw a city *comme il faut dans l'Amerique.*

The ideas of this artist were ideas from long ago,
Out of scenery in an opera, "Cortez in the Mexico."

Therefore all his work expanded with expensive fallacies:
Castles, towered walls, pavilions, real-estately palaces.

In the foreground lofty palm-trees, as if full of soaring love,
Bore up coco-nuts and monkeys to the smiling heaven above;
Jet-black Indian chieftains, at their feet too lovely girls were sighin,
With an elephant beyond them—here and there a casual lion.

You have seen in *Pilgrim's Progress* the Celestial City stand
Like a hub in half a cart-wheel raying light o'er all the land.
Well, in *that*, it is the felloes of the wheel which cause the blaze;
So in Gloryville the fellows were the ones who made the rays.

When these views were well matured the Governor went to
      Amsterdam,
Where to Mynheer Schmuel Ganef first of all he made his slam:
At a glance each "saw" the other—at a glance they went aside,
And without a word of bother soon the plan was cut and dried.

For one hundred thousand dollars then the Governor at will
Gave away the full fee-simple of the town of Gloryville.
"Dat for you," said Schmuel Ganef, "is, I dink, not much too much,
But I makesh de shtock a million ven I sells him to the Dutch."

And the secret of his selling was upon the artful plan
Known to the police in Paris as the *vol Americain*,
Whereby he who does the spilling manages the man who's spilt
Very nicely, for he makes him an accomplice in the guilt.

Even as of old great sages managed the Parisian *fonds*,
So in Amsterdam Heer Ganef peddled out his Glory bonds;
And to all he slyly whispered, "I will let you in de first
On de ground-floor—sell out quickly—for you know de ding may
      burst."

Woe to you who live by thieving, though you be of rogues the chief,
Even the greatest will discover in due time his master-thief.
True, he "let them in," and truly on the very bottom floor,
But was with the Gloryvillins in the cellar long before.

And to tell you how the biters all got bitten were in vain;
Here the Governor leaves my story, and he comes not in again.
I will pass to later ages, when all Gloryville, you bet,
Found itself extreme encumbered with an extra booming debt.

Those who sold the bonds had vanished, those who hadn't held the
      town,

Little knew they of its glory over seas or great renown.
They had nothing of the fruitage, though, alas! they held the plant,
Nothing saw they of the picture, save, indeed, the Elephant.

He who had been in the background now came trampling to the
     fore;
Terribly he trampled on them, very awful was his roar!
Very dreadful is the silence when no human voice responds
To a legal requisition for the interest of our bonds.

But ere long a shrewd reflection unto Moses Adams came—
"Darned ef I'm a-gwine to suffer fur another party's game;
Wings is given to muskeeters—like muskeeters men can fly;
Ef a strawberry-vine can travel with its roots, then why not I?"

Silently, in secret Moses to himself a plan reveals,
Got a three-inch plank and sawed it into surreptitious wheels,
And when night in solemn mystery had succeeded unto day,
Put his hut and things on axles, and quite lonely drove away

To a place just over yonder by the old Coyote Road;
There, no more a man of glory, Moses Adams dropped his load,
And when resting from his labour and refreshing from his jug,
Having known a town called Julesberg called his shanty
     Splendourbug.

On the following morn as usual in due time arose the sun,
And the Gloryvillins followed his example one by one;
While he smiled upon the city, as on other things beneath,
'Twas observed one snag was wanting in the double row of teeth.

Little said the Left-behinders, but they seemed to take the hint,
And each man surveyed his neighbour with a shrewd and genial
     squint;
All day long there was a sound of sawing timber up and down,
Seven more houses in the morning were a-wanting in the town.

And before the week departed all the town departed too,
Just like the swallows in the autumn to another soil they flew;
Only that, unlike the swallows which we hear of in the song,
When the Gloryvillins squandered each one took his nest along.

All except one ancient darkey, obstinate and blind and lame,
Who for want of wheels and credit could not follow up the game;
So the others had to leave him, which they did without regret,
Left him there without a copper—just one million deep in debt.

If you seek them you may find them comfortable as in a rug,
All of them at length established in the town of Splendourbug;
And the driver to the traveller as by Gloryville he goes,
Points him out, an ancient darkey who a million dollars owes.

Zion Jersey Boggs
A Legend of Philadelphia

Before the telegraphic wires
   Had ever run from pole to pole,
Or telegirls sent telegrams
   To cheer the weary waiting soul;
When all things went about as slow
   As terrapins could run on clogs,
     Was played a game
     By one whose name
   Was Mister Zion Jersey Boggs.

A Philadelphia newspaper
   Was printed then on Chestnut Street,
While 'crost the way, just opposite,
   There lived a sufferin' rival sheet,
Whose editors could get no news,
   Which made 'em cross as starvin' hogs;
     The first, I guess,
     Had an express
   Which kind o' b'longed to Mister Boggs.

But in those days the only news
   Which reëly opened readers' eyes,
Was of the New York lottery,
   And who by luck had got a prize.
All other news, for all they cared,
   Might travel to the orful dogs;
     And this they got
     All piping hot—
   Though surreptitiously—from Boggs.

For of the crew no party knew
   That Boggs did any horses own.

All sportin' amputations he
  Did most concussively disown;
For he had serious subtle aims,
    His wheels were full of secret cogs,—
      Well oiled and slow,
      Yet sure to go,
    Was Mister Zion Jersey Boggs.

One mornin' he, mysteriously,
  An' smilin' quite ironical,
Spoke to the other editor,
  The man who run the *Chronicle*:
"The *Ledger* has a hoss express
  By which your lottery news he flogs."
    "Yes, that is true,
    But what's to do?"
  Replied the man to Mister Boggs.

Then Mister Boggs let down his brows,
  And with a long deep knowing wink,
Said, "Hosses travel mighty fast,
  But ther air faster things, I think:
An' kerrier-pidgings, as you know,
  Kin find their way thro' storm and fogs:
    Them air the bugs
    To fly like slugs!"
  Said Mister Zion Jersey Boggs.

"And in my glorious natyve land,
  Which lies acrost the Delaware,
I hev a lot upon the spot,—
  Just twenty dollars fur a pair.
These gentle insects air the things
  To make the *Ledger* squeal like hogs;
    That is the game
    To hit 'em lame!"
  Said Mister Zion Jersey Boggs.

The editor looked back again,
  And saw him better on his wink.
"It is the crisis of our fate—
  Say, Boggs, what is your style of drink?

Step to the bar of Congress Hall;—
   We'll try your poultry on, by Gogs!
     An' let 'em fly
     Tarnation high!"
   "Amen!" said Zion Jersey Boggs.

The pidgins came, the pidgins flew,
   They lit upon the lofty wall;
They made their five an' ninety miles
   In just about no time at all.
Compared to them, the *Ledger* team
   Went just as slow as haulin' logs.
     But all was mum,
     Shut close an' dum,
   By the request of Mister Boggs.

Then on the follerin' Monday he,
   Lookin' profounder as he prowled,
This son of sin an' mystery,
   Into the *Ledger* orfice owled.
"An' oh! to think," he sadly groaned,
   "That earth should bear setch skalliwogs!
     Setch all-fired snakes,
     And no mistakes!"
   Said Mister Zion Jersey Boggs.

"Why, what is up?" asked Mr. Swain;
   "It seems you've had some awful shoves."
"The *Chronicle*," his agent cried,
   "Has went an' bin an' bought some doves!
Them traitors, wretches, swindlers, cheats,
   Hev smashed us up like polywogs.
     They've knocked, I guess,
     Our hoss express
   Higher than any kite," said Boggs.

"Have you no plan?" asked Mister Swain,
   "To keep the fellows off our walks?"
"I *hev*," said Boggs, as grim as death;
   "What do you think of pidging-horks?
For in my glorious natyve land,
   Acrost the river, 'mong the frogs,

I hev a lot
    All sharply sot
To eat them pidgings up," said Boggs.
"They are the chosen birds of wrath,
    They fly like arrers through the air,
Or angels sent by orful Death—
    Jist fifty dollars fur a pair;
An' cheap to keep, because, you see,
    Upon the enemy they progs."
        "Well, try it on,
        And now begone!"
Said Mister Swain to Mister Boggs.

The autumn morn was bright and fair,
    Fresh as a rose with recent rain.
The pidgins tortled through the air,
    But nary one came home again.
Some feathers dropped in Chestnut Street,
    Some bills and claws among the logs:
        Wipin' a tear,
        "I greatly fear
That all's not right," said Mr. Boggs.

Into the *Chronicle* he went,
    Twice as mysterious as before,
"And *hev* you heard the orful news?"
    He whispered as he shet the door.
"Oh, I hev come to tell a tale
    Of crime, which all creation flogs,
        Of wretchery
        And treachery
    That bangs tarnation sin," said Boggs.

"Them *Ledger* fellers with their tricks,
    Hev slopped clean over crime's dark cup.
They've bin an' bought some pidging-horks,
    And they hev *et* our pidgings up.
Oh, whut is life wuth livin' fur
    When editors behave like hogs?
        An' ragin' crime
        Makes double time;
    Oh, darn setch villany!" cried Boggs.

"But hark! bee-hold, to-morrer, thou
    In deep revenge may dry your tears;
I hev a plan, which, you'll allow,
    Beats all-git-out when it eppears.
The ragin' eagle of the North,
    The bird which all creation flogs,
      Will cause them horks
      To walk ther chalks,
    An' give us grand revenge," said Boggs.

'Them glorious birds of liberty,
    Them symbols of our country's fame,
Wild, sarsy, furious, and free,
    Indeliably rowdy game;
They shall revenge them gentile doves,
    Our harmless messengers, by Gogs!
      In which the horks
      Hev stuck ther forks,"
    Cried Mister Zion Jersey Boggs.

"For in my glorious natyve land
    Acrost the river, down below,
I hev a farm, and in the barn
    Six captyve eagles in a row;
One hundred dollars fur a pair;
    Fetch out the flimsies frum your togs
      An' up on high
      I'll make 'em fly,"
    Said Mister Zion Jersey Boggs.

But this same editor had heard
    Some hint or rumour, faint or dim,
How Mister Boggs, it was averred,
    Was coming Paddy over him.
An earlier tale of soapy deeds
    Then gave his memory startling jogs,
      And full of wrath
      Right in his path
    He went for Zion Jersey Boggs.

"Horses and pidgins—pidgin-horks"—
    That was enough to raise his Dutch:
He saw it all—and also saw

The eagle—"Just one bird too much."
Too mad to mind his shootin'-iron,
    And throw good powder to the dogs,
      He grabbed his chair,
      And then and there
    Corrected Zion Jersey Boggs.

After long years had rolled away,
    And Morse's telegraph came in,
Still on the facing rival roofs
    Two grey old cages could be seen,
And young reporters o'er their drinks
    Would tell each other—jolly dogs—
      Of ancient time
      What in this rhyme
I've told of Zion Jersey Boggs.

The Story of Mr. Scroper, Architect

Yes, I'll tell you how it happened—that, too, with all due respect
To the memory of Scroper, late departed architect—
How it came that he departed so abruptly in the train;
Why it was he's been so late, too, in returnin' back again.

Now some folks are born to greatness, some achieve it, as you've
    read
And some justly stand and take it as it dollops on their head;
But in this sublime Republic, where it's help and help again,
We all generally make it in cahoot with other men.

Scroper was a fine young fellow, of a monstrous enterprise;
Likewise really ambitious, for he was so bound to rise,
And he left no stone unturned—nor a log—he rolled 'em all,
Till at last he got the contract for our new great City Hall.

Now, of all our mortal actors here upon this earthly stage,
The contractors have the hardest parts to play, I will engage;
Specially in bran-new cities, just between the knead and bake,
And where all the population are severely on the make.

What between the Common Council, and the more uncommon sort,
Politicians, Press, and preachers, Scroper fell uncommon short.

All of such as come a-plummin' when a puddin's to be had;
All against his best contractin' counteractin' mighty bad.

Therefore when this edificial had got up his edifice,
All who'd not been edifishing with him soon got up a hiss;
Said the stuff upon the buildin' was the worst that could be had,
Likewise called the architexture architechnically bad.

So it came one solemn evenin' in a Presbyterian rain
Mr. Scroper all in silence gently took the Northern train;
All he left was one small message to a friend who shared his home,—
When the darned affair blows over, telegraph for me to come.

So he sat one summer mornin', far away in Montreal,
Musin' on his recent patrons, while at heart he darned 'em all,
When there came a little letter datin' from his recent home,—
"All the thing is quite blown over, back again we bid you come.

"For last night we had a tempest,—while the mighty thunder rang,
Up there came a real guster, which blew down the whole shebang.
(*Shebang*'s a word from Hebrew, meanin' Seven, sayeth Krupp,
And applied to any shanty where they play at seven-up.)

"Truly it was well blown over all to splinters in the night,
And the winds of heaven are blowing o'er the ruins as I write."
Gentlemen, the story's over. It would last for many a day
If it told of every buildin' built upon the swindlin' lay.

Samuel L. Clemens (Mark Twain)

Samuel L. Clemens (1835–1910), "Mark Twain," although frequently identified as a southwestern or western writer representing the frontier spirit, shows the characteristics of the northeastern literary humorists in these burlesque treatments of social and personal interests approached through the medium of national political rhetoric. *The Gilded Age* (1873), written with the Hartford humorist Charles Dudley Warner, extended the fictionalization of shoddy personal interests, allowing Twain to describe corporate, governmental, and religious deficiencies in comic moments and rhetorical irony close to the pieces published in the late 1860s.

"Barnum's First Speech in Congress" appeared in the New York *Evening Express* (March 5, 1867) and was not reprinted by Twain; similarly, "Female Suffrage" under the heading "Petticoat Government" was published in the New York *Sunday Mercury* (April 7, 1867) and nowhere else in Twain's collected works. I am indebted to Louis J. Budd of Duke University for making copies of these selections available; they will appear with related pieces in his collection of Twain's newspaper writings from the 1860s as part of the complete edition of Mark Twain's works being published by the University of California Press. "Cannibalism in the Cars" first appeared in the (London) *Broadway*, n.s., I (September, 1868–February, 1869), 189–94. "Mark Twain on his Muscle" is a letter to the editor of the New York *World* published on February 18, 1877. It exemplifies the moral diatribes that Twain addressed to Vanderbilt, King Leopold, and other major figures. Twain describes his sense of his own ethical growth in relation to the comic scenes at the opening of *The Innocents Abroad* (1869); Twain's disdain for priggish social conventions matured into Huck Finn and the doctor in "Was It Heaven? Or Hell?" It is consequently interesting to see him apply his moral yardstick to himself. In *Mark Twain as a Literary Comedian* (Baton Rouge, 1979), I have described Twain's relationship to the literary comedians and particularly to Artemus Ward, the outstanding representative of that school of humor. Other valuable works on Twain are far too numerous to list here.

Barnum's First Speech in Congress

Mr. P. T. Barnum will find the House of Representatives a most excellent advertising medium, in case he is elected to Congress. He will certainly not forget the high duties to his country devolving upon him, and it will be a pity if he forgets his private worldly affairs,—a genuine pity if his justly-famed sagacity fails to point out to him how he can dovetail business and patriotism together to the mutual benefit of himself and the Great Republic. I am informed by the Spirits that his first speech in Congress will read as follows:

"Mr. Speaker—What do we do with a diseased limb? Cut it off! What do I do with a diseased curiosity? Sell him! What do we do with any speculation of any kind whatever that don't pay? Get rid of it— get out of it! Of course. Simply because I have got the most superb collection of curiosities in the world—the grandest museum ever conceived of by man—containing the dwarf elephant, Jenny Lind, and the only living giraffe on this continent, (that noble brute, which sits upon its hams in an attitude at once graceful and picturesque, and eats its hay out of the second-story window,)—because I have got these things, and because admission is only thirty cents, children and servants half-price, open from sunrise till 10 P.M., peanuts and all the other luxuries of the season to be purchased in any part of the house,—the proprietor, at enormous expense, having fitted up two peanut stands to each natural curiosity,—because I have got these things, shall I revel in luxurious indolence when my voice should sound a warning to the nation? No! Because the Wonderful Spotted Human Phenomenon, the Leopard Child from the wilds of Africa, is mine, shall I exult in my happiness and be silent when my country's life is threatened? No! Because the Double Humpbacked Bactrian Camel takes his oats in my menagerie, shall I surfeit with bliss and lift not up my voice to save the people? No!—Because among my possessions are dead loads of Royal Bengal Tigers, White Himalaya Mountain Bears, so interesting to Christian families from being mentioned in the Sacred Scriptures, Silver-striped Hyenas, Lions, Tigers, Leopards, Wolves,

Sacred Cattle from the sacred hills of New Jersey, Panthers, Ibexes, Performing Mules and Monkeys, South American Deer, and so-forth, and so-forth, shall I gloat over my blessings in silence, and leave Columbia to perish? No! Because I have secured the celebrated Gordon Cumming collection, consisting of oil portraits of the two negroes and a child who rescued him from impending death, shall I wrap me. in mute ecstacy and let my country rush unwarned to her destruction? No! Because unto me belong the monster living alligator, over 12 feet in length, and four living speckled brook trout, weighing 20 pounds, shall these lips sing songs of gladness and peal no succoring cry unto a doomed nation? No! Because I have got Miller's grand national bronze portrait gallery, consisting of two plaster of Paris Venuses and a varnished mud-turtle, shall I bask in mine own bliss and be mute in the season of my people's peril? No! Because I possess the smallest dwarfs in the world, and the Nova Scotian giantess, who weighs a ton and eats her weight every forty-eight hours; and Herr Phelim O'Flannigan the Norwegian Giant, who feeds on the dwarfs and ruins business; and the lovely Circassian girls and the celebrated Happy Family, consisting of animals of the most diverse principles and dispositions, dwelling together in peace and unity, and never beheld by the religious spectator acquainted with Eden before the Fall, without emotions too profound for utterance; and 250,000 other curiosities, chiefly invisible to the naked eye—all to be seen for the small sum of 30 cents, children and servants half price—staircases arranged with special reference to limb displays—shall I hug my happiness to my soul and fail to cry aloud when I behold my country sinking to destruction and the grave? No!—a thousand times No!

NO! Even as one sent to warn ye of fearful peril, I cry help! help! for the stricken land! I appeal to you—and to you—and to you, sir—to every true heart in this august menagerie! Demagogues threaten the Goddess of Liberty!—they beard the starry-robed woman in her citadel! and to you the bearded woman looks for succor! Once more grim Treason towers in our midst, and once more helpless loyalty scatters into corners as do the dwarfs when the Norwegian giant strides among them! The law-making powers and the Executive are at daggers drawn, State after State flings defiance at the Amendment, and lo! the Happy Family of the Union is broken up! Woe is me!

"Where is the poor negro? How hath he fared? Alas! his regeneration is incomplete; he is free, but he cannot vote; ye have only made him white in spots, like my wonderful Leopard Boy from the wilds of Africa! Ye promised him universal suffrage, but ye have given him universal suffering instead! Woe is me!

"The country is fallen! The boss monkey sits in the feed-tub, and the tom-cats, the raccoons and the gentle rabbits of the once happy family stand helpless and afar off, and behold him gabble the provender in the pride of his strength! Woe is me!

"Ah, gentlemen, our beloved Columbia, with these corroding distresses upon her, must soon succumb! The high spirit will depart from her eye, the bloom from her cheek, the majesty from her step, and she will stand before us gaunt and worn, like my beautiful giantess when my dwarfs and Circassians prey upon her rations! Soon we shall see the glory of the realm pass away as did the grandeur of the Museum amid the consuming fires, and the wonders the world admires shall give place to trivialities, even as in the proud Museum the wonders that once amazed have given place to cheap stuffed reptiles and peanut stands! Woe is me!

"O, spirit of Washington! forgotten in these evil times, thou art banished to the dusty corridors of memory, a staring effigy of wax, and none could recognize thee but for the label pinned upon thy legs! O, shade of Jackson! O, ghost of gallant Lafayette! ye live only in museums, and the sublime lessons of your lives are no longer heeded by the slumbering nation! Woe is me!

"Rouse ye, my people, rouse ye! rouse ye! rouse ye! Shake off the fatal stupor that is upon ye, and hurl the usurping tyrant from his throne! Impeach! impeach! impeach!—Down with the dread boss monkey! O, snake the seditious miscreant out of the national feed-tub and reconstruct the Happy Family!

Such is the speech as imparted to me in advance from the spirit land.

Petticoat Government

Our contributor, like many other sagacious people, is evidently afraid that if women should find an official entrance to the halls of legislation, there would occur almost as disgraceful scenes as have lately blurred the record of Congressional proceedings.

Female Suffrage

Ed. T. T.:—The women of Missouri are bringing a tremendous pressure to bear in an endeavor to secure to themselves the right to vote and hold office. Their petitions to the legislature are scattered abroad, and are filled with signers. Thirty-nine members of the Missouri Legislature have declared in favor of the movement. This thing looks ominous. Through an able spiritual medium I have been permitted to see a Missouri Legislature of five years hence in session. Here is a report of the proceedings:

The P. R. R. Appropriation Bill being the special order for the day, and the hour for its discussion having arrived:

Miss Belcher, of St. Louis, said—Madam Speaker, I call for the special order for to-day.

Madam Speaker.—The clerk will read—

Clerk.—An act supplementary to an Act entitled An Act amendatory of an Act entitled An Act to Appropriate Five millions of dollars in aid of the Pacific Railroad, etc., etc.

Miss Belcher.—Madame Speaker, it is with the keenest pain that I observe the diminishing esteem in which gored-dresses are held. It is with pain which these lips are indeed powerless to express. The gored-dress of two years ago, Madam, with its long, graceful sweep—

Mr. Jones, of St. Joseph.—Madam Speaker, I rise to a point of order. The lady is not confining herself to the question before the house. What in the nation has these cussed gored dresses and stuff got to do with the great Pacif—

Madam Speaker (amid piping female voices all over the house, shrieking angrily).—Sit down, Sir! Take your seat, Sir, and don't you presume to interrupt again! Go on, Miss Belcher.

Miss Belcher.—I was remarking, Madam, when the unprincipled bald-headed outlaw from St. Joseph interrupted me, that it pained me to see the charming and attractive gored dress we all were once so fond of, going out of fashion. And what, I ask, are we to have in place of it? What is offered to recompense us for its loss? Why, nothing, Madam, but the wretched, slimprey, new-fangled street-dress, hoopless, shapeless, cut bias, hem-stitched, with the selvedge edge turned down; and all so lank, so short, so cadaverous, and so disgraceful! Excuse these tears. Who can look without emotion upon such a garment? Who can look unmoved upon a dress which exposes feet at every step which shrink from inspection? Who can consent to countenance a dress which—

Mr. Slawson, of St. Genevieve.—Madam Speaker, This is absurd. What will such proceedings as these read like in the newspapers? We take up the discussion of a measure of vast consequence—a measure of tremendous financial importance—and a member of this body, totally ignoring the question before the House, launches out into a tirade about womanly apparel!—a matter trivial enough at any time, God knows, but utterly insignificant in presence of so grave a matter as the behests of the Great Pacific Rail—

Madam Speaker.—Consider yourself under arrest, Sir! Sit down, and dare to speak again at your peril! The honorable lady from St. Louis will proceed.

Miss Belcher.—Madam Speaker, I will dismiss the particular section of my subject upon which I was speaking when interrupted by the degraded ruffian from St. Genevieve, and pass to the gist of the matter. I propose, Madam, to prohibit, under heavy penalties, the wearing of the new street-dress, and to restore the discarded gored dress by legislative enactment, and I beg leave to introduce a bill to that end, and without previous notice, if the courtesy of this honorable body will permit it.

Mr. Walker, of Marion.—Madam Speaker, this is an outrage! it is damnable! The Pacific Railroad—

Madam Speaker.—Silence! Plant yourself, Sir! Leave is granted to introduce the Bill. If no objection is made, it will be referred to the Standing Committee on Public Improvements. Reports of Committees are now in order.

Mrs. Baker, of Ralls.—Madam Speaker, the Select Committee of Five, to whom was referred an Act Amendatory of An act Establishing the Metes and Bounds of School Lands, and to which was added a clause Establishing the Metes and Bounds of Water Privileges, have been unable to agree. The younger members of the committee contend that the added clause is of sufficient latitude to permit of legislation concerning ladies' waterfalls, and they have reported upon that clause alone to the exclusion of all other matters contemplated in the bill. There is no majority-report, Madam, and no minority-report.

Mr. Bridgewater, of Benton.—There are five women on the committe, ain't there?

Mrs. Baker.—Yes.

THE WIFE AND MOTHER AT A PRIMARY,

Both Mark Twain and Marietta Holley wrote about the domestic consequences of women in politics. "The Wife and Mother at a Primary" appeared
in Holley's *My Opinions and Betsey Bobbet's* (1873).

Mr. Bilgewater.—Each of 'em made a report by herself, hasn't she?

Mrs. Baker.—Yes, Sir.

Mr. Bilgewater.—Why, certainly. Five women's bound to have five opinions. It's like 'em.

[With the last word the gentleman from Benton darted out at the window, and eleven inkstands followed him.]

The several reports were received and tabled, after considerable discussion. Third reading and final passage of bills being next in order, an Act for Amending the Common School System was taken up, but it was found to be so interlarded with surreptitious clauses for remodeling and establishing fashion for ladies' bonnets, that neither head nor tail could be made out of it, and it had to be referred back to the Committee of the Whole again. An Act to Provide Arms for the State Militia was discovered to be so hampered with clauses for the protection of Sewing Societies and Tea Drinkings, that it had to go back to the file also. Every Bill on the third-reading list was found to be similarly mutilated, until they got down to an Act to Compel Married Gentlemen to be at Home by Nine of the Clock, every evening; an Act to Abolish the Use of Tobacco in any form; and an Act to Abolish the Use of Intoxicating Liquors. These had not been meddled with, and were at once put to vote, and passed over the heads of the male members, who made a gallant fight, but were overcome by heartless and tyrannical members.

Mr. Green, of Cape Girardeau, then rose in his place and said.—"I now shake the dust of this House from my feat, and take my eternal leave of it. I never will enter its doors again, to be snubbed and harried by a pack of padded, scraggy, dried-up, snuff-dipping, toothless oldmaids, who—"

He never got any further. A howl went up that shook the building to its foundation, and in the midst of struggling forms, fiery eyes, distorted countenances, and dismembered waterfalls, I saw the daring legislator yield and fall; and when at last he reappeared, and fled toward the door, his shirt-front was in ribbons, his cravat knot under his ear, his face scratched red and white like the national flag, and hardly hair enough left on his head to make a toothbrush.

I shudder now. Is it possible that this revelation of the spirits is a prophecy.

Cannibalism in the Cars

I visited St. Louis lately, and on my way west, after changing cars at Terre Haute, Indiana, a mild, benevolent-looking gentleman of about forty-five, or may be fifty, came in at one of the way-stations and sat down beside me. We talked together pleasantly on various subjects for an hour, perhaps, and I found him exceedingly intelligent and entertaining. When he learned that I was from Washington, he immediately began to ask questions about various public men, and about Congressional affairs; and I saw very shortly that I was conversing with a man who was perfectly familiar with the ins and outs of political life at the Capital, even to the ways and manners, and customs of procedure of Senators and Representatives in the Chambers of the National Legislature. Presently two men halted near us for a single moment, and one said to the other:

"Harris, if you'll do that for me, I'll never forget you, my boy."

My new comrade's eyes lighted pleasantly. The words had touched upon a happy memory, I thought. Then his face settled into thoughtfulness—almost into gloom. He turned to me and said, "Let me tell you a story; let me give you a secret chapter of my life—a chapter that has never been referred to by me since its events transpired. Listen patiently, and promise that you will not interrupt me."

I said I would not, and he related the following strange adventure, speaking sometimes with animation, sometimes with melancholy, but always with feeling and earnestness.

The Stranger's Narrative

On the 19th December, 1853, I started from St. Louis in the evening train, bound for Chicago. There were only twenty-four passengers, all told. There were no ladies and no children. We were in excellent spirits, and pleasant acquaintanceships were soon formed. The journey bade fair to be a happy one, and no individual in the party, I think, had even the vaguest presentiment of the horrors we were soon to undergo.

At 11 P.M. it began to snow hard. Shortly after leaving the small village of Welden, we entered upon that tremendous prairie solitude that stretches its leagues on leagues of houseless dreariness far away towards the Jubilee Settlements. The winds unobstructed by trees or hills, or even vagrant rocks, whistled fiercely across the level desert, driving the falling snow before it like spray from the crested waves of a stormy sea. The snow was deepening fast, and we knew, by the diminished speed of the train, that the engine was ploughing through it with steadily increasing difficulty. Indeed it almost came to a dead halt sometimes, in the midst of great drifts that piled themselves like colossal graves across the track. Conversation began to flag. Cheerfulness gave place to grave concern. The possibility of being imprisoned in the snow, on the bleak prairie, fifty miles from any house, presented itself to every mind, and extended its depressing influence over every spirit.

At two o'clock in the morning I was aroused out of an uneasy slumber by the ceasing of all motion about me. The appalling truth flashed upon me instantly—we were captives in a snowdrift! "All hands to the rescue!" Every man sprang to obey. Out into the wild night, the pitchy darkness, the billowing snow, the driving storm, every soul leaped, with the consciousness that a moment lost now might bring destruction to us all. Shovels, hands, boards—anything, everything that could displace snow, was brought into instant requisition. It was a weird picture, that small company of frantic men fighting the banking snows, half in the blackest shadow and half in the angry light of the locomotive's reflector.

One short hour sufficed to prove the utter uselessness of our efforts. The storm barricaded the track with a dozen drifts while we dug one away. And worse than this, it was discovered that the last grand charge the engine had made upon the enemy had broken the fore-and-aft shaft of the driving-wheel! With a free track before us we should still have been helpless. We entered the car wearied with labour, and very sorrowful. We gathered about the stoves, and gravely canvassed our situation. We had no provisions whatever—in this lay our chief distress. We could not freeze, for there was a good supply of wood in the tender. This was our only comfort. The discussion ended at last in accepting the disheartening decision of the conductor,—viz.: That it would be death for any man to attempt to travel fifty miles on foot through snow like that. We could not send for help, and even if we could, it could not come. We must submit and await, as patiently as we might, succour or starvation! I think the stoutest heart there felt a momentary chill when those words were uttered.

Within the hour conversation subsided to a low murmur here and there about the car, caught fitfully between the rising and falling of the blast; the lamps grew dim; and the majority of the castaways settled themselves among the flickering shadows to think—to forget the present if they could—to sleep, if they might.

The eternal night—it surely seemed eternal to us—wore its lagging hours away at last, and the cold grey dawn broke in the east. As the light grew stronger the passengers began to stir and give signs of life, one after another, and each in turn pushed his slouched hat up from his forehead, stretched his stiffened limbs, and glanced out at the windows upon the cheerless prospect. It was cheerless indeed!—not a living thing visible anywhere, not a human habitation; nothing but a vast white desert; uplifted sheets of snow drifting hither and thither before the wind—a world of eddying flakes shutting out the firmament above.

All day we moped about the cars, saying little, thinking much. Another lingering, dreary night—and hunger.

Another dawning—another day of silence, sadness, wasting hunger, hopeless watching for succour that could not come. A night of restless slumber, filled with dreams of feasting—wakings distressed with the gnawings of hunger.

The fourth day came and went—and the fifth! Five days of dreadful imprisonment! A savage hunger looked out at every eye. There was in it a sign of awful import—the foreshadowing of a something that was vaguely shaping itself in every heart—a something which no tongue dared yet to frame into words.

The sixth day passed—the seventh dawned upon as gaunt and haggard and hopeless a company of men as ever stood in the shadow of death. It must out now! That thing which had been growing up in every heart was ready to leap from every lip at last! Nature had been taxed to the utmost—she must yield. RICHARD H. GASTON, of Minnesota, tall, cadaverous, and pale, rose up. All knew what was coming. All prepared—every emotion, every semblance of excitement was smothered—only a calm, thoughtful seriousness appeared in the eyes that were lately so wild.

"Gentlemen,—It cannot be delayed longer! The time is at hand! We must determine which of us shall die to furnish food for the rest!"

Mr. JOHN J. WILLIAMS, of Illinois, rose and said: "Gentlemen,—I nominate the Rev. James Sawyer, of Tennessee."

Mr. WM. R. ADAMS, of Indiana, said: "I nominate Mr. Daniel Slote, of New York."

Mr. CHARLES J. LANGDON: "I nominate Mr. Samuel A. Bowen, of St. Louis."

Mr. SLOTE: "Gentlemen,—I desire to decline in favour of Mr. John A. Van Nastrand, jun., of New Jersey."

Mr. GASTON: "If there be no objection, the gentleman's desire will be acceded to."

Mr. VAN NASTRAND objecting, the resignation of Mr. Slote was rejected. The resignations of Messrs. Sawyer and Bowen were also offered, and refused upon the same grounds.

Mr. A. L. BASCOM, of Ohio: "I move that the nominations now close, and that the House proceed to an election by ballot."

Mr. SAWYER: "Gentlemen,—I protest earnestly against these proceedings. They are, in every way, irregular and unbecoming. I must beg to move that they be dropped at once, and that we elect a chairman of the meeting and proper officers to assist him, and then we can go on with the business before us understandingly."

Mr. BELKNAP, of Iowa: "Gentlemen,—I object. This is no time to stand upon forms and ceremonious observances. For more than seven days we have been without food. Every moment we lose in idle discussion increases our distress. I am satisfied with the nominations that have been made—every gentleman present is, I believe—and I, for one, do not see why we should not proceed at once to elect one or more of them. I wish to offer a resolution—"

Mr. GASTON: "It would be objected to, and have to lie over one day under the rules, thus bringing about the very delay you wish to avoid. The gentleman from New Jersey—"

Mr. VAN NASTRAND: "Gentlemen, I am a stranger among you; I have not sought the distinction that has been conferred upon me, and I feel a delicacy."

Mr. MORGAN, of Alabama: "I move the previous question."

The motion was carried, and further debate shut off, of course. The motion to elect officers was passed, and under it Mr. Gaston was chosen Chairman, Mr. Blake, Secretary, Messrs. Holcomb, Dyer, and Baldwin, a Committee on nominations, and Mr. R. M. Howland, Purveyor, to assist the committee in making selections.

A recess of half an hour was then taken, and some little caucusing followed. At the sound of the gavel the meeting reassembled, and the committee reported in favour of Messrs. George Ferguson, of Kentucky, Lucien Hermann, of Louisiana, and W. Messick, of Colorado, as candidates. The report was accepted.

Mr. ROGERS, of Missouri: Mr. President,—The report being properly before the House now, I move to amend it by substituting for the name of Mr. Hermann that of Mr. Lucius Harris, of St. Louis, who is well and honourably known to us all. I do not wish to be understood as casting the least reflection upon the high character and standing of the gentleman from Louisiana—far from it. I respect and esteem him as much as any gentleman here present possibly can; but none of us can be blind to the fact that he has lost more flesh during the week that we have lain here than any among you—none of us can be blind to the fact that the committee has been derelict in its duty, either through negligence or a graver fault, in thus offering for our suffrages a gentleman who, however pure his own motives may be, has really less nutriment in him—

THE CHAIR: The gentleman from Missouri will take his seat. The Chair cannot allow the integrity of the Committee to be questioned save by the regular course, under the rules. What action will the House take upon the gentleman's motion?

Mr. HALLIDAY, of Virginia: I move to further amend the report by substituting Mr. Harvey Davis, of Oregon, for Mr. Messick. It may be urged by gentlemen that the hardships and privations of a frontier life have rendered Mr. Davis tough; but, gentlemen, is this a time to cavil at toughness? is this a time to be fastidious concerning trifles? is this a time to dispute about matters of paltry significance? No, gentlemen, bulk is what we desire—substance, weight, bulk—these are the supreme requisites now—not talent, not genius, not education. I insist upon my motion.

Mr. MORGAN (excitedly): Mr. Chairman,—I do most strenuously object to this amendment. The gentleman from Oregon is old, and furthermore is bulky only in bone—not in flesh. I ask the gentleman from Virginia if it is soup we want instead of solid sustenance? if he would delude us with shadows? if he would mock our suffering with an Oregonian spectre? I ask him if he can look upon the anxious faces around him, if he can gaze into our sad eyes, if he can listen to the beating of our expectant hearts, and still thrust this famine-stricken fraud upon us? I ask him if he can think of our desolate state, of our past sorrows, of our dark future, and still unpityingly foist upon us this wreck, this ruin, this tottering swindle, this gnarled and blighted and sapless vagabond from Oregon's inhospitable shores? Never! (Applause.)

The amendment was put to vote, after a fiery debate, and lost. Mr. Harris was substituted on the first amendment. The balloting then began. Five ballots were held without a choice. On the sixth, Mr. Harris was elected, all voting for him but himself. It was then moved that his

election should be ratified by acclamation, which was lost, in consequence of his again voting against himself.

Mr. RADWAY moved that the House now take up the remaining candidates, and go into an election for breakfast. This was carried.

On the first ballot there was a tie, half the members favouring one
candidate on account of his youth, and half favouring the other on
account of his superior size. The President gave the casting vote for the
latter, Mr. Messick. This decision created considerable dissatisfaction
among the friends of Mr. Ferguson, the defeated candidate, and there
was some talk of demanding a new ballot; but in the midst of it, a
motion to adjourn was carried, and the meeting broke up at once.

The preparations for supper diverted the attention of the Ferguson
faction from the discussion of their grievance for a long time, and
then, when they would have taken it up again, the happy announcement that Mr. Harris was ready, drove all thought of it to the winds.

We improvised tables by propping up the backs of car-seats, and sat
down with hearts full of gratitude to the finest supper that had blessed
our vision for seven torturing days. How changed we were from what
we had been a few short hours before! Hopeless, sad-eyed misery, hunger, feverish anxiety, desperation, then—thankfulness, serenity, joy
too deep for utterance now. That I know was the cheeriest hour of my
eventful life. The wind howled, and blew the snow wildly about our
prison-house, but they were powerless to distress us any more. I liked
Harris. He might have been better done, perhaps, but I am free to say
that no man ever agreed with me better than Harris, or afforded me so
large a degree of satisfaction. Messick was very well, though rather
high-flavoured, but for genuine nutritiousness and delicacy of fibre,
give me Harris. Messick had his good points—I will not attempt to
deny it, nor do I wish to do it—but he was no more fitted for breakfast
than a mummy would be, sir—not a bit. Lean?—why, bless me!—and
tough? Ah, he was very tough! You could not imagine it,—you could
never imagine anything like it.

"Do you mean to tell me that—"

Do not interrupt me, please. After breakfast we elected a man by the
name of Walker, from Detroit, for supper. He was very good. I wrote
his wife so afterwards. He was worthy of all praise. I shall always remember Walker. He was a little rare, but very good. And then the next
morning we had Morgan, of Alabama, for breakfast. He was one of
the finest men I ever sat down to,—handsome, educated, refined,
spoke several languages fluently—a perfect gentleman—he was a per-

fect gentleman, and singularly juicy. For supper we had that Oregon patriarch, and he *was* a fraud, there is no question about it—old, scraggy, tough—nobody can picture the reality. I finally said, gentlemen, you can do as you like, but *I* will wait for another election. And Grimes of Illinois, said, "Gentlemen, *I* will wait also. When you elect a man that has *something* to recommend him, I shall be glad to join you again." It soon became evident that there was general dissatisfaction with Davis, of Oregon, and so, to preserve the good-will that had prevailed so pleasantly since we had Harris, an election was called, and the result of it was that Baker, of Georgia, was chosen. He was splendid! Well, well—after that we had Doolittle and Hawkins, and McElroy (There was some complaint about McElroy, because he was uncommonly short and thin), and Penrod, and two Smiths, and Bailey (Bailey had a wooden leg, which was clear loss, but he was otherwise good), and an Indian boy, and an organ-grinder, and a gentleman by the name of Buckminster—a poor stick of a vagabond that wasn't any good for company and no account for breakfast. We were glad we got him elected before relief came.

"And so the blessed relief *did* come at last?"

Yes, it came one bright sunny morning, just after election. John Murphy was the choice, and there never was a better, I am willing to testify; but John Murphy came home with us, in the train that came to succour us, and lived to marry the widow Harris—

"Relict of—"

Relict of our first choice. He married her, and is happy and respected and prosperous yet. Ah, it was like a novel, sir—it was like a romance. This is my stopping-place, sir; I must bid you good-bye. Any time that you can make it convenient to tarry a day or two with me, I shall be glad to have you. I like you, sir; I have conceived an affection for you. I could like you as well as I liked Harris himself, sir. Good day, sir, and a pleasant journey."

He was gone. I never felt so stunned, so distressed, so bewildered in my life. But in my soul I was glad he was gone. With all his gentleness of manner and his soft voice, I shuddered whenever he turned his hungry eye upon me; and when I heard that I had achieved his perilous affection, and that I stood almost with the late Harris in his esteem, my heart fairly stood still!

I was bewildered beyond description. I did not doubt his word; I could not question a single item in a statement so stamped with the earnestness of truth as his; but its dreadful details overpowered me, and threw my thoughts into hopeless confusion.

I saw the conductor looking at me. I said, "Who is that man?"

"He was a member of Congress once, and a good one. But he got caught in a snowdrift in the cars, and like to been starved to death. He got so frost-bitten and frozen up generally, and used up for want of something to eat, that he was sick and out of his head two or three months afterwards. He is all right now, only he is a monomaniac, and when he gets on that old subject he never stops till he has eat up that whole car-load of people he talks about. He would have finished the crowd by this time, only he had to get out here. He has got their names as pat as A. B. C. When he gets them all eat up but himself, he always says:—'Then the hour for the usual election for breakfast having arrived, and there being no opposition, I was duly elected, after which, there being no objections offered, I resigned. Thus I am here.' "

I felt inexpressibly relieved to know that I had only been listening to the harmless vagaries of a madman, instead of the genuine experiences of a bloodthirsty cannibal.

Mark Twain on His Muscle

Emulating Macbeth, He Kills Duncan Over Again
The "Innocent" at Home Tells the Story of His Crimes
Abroad

To the Editor of *The World*.

Sir: I see by your report of a lecture delivered in your neighborhood recently, that a bit of my private personal history has been revealed to the public. The lecturer was head-waiter of the Quaker City Excursion of ten years ago. I do not repeat his name for the reason that I think he wants a little notoriety as a basis for introduction to the lecture platform, and I don't wish to contribute. I harbor this suspicion because he calls himself "captain" of that expedition.

The truth is, that as soon as the ship was fairly at sea, he was degraded from his captaincy by Mr. Leary (owner of the vessel) and Mr. Bunsley (executive officer.) As he was not a passenger, and had now ceased to be an officer, it was something of a puzzle to define his position. However, as he still had authority to discharge waiter-boys—an authority which the passengers did not possess—it was presently decided, privately, that he must naturally be the "head-waiter;" and thus was he dubbed. During the voyage he gave orders to none but his under-waiters; all the excursionists will testify to this. It may be humorous enough to call himself "captain," but then it is calculated to deceive the public.

The "captain" says that when I came to engage passage in the Quaker City I "seemed to be full of whiskey, or something," and filled his office with the "fumes of bad whiskey." I hope this is true, but I cannot say, because it is so long ago; at the same time I am not depraved enough to deny that for a ceaseless, tireless, forty-year public advocate of total abstinence the "captain" is a mighty good judge of whiskey at second-hand.

He charges that I couldn't tell the Quaker City tea from coffee. Am I a god, that I can solve the impossible?

He charges that I uttered a libel when I said he made this speech at a Fourth of July dinner on shipboard: "Ladies and gentlemen, may you all live long and prosper; steward, pass up another bottle of champagne."

Well, the truth is often a libel, and this may be one; yet it is the truth nevertheless. I did not publish it with malicious intent, but because it showed that even a total-abstinence gladiator can have gentle instincts when he is removed from hampering home influences.

The "captain" charges that when I came to his office to engage passage I represented myself to be a Baptist minister cruising after health. No; Mr. Edward H. House told him that, without giving me any warning, that he was going to do it. But no matter, I should have done it myself if I had thought of it. Therefore I lift this crime from Mr. House's shoulders and transfer it to mine. I was without conscience in those old days. It had been my purpose to represent that I was a son of the captain's whom he had never met, and consequently hadn't classified, and by this means I hoped to get a free passage; but I was saved from this great villainy by the happy accident of Mr. House's getting in his milder rascality ahead of me. I often shudder to think how near I came to saddling an old father on to myself forever whom I never could have made any use of after that excursion was finished. Still, if I had him now, I would make him lecture his head off at his customary 25 cents before I would support him in idleness. I consider idleness an immoral thing for the aged.

Certain of my friends in New York have been so distressed by the "captain's" charges against me that they have simply forced me to come out in print. But I find myself in a great difficulty by reason of the fact that I don't find anything in the charges that discomforts me. Why should I worry over the "bad whiskey?" I was poor—I couldn't afford good whiskey. How could I know that the "captain" was so particular about the quality of a man's liquor? I didn't know he was a purist in that matter, and that the difference between 5-cent and 40-cent toddy would remain a rankling memory with him for ten years.

The tea and champagne items do not trouble me—both being true and harmless. The Baptist minister fraud does not give me any anguish, since I did not invent it.

What I need now that I am going into print, is a text. These little things do not furnish it. Why does the "captain" make no mention of the highway robbery which I committed on the road between Damascus and the Dead Sea? He must have heard of it—the land was full of it. Why does he make no mention of the fact that during the entire excursion I never drew a sober breath except by proxy? Why does he conceal the fact that I killed a cripple in Caïro because I thought he had an unpleasant gait? Why is he silent about my skinning a leper in Smyrna in order that I might have a little something to start a museum with when I got home? What is the use of making "charges" out of a man's few little virtuous actions when that man has committed real indiscretions by the dozens?

But where is the use in bothering about what a man's character was ten years ago, anyway? Perhaps the "captain" values his character of ten years ago? I never have heard of any reason why he should; but still he may possibly value it. No matter. I do not value my character of ten years ago. I can go out any time and buy a better one for half it cost me. In truth, my character was simply in course of construction then. I hadn't anything up but the scaffolding, so to speak. But I have finished the edifice now and taken down that worm-eaten scaffolding. I have finished my moral edifice, and frescoed it and furnished it, and I am obliged to admit that it is one of the neatest and sweetest things of the kind that I have ever encountered. I greatly value it, and I would feel like resenting any damage done to it. But that old scaffolding is no longer of any use to me; and inasmuch as the "captain" seems able to use it to advantage, I hereby make him a present of it. It is a little shaky, of course, but if he will patch it here and there he will find that it is still superior to anything of the kind he can scare up upon his own premises.

⚜ John W. DeForest ⚜

John W. DeForest (1826–1906) of New Haven has attracted more attention than many of the writers in this collection because of his early realism in *Miss Ravenal's Conversion* (1867). James F. Light, in *John William DeForest* (New York, 1965), has described him as desperately seeking a style and consistent subject matter in a career tipping ambivalently from realism to romance writing, but the series of comic writings in the late 1860s and early 1870s is marked by a boldly defined sarcastic style that welds Miltonic allusions to democratic rhetoric. *Honest John Vane*—published in 1875 after running serially in the *Atlantic Monthly* in the fall of 1873—depicted a corruptible congressman with the moral sensitivity of a sparerib, a guerrilla fighter for the special interests, which DeForest saw as threatening the overthrow of democracy in the face of capitalists' demands for easy profits. "As the mountain brigands of Greece and the municipal highwaymen of New York can both testify—it is not the custom of some communities to execute justice upon criminals."

"An Inspired Lobbyist," reprinted here from the *Atlantic Monthly*, XXX (December, 1872), 676–84, like the later novel, packs burlesque, anticlimax, and repellent metaphor—greenbacks laid in a wallet like a corpse in a coffin—into a plot based on contemporary events, in this case the contest between Hartford and New Haven to be the permanent capitol of Connecticut. "The Colored Member," published in the *Galaxy* (1872), belongs with this group of comic political stories. DeForest corresponded with Mark Twain unsuccessfully about a joint volume of short stories at this time; despite the support of William Dean Howells, DeForest never achieved an outstanding success as a writer, and the darkly sarcastic melodramatized realism of his comic stories hardly offers enough of an optimistic vision to entice readers. James W. Gargano (ed.), *Critical Essays on John William DeForest* (Boston, 1981), is the first collection of criticism on DeForest, and

Joseph J. Rubin's Introduction in *Honest John Vane* (State College, Pa., 1960) is also valuable.

An Inspired Lobbyist

A certain fallen angel (politeness toward his numerous and influential friends forbids me to mention his name abruptly) lately entered into the body of Mr. Ananias Pullwool, of Washington, D.C.

As the said body was a capacious one, having been greatly enlarged circumferentially since it acquired its full longitude, there was accommodation in it for both the soul of Pullwool himself (it was a very little one) and for his distinguished visitant. Indeed, there was so much room in it that they never crowded each other, and that Pullwool hardly knew, if he even so much as mistrusted, that there was a chap in with him. But other people must have been aware of this double tenantry, or at least must have been shrewdly suspicious of it, for it soon became quite common to hear fellows say, "Pullwool has got the Devil in him."

There was, indeed, a remarkable change—a change not so much moral as physical and mental—in this gentleman's ways of deporting and behaving himself. From being logy in movement and slow if not absolutely dull in mind, he became wonderfully agile and energetic. He had been a lobbyist, and he remained a lobbyist still, but such a different one, so much more vigorous, eager, clever, and impudent, that his best friends (if he could be said to have any friends) scarcely knew him for the same Pullwool. His fat fingers were in the buttonholes of congressmen from the time when they put those buttonholes on in the morning to the time when they took them off at night. He seemed to be at one and the same moment treating some honorable member in the bar-room of the Arlington, and running another honorable member to cover in the committee-rooms of the Capitol. He log-rolled bills which nobody else believed could be log-rolled, and he pocketed fees which absolutely and point-blank refused to go into other people's pockets. During this short period of his life he was the most successful and famous lobbyist in Washington, and the most sought after by the most rascally and desperate claimants of unlawful millions.

But, like many another man who has the Devil in him, Mr. Pullwool ran his luck until he ran himself into trouble. An investigating committee pounced upon him; he was put in confinement for refusing to answer questions; his filchings were held up to the execration of the envious both by virtuous members and a virtuous press; and when he at last got out of durance he found it good to quit the District of Columbia for a season. Thus it happened that Mr. Pullwool and his eminent lodger took the cars and went to and fro upon the earth seeking what they might devour.

In the course of their travels they arrived in a little State, which may have been Rhode Island, or may have been Connecticut, or may have been one of the Pleiades, but which at all events had two capitals. Without regard to Morse's Gazetteer, or to whatever other Gazetteer may now be in currency, we shall affirm that one of these capitals was called Slowburg and the other Fastburg. For some hundreds of years (let us say five hundred, in order to be sure and get it high enough) Slowburg and Fastburg had shared between them, turn and turn about, year on and year off, all the gubernatorial and legislative pomps and emoluments that the said State had to bestow. On the 1st of April of every odd year, the governor, preceded by citizen soldiers, straddling or curvetting through the mud,—the governor, followed by twenty barouches full of eminent citizens, who were not known to be eminent at any other time, but who made a rush for a ride on this occasion as certain old ladies do at funerals,—the governor, taking off his hat to pavements full of citizens of all ages, sizes, and colors, who did not pretend to be eminent,—the governor, catching a fresh cold at every corner, and wishing the whole thing were passing at the equator,—the governor triumphally entered Slowburg,—observe, Slowburg—read his always enormously long message there, and convened the legislature there. On the 1st of April of every even year the same governor, or a better one who had succeeded him, went through the same ceremonies in Fastburg. Each of these capitals boasted, or rather blushed over, a shabby old barn of a State-House, and each of them maintained a company of foot-guards, and ditto of horse-guards, the latter very loose in their saddles. In each the hotels and boarding-houses had a full year and a lean year, according as the legislature sat in the one or in the other. In each there was a loud call for fresh shad and stewed oysters, or a comparatively feeble call for fresh shad and stewed oysters, under the same biennial conditions.

Such was the oscillation of grandeur and power between the two cities. It was an old-time arrangement, and like many other old-fashioned things, as for instance wood fires in open fireplaces, it had not only its substantial merits but its superficial inconveniences. Every year certain ancient officials were obliged to pack up hundreds of public documents and expedite them from Fastburg to Slowburg, or from Slowburg back to Fastburg. Every year there was an expense of a few dollars on this account, which the State treasurer figured up with agonies of terror, and which the opposition roared at as if the administration could have helped it. The State-Houses were two mere deformities of patched plaster and leprous whitewash; they were such shapeless, graceless, dilapidated wigwams, that no sensitive patriot could look at them without wanting to fly to the uttermost parts of the earth; and yet it was not possible to build new ones, and hardly possible to obtain appropriations enough to shingle out the weather; for Fastburg would vote no money to adorn Slowburg, and Slowburg was equally niggardly towards Fastburg. The same jealousy produced the same frugality in the management of other public institutions, so that the patients of the lunatic asylum were not much better lodged and fed than the average sane citizen, and the gallows-birds in the State's prison were brought down to a temperance which caused admirers of that species of fowl to tremble with indignation. In short, the two capitals were as much at odds as the two poles of a magnet, and the results of this repulsion were not all of them worthy of hysterical admiration.

But advantages seesawed with disadvantages. In this double-ender of a State, political jobbery was at fault, because it had no headquarters. It could not get together a ring; it could not raise a corps of lobbyists. Such few axe-grinders as there were had to dodge back and forth between the Fastburg grindstone and the Slowburg grindstone, without ever fairly getting their tools sharpened. Legislature here and legislature there; it was like guessing at a pea between two thimbles; you could hardly ever put your finger on the right one. Then what one capital favored the other disfavored; and between them appropriations were kicked and hustled under the table; the grandest of railroad schemes shrunk into waste-paper baskets; in short, the public treasury was next door to the unapproachable. Such, indeed, was the desperate condition of lobbyists in this State, that, had it contained a single philanthropist of the advanced radical stripe, he would surely have brought in a bill for their relief and encouragement.

Into the midst of this happily divided community dropped Mr. Ananias Pullwool with the Devil in him. It remains to be seen whether this pair could figure up anything worth pocketing out of the problem of two capitals.

It was one of the even years, and the legislature met in Fastburg, and

the little city was brimful. Mr. Pullwool with difficulty found a place
for himself without causing the population to slop over. Of course he
went to a hotel, for he needed to make as many acquaintances as possible, and he knew that a bar was a perfect hot-house for ripening such
friendships as he cared for. He took the best room he could get; and as
soon as chance favored, he took a better one, with parlor attached;
and on the sideboard in the parlor he always had cigars and decanters.
The result was that in a week or so he was on jovial terms with several
senators, numerous members of the lower house, and all the members
of the "third house." But lobbying did not work in Fastburg as
Mr. Pullwool had found it to work in other capitals. He exhibited the
most dazzling double-edged axes, but nobody would grind them; he
pointed out the most attractive and convenient of logs for rolling, but
nobody would put a lever to them.

"What the doose does this mean?" he at last inquired of Mr. Josiah
Dicker, a member who had smoked dozens of his cigars and drunk
quarts out of his decanters. "I don't understand this little old legislature at all, Mr. Dicker. Nobody wants to make any money; at least,
nobody has the spirit to try to make any. And yet the State is full;
never been bled a drop; full as a tick. What does it mean?"

Mr. Dicker looked disconsolate. Perhaps it may be worth a moment's time to explain that he could not well look otherwise. Broken
in fortune and broken in health, he was a failure and knew it. His large
forehead showed power, and he was in fact a lawyer of some ability;
and still he could not support his family, could not keep a mould of
mortgages from creeping all over his house-lot, and had so many creditors that he could not walk the streets comfortably. The trouble lay
in hard drinking, with its resultant waste of time, infidelity to trust,
and impatience of application. Thin, haggard, duskily pallid, deeply
wrinkled at forty, his black eyes watery and set in baggy circles of a
dull brown, his lean dark hands shaky and dirty, his linen wrinkled
and buttonless, his clothing frayed and unbrushed, he was an imper-
sonation of failure. He had gone into the legislature with a desperate
hope of somehow finding money in it, and as yet he had discovered
nothing more than his beggarly three dollars a day, and he felt himself
more than ever a failure. No wonder that he wore an air of profound
depression, approaching to absolute wretchedness and threatening
suicide.

He looked the more cast down by contrast with the successful Mr.
Pullwool, gaudily alight with satin and jewelry, and shining with con-

ceit. Pullwool, by the way, although a dandy (that is, such a dandy as one sees in gambling-saloons and behind liquor-bars), was far from being a thing of beauty. He was so obnoxiously gross and shapeless, that it seemed as if he did it on purpose and to be irritating. His fat head was big enough to make a dwarf of, hunchback and all. His mottled cheeks were vast and pendulous to that degree that they inspired the imaginative beholder with terror, as reminding him of avalanches and landslides which might slip their hold at the slightest shock, and plunge downward in a path of destruction. One puffy eyelid drooped in a sinister way; obviously that was the eye that the Devil had selected for his own; he kept it well curtained for purposes of concealment. Looking out of this peep-hole, the Satanic badger could see a short, thick nose, and by leaning forward a little, he could get a glimpse of a broad chin of several stories. Another unpleasing feature was a full set of false teeth, which grinned in a ravenous fashion that was truly disquieting, as if they were capable of devouring the whole internal revenue. Finally, this continent of a physiognomy was diversified by a gigantic hairy wart, which sprouted defiantly from the temple nearest the game eye, as though Lucifer had accidentally ,poked one of his horns through. Mr. Dicker, who was a sensitive, squeamish man (as drunkards sometimes are, through bad digestion and shaky nerves), could hardly endure the sight of this wart, and always wanted to ask Pullwool why he didn't cut it off.

"What's the meaning of it all?" persisted the Washington wire-puller with bland superiority, much as the city mouse may have surveyed the country mouse.

"Two capitals," responded Dicker, withdrawing his nervous glance from the wart, and locking his hands over one knee to quiet their trembling.

Mr. Pullwool, having the Old Harry in him, and being consequently full of all malice and subtlety, perceived at once the full scope and force of the explanation.

"I see," he said, dropping gently back into his arm-chair, with the plethoric, soft movement of a subsiding pillow. The puckers of his cumbrous eyelids drew a little closer together; his bilious eyes peered out cautiously between them, like sallow assassins watching through curtained windows; for a minute or so he kept up what might without hyperbole be called a devil of a thinking.

"I've got it," he broke out at last. "Dicker, I want you to bring in a bill to make Fastburg the only capital."

"What is the use?" asked the legislator, looking more disconsolate, more hopeless than ever. "Slowburg will oppose it and beat it."

"Never you mind," persisted Mr. Pullwool. "You bring in your little bill and stand up for it like a man. There's money in it. You don't see it? Well, I do; I'm used to seeing money in things; and in this case I see it plain. As sure as whiskey is whiskey, there's money in it."

Mr. Pullwool's usually dull and, so to speak, extinct countenance was fairly alight and aflame with exultation. It was almost a wonder that his tallowy person did not gutter beneath the blaze, like an over-fat candle under the flaring of a wick too large for it.

"Well, I'll bring in the bill," agreed Mr. Dicker, catching the enthusiasm of his counsellor and shaking off his lethargy. He perceived a dim promise of fees, and at the sight his load of despondency dropped away from him, as Christian's burden loosened in presence of the cross. He looked a little like the confident, resolute Tom Dicker, who twenty years before had graduated from college, the brightest, bravest, most eloquent fellow in his class, and the one who seemed to have before him the finest future.

"Snacks!" said Mr. Pullwool.

At this brazen word Mr. Dicker's countenance fell again; he was ashamed to talk so frankly about plundering his fellow-citizens; "a little grain of conscience turned him sour."

"I will take pay for whatever I can do as a lawyer," he stammered.

"Get out!" laughed the Satanic one. "You just take all there is a going! You need it bad enough. I know when a man's hard up. I know the signs. I've been as bad off as you; had to look all ways for five dollars; had to play second fiddle and say thanky. But what I offer you ain't a second fiddle. It's as good a chance as my own. Even divides. One half to you, and one half to me. You know the people and I know the ropes. It's a fair bargain. What do you say?"

Mr. Dicker thought of his decayed practice and his unpaid bills; and, flipping overboard his little grain of conscience, he said, "Snacks."

"All right," grinned Pullwool, his teeth gleaming alarmingly. "Word of a gentleman," he added, extending his pulpy hand, loaded with ostentatious rings, and grasping Dicker's recoiling fingers. "Harness up your little bill as quick as you can and drive it like Jehu. Fastburg to be the only capital. Slowburg no claims at all, historical, geographical, or economic. The old arrangement a humbug; as inconvenient as a fifth wheel of a coach; costs the State thousands of greenbacks every year. Figure it all up statistically and dab it over with your shiniest rhetoric and make a big thing of it every way. That's what you've got to do; that's your little biz. I'll tend to the rest."

"I don't quite see where the money is to come from," observed Mr. Dicker.

"Leave that to me," said the veteran of the lobbies; "my name is Pullwool and I know how to pull the wool over men's eyes, and then I know how to get at their britches-pockets. You bring in your bill and make your speech. Will you do it?"

"Yes," answered Dicker, bolting all scruples in another half-tumbler of brandy.

He kept his word. As promptly as parliamentary forms and mysteries would allow, there was a bill under the astonished noses of honorable lawgivers, removing the seat of legislation from Slowburg and centring it in Fastburg. This bill Mr. Thomas Dicker supported with that fluency and fiery enthusiasm of oratory which had for a time enabled him to show as the foremost man of his State. Great was the excitement, great the rejoicing and anger. The press of Fastburg sent forth shrieks of exultation, and the press of Slowburg responded with growlings of disgust. The two capitals and the two geographical sections which they represented were ready to fire Parrot guns at each other, without regard to life and property in the adjoining regions of the earth. If there was a citizen of the little Commonwealth who did not hear of this bill and did not talk of it, it was because that citizen was as deaf as a post and as dumb as an oyster. Ordinary political distinctions were forgotten, and the old party-whips could not manage their very wheel-horses, who went snorting and kicking over the traces in all directions. In short, both in the legislature and out of it, nothing was thought of but the question of the removal of the capital.

Among the loudest of the agitators was Mr. Pullwool; not that he cared one straw whether the capital went to Fastburg, or to Slowburg, or to Ballyhack; but for the money which he thought he saw in the agitation he did care mightily, and to get that money he labored with a zeal which was not of this world alone. At the table of his hotel and in the bar-room of the same institution and in the lobbies of the legislative hall and in editorial sanctums and barbers' shops and all other nooks of gossip, he trumpeted the claims of Fastburg as if that little city were the New Jerusalem and deserved to be the metropolis of the sidereal universe. All sorts of trickeries, too; he sent spurious telegrams and got fictitious items into the newspapers; he lied through every medium known to the highest civilization. Great surely was his success, for the row which he raised was tremendous. But a row alone was not enough; it was the mere breeze upon the surface of the waters; the treasure-ship below was still to be drawn up and gutted.

"It will cost money," he whispered confidentially to capitalists and land-owners. "We must have the sinews of war, or we can't carry it on. There's your city lots goin' to double in value, if this bill goes through. What per cent will you pay on the advance? That's the question. Put your hands in your pockets and pull 'em out full, and put back ten times as much. It's a sure investment; warranted to yield a hundred per cent; the safest and biggest thing agoing."

Capitalists and land-owners and merchants harkened and believed and subscribed. The slyest old hunks in Fastburg put a faltering fore-finger into his long pocket-book, touched a greenback which had been laid away there as neatly as a corpse in its coffin, and resurrected it for the use of Mr. Pullwool. By tens, by twenties, by fifties, and by hundreds the dollars of the ambitious citizens of the little metropolis were charmed into the porte monnaie of this rattlesnake of a lobbyist.

"I never saw a greener set," chuckled Pullwool. "By jiminy, I believe they'd shell out for a bill to make their town a seaport, if it was a hundred miles from a drop of water."

But he was not content with individual subscriptions, and conscientiously scorned himself until he had got at the city treasury.

"The corporation must pony up," he insisted, with the mayor. "This bill is just shaking in the wind for lack of money. Fastburg must come down with the dust. You ought to see to it. What are you chief magistrate for? Ain't it to tend to the welfare of the city? Look here, now; you call the common council together; secret session, you understand. You call 'em together and let me talk to 'em. I want to make the loons comprehend that it's their duty to vote something handsome for this measure."

The mayor hummed and hawed one way, and then he hawed and hummed the other way, and the result was that he granted the request. There was a secret session in the council-room, with his honor at the top of the long, green table, with a row of more or less respectable functionaries on either side of it, and with Mr. Pullwool and the Devil at the bottom. Of course, it is not to be supposed that this last-named personage was visible to the others, or that they had more than a vague suspicion of his presence. Had he fully revealed himself, had he plainly exhibited his horns and hoofs, or even so much as uncorked his perfume-bottle of brimstone, it is more than probable that the city authorities would have been exceedingly scandalized, and they might have adjourned the session. As it was, seeing nothing more disagreeable than the obese form of the lobbyist, they listened calmly while he unfolded his project.

Mr. Pullwool spoke at length, and to Fastburg ears eloquently, Fastburg must be the sole capital; it had every claim, historical and geographical, and commercial, to that distinction; it ought, could, would, and should be the sole capital; that was about the substance of his exordium.

"But, gentlemen, it will cost," he went on. "There is an unscrupulous and furious opposition to the measure. The other side—those fellows from Slowburg and vicinity—are putting their hands into their britches-pockets. You must put your hands into yours. The thing will be worth millions to Fastburg. But it will cost thousands. Are you ready to fork over? *Are* you ready?"

"What's the figure?" asked one of the councilmen. "What do you estimate?"

"Gentlemen, I shall astonish *some* of you," answered Mr. Pullwool, cunningly. It was well put; it was as much as to say, "I shall astonish the green ones; of course, the really strong heads among you won't be in the least bothered." "I estimate," he continued, "that the city treasury will have to put up a good round sum, say a hundred thousand dollars, be it more or less."

A murmur of surprise, of chagrin, and of something like indignation ran along the line of official mustaches. "Nonsense," "The dickens," "Can't be done," "We can't think of it," broke out several councilmen, in a distinctly unparliamentary manner.

"Gentlemen, one moment," pleaded Pullwool, passing his greasy smile around the company, as though it were some kind of refreshment. "Look at the whole job; it's a big job. We must have lawyers; we must have newspapers in all parts of the State; we must have writers to work up the historical claims of the city; we must have fellows to buttonhole honorable members; we must have fees for honorable members themselves. How can you do it for less?"

Then he showed a schedule; so much to this wire-puller and that and the other; so much apiece to so many able editors; so much for eminent legal counsel; finally, a trifle for himself. And one hundred thousand dollars or thereabouts was what the schedule footed up, turn it whichever way you would.

Of course, this common council of Fastburg did not dare to vote such a sum for such a purpose. Mr. Pullwool had not expected that it would; all that he had hoped for was the half of it; but that half he got.

"Did they do it?" breathlessly inquired Tom Dicker of him, when he returned to the hotel.

"They done it," calmly, yet triumphantly, responded Mr. Pullwool.

"Thunder!" exclaimed the amazed Dicker. "You are the most extraordinary man! You must have the very Devil in you!"

Instead of being startled by this alarming supposition, Mr. Pullwool looked gratified. People thus possessed generally do look gratified when the possession is alluded to.

But the inspired lobbyist did not pass his time in wearing an aspect of satisfaction. When there was money to get and to spend he could run his fat off almost as fast as if he were pouring it into candle-moulds. The ring—the famous capital ring of Fastburg—must be seen to, its fingers greased, and its energy quickened. Before he rolled his apple-dumpling of a figure into bed that night, he had interviewed Smith and Brown the editors, Jones and Robinson the lawyers, Smooth and Slow the literary characters, various lobbyists and various lawgivers.

"Work, gentlemen, and capitalize Fastburg and get your dividends," was his inspiring message to one and all. He promised Smith and Brown ten dollars for every editorial, and five dollars for every humbugging telegram, and two dollars for every telling item. Jones and Robinson were to have five hundred dollars apiece for concurrent legal statements of the claim of the city; Smooth and Slow, as being merely authors and so not accustomed to obtain much for their labor, got a hundred dollars between them for working up the case historically. To the lobbyists and members Pullwool was munificent; it seemed as if those gentlemen could not be paid enough for their "influence"; as if they alone had that kind of time which is money. Only, while dealing liberally with them, the inspired one did not forget himself. A thousand for Mr. Sly; yes, Mr. Sly was to receipt for a thousand; but he must let half of it stick to the Pullwool fingers. The same arrangement was made with Mr. Green and Mr. Sharp and Mr. Bummer and Mr. Pickpurse and Mr. Buncombe. It was a game of snacks, half to you and half to me; and sometimes it was more than snacks,—a thousand for you two and a thousand for me too.

With such a greasing of the wheels, you may imagine that the machinery of the ring worked to a charm. In the city and in the legislature and throughout the State there was the liveliest buzzing and humming and clicking of political wheels and cranks and cogs that had ever been known in those hitherto pastoral localities. The case of Fastburg against Slowburg was put in a hundred ways and proved as sure as it was put. It really seemed to the eager burghers as if they already heard the clink of hammers on a new State-House and beheld a perpetual legislature sitting on their fences and curbstones until the edifice should be finished. The great wire-puller and his gang of stipendiaries were the objects of popular gratitude and adoration. The landlord of the hotel which Mr. Pullwool patronized actually would not take pay for that gentleman's board.

"No, sir!" declared this simple Boniface, turning crimson with enthusiasm. "You are going to put thousands of dollars into my purse, and I'll take nothing out of yours. And any little thing in the way of cigars and whiskey that you want, sir, why, call for it. It's my treat, sir."

"Thank you, sir," kindly smiled the great man. "That's what I call the square thing. Mr. Boniface, you are a gentleman and a scholar; and I'll mention your admirable house to my friends. By the way, I shall have to leave you for a few days."

"Going to leave us!" exclaimed Mr. Boniface, aghast. "I hope not till this job is put through."

"I must run about a bit," muttered Pullwool, confidentially. "A little turn through the State, you understand, to stir up the country districts. Some of the members ain't as hot as they should be, and I want to set their constituents after them. Nothing like getting on a few deputations."

"O, exactly!" chuckled Mr. Boniface, ramming his hands into his pockets and cheerfully jingling a bunch of keys and a penknife, for lack of silver. It was strange indeed that he should actually see the Devil in Mr. Pullwool's eye and should not have a suspicion that he was in danger of being humbugged by him. "And your rooms?" he suggested. "How about them?"

"I keep them," replied the lobbyist, grandly, as if blaspheming the expense—to Boniface. "Our friends must have a little hole to meet in. And while you are about it, Mr. Boniface, see that they get something to drink and smoke; and we'll settle it between us."

"Pre-cisely!" laughed the landlord, as much as to say, "My treat!"

And so Mr. Pullwool, that Pericles and Lorenzo de' Medici rolled in one, departed for a season from the city which he ruled and blessed. Did he run about the State and preach and crusade in behalf of Fastburg, and stir up the bucolic populations to stir up their representatives in its favor? Not a bit of it; the place that he went to and the only place that he went to was Slowburg; yes, covering up his tracks in his usual careful style, he made direct for the rival of Fastburg. What did he propose to do there? O, how can we reveal the whole duplicity and turpitude of Ananias Pullwool? The subject is too vast for a merely human pen; it requires the literary ability of a recording angel. Well, we must get our feeble lever under this boulder of wickedness as we can, and do our faint best to expose all the reptiles and slimy things beneath it.

The first person whom this apostle of lobbyism called upon in Slowburg was the mayor of that tottering capital.

"My name is Pullwool," he said to the official, and he said it with an almost enviable ease of impudence, for he was used to introducing himself to people who despised and detested him. "I want to see you confidentially about this capital ring which is making so much trouble."

"I thought you were in it," replied the mayor, turning very red in the face, for he had heard of Mr. Pullwool as the leader of said ring; and being an iracund man, he was ready to knock his head off.

"In it!" exclaimed the possessed one. "I wish I was. It's a fat thing. More than fifty thousand dollars paid out already!"

"Good gracious!" exclaimed the mayor, in despair.

"By the way, this is between ourselves," added Pullwool. "You take it so, I hope. Word of honor, eh?"

"Why, if you have anything to communicate that will help us, why, of course I promise secrecy," stammered the mayor. "Yes, certainly; word of honor."

"Well, I've been looking about among those fellows a little," continued Ananias. "I've kept my eyes and ears open. It's a way I have. And I've learned a thing or two that it will be to your advantage to know. Yes, sir! fifty thousand dollars!—the city has voted it and paid it, and the ring has got it. That's why they are all working so. And depend upon it, they'll carry the legislature and turn Slowburg out to grass, unless you wake up and do something."

"By heavens!" exclaimed the iracund mayor, turning red again. "It's a piece of confounded rascality. It ought to be exposed."

"No, don't expose it," put in Mr. Pullwool, somewhat alarmed. "That game never works. Of course they'd deny it and swear you down, for bribing witnesses is as easy as bribing members. I'll tell you what to do. Beat them at their own weapons. Raise a purse that will swamp theirs. That's the way the world goes. It's an auction. The highest bidder gets the article."

Well, the result of it all was that the city magnates of Slowburg did just what had been done by the city magnates of Fastburg, only, instead of voting fifty thousand dollars into the pockets of the ring, they voted sixty thousand. With a portion of this money about him, and with authority to draw for the rest on proper vouchers, Mr. Pullwool, his tongue in his cheek, bade farewell to his new allies. As a further proof of the ready wit and solid impudence of this sublime politician and model of American statesmen, let me here introduce a brief anecdote. Leaving Slowburg by the cars, he encountered a gentleman from Fastburg, who saluted him with tokens of amazement, and said, "What are you doing here, Mr. Pullwool?"

"O, just breaking up these fellows a little," whispered the man with the Devil in him. "They were making too strong a fight. I had to *see* some of them," putting one hand behind his back and rubbing his fingers together, to signify that there had been a taking of bribes. "But be shady about it. For the sake of the good cause, keep quiet. Mum's the word."

The reader can imagine how briskly the fight between the two capitals re-opened when Mr. Pullwool re-entered the lobby. Slowburg now had its adherents, and they struggled like men who saw money in their warfare, and they struggled not in vain. To cut a very long story very short, to sum the whole of an exciting drama in one sentence, the legislature kicked overboard the bill to make Fastburg the sole seat of government. Nothing had come of the whole row, except that the pair of simple little cities had spent over one hundred thousand dollars, and that the capital ring, fighting on both sides and drawing pay from both sides, had lined its pockets, while the great creator of the ring had crammed his to bursting.

"What does this mean, Mr. Pullwool?" demanded the partially honest and entirely puzzled Tom Dicker, when he had discovered by an unofficial count of noses how things were going. "Fastburg has spent all its money for nothing. It won't be sole capital after all."

"I never expected it would be," replied Pullwool, so tickled by the

Devil that was in him that he could not help laughing. "I never wanted it to be. Why, it would spoil the little game. This is a trick that can be played every year."

"Oh!!" exclaimed Mr. Dicker, and was dumb with astonishment for a minute.

"Didn't you see through it before?" grinned the grand master of all guile and subtlety.

"I did not," confessed Mr. Dicker, with a mixture of shame and abhorrence. "Well," he presently added, recovering himself, "shall we settle?"

"O, certainly, if you are ready," smiled Pullwool, with the air of a man who has something coming to him.

"And what, exactly, will be my share?" asked Dicker, humbly.

"What do you mean?" stared Pullwool, apparently in the extremity of amazement.

"You said *snacks*, didn't you?" urged Dicker, trembling violently.

"Well, *snacks* it is," replied Pullwool. "Haven't you had a thousand?"

"Yes," admitted Dicker.

"Then you owe me five hundred?"

Mr. Dicker did not faint, though he came very near it, but he staggered out of the room as white as a sheet, for he was utterly crushed by this diabolical impudence.

That very day Mr. Pullwool left for Washington, and the Devil left for *his* place, each of them sure to find the other when he wanted him, if indeed their roads lay apart.

Marietta Holley (Josiah Allen's Wife)

Marietta Holley (1836–1926), an unmarried champion of women's suffrage who wrote under the name of "Josiah Allen's Wife," published twenty-one volumes of humorous Samantha Allen stories and travel narratives, beginning in 1873 with *My Adventures and Betsey Bobbet's*—published by the American Publishing Company, which had successfully merchandized Twain's volumes by door-to-door subscription sales. As a "wimmin's rights" reformer, Holley stood for equality of the sexes and equal rights for all, but stories like Jenette Finster's adhere to Victorian humorous stereotypes. The hero, Joe, is a little boy mothered and controlled by the long-suffering Jenette. Although Holley seldom left her home in upstate New York, the peripatetic Samantha applied her critical eye to the social issues of slavery in the South and meanness and social irresponsibility in a wide variety of national and even international situations.

"Jenette Finster's Story," reprinted from *Samantha Among the Brethren* (New York, 1890), focuses on the "happy" outcome of self-interest and religious delusion when corrected by the natural flow of events. The nonoccurrence of the judgment day is but a grotesque intrusion subordinated to localist values and sympathies that Samantha embodies as observer. Holley was a sophisticated and even haughtily aristocratic dowager by the standards of her neighbors; yet her preference for simplistic reverence and individual restraint caused her popularity to wane rapidly at the turn of the century, when changing agricultural conditions and the diminishing quality of village life established the conditions for the revolt-from-the-village school of writers. Katherine Blyly's "Marietta Holley" (Ph.D. dissertation, University of Pittsburgh, 1936) remains definitive, and an essay on Holley appears in *American Humorists, 1800–1950* (Detroit, 1982).

Jenette Finster's Story

Chapter XII

Submit wuz very skairt to heern him go on (she felt more nervus on account of an extra hard day's work), and I myself wuz beat out, but I wuzn't afraid at all of him, though he did go on elegant, and dretful empressive and even skairful.

He stood up on the same old ground that men have aleys stood up on, the ground of man's great strength and capability, and wimmen's utter weekness, helplessness, and incapacity. Josiah enlarged almost wildly on the subject of how high, how inaccessibley lofty the Conference wuz, and the utter impossibility of a weak, helpless, fragile bein' like a women ever gettin' up on it, much less settin' on it.

And then, oh how vividly he depictered it, how he and every other male Methodist in the land loved wimmen too well, worshipped 'em too deeply to put such a wearin' job onto 'em. Oh how Josiah Allen soared up in eloquence. Submit shed tears, or, that is, I thought she did—I see her wipe her eyes any way. Some think that about the time the Samuel Danher anniversary comes round, she is more nervus and depressed. It wuz very near now, and take that with her hard work that day, it accounts some for her extra depression—though, without any doubt, it wuz Josiah's talk that started the tears.

I couldn't bear to see Submit look so mournful and depressed, and so, though I wuz that tired myself that I could hardly hold my head up, yet I did take my bits in my teeth, es you may say, and asked him—

What the awful hard job wuz that he and other men wuz so anxus to ward offen wimmen.

And he sez, "Why, a settin' on the Conference."

And I sez, "I don't believe that is such a awful hard job to tackle."

"Yes, indeed, it is," sez Josiah in his most skairful axent, "yes, it is."

And he shook his head meenin'ly and impressively, and looked at me and Submit in as mysterius and strange a way, es I have ever been looked at in my life, and I have had dretful curius looks cast onto me, from first to last. And he sez in them deep impressive axents of hisen.

"You jest try it once, and see—I have sot on it, and I know."

Josiah wuz sent once as a delegate to the Methodist Conference, so I spozed he did know.

But I sez, "Why you come home the secent day when you sot as

"The Methodist Conference had decided that wimmen wuz to weak to set."
As the women labor to renovate their church building, male elders burst in
with the news that the Methodist Conference has decided that women are too
weak to sit in conference on complicated church matters.

happy as a king, and you told me how you had rested off durin' the
two days, and how you had visited round at Uncle Jenkins'es, and
Cousin Vunn's, and you said that you never had had such a good time
in your hull life, es you did when you wuz a settin'. You looked es
happy es a king, and acted so."

Josiah looked dumbfounded for most a quarter of a minute. For he
knew my words wuz as true es anything ever sot down in Matthew,
Mark, or Luke, or any of the other old patriarks. He knew it wuz Gos-
pel truth, that he had boasted of his good times a settin', and es I

say for nearly a quarter of a minute he showed plain signs of mortification.

But almost imegietly he recovered himself, and went on with the doggy obstinacy of his sect:

"Oh, wall! Men can tackle hard jobs, and get some enjoyment out of it too, when it is in the line of duty. One thing that boys em' up, and makes em' happy, is the thought that they are a keepin' trouble and care offen wimmen. That is a sweet thought to men, and always wuz. And there wuz great strains put onto our minds, us men that sot, that wimmen couldn't be expected to grapple with, and hadn't ort to try to. It wuz a great strain onto us."

"What was the nater of the strain?" sez I. "I didn't know as you did a thing only sot still there and go to sleep. You wuz fast asleep there most the hull of the time, for it come straight to me from them that know. And all that Deacon Bobbet did who went with you wuz to hold up his hand two or three times a votin'. I shouldn't think that wuz so awful wearin'."

And agin I sez, "What wuz the strain?"

But Josiah didn't answer, for that very minute he remembered a pressin' engagement he had about borrowin' a plow. He said he had got to go up to Joe Charnick's to get his plow. (*I* don't believe he wanted a plow that time of night.)

But he hurried away from the spot. And soon after Submit went home lookin' more depressed and down-casted than ever.

And Josiah Allen didn't get home till *late* at night. I dare presume to say it wuz as late as a quarter to nine when that man got back to the bosom of his family.

And I sot there all alone, and a-meditatin' on things, and a-wonderin' what under the sun he wuz a-traipsin up to Joe Charnick's for at that time of night, and a-worryin' some for fear he wuz a-keepin' Miss Charnick up, and a-spozin' in my mind what Miss Charnick would do, to get along with the meetin' house, and the Conference question, if she wuz a member. (She is a *very* sensible woman, Jenette Charnick is, *very*, and a great favorite with me, and others.)

And I got to thinkin' how prosperus and happy she is now, and how much she had went through. And I declare the hull thing come back to me, all the strange and curius circumstances connected with her courtship and marriage, and I thought it all out agin, the hull story, from beginnin' to end.

The way it begun wuz—and the way Josiah Allen and me come to have any connectin with the story wuz as follers:

Some time ago, and previus, we had a widder come to stay with us a spell, she that wuz Tamer Shelmadine, Miss Trueman Pool that now is.

Her husband died several years ago, and left her not over and above well off. And so she goes round a-visitin', and has went ever sense his death. And finds sights of faults with things wherever she is, sights of it.

Trueman wuz Josiah's cousin, on his own side, and I always made a practice of usin' her quite well. She used to live neighbor to me before I wuz married, and she come and stayed nine weeks.

She is a tall spindlin' woman, a Second Adventist by perswasion, and weighs about ninety-nine pounds.

Wall, as I say, she means middlin' well, and would be quite agreeable if it wuzn't for a habit she has of thinkin' what she duz is a leetle better than anybody else can do, and wantin' to tell a leetle better story than anybody else can.

Now she thinks she looks better than I do. But Josiah sez she can't begin with me for looks, an I don't spoze she can, though of course it hain't to be expected that I would want it told of that I said so. No, I wouldn't want it told of pro or con, especially con. But I know Josiah Allen has always been called a pretty good judge of wimmen's looks.

And now she thinks she can set hens better than I can—and make better riz biscuit. She jest the same as told me so. Any way, the first time I baked bread after she got here, she looked down on my loaves real haughty, yet with a pityin' look, and sez:

"It is very good for yeast, but I always use milk emptin's."

And she kinder tosted her head, and sort o' swept out of the room, not with a broom, no, she would scorn to sweep out a room with a broom or help me in any way, but she sort o' swept it out with her mean. But I didn't care, I knew my bread wuz good.

Now if anybody is rich, she will always tell of times when she has been richer. She boasts of layin' three nights and two days in a fit. But we don't believe it, Josiah and me don't. That is, we don't believe she lay there so long, a-runnin', so she sez, and she has said it so long, that we spoze, Josiah and me do, that she believes it herself now.

Chapter XIII

Curius, hain't it? How folks will get to tellin' things, and finally tell 'em so much, that finally they will get to believin' of 'em themselves—boastin' of bein' rich, etc., or bad. Now I have seen folks boast over that, act real haughty because they had been bad and got over it. We seen temperance lectures and religious exhorters boast sights and sights over how bad they had been. But they wuzn't tellin' the truth, though they had told the same thing so much that probable they had got to thinkin' so.

But in the case of one man in pertickuler, I found out for myself, for I didn't believe what he wuz a sayin' any of the time.

Why, he made out in evenin' meetin's, protracted and otherwise, that he had been a awful villain. Why no pirate wuz ever wickeder than he made himself out to be, in the old times before he turned round and become pious.

But I didn't believe it, for he had a good look to his face, all but the high headed look he had, and sort o' vain.

But except this one look, his face wuz a good moral face, and I knew that no man could cut up and act as he claimed that he had, without carryin' some marks on the face of the cuttin' up, and also of the actin'.

And so, as it happened, I went a visitin' (to Josiah's relations) to the very place where he had claimed to do his deeds of wild badness, and I found that he had always been a pattern man—never had done a single mean act, so fur as wuz known.

Where wuz his boastin' then? As the Bible sez, why, it wuz all vain talk. He had done it to get up a reputation. He had done it because he wuz big feelin' and vain. And he had got so haughty over it, and had told of it so much, that I spoze he believed in it himself.

Curius! hain't it? But I am a eppisodin', and to resoom. Trueman's wife would talk jest so, jest so haughty and high headed, about the world comin' to a end.

She'd dispute with everybody right up and down if they disagreed with her—and specially about that religion of hern. How sot she wuz, how extremely sot.

But then, it hain't in me, nor never wuz, to fight anybody for any pertickuler religion of theirn.

There is sights and sights of different religions round amongst different friends of mine, and most all on 'em quite good ones.

That is, they are agreeable to the ones who believe in 'em, and not over and above disagreeable to me.

Now it seems to me that in most all of these different doctrines and beliefs, there is a grain of truth, and if folks would only kinder hold onto that grain, and hold themselves stiddy while they held onto it, they would be better off.

But most folks when they go to follerin' off a doctrine, they foller too fur, they hain't megum enough.

Now, for instance, when you go to work and whip anybody, or hang 'em, or burn 'em up for not believin' as you do, that is goin' too fur.

It has been done though, time and agin, in the world's history, and mebby will be agin.

But it hain't reasonable. Now what good will doctrines o' any kind do to anybody after they are burnt up or choked to death?

You see such things hain't bein' megum. Because I can't believe jest as somebody else duz, it hain't for me to pitch at 'em and burn 'em up, or even whip 'em.

No, indeed! And most probable if I should study faithfully out their beliefs, I would find one grain, or mebby a grain and a half of real truth in it.

Now, for instance, take the doctrines of Christi'n Healin', or Mind Cure.

Now I can't exactly believe that ef I fell down and hurt my head on a stun—I cannot believe as I am a layin' there, that I hain't fell, and there hain't no stun—and while I am a groanin' 'and a bathin' the achin' bruise in anarky and wormwood, I can't believe that there hain't no such thing as pain, nor never wuz.

No, I can't believe this with the present light I have got on the subject.

But yet, I have seen them that this mind cure religion had fairly riz right up, and made 'em nigher to heaven every way—so nigh to it that seemin'ly a light out of some of its winders had lit up their faces with its glowin' repose, its sweet rapture.

We seen 'em, seen 'em as the Patent Medicine Maker observes so frequently, "before and after takin'."

Folks that wuz despondent and hopeless, and wretched actin', why, this belief made 'em jest blossom right out into a state of hopefulness, and calmness, and joy—refreshin' indeed to contemplate.

Wall now, the idee of whippin' anybody for believin' anything that brings such a good change to 'em, and fills them and them round 'em with so much peace and happiness.

Why, I wouldn't do it for a dollar bill. And as for hangin' 'em, and brilin' 'em on gridirons, etc., why, that is entirely out of the question, or ort to be.

And now, it don't seem to me that I ever could make a tree walk off, by lookin' at it, and commandin' it to—or call some posys to fall down into my lap, right through the plasterin'—

Or send myself, or one of myselfs, off to Injy, while the other one of me stayed to Jonesville.

Now, honestly speakin', it don't seem to me that I ever could learn to do this, not at my age, any way, and most dead with rheumatiz a good deal of the time.

I most know I couldn't.

But then agin I have seen believers in Theosipey that could do wonders, and seemed indeed to have got marvelous control over the forces of Natur.

And now the idee of my whippin' 'em for it. Why you wouldn't ketch me at it.

And Speritualism now! I spoze, and I about know that there are lots of folks that won't ever see into any other world than this, till the breath leaves their body.

Yet we seen them pure sweet souls too, es I ever see, where eyes beheld blessed visions withheld from more material gaze.

Yes, we neighbored with about all sorts of religius believers, and never disputed that they had a right to their own religion.

And we seen them too that didn't make a practice of goin' to any meetin' houses much, who lived so near to God and his angels that they felt the touch of angel hands on their forwards every day of their lives, and you could see the glow of the Fairer Land in their rapt eyes.

They had outgrown the outward forms of religion that had helped them at first, jest as children outgrow the primers and A B C books of their childhood and advance into the higher learnin'.

We seen them folks we neighbored with 'em. Human faults they had, or God would have taken them to His own land before now. Their imperfections, I spoze sort o' anchored 'em here for a spell to a imperfect world.

But you could see, if you got nigh enough to their souls to see anything about 'em—you could see that the anchor chains wuz slight after all, and when they wuz broke, oh how lightly and easily they would sail away, away to the land that their rapt souls inhabited even now.

Yes, we seen all sorts of religius believers and I wuzn't goin' to be too hard on Tamer for her belief, though I couldn't believe es she did.

Chapter XIV

She come to our house a visitin' along the first week in June, and the last day in June wuz the day they had sot for the world to come to an end. I, myself, didn't believe she knew positive about it, and Josiah didn't either. And I sez to her, "The Bible sez that it hain't agoin' to be revealed to angels even, or to the Son himself, but only to the Father when that great day shall be." And sez I to Trueman's wife, sez I, "How should *you* be expected to know it?"

Sez she, with that same collected together haughty look to her, "My name wuzn't mentioned, I believe, amongst them that *wuzn't* to know it!"

And of course I had to own up that it wuzn't. But good land! I didn't believe she knew a thing more about it than I did, but I didn't dispute with her much, because she wuz one of the relatives on his side—you know you have to do different with 'em than you do with them on your own side—you have to. And then agin, I felt that if it didn't come to an end she would be convinced that she wuz in the wrong on't, and if she did we should both of us be pretty apt to know it, so there wuzn't much use in disputin' back and forth.

But she wuz firm es iron in her belief. And she had come up visitin' to our home, so's to be nigh when Trueman riz. Trueman wuz buried in the old Risley deestrict, not half a mile from us on a back road. And she naterally wanted to be round at the time.

She said plain to me that Trueman never could seem to get along without her. And though she didn't say it right out, she carried the idea (and Josiah resented it because Trueman was a favorite cousin of his'n on his own side.) She jest the same es said right out that Trueman, if she wuzn't by him to tend to him, would be jest as apt to come up wrong end up es any way.

Josiah didn't like it at all.

Wall, she had lived a widowed life for a number of years, and had said right out, time and time agin, that she wouldn't marry agin. But Josiah thought, and I kinder mistrusted myself, that she wuz kinder on the lookout, and would marry agin if she got a chance—not fierce, you know, or anything of that kind, but kinder quietly lookin' out and standin' ready. That wuz when she first come; but before she went away she acted fierce.

Wall, there wuz sights of Adventists up in the Risley deestrict, and amongst the rest wuz an old bachelder, Joe Charnick.

And Joe Charnick, wuz, I s'poze, of all Advents, the most Adventy. He jest *knew* the world wuz a comin' to a end that very day, the last day of June, at four o'clock in the afternoon. And he got his robe all made to go up in. It wuz made of a white book muslin, and Jenette Finster made it. Cut it out by one of his mother's nightgowns—so she told me in confidence, and of course I tell it jest the same; I want it kep.

She was afraid Joe wouldn't like it, if he knew she took the nightgown for a guide, wantin' it, es he did, for a religious purpose.

But, good land! as I told her, religion or not, anybody couldn't cut anything to look anyhow without sumpthin' for a guide, and she bein' an old maiden felt a little delicate about measurin' him.

His mother wuz es big round es he wuz, her weight bein' 230 by the steelyards, and she allowed 2 fingers and a half extra length—Joe is tall. She gathered it in full round the neck, and the sleeves (at his request) hung down like wings, a breadth for each wing wuz what she allowed.

Jenette owned up to me (though she wouldn't want it told of for the world, for it had been spared for years, that he and she had a likin' for each other, and mebby would make a match some time, though what they had been a-waitin' for for the last 10 years nobody knew). But she allowed to me that when he got his robe on, he wuz the worst lookin' human bein' that she ever laid eyes on, and sez she, for she likes a joke, Jenette duz: "I should think if Joe looked in the glass after he got it on, his religion would be a comfort to him; I should think he would be glad the world *wuz* comin' to a end."

But he *didn't* look at the glass, Jenette said he didn't; he wanted to see if it wuz the right size round the neck. Joe hain't handsome, but he is kinder good-lookin', and he is a good feller and got plenty to do with, but bein' kinder big-featured, and tall, and hefty, he must have looked like fury in the robe. But he is liked by everybody, and everybody is glad to see him so prosperous and well off.

He has got 300 acres of good land, "be it more or less," as the deed reads; 30 head of cows, and 7 head of horses (and the hull bodies of 'em). And a big sugar bush, over 1100 trees, and a nice little sugar house way up on a pretty side hill amongst the maple trees. A good, big, handsome dwellin' house, a sort of cream color, with green blinds; big barn, and carriage house, etc., etc., and everything in the very best of order. He is a pattern farmer and a pattern son—yes, Joe couldn't be a more pattern son if he acted every day from a pattern.

He treats his mother dretful pretty, from day to day. She thinks that there hain't nobody like Joe; and it wuz s'pozed that Jenette thought so too.

But Jenette is, and always wuz, runnin' over with common sense, and she always made fun and laughed at Joe when he got to talkin' about his religion, and about settin' a time for the world to come to a end. And some thought that that wuz one reason why the match didn't go off, for Joe likes her, everybody could see that, for he wuz jest such a great, honest, open-hearted feller, that he never made any secret of it. And Jenette liked Joe *I* knew, though she fooled a good many on the subject. But she wuz always a great case to confide in me, and though she didn't say so right out, which wouldn't have been her way, for, es the poet sez, she wuzn't one "to wear her heart on the sleeves of her back waist," still, I knew es well es I wanted to, that she thought her eyes of him. And old Miss Charnick jest about worshipped Jenette, would have her with her, sewin' for her, and takin' care of her—she wuz sick a good deal, Mother Charnick wuz. And she would have been tickled most to death to have had Joe marry her and bring her right home there.

And Jenette wuz a smart little creeter, "smart as lightnin'," as Josiah always said.

She had got along in years, Jenette had, without marryin', for she staid to hum and took care of her old father and mother and Tom. The other girls married off, and left her to hum, and she had chances, so it wuz said, good ones, but she wouldn't leave her father and mother, who wuz gettin' old, and kinder bed-rid, and needed her. Her father, specially, said he couldn't live, and wouldn't try to, if Jenette left 'em, but he said, the old gentleman did, that Jenette should be richly paid for her goodness to 'em.

That wuzn't what made Jenette good, no, indeed; she did it out of the pure tenderness and sweetness of her nature and lovin' heart. But I used to love to hear the old gentleman talk that way, for he wuz well off, and I felt that so far as money could pay for the hull devotion of a life, why, Jenette would be looked out for, and have a good home, and enough to do with. So she staid to hum, es I say, and took care of 'em night and day; sights of watching and weerisome care she had, poor little creeter; but she took the best of care of 'em, and kep 'em kinder comforted up, and clean, and brought up Tom, the youngest boy, by hand, and thought her eyes on him.

And he wuz a smart chap—awful smart, es it proved in the end; for he married when he wuz 21, and brought his wife (a disagreeable creeter) home to the old homestead, and Jenette, before they had been there 2 weeks, wuz made to feel that her room wuz better than her company.

That wuz the year the old gentleman died; her mother had died 3 months prior and beforehand.

Her brother, es I said, wur smart, and he and his wife got round the old man in some way and sot him against Jenette, and got everything he had.

He wuz childish, the old man wuz; used to try to put his pantaloons on over his head, and got his feet into his coat sleeves, etc., etc.

And he changed his will, that had gi'n Jenette half the property, a good property, too, and gi'n it all to Tom, every mite of it, all but one dollar, which Jenette never took by my advice.

For I wuz burnin' indignant at old Mr. Finster and at Tom. Curius, to think such a girl as Jenette had been—such a patient, good creeter, and such a good-tempered one, and everything—to think her pa should have forgot all she had done, and suffered, and gi'n up for 'em, and give the property all to that boy, who had never done anything only to spend their money and make Jenette trouble.

But then, I s'poze it wuz old Mr. Finster's mind, or the lack on't, and I had to stand it, likewise so did Jenette.

But I never sot a foot into Tom Finster's house, not a foot after that day that Jenette left it. I wouldn't. But I took her right to my house, and kep her for 9 weeks right along, and wuz glad to.

That wuz some 10 years prior and before this, and she had gone round sewin' ever sense. And she wuz beloved by everybody, and had gone round highly respected, and at seventy-five cents a day.

Her troubles, and everybody that knew her, knew how many she had of 'em, but she kep 'em all to herself, and met the world and her neighbors with a bright face.

If she took her skeletons out of the closet to air 'em, and I s'poze she did, everybody duz; they have to at times, to see if their bones are in good order, if for nothin' else. But if she ever did take 'em out and dust 'em, she did it all by herself. The closet door wuz shet up and locked when anybody wuz round. And you would think, by her bright, laughin' face, that she never heard the word skeleton, or ever listened to the rattle of a bone.

And she kep up such a happy, cheerful look on the outside, that I s'poze it ended by her bein' cheerful and happy on the inside.

The stiddy, good-natured, happy spirit that she cultivated at first by

hard work, so I s'poze; but at last it got to be second nater, the quali-
ties kinder struck in and she *wuz* happy, and she *wuz* contented—that
is, I s'poze so.

Though I, who knew Jenette better than anybody else, almost, knew
how tuff, how fearful tuff it must have come on her, to go round from
home to home—not bein' settled down at home anywhere. I knew jest
what a lovin' little home body she wuz. And how her sweet nater, like
the sun, would love to light up one bright lovin' home, and shine
kinder stiddy there, instead of glancin', and changin' about from one
place to another, like a meteor.

Some would have liked it; some like change and constant goin'
about, and movin' constantly through space—but I knew Jenette
wuzn't made on the meteor plan. I felt sorry for Jenette, down deep in
my heart, I did; but I didn't tell her so; no, she wouldn't have liked it;
she kep a brave face to the world. And es I said, her comin' wuz looked
for weeks and weeks ahead, in any home where she wuz engaged to
sew by the day.

Everybody in the house used to feel the presence of a sunshiny,
cheerful spirit. One that wuz determined to turn back onto troubles
she couldn't help and keep her face sot towards the Son of Happiness.
One who felt good and pleasant towards everybody, wished everybody
well. One who could look upon other folks'es good fortune without a
mite of jealousy or spite. One who loved to hear her friends praised
and admired, loved to see 'em happy. And if they had a hundred times
the good things she had, why, she was glad for their sakes, that they
had 'em, she loved to see 'em enjoy 'em, if she couldn't.

And she wuz dretful kinder cunnin' and cute, Jenette wuz. She
would make the oddest little speeches; keep everybody laughin' round
her, when she got to goin'.

Yes, she wuz liked dretful well, Jenette wuz. Her face had a kind of a
pert look on to it, her black eyes snap, a good-natured snap, though,
and her nose turns up jest enough to look kinder cunnin', and her hair
curls all over her head.

Smart round the house she is, and Mother Charnick likes that, for
she is a master good housekeeper. Smart to answer back and joke. Joe
is slow of speech, and his big blue eyes won't fairly get sot onto anything, before Jenette has looked it all through, and turned it over, and
examined it on the other side, and got through with it.

Wall, she wuz to work to Mother Charnick's makin' her a black al-
packa dress, and four new calico ones, and coverin' a parasol.

A good many said that Miss Charnick got dresses a purpose for Jenette to make, so's to keep her there. Jenette wouldn't stay there a minute only when she wuz to work, and es they always kep a good, strong, hired girl, she knew when she wuz needed, and when she wuzn't. But, of course, she couldn't refuse to sew for her, and at what she wuz sot at, though she must have known and felt that Miss Charnick wuz lavish in dresses. She had 42 calico dresses, and everybody knew it, new ones, besides woosted. But, anyway, there she was a sewin' when the word came that the world was a comin' to a end on the 30th day of June, at 4 o'clock in the afternoon.

Miss Charnick wuz a believer, but not to the extent that Joe was. For Jenette asked her if she should stop sewin', not sposin' that she would need the dresses, specially the four calico ones, and the parasol in case of the world's endin'. And she told Jenette, and Jenette told me, so's I know it is true, "that she might go right on, and get the parasol cover and the trimmins to the dresses, cambrick, and linin' and things, and hooks and eyes."

And Miss Charnick didn't prepare no robe. But Jenette mistrusted that Miss Charnick is closemouthed, and didn't say nothin', but Jenette mistrusted that she laid out, when she sees signs, to use a nightgown.

She had piles of the nicest ones, that Jenette had made for her from time to time, over 28, all trimmed off nice enough for day dresses, so Jenette said, trimmed with tape trimmin's, some of 'em, and belted down in front.

Wall, they had lots of meetin's at the Risley school-house, es the time drew near. And Miss Trueman Pool went to every one on 'em.

She had been too weak to go out to the well, or to the barn. She wanted dretfully to see some new stanchils that Josiah had been a makin', jest like some that Pool had had in his barn. She wanted to see 'em dretful, but was too weak to walk. And I had had kind of a tussle in my own mind, whether or not I should offer to let Josiah carry her out; but kinder hesitated, thinkin' mebby she would get stronger.

But I hain't jealous, not a mite. It is known that I hain't all through Jonesville and Loontown. No, I'd scorn it. I thought Pool's wife would get better and she did.

One evenin' Joe Charnick came down to bring home Josiah's augur, and the conversation turned onto Adventin'. And Miss Pool see that Joe wuz congenial on that subject; he believed jest as she did, that the world would come to an end the 30th. This was along the first part of the month.

He spoke of the good meetin's they wuz a-havin' to the Risley school-house, and how he always attended to every one of 'em. And the next mornin' Miss Trueman Pool gin out that she wuz a-goin' that evenin'. It wuz a good half a mile away, and I reminded her that Josiah had to be away with the team, for he wuz a-goin' to Loontown, heavy loaded, and wouldn't get back till along in the evenin'.

But she said "that she felt that the walk would do her good."

I then reminded her of the stanchils, but she said "stanchils and religion wuz two separate things." Which I couldn't deny, and didn't try to. And she sot off for the school-house that evenin' a-walkin' a foot. And the rest of her adventins and the adventins of Joe I will relate in another epistol; and I will also tell whether the world come to an end or not. I know folks will want to know, and I don't care to keep folks in onxiety—it hain't my way.

Chapter XV

Wall, from that night, Miss Trueman Pool attended to the meetins at the Risley school-house, stiddy and constant. And before the week wuz out Joe Charnick had walked home with her twice. And the next week he carried her to Jonesville to get the cloth for her robe, jest like his'n, white book muslin. And twice he had come to consult her on a Bible passage, and twice she had walked up to his mother's to consult with her on a passage in the Apockraphy. And once she went up to see if her wings wuz es deep and full es his'n. She wanted 'em jest the same size.

Miss Charnick couldn't bear her. Miss Charnick wuz a woman who had enjoyed considerable poor health in her life, and she had now, and had been havin' for years, some dretful bad spells in her stomach—a sort of a tightness acrost her chest.

And Trueman's wife argued with her that her spells had been worse, and her chest had been tighter. And the old lady didn't like that at all, of course. And the old lady took thoroughwert for 'em, and Trueman's wife insisted on't that thoroughwert wuz tightenin'.

And then there wuz some chickens in a basket out on the stoop, that the old hen had deserted, and Miss Charnick wuz a bringin' 'em up by hand. And Mother Charnick went out to feed 'em while Trueman's wife tosted her head and said, "she didn't approve of it—she thought a chicken ought to be brung up by a hen."

But Miss Charnick said, "Why, the hen deserted 'em; they would have perished right there in the nest."

But Trueman's wife wouldn't gin in, she stuck right to it, "that it wuz a hen's business, and nobody else's."

And of course she had some sense on her side, for of course it is a hen's business, her duty and her prevelege to bring up her chickens. But if she won't do it, why, then, somebody else has got to—they ought to be brung.

I say Mother Charnick wuz in the right on't. But Trueman's wife had got so in the habit of findin' fault, and naggin' at me, and the other relations on Trueman's side, and hern, that she couldn't seem to stop it when she knew it wuz for her interest to stop.

And then she ketched a sight of the alpaker dress Jenette wuz a-makin' and she said "that basks had gone out."

And Miss Charnick was over partial to 'em (most too partial, some thought), and thought they wuz in the height of the fashion. But Trueman's wife ground her right down on it.

"Basks *wuz out*, fer she knew it, she had all her new ones made polenay."

And hearin' 'em argue back and forth for more'n a quarter of an hour, Jenette put in and sez (she thinks all the world of Mother Charnick), "Wall, I s'pose you won't take much good of your polenays, if you have got so little time to wear 'em."

And then Trueman's wife (she wuz meen-dispersitioned, anyway) said somethin' about "hired girls keepin' their place."

And then Mother Charnick flared right up and took Jenette's part. And Joe's face got red; he couldn't bear to see Jenette put upon, if she wuz makin' fun of his religeon. And Trueman's wife see that she had gone too fur, and held herself in, and talked good to Jenette, and flattered up Joe, and he went home with her and staid till ten o'clock.

They spent a good deal of this time a-huntin' up passages, to prove their doctrine, in the Bible, and the Apockraphy, and Josephus, and others.

It beat all how many Trueman's wife would find, and every one she found Joe would seem to think the more on her. And so it run along, till folks said they wuz engaged, and Josiah and me thought so, too.

And though Jenette wuzn't the one to say anything, she began to look kinder pale and mauger. And when I spoke of it to her, she laid it to her liver. And I let her believe I thought so too. And I even went so far es to recommend tansey and camomile tea, with a little catnip mixed in—I did it fer blinders. I knew it wuzn't her liver that ailed her. I knew it wuz her heart. I knew it wuz her heart that wuz a-achin'.

Wall, we had our troubles, Josiah and me did. Trueman's wife wuz dretful disagreeable, and would argue us down, every separate thing we tried to do or say. And she seemed more high-header and disagreeable than ever sence Joe had begun to pay attention to her. Though what earthly good his attention wuz a-goin' to do, wuz more than I could see, accordin' to her belief.

But Josiah said, "he guessed Joe wouldn't have paid her any attention, if he hadn't thought that the world wuz a-comin' to a end so soon. He guessed he wouldn't want her round if it wuz a-goin' to stand."

Sez I, "Josiah, you are a-judgin' Joe by yourself." And he owned up that he wuz.

Wall, the mornin' of the 30th, after Josiah and me had eat our breakfast, I proceeded to mix up my bread. I had set the yeast overnight, and I wuz a mouldin' it out into tins when Trueman's wife come down-stairs with her robe over her arm. She wanted to iron it out and press the seams.

I had baked one tin of my biscuit for breakfast, and I had kep 'em warm for Trueman's wife, for she had been out late the night before to a meetin' to Risley school-house, and didn't come down to breakfast. I had also kep some good coffee warm for her, and some toast and steak.

She laid her robe down over a chair-back, and sot down to her breakfast, but begun the first thing to find fault with me for bein' to work on that day. She sez, "The idee, of the last day of the world, and you a-bein' found makin' riz biscuit, yeast ones!" sez she.

"Wall," sez I, "I don't know but I had jest es soon be found a-makin' riz biscuit, a-takin' care of my own household, es the Lord hes commanded me to, es to be found a-sailin' round in a book muslin Mother Hubbard."

"It hain't a Mother Hubbard!" sez she.

"Wall," sez I, "I said it fer oritory. But it is puckered up some like them, and you know it." Hers wuz made with a yoke.

And Josiah sot there a-fixin' his plantin' bag. He wuz a-goin' out that mornin' to plant over some corn that the crows had pulled up.

And she bitterly reproved him. But he sez, "If the world don't come to a end, the corn will be needed."

"But it will," she sez in a cold, haughty tone.

"Wall," sez he, "if it does, I may as well be a-doin' that es to be settin' round." And he took his plantin' bag and went out. And then she jawed me for upholdin' him.

And sez she, es she broke open a biscuit and spread it with butter previous to eatin' it, sez she, "I should think *respect*, respect for the great and fearful thought of meetin' the Lord, would scare you out of the idea of goin' on with your work."

Sez I calmly, "Does it scare you, Trueman's wife?"

"Wall, not exactly scare," sez she, "but lift up, lift up far above bread and other kitchen work."

And again she buttered a large slice, and I sez calmly, "I don't s'poze I should be any nearer the Lord than I am now. He sez He dwells inside of our hearts, and I don't see how He could get any nearer to us than that. And anyway, what I said to you I keep a-sayin', that I think He would approve of my goin' on calm and stiddy, a-doin' my best for the ones He put in my charge here below, my husband, my children, and my grandchildren." (I some expected Tirzah Ann and the babe home that day to dinner.)

"Wall, you feel very diffrent from some wimmen that wuz to the school-house last night, and act very diffrent. They are good Christian females. It is a pity you wuzn't there. P'raps your hard heart would have melted, and you would have had thoughts this mornin' that would soar up above riz biscuit."

And es she sez this she begun on her third biscuit, and poured out another cup of coffee. And I, wantin' to use her well, sez, "What did they do there?"

"Do!" sez she, "why, it wuz the most glorious meetin' we ever had. Three wimmen lay at one time perfectly speechless with the power. And some of em' screemed so you could hear 'em fer half a mile."

I kep on a-mouldin' my bread out into biscuit (good shaped ones, too, if I do say it), and sez calmly, "Wall, I never wuz much of a screemer. I have always believed in layin' holt of the duty next to you, and doin' *some* things, things He has *commanded*. Everybody to their own way. I don't condemn yourn, but I have always seemed to believe more in the solid, practical parts of religion, than the ornamental. I have always believed more in the power of honesty, truth, and justice, than in the power they sometimes have at camp and other meetins. Howsumever," sez I, "I don't say but what that power is powerful, to the ones that have it, only I wuz merely observin' that it never wuz *my* way to lay speechless or holler much—not that I consider hollerin' wrong, if you holler from principle, but I never seemed to have a call to."

"You would be far better if you did," sez Trueman's wife, "far better. But you hain't good enough."

"Oh!" sez I, reservedly, "I could holler if I wanted to, but the Lord hain't deef. He sez specilly, that He hain't, and so I never could see the *use* in hollerin' to Him. And I never could see the use of tellin' Him in public so many things es some do. Why He *knows* it. He *knows* all these things. He don't need to have you try to enlighten Him es if you wuz His gardeen—es I have heard folks do time and time again. He *knows* what we are, what we need. I am glad, Trueman's wife," sez I, "that He can look right down into our hearts, that He is right there in 'em a-knowin' all about us, all our wants, our joys, our despairs, our temptations, our resolves, our weakness, our blindness, our defects, our regrets, our remorse, our deepest hopes, our inspiration, our triumphs, our glorys. But when He *is* right there, in the midst of our soul, our life, why, *why* should we kneel down in public and holler at Him?"

"You would be glad to if you wuz good enough," sez she; "if you had attained unto a state of perfection, you would feel like it."

That kinder riled me up, and I sez, "Wall, I have lived in this house with them that wuz perfect, and that is bad enough for me, without bein' one of 'em myself. For more disagreeable creeters," sez I, a prickin' my biscuit with a fork, "more disagreeable creeters I never laid eyes on."

Trueman's wife thinks she is perfect, she has told me so time and agin—thinks she hain't done anything wrong in upwards of a number of years.

But she didn't say nothin' to this, only begun agin about the wickedness and immorality of my makin' riz biscuit that mornin', and the deep disgrace of Josiah Allen keepin' on with his work.

But before I could speak up and take his part, for I *will* not hear my companion found fault with by any female but myself, she had gathered up her robe, and swept upstairs with it, leavin' orders for a flatiron to be sent up.

Wall, the believers wuz all a-goin' to meet at the Risley school-house that afternoon. They wuz about 40 of 'em, men and wimmen. And I told Josiah at noon, I believed I would go down to the school-house to the meetin'. And he a-feelin', I mistrust, that if they should happen to be in the right on't, and the world should come to a end, he wanted to be by the side of his beloved pardner, he offered to go too. But he never had no robe, no, nor never thought of havin'.

The Risley school-house stood in a clearin', and had tall stumps round it in the door-yard. And we had heard that some of the believers wuz goin' to get up on them stumps, so's to start off from there. And sure enough, we found it wuz the calculation of some on 'em.

The school-boys had made steps up the sides of some of the biggest stumps, and lots of times in political meetin's men had riz up on 'em to talk to the masses below. Why I s'poze a crowd of as many es 45 or 48, had assembled there at one time durin' the heat of the campain.

But them politicians had on their usual run of clothes, they didn't have on white book muslin robes. Good land!

Chapter XVI

Wall, lots of folks had assembled to the school-house when we got there, about 3 o'clock P.M.—afternoon. Believers, and world's people, all a-settin' round on seats and stumps, for the school-house wuz small and warm, and it wuz pleasanter outdoors.

We had only been there a few minutes when Mother Charnick and Jenette walked in. Joe had been there for sometime, and he and the Widder Pool wuz a-settin' together readin' a him out of one book. Jenette looked kinder mauger, and Trueman's wife looked haughtily at her, from over the top of the him book.

Mother Charnick had a worsted work-bag on her arm. There might have been a nightgown in it, and there might not. It wuz big enough to hold one, and it looked sort o' bulgy. But it wuz never known—Miss Charnick is a smart woman. It never wuz known what she had in the bag.

Wall, the believers struck up a him, and sung it through—es mournful, skeerful sort of a him es I ever hearn in my hull life; and it swelled out and riz up over the pine trees in a wailin', melancholy sort of a way, and wierd—dretful wierd.

And then a sort of a lurid, wild-looking chap, a minister, got up and preached the wildest and luridest discourse I ever hearn in my hull days. It wuz enough to scare a snipe. The very strongest and toughest men there turned pale, and wimmen cried and wept on every side of me, and cried and wept.

I, myself, didn't weep. But I drawed neerer to my companion, and kinder leaned up against him, and looked off on the calm blue heavens, the serene landscape, and the shinin' blue lake far away, and thought—jest es true es I live and breathe, I thought that I didn't care much, if God willed it to be so, that my Josiah and I should go side by side, that very day and minute, out of the certainties of this life into the mysteries of the other, out of the mysteries of this life into the certainties of the other.

For, thinks I to myself, we have got to go into that other world pretty soon, Josiah and me have. And if we went in the usual way, we had got to go alone, each on us. Terrible thought! We who had been together under shine and shade, in joy and sorrow. Our two hands that had joined at the alter, and had clung so clost-together ever sence, had got to leggo of each other down there in front of the dark gateway.

Solemn gateway! So big that the hull world must pass through it— and yet so small that the hull world has got to go through it alone, one at a time.

My Josiah would have to stand outside and let me go down under the dark, mysterious arches, alone—and he knows jest how I hate to go anywhere alone, or else I would have to stop at the gate and bid him good-by. And no matter how much we knocked at the gate, or how many tears we shed onto it, we couldn't get through till our time come, we had *got* to be parted.

And now if we went on this clear June day through the crystal gateway of the bendin' heavens—we two would be together for weal or for woe. And on whatever new, strange landscape we would have to look on, or wander through, he would be right by me. Whatever strange inhabitants the celestial country held, he would face 'em with me. Close, close by my side, he would go with me through that blue, lovely gateway of the soft June skies into the City of the King. And it wuz a sweet thought to me.

Not that I really *wanted* the world to come to a end that day. No, I kinder wanted to live along for some time, for several reasons: My pardner, the babe, the children, etc.; and then I kinder like to live for the *sake* of livin'. I enjoy it.

But I can say, and say with truth, and solemnity, that the idee didn't scare me now. And es my companion looked down in my face es the time approached, I could see the same thoughts that wuz writ in my eyes a-shinin' in his'n.

Wall, es the pinter approached the hour, the excitement grew nearly, if not quite rampant. The believers threw their white robes on over their dresses and coats, and es the pinter slowly moved round from half-past three to quarter to 4—and so on—they shouted, they sung, they prayed, they shook each other's hands—they wuz fairly crazed with excitement and ferver, which they called religion—for they wuz in earnest, nobody could dispute that.

Joe and Miss Pool kinder hung together all this time—though I ketched him givin' several wistful looks at Jenette, as much as to say, "Oh, how I hate to leave you, Jenette!"

But Miss Pool would roust him up agin, and he would shout and sing with the frienziedest and most zealousest of 'em.

Mother Charnick stood with her bag in her hand, and the other hand on the puckerin' string. I don't say what she had in the bag, but I do say this, that she had it fixed so's she could have ondone it in a secent's time. And her eyes wuz intent on the heavens overhead. But they kep calm and serene and cloudless, nothin' to be seen there—no sign, no change—and Ma Charnick kep still and didn't draw the puckerin' string.

But oh how excitement reined and grew rampant around that school-house! Miss Pool and Joe seemin' to outdo all the rest (she always did try to), till at last, jest es the pinter swung round to the very minute, Joe, more than half by the side of himself, with the excitement he had been in fer a week, and bein' urged onto it by Miss Pool, es he sez to this day, he jumped up onto the tall stump he had been a standin' by, and stood there in his long white robe, lookin' like a spook, if anybody had been calm enough to notice it, and he sung out in a clear voice—his voice always did have a good honest ring to it:

> Farewell my friends,
> Farewell my foes;
> Up to Heaven
> Joe Charnick goes.

And jest es the clock struck, and they all shouted and screamed, he waved his arms, with their two great white wings a-flutterin', and sprung upwards, expectin' the hull world, livin' and dead, would foller him—and go right up into the heavens.

And Trueman's wife bein' right by the stump, waved her wings and

"Farewell my friends, Farewell my foes" shows Joe Charnick in "Jenette Fin-ster's Story" ready to leap into resurrection; his mother cautiously keeps her hand in her reticule just in case she needs the ascension robe stashed inside.

jumped too—jest the same direction es he jumped. But she only stood on a camp chair, and when she fell, she didn't crack no bones, it only jarred her dretfully, and hurt her across the small of her back, to that extent that I kep bread and milk poultices on day and night for three weeks, and lobelia and catnip, half and half; she a-arguin' at me every single poultice I put on that it wuzn't her way of makin' poultices, nor her way of applyin' of 'em.

I told her I didn't know of any other way of applyin' 'em to her back, only to put 'em on it.

But she insisted to the last that I didn't apply 'em right, and I didn't crumble the bread into the milk right, and the lobelia wuzn't picked right, nor the catnip.

Not one word did she ever speak about the end of the world—not a word—but a-naggin' about everything else.

Wall, I healed her after a time, and glad enough wuz I to see her healed, and started off.

But Joe Charnick suffered worse and longer. He broke his limb in two places and cracked his rib. The bones of his arm wuz a good while a-healin', and before they wuz healed he was wounded in a new place.

He jest fell over head and ears in love with Jenette Finster. For bein' shet up to home with his mother and her (his mother wouldn't hear to Jenette leavin' her for a minute) he jest seemed to come to a full realizin' sense of her sweet natur' and bright, obleegin' ways; and his old affection for her bloomed out into the deepest and most idolatrous love—Joe never could be megum.

Jenette, and good enough for her, held him off for quite a spell—but when he got cold and relapsted, and they thought he wuz goin' to die, then she owned up to him that she worshipped him—and always had.

And from that day he gained out. Mother Charnick wuz tickled most to death at the idea of havin' Jenette for her own girl—she thinks her eyes on her, and so does Jenette of her. So it wuz agreeable es anything ever wuz all around specilly, if not agreeabler.

Jest as quick es she got well enough to walk, and before he got out of his bed, Trueman's wife walked over to see Joe. And Joe's mother hatin' her so, wouldn't let her step her foot into the house. And Joe wuz glad on't, so they say.

Mother Charnick wuz out on the stoop in front of the house, when Trueman's wife got there, and told her that they had to keep the house still; that is, they say so, I don't know for certain, but they say that Ma Charnick offered to take Trueman's wife out to see her chickens, the ones she had brought up by hand, and Trueman's wife wantin' to please her, so's to get in, consented. And Miss Charnick showed her the hull 13 of 'em, all fat and flourishin',—they wuz well took care of. And Miss Charnick looked down on 'em fondly, and sez:

"I lay out to have a good chicken pie the day that Joe and Jenette are married."

"Married!" sez Trueman's wife, in faint and horrified axcents.

"Yes, they are goin' to be married jest as soon as my son gets well enough. Jenette is fixin' a new dress for me to wear to the weddin'—with a bask," sez she with emphasis. And es she said it, they say she stooped down and gathered some sprigs of thoroughwert, a-mentionin' how much store she set by it for sickness.

But if she did, Trueman's wife didn't sense it, she wuz dumbfounded and sot back by the news. And she left my home and farewell the week before the weddin'.

They had been married about a year, when Jenette wuz here a-visitin' —and she asked me in confidence (and it *must* be kep, it stands to reason it must), "if I s'posed that book muslin robe would make two little dresses?"

And I told her, "Good land! yes, three on 'em," and it did.

She dresses the child beautiful, and I don't know whether she would want the neighbors to know jest what and when and where she gets the materials—

It looks some like her and some like Joe—and they both think their eyes on it—but old Miss Charnick worships it—

Wall, though es I said (and I have eppisoded to a extent that is almost onprecidented and onheard on).

Though Josiah Allen made a excuse of borrowin' a plow (a *plow*, that time of night) to get away from my argiments on the Conference, and Submit's kinder skairt face, and so forth, and so on—

He resumed the conversation the next mornin' with more energy than ever. (He never said nuthin' about the plow, and I never see no sign on it, and don't believe he got it, or wanted it.)

He resumed the subject, and kep on a-resumin' of it from day to day and from hour to hour.

He would nearly exhaust, the subject at home, and then he would tackle the wimmen on it at the Methodist Meetin' House, while we Methodist wimmen wuz to work.

After leavin' me to the meetin' house, Josiah would go on to the post-office for his daily *World*, and then he would stop on his way back to give us female wimmen the latest news from the Conference, and give us his idees on't.

And sometimes he would fairly harrow us to the very bone, with his dretful maginins' and fears that wimmen would be allowed to overdo herself, and ruin her health, and strain her mind, by bein' permitted to set!

Why Submit Tewksbury, and some of the other weaker sisters, would look fairly wild-eyed for some time after he would go.

He never could stay long. Sometimes we would beset him to stay and do some little job for us, to help us along with our work, such as liftin' somethin' or movin' some bench, or the pulpit, or somethin'.

But he never had the time; he always had to hasten home to get to work. He wuz in a great hurry with his spring's work, and full of care about that buzz saw mill.

And that wuz how it wuz with every man in the meetin' house that wuz able to work any. They wuz all in a hurry with their spring's work, and their buzz saws, and their inventions, and their agencys, etc., etc., etc.

And that wuz the reason why we wimmen wuz havin' such a hard job on the meetin' house.

Further Selections from Various Sources

The selections included here are not intended to offer a complete survey of the kinds of humorous literature produced in the Northeast during the nineteenth century. The literary comedians of the Civil War era are only modestly represented by Artemus Ward and Josh Billings, whose works have been collected elsewhere. The other works presented here are more obscure. They represent a tradition of comic scepticism that affirms progress and decency even while history and economic relations are matters of notice. Needless to say, the values expressed actually vary widely, but the matter—railroads, land deals, maritime adventures, and the Civil War—is northern in every respect.

An excerpt from Lord Timothy Dexter's *A Pickle for the Knowing Ones; or, Plain Truth in a Homespun Dress*, published in 1802, is reprinted here from Samuel L. Knapp, *Life of Lord Timothy Dexter, Etc.* (Boston, 1858). Dexter describes the mansion he erected, which is decorated with a group of fifty-two wooden statues of political greats, his motif for a world congress of peace. The "Speech of David Wood," from Joseph Dennie (ed.), *The Spirit of the Farmer's Museum and Lay Preacher's Gazette* (Walpole, N.H., 1801), was discussed in the Introduction as representative of the conflict between individualism and large-scale economics, a topic also important to Artemus Ward and Mark Twain. Two poems from the *New Havener*, III (November 18, 1837), 148, entitled "Pickpocket Training Poem on Credit," which ran under the heading "Odds and Ends" reflect the economic effects of the Panic of 1837 in comic literature. "A Muggy Morning Off Sandy Hook: A Yarn Spun by a Yankee Tar," from the *New Mirror*, I (July 8, 1843), 209–10, is particularly interesting in showing the northeastern tradition of sentimental courage, nautical and trade settings, and happy endings—sharply different from the southwestern humor of fights and village low-lifes. "Soliloquy of a Low Thief" and "The Prince of Wales" appeared in [Charles F. Browne], *Artemus Ward: His Book*

(1862); they are reprinted here from [Charles F. Browne], *The Complete Works of Artemus Ward* (London, 1922). "The First Locomotive" makes an interesting contrast to Edgar Allen Poe's method; instead of mood, external details are stressed, and the sanctum of Jabez Doolittle produces a wildly active machine. "Picketing—an Affecting War Incident" is from the same source, *The Railway Anecdote Book: A Collection of Anecdotes and Incidents of Travel by River and Rail* (New York, 1864), 21–23, 199. "Amerikan Aristokrasy" was taken from Henry W. Shaw, *Josh Billings on Ice: And Other Things* (New York, 1870). "The American Turkey," from Street and Smith's *New York Weekly* (January 15, 1872), 4, is representative of the sort of humorous columns published there by Doesticks, Josh Billings, and a host of others. "Why She Could Not Be His Wife" is taken from *Chill Blains* (New York, 1883), 52.

Timothy Dexter

From *A Pickle for the Knowing Ones; or, Plain Truth in a Homespun Dress*

The Pickle; from the Museum of Lord Timothy Dexter

Lord Dexter relates how he was created Lord by the People, announces his intention of forming a Museum of great men, that shall be the wonder of the world, and shall confound his enemies.

Ime the first Lord in the younited States of A mercury Now of Newburyport it is the voise of the peopel and I cant Help it and so Let it goue Now as I must be Lord there will foller many more Lords pretty soune for it Dont hurt A Cat Nor the mouse Nor the son Nor the water Nor the Eare then goue on all is Easey Now bons broaken all is well all in Love Now I be gin to Lay the corner ston and the kee ston with grat Remembrence of my father Jorge Washington the grate herow 17 sentreys past before we found so good a father to his shildren and Now gone to Rest Now to shoue my Love to my father and grate Caricters I will shoue the world one of the grate Wonders of the world in 15 months if now man mourders me in Dors or out Dors such

A mouserum* on Earth will announce O Lord thou knowest to be troue fourder hear me good Lord I am A goueing to Let or shildren know Now to see good Lord what has bin in the world grat wase back to owr fore fathers Not old plimeth† but stop to Addom & Eave to shone 45 figures two Leged and fore Leged because we Cant Doue weel with out fore Leged in the first plase they are our foude in the Next plase to make out Dexters mouseum I wants 4 Lions to defend thous grat and mistry men from East to wist from North to South which Now are at the plases Rased the Lam is Not Readey in short meater if Agreabel I forme A good and peasabel government on my Land in Newburyport Compleat I taks 3 presedents hamsher govenor all to Noue york and the grate mister John Jay is one, that maks 2 in that state the king of grat britton mister pitt Roufes king Cros over to france Loues the 16 and then the grate bonnepartey the grate and there segnetoure Crow biddey—I Command pease and the gratest brotherly Love and Not fade be Linked to gether with that best of troue Love so as to govern all nasions on the fass of the gloub not to tiranize over them but to put them to order if any Despout shall A Rise** as to boundreys or Any maturs of Importance it is Left france and grat britton and Amacarey to be setteled A Congress to be allways in france all Despouts is to be thare settled and this may be Dun this will balless power and then all wars Dun A way there-fore I have the Lam to Lay Dow with the Lion Now this may be Dun if thos three powers would A geray to Lay what is called Devel one side and Not Carry the gentelman pack hors Any longer but shake him of as dust on your feet and Laff at him there is grate noise Aboute a toue Leged Creter he says I am going to set sade black Divel there stop he would scare the womans so there would be No youse for the bilding, I should have to erect sum Noue won Now I stop hear I puts the Devil Long with the bull for he is a bulling 2 Leged Annemal stop put him one side Near Soloman Looking with Soloman to Ladey venus Now stop wind up there is grat ods in froute I will Let you know the sekret houe you may

---

*Museum.
†Plymouth.
**Here the learned author makes a plunge into the sea of political discussion. The wisdom he displays cannot be too much admired. If the princes and potentates of the earth would but take a fool's advice they might save themselves the trouble of fighting. The "Pickle for the Knowing Ones," will teach them how they may compose their differences without bloodshed. Should any one inquire who invented Peace Societies, we can reply, "Lord Dexter." The whole scheme of the "Congress of Nations" is to be found in the lines which follow: yet we dare say, Dexter had never read the Abbé St. Pierre.

see the Devel stand on your head before a Loucking glass and take a bibel in to your bousum fast 40 owers and look in the loucking glass, there is no Devel if you dont see the ould fellow but I affirm you will see that old Devel

Unto you all mankind Com to my hous to mock and sneare whi ye Dont you Lafe be fore hevvn or I meane your betters think the heir power Dont know thorts and Axsions Now I will tell you good and bad it is not pelite to Com to see what the bare walls keep of my ground if you are gentel men you would stay Away when all is Dun in marble Expect to goue out my selfe to Help it thous grat men will send on there Likeness all over the younited States I wish all the printers would send on there Likenesses in 40 Days to Timothy Dexter I mean I want the printers to give Notis if pleases to inform by printen in the Nouspapers for the good of the holl of mankind—

I wans to make my Enemys grin in time Lik A Cat over A hot pudding and goue Away and hang there heads Doun Like a Dogg bin After sheep gilty stop see I am Afrade I Rite toue hash my peopel Complane of backker spittel maks work to Cleane it up—in the women skouls A bout it spit in ther hankershif or not spit A tall I must say sumthing or I should say Nothing there fore make sum Noise in the world when I git so ouely to Nash my goms and griyng for water and that is salt water when brot A young Devel to bring it and A Scoyer*** to wate and tend on gentelmen A black Suier his breth Smelt wos than bram stone by far but Let the Devel goue in to Darknes and take his due to Descare mankind for A Littel while this Cloven foot is seen by sum but the trap will over hall the Devel in tim, I pittey this poore black man†† I thinc his master wants purging A Littel to har ber mr Devel A most but I did Not say Let him Run A way good Nit mr Devel Cary††† the sword and money with you tak John mekel Jentel man good Nit

Lord Dexter Against Colleges and Priests

Noue mister printer *sir* I was at Noue haven 7 years and seven monts past at commencement Degress on 40 boys was tuck degrees to doue

***Squire.

††*I pittey this poore black man.* There is the same touch of pathos in Tristram Shandy. "The devil is damned to all eternity," quoth Dr. Slop. "I am sorry for it," said my uncle Toby.

†††Mr. Cary was a clergyman of Newburyport, with whom Dexter had a quarrel.

good or Not good the old man with the hat on told them to sueday houeman Nater* walk as A band of brothers from that time to this day I thort that all thous that was brot up to Coleage the meaning was to git there Liveing out of the Labeer If the Coleages was to continer one sentry and keep up the game recken the cost of all from there cradel to 22 years old all there fathers and gurdEands† to Lay out one houndred years intress upon intress gess at it & cast it see houe many houndred thousand millions of Dolors it would com to to make Rougs and thieves to plunder the Labering man that sweats to get his bread good common Laning is the best sum good books is best well under stoud be onnest dont be preast Riden it is a cheat all be onnest in all things Now feare Let this goue as you find it my way speling houe is the strangest man

(Note to Dexter's Second Edition)

fouder mister printer the Nowing ones complane of my book the fust edition had no stops I put in A Nuf here and thay may peper and solt it as they plese

,,
,,
;;
::
....!!!!!!!!!!!!!!!!!!!.......................................
.... !!!!!!!!!!!! ....
.... !!!!! ....
.... ! ....
,,
.... ?? ....
:::::::::::::::::::::: ,, ::::::::::::::::::::::
:::::::::::::::::::::: ,,,,,,,,,,,,,,,,,,,,,,,,,,,,,,,,,, ::::::::::::::::::::::
:::::::::::::::::::::: ,,,,,,,,,,,,,,,,,,,, ::::::::::::::::::::::
:::::::::::::::::::::: ,,,,,,,,,,,,,,,,,,,,,,,,,,,,,, ::::::::::::::::::::::
:::::::::::::::::::::: ,, ::::::::::::::::::::::
:::::::::::::::::: -,,,,,,,,,,-;;;;;;;;;;;;;;;;;;;;;;;;;-,,,,,,,,,,- ::::::::::::::::::
;;;;;;;;;;;;;;;;;;;;;;;;;;;;;;; -??????????-!!!!!!!-??????????- ;;;;;;;;;;;;;;;;;;;;;;;;;;;;;;;
;;;;;;;;;;;; -??????????-!!!!!!!!!!!!!!!!!!!!!!!!!!!!!!-??????????- ;;;;;;;;;;;;

*Study human nature.
†Guardians.

```
?????????????????? -!!!!!!!!!!!!!!!!!!!!!!!!!!!!!!!!!!!!!!!!!!!!!!!- ???????????????????
"—"_____"—"_____"—"_____ !!!!!!!!!!!! _____"—"_____"—"_____"—"
"—"_____"—"_____"—"_____ ()()()()() _____"—"_____"—"_____"—"
_____ _____ _____ _____ ()()()()()()()() _____ _____ _____ _____ _____
[][][][] ⌒⌒⌒  — ⌒⌒  — ⌒⌒  — ⌒ [][][][]
...................................... ---------- ......................................
..................... ----------------------------------------- .....................
----------------------------------------- ,,,,,,,,,,,,,,,,,,,,, -----------------------------------------
..................... .....................
†††********* ¶¶¶   ‡   §§§§‡‡¶¶¶         *********†††
???????? :?!,,.!,?.:-,.:,,.:',,,?.!"!",?.?.:!.,"."?:!.?,.!!.?"-"??.?.  ,,,,,,,,,,,,
?????????????????? !.?:?:.,-;!?.!,?.,.?.,?:_.?,,?.,.;;:?,.?... ???????????????????
```

Speech of David Wood While Standing in the Pillory at Charlestown, N.H., May 27th, 1797, for Forging a Deed

Anonymous

Sympathizing Friends,

You come here this day to see a sad sight; a poor old man publicly disgraced for attempting to make a penny out of fifty acres of Vermont rocks; and yet I see some here in gay coats, mounted on naggish horses, who have made thousands out of lands, to which you had no more title, than I to David Dray's rocks. But you are great rogues, and wear silver spurs, and white beaver hats, and flourish your loaded whips, forget what you once were, drink your Madeira, and talk of your millions of acres, and sit at your ease; while poor I, who have speculated a little in a fifty acre lot, which would not maintain a wood-chuck, must stand here; for I am a little rogue, and have no pretensions to be a great speculator.

Let me ask you, what is the difference, as to sin, between a man, who forges a deed and sells lands under it, and a man who sells lands, to which he knows he has no title? You all know the great 'Squire ———, he bought lands in Boston at the time all their great men got caught in the Georgia land trap. The 'Squire came home by the way of Hartford, at the very moment when the Hartford foxes were wailing for the loss of their tails, in the same spring trap. The 'Squire found he had bought the Devil, and was determined to sell him again on the best terms he could. He put spurs to his old mare, rode before the news, and sold to the widow Lowly and her two sons, who had just come of age, about fifty thousand acres of land, which lay the Lord knows where, and to which he knew he had no title, and took all their father, the old deacon's farm in mortgage, and threatens to turn the poor widow upon the town, and her two boys upon the world; but this is the way of the world. The 'Squire is a great speculator, he is of the quorum, can sit on the sessions, and fine poor girls for natural misteps; but I am a little rogue, who speculated in only fifty acres of rocks, and must stand here in the pillory.

Then there is the state of Georgia. They sold millions of acres, to which they had no more title, than I to David Dray's land. Their great men pocketed the money; and their Honourable Assembly publicly burnt all the records of their conveyance, and are now selling the lands again. But Georgia is a great Honourable State. They can keep Negro slaves, race horses, gouge out eyes, send members to fight duels at Congress, and cry out for France and the guillotine, and be honoured in the land; while poor I, who never murdered any one, who never fought a duel or gouged an eye; *and had too much honour to burn my forged deed, when I had once been wicked enough to make it*, must stand here in the pillory, for I am a little rogue. Take warning by my sad fate; and if you must speculate in lands, let it be in millions of acres; and if you must be rogues, take warning by my unhappy fate and become great rogues.—For as it is said in a pair of verses I read when I was a boy,

> Little villains must submit to fate,
> That great ones may enjoy the world in state.

And again,

> A little knavery is a dangerous thing,
> Great cheats will flourish, while the small ones swing.

Pickpocket Training Poem on Credit

Anonymous

Hints to singers.—This song published a great many years since, and by no means difficult to be understood in our times, would not go

amiss to more than one celebrated tune; and we recommend it to the
attention of our sentimental singers;

"What's this dull town to me?
　　No cash is here!
Things that we used to see,
　　Now don't appear!
Where's all the current bills?
Silver dollars, cents and mills!
Oh! we must check our wills,
　　No cash is here!

"What made the city shine?
　　Money was here!
What makes the lads repine?
　　No cash is here!
What makes the planters sad?
Factors crazy, merchants mad?
Oh! times are very bad,
　　No cash is here!

"Oh! curse upon the banks!
　　No credit's there!
They issue nought but blanks!
　　No cash is there!
Hard times, the men do cry;
Hard times, the women sigh—
Ruin and misery!
　　No cash is here!

Nor do we think the following, to the tune of "The Galley Slave,"
and published at Cincinnati, when Cincinnati was a baby city, will be
considered more inaposite to the times, than the one just quoted:

O think on my fate, once I credit enjoyed,
　　And few men were trusted like me;
But my cash is all gone, and my credit destroyed,
　　I failed and a bankrupt I be;
My goods were attached and were all borne away,
　　And I never shall measure them more,
When thought brings to mind what I sold on each day,
　　I sigh for the fate of my store!

Hard, hard is my fate, O how galling my chains,
　　Confined in the county jail yard,

And though of the sherif I never complain,
    My limits I still must regard.
I never reply though my comrades will grin,
    When they think how I figured before;
Oh! around me the writs in profusion are seen,
    And I sigh when I think on my store!

How fortune deceives; I had profit in tow,
    Which I thought to sow close in my drawer,
But my creditors drained me, and bothered me so,
    I fairly was touched in the craw;
My shop it was entered, and I forced away,
    And shall see the shelves crowded no more;
And what's worse, all my debts I never can pay;
    I weep at the thoughts of my store."

A Muggy Morning Off Sandy Hook
A Yarn Spun by a Yankee Tar

Anonymous

Of all human beings, the most proverbially daring and courageous are
seamen. Inured to danger in its most appalling shape, while battling
with the mighty spirit of the storm they risk their lives with reckless
temerity. Cool, collected, and, above all, obedient to command, in the
most trying extremities, not one refuses the point of duty the exigencies of the moment obliges him to maintain; but all strenuously work
with a will, when to the landsman hope appears to be departed, and
inevitable that most fearful of all deaths, the sudden quenching of the
life-spark in the full health and vigour of youth, with the blood flowing freely through the veins, and every sense in full activity.

    Yet, despite of all this bravery, no mass of men are more easily
panic-stricken by any circumstance which, for the time being, should
seem to them strange or unaccountable; superstitious to an extent
hardly conceivable to those who have not lived and moved amongst
them, signs and omens, favourable or inauspicious, sway them to a
man. The shape of a cloud is full of meaning; the movements of fish
important; the very slightest matter at all out of the common run of

events, as would naturally be expected amidst the monotony of a sea-faring life, is eagerly seized upon, and its influence discussed; generally referred to one sagacious individual, who, if he cannot positively explain the phenomenon, usually contrives, by sundry expressive head-shakes to give a degree of immense importance to the event—for your ship-oracle never confesses ignorance upon any subject whatever, but makes his bold assertion in that I-know-all-about-it sort of way, utterly uncontradictable.

A curious exemplification of the rapidity with which a panic will spread through a body of sailors, occurred not many years ago in the neighborhood of New York. Several vessels happened to be making what way they could, slowly and sluggishly, toward New York harbour. They were of various descriptions and from various places, but all creeping slowly on toward their common destination. It was a dull spring morning, very early. The night had been wet, and the gray dawn, long protracted, seemed to have usurped the day's prerogative. A thick, heavy haze settled on the surface of the water, causing that indefinite appearance when the two elements commingle: no sea limit, no horizon, but all round one impenetrable leaden medium; varied only by suddenly looming masses of thicker fog, which rolled cloud-like over, soaking everything in its progress. At last the haze began partially to clear away, and soon a pale, spiritless, washed-out looking sun tried to struggle through the dense veil; showing, however, enough of his face to animate the chilled crew of the good ship Enterprise, Captain Peanut, commander—both fictitious names, for, between you and me, my worthy friend dislikes exceedingly the notoriety of print, beyond the ship's advertisement. Well, the captain, in his choicest nautical phraseology, (which, perhaps, you'll excuse me from repeating literally,) intimated, that as there was not, I think he said, a cap-full of wind, and that little unfavourable, they might as well take in sail, cast anchor, and wait the arrival of the steam-tug. Steam was then in its infancy, and there was no competition. Of course the captain was obeyed instanter; and, in company with half-a-dozen or more vessels similarly situated, remained stationary.

About an hour had elapsed, and my friend P., having finished the discussion of a substantial sea-breakfast, was busily calculating market contingencies, when he heard the tail of a dialogue on deck, which indicated that there was something uncommon afloat.

"Well," said one voice, "if I can make out what she is, I'm—" blessed, he ought to have said, but he didn't.

"Nor I," said another.

At that moment there was the sound of a dull, distant crash.

"Look, look!" said one; "blow my wig if she hasn't run bang into that ere sloop."

The captain got curious, and on reaching the deck saw a clumsy, Dutch-built craft, crawling along on the top of the tide, in a lubberly, unseaman-like way, all no how. She looked as though she had been slightly injured; had lost her foretopsail and part of her bowsprit, over which her jib hung trailing; altogether, she was rigged in a patchy, unaccountable way. There was evidently something wrong. The captain couldn't make it out; and the mysterious craft was as much the wonder of the surrounding ships, for their decks were crowded with men, watching the stranger as she floated by. On she came, clearing the other vessels by a kind of miracle; making directly for the Enterprise, in a dead line. The captain got nervous, seized his trumpet, and nautically roared to the Dutchman to alter his line of conduct; but the ship was deaf as well as blind. On she came; consternation fell upon the crew; the weather, still being rather muggy, magnifying the danger. One false move would have been productive of serious damage; and it was only by exercising some skilful manoeuvre that they at length succeeded in getting out of the stranger's way. This dilemma over, speculation became rife as to what the deuse she could be. Some said, the Flying Dutchman; some one thing, some another. Meantime, a boat's crew arrived, with some captain's compliments, and requesting an elucidation of the affair. None could be given; and a council being held, it was resolved to send a boat to reconnoitre: a proceeding which appeared to have been simultaneously adopted by nearly all the neighboring vessels; and soon several boats were seen making for the stranger. However, the four men who started from the Enterprise were the first to approach her. Anxiously watched from the deck, they were seen to near the vessel. A cry was heard; and, backing off from the ship, the men rowed away with frightful speed, as if avoiding some dread sight. Pale, agitated and exhausted, they returned; and it was some minutes before the spokesman could utter a word, all the crew being grouped round him in wondering suspense. At length he told his tale, which was—that as they came up to the head of the ship they saw nothing remarkable, except that the rigging gave sufficient proof that hands were scarce; but, upon rowing round towards her quarter, what was their horror to see three or four dead sailors hanging over the mainyard arm!

"They must have hung there a long time," said the fellow, "for their heads were gone; and their hands and feet had also disappeared!"

This steel engraving titled *A Muggy Morning Off Sandy Hook* was the frontis-piece for the *New Mirror*, I (July 8, 1843).

White with fear, every soul on board stood awe-stricken, while the captain slowly and solemnly ejaculated—

"Men, she's a *Plague-ship!*"

A cold shudder ran through the group.

"What's to be done?" said they.

"Something must," replied the captain, "and instantly, or else she'll float right into the harbour, carrying a cargo of pestilence. There can't be a living soul on board. What little wind there is, is dead ahead. Let us get a long hawser, tow her ashore, and burn her. It's a dangerous service, so I'll be the first volunteer."

But, before he could put his intent into execution, six determined fellows and the mate, each with a fresh plug in his jaw, jumped into the boat, and for once disobeyed orders, leaving the captain on board.

"Noble fellows!" said he, as he watched them, and not without a glistening eye.

And now they neared the devoted ship. Every man's breath was hushed as the grapnel was made fast; but when they turned her head in-shore, a general cheer burst from every ship around, that might have woke—nay, that did wake—the skipper of the mysterious craft himself, who, rushing up on deck to see what was the matter, astonished the rowers by crying out—

"Yollo, dere! Donder and Blitzen, vot vor de dyvel are you bullen myn chips?"

"Why, then," said our friend the mate, "may the devil sweep flames wid ye, and burn the broom, you vagabone Dutch pickled herrin'. What a fright you guv us!"

I needn't say what countryman he was.

"Why don't you bury your dead, you blaggard?" he continued, pointing up to the dismal spectacle on the yard-arm.

"Pig vools you," replied Mynheer. "Vot vor? I bury jackeds and drowzers."

The mystery was over. They rowed back, not a little delighted at the explanation, and the Dutch Plague-ship was a favourite yarn on board the Enterprise for many a long day.

Charles F. Browne (Artemus Ward)

Soliloquy of a Low Thief

My name is Jim Griggins. I'm a low thief. My parients was ignorant folks, and as poor as the shadder of a bean pole. My advantages for gettin' a eddycation was exceedin' limited. I growed up in the street, quite loose and permiskis, you see, and took to vice because I had nothing else to take to, and because nobody had never given me a sight at virtue.

I'm in the penitentiary. I was sent here onct before for priggin' a watch. I served out my time, and now I'm here agin, this time for stealin' a few insignificant clothes.

I shall always blame my parients for not eddycatin' me. Had I been liberally eddycated I could, with my brilliant native talents, have bin a big thief—I b'leeve they call 'em defaulters. Instead of confinin' myself to priggin' clothes, watches, spoons, and sich like, I could have plundered princely sums—thousands and hundreds of thousands of dollars—and that old humbug, the Law, wouldn't have harmed a hair on my head! For, you see, I should be smart enough to get elected State

Treasurer, or have something to do with Banks or Railroads, and perhaps a little of both. Then, you see, I could ride in my carriage, live in a big house with a free stun frunt, drive a fast team, and drink as much gin and sugar as I wanted. A inwestigation might be made, and some of the noosepapers might come down on me heavy, but what the d——l would I care about that, havin' previously taken precious good care of the stolen money? Besides, my "party" would swear stout that I was as innersunt as the new-born babe, and a great many people would wink very pleasant, and say, "Well, Griggins understands what *he's* 'bout, HE does!'"

But havin' no eddycation, I'm only a low thief—a stealer of watches and spoons and sich—a low wretch, anyhow—and the Law puts me through without mercy.

It's all right, I s'pose, and yet I sometimes think it's weery hard to be shut up here, a wearin' checkered clothes, a livin' on cold vittles, a sleepin' on iron beds, a lookin' out upon the world through iron muskeeter bars, and poundin' stun like a galley slave, day after day, week after week, and year after year, while my brother thieves (for to speak candid, there's no difference between a thief and a defaulter, except that the latter is forty times wuss), who have stolen thousands of dollars to my one cent, are walkin' out there in the bright sunshine— dressed up to kill, new clothes upon their backs and piles of gold in their pockets! But the law don't tech 'em. They are too big game for the Law to shoot at. It's as much as the Law can do to take care of us ignorant theives.

Who said there was no difference 'tween tweedledum and tweedledee! He lied in his throat, like the villain as he was! I tell ye there's a tremendous difference.

Oh that I had been liberally eddycated!

Sing-sing, 1860   Jim Griggins

The Prince of Wales

To My Friends of the Editorial Corpse:—

I rite these lines on British sile. I've bin follerin Mrs Victory's hopeful sun Albert Edward threw Kanady with my onparaleled Show, and tho I haint made much in a pecoonery pint of vew, I've lernt sumthin new, over hear on British Sile, whare they bleeve in Saint Gorge and the Dragoon. Previs to cumin over hear I tawt my organist how to grind Rule Britanny and other airs which is poplar on British Sile. I likewise fixt a wax figger up to represent Sir Edmun Hed the Govner Ginral. The statoot I fixt up is the most versytile wax statoot I ever saw. I've showd it as Wm. Penn, Napoleon Bonypart, Juke of Welling-ton, the Beneker Boy, Mrs Cunningham, & varis other notid persons, & also for a sertin pirut named Hix. I've bin so long amung wax statoots that I can fix 'em up to soot the tastes of folks, & with sum paints I hav I kin giv their facis a beneverlent or fiendish look as the kase requires. I giv Sir Edmun Hed a beneverlent look, & when sum folks who thawt they was smart sed it didn't look like Sir Edmund Hed anymore than it did anybody else, I sed, "That's the pint. That's the beauty of the Statoot. It looks like Sir Edmun Hed or any other man. You may kall it what you pleese. Ef it don't look like anybody that ever lived, then it's sertinly a remarkable Statoot & well worth seein. I kall it Sir Edmun Hed. *You* may kall it what you darn pleese!" [I had 'em thare.]

At larst I've had a interview with the Prince, tho it putty nigh cost me my vallerble life. I cawt a glimpse of him as he sot on the Pizarro of the hotel in Sarnia, & elbowed myself threw a crowd of wimin, chil-dren, sojers, & Injins that was hangin round the tavern. I was drawin near to the Prince when a red faced man in Millingtery close grabd holt of me and axed me whare I was goin all so bold?

"To see Albert Edard the Prince of Wales," sez I; "who are you?"

He sed he was Kurnal of the Seventy Fust Regiment, Her Magisty's troops. I told him I hoped the Seventy Onesters was in good health, and was passin by when he ceased hold of me agin, and sed in a tone of indigent cirprise:

"What? Impossible! It kannot be! Blarst my hize, sir, did I understan you to say that you was actooally goin into the presents of his Royal Iniss?"

"That's what's the matter with me," I replide.

"But blarst my hize, sir, its onprecedented. It's orful, sir. Nothin' like it hain't happened sins the Gun Power Plot of Guy Forks. Owdashus man, who air yu?"

"Sir," sez I, drawin myself up & puttin on a defiant air, "I'm a Amerycan sitterzen. My name is Ward. I'm a husband & the father of twins, which I'm happy to state they look like me. By perfeshun I'm a exhibiter of wax works & sich."

"Good God!" yelled the Kurnal, "the idee of a exhibiter of wax fig-gers goin into the presents of Royalty! The British Lion may well roar with raje at the thawt!"

Sez I, "Speakin of the British Lion, Kurnal, I'd like to make a bargin with you fur that beast fur a few weeks to add to my Show." I didn't mean nothin by this. I was only gettin orf a goak, but you orter hev seen the Old Kurnal jump up & howl. He actooally fomed at the mowth.

"This can't be real," he showtid. "No, no. It's a horrid dream. Sir, you air not a human bein—you hav no existents—yure a Myth!"

"Wall," sez I, "old hoss, yule find me a ruther onkomfortable Myth ef you punch my inards in that way agin." I began to git a little riled, fur when he called me a Myth he puncht me putty hard. The Kurnal now commenst showtin fur the Seventy Onesters. I at fust thawt I'd stay & becum a Marter to a British Outraje, as sich a course mite git ny name up, & be a good advertisement fur my Show; but it occurred to me that ef enny of the Seventy Onesters should happen to insert a barronet into my stummick, it mite be onplesunt, & I was on the pint of runnin orf when the Prince hisself kum up & axed me what the matter was. Sez I, "Albert Edard, is that you?" & he smilt & sed it was. Sez I, "Albert Edard, hears my keerd. I cum to pay my respecks to the futer King of Ingland. The Kurnal of the Seventy Onesters hear is ruther smawl pertaters, but of course you ain't to blame fur that. He puts on as many airs as tho he was the Bully Boy with the glass eye."

"Never mind," sez Albert Edard; "I'm glad to see you, Mister Ward, at all events," & he tuk my hand so plesunt like & larfed so sweet that I fell in love with him to onct. He handed me a segar & we sot down on the Pizarro & commenst smokin rite cheerful. "Wall," sez I, "Al-bert Edard, how's the old folks?"

"Her majesty & the Prince are well," he sed.

"Duz the old man take his Lager beer reglar?" I inquired.

The Prince larfed, & intermatid that the old man didn't let many kegs of that bevridge spile in the sellar in the coarse of a year. We sot & tawked there sum time abowt matters & things, & bimeby I axed him how he liked bein Prince as fur as he'd got.

"To speak plain, Mister Ward," he sed, "I don't much like it. I'm sick of all this bowin & scrapin & crawlin & hurrain over a boy like me. I would rather go through the country quietly & enjoy myself in my own way, with the other boys, & not be made a Show of to be garped at by everybody. When the *peple* cheer me I feel pleesed, fur I know they meen it, but if these one-horse offishuls coold know how I see threw all their moves & understan exackly what they air after, & knowd how I larft at 'em in private, theyd stop kissin my hands & fawnin over me as thay now do. But you know Mr Ward I can't help bein a Prince, & I must do all I kin to fit myself fur the persishun I must sumtime ockepy."

"That's troo," sez I; "sickness and the doctors will carry the Queen orf one of these dase, sure's yer born."

The time hevin arove fur me to take my departer, I rose up & sed: "Albert Edard, I must go, but previs to doin so I will obsarve that you soot me. Yure a good feller, Albert Edard, & tho I'm agin Princes as a gineral thing, I must say I like the cut of your Gib. When you git to be King try and be as good a man as yure muther has bin! Be just & be Jenerus, espeshully to showmen, who hav allers bin aboozed sins the dase of Noah, who was the fust man to go into the Menagery bizniss, & ef the daily papers of his time air to be beleeved Noah's colleckshun of livin wild beests beet ennything ever seen sins, tho I make bold to dowt ef his snaiks was ahead of mine. Albert Edard, adoo!" I tuk his hand which he shook warmly, & givin him a perpetooal free pars to my show, & also parses to take hum for the Queen & Old Albert, I put on my hat and walkt away.

"Mrs Ward," I solilerquized, as I walkt along, "Mrs Ward, ef you could see your husband now, just as he prowdly emerjis from the presunts of the futur King of Ingland, you'd be sorry you called him a Beest jest becaws he cum home tired 1 nite, and wantid to go to bed without takin orf his boots. You'd be sorry for tryin to deprive yure husband of the pricelis Boon of liberty, Betsy Jane!"

Jest then I met a long perseshun of men with gownds onto 'em. The leader was on horseback, & ridin up to me he sed, "Air you Orange?"

Sez I, "Which?"

"Air you a Orangeman?" he repeated, sternly.

"I used to peddle lemins," sed I, "but I never delt in oranges. They are apt to spile on yure hands. What particler Loonatic Asylum hev you & yure frends escaped frum, ef I may be so bold?" Just then a sudden thawt struck me, & I sed, "Oh yure the fellers who air worryin the Prince so & givin the Juke of Noocastle cold sweats at nite, by your infernal catawalins, air you? Wall, take the advice of a Amerykin sitterzin: take orf them gownds & don't try to get up a religious fite, which is 40 time wuss nor a prize fite, over Albert Edard, who wants to receive you all on a ekal footin, not keerin a tinker's cuss what

meetin house you sleep in Sundays. Go home and mind yure bizniss &
not make noosenses of yourselves." With which observashuns I left
'em.

I shall leeve British sile 4thwith.

The First Locomotive

Anonymous

In the year 1808, I enjoyed the never-to-be forgotten gratification of a
paddle up the Hudson, on board the aforesaid first steamboat that
ever moved on the waters of any river with passengers. Among the
voyagers was a man I had known for some years previous, by the name
of Jabez Doolittle. He was an industrious and ingenious worker in
sheet-iron, tin, and wire; but his greatest success lay in wirework, especially in making "rat-traps," and for this and best invention in that
line, he had just secured a patent; and with a specimen of his work he
was on a journey through the State of New York, for the purpose of
disposing of what he called "county rights;" or, in other words, to sell
the privilege of catching rats, according to his patent trap. It was a very
curious trap, as simple as it was ingenious, as most ingenious things
are after they are invented. It was an oblong wire-box, divided into
two compartments; a rat enters into one end, where the bait was hung,
which he no sooner touched than the door at which he entered fell.
His only apparent escape was by a funnel-shaped hole into the other
apartment, in passing which he moved another wire, which instantly
reset the trap; and thus rat after rat was furnished the means of "following his illustrious predecessor," until the trap was full. Thus it was
not simply a trap to catch a rat, but a trap in which rats trapped rats *ad
infinitum*. And now that the recollection of that wonderful trap is re-
called to my memory, I would respectfully recommend it to the attention of the treasury department as an appendage to the sub-treasury
system. The "specification" may be found on file in the patent office,
number eleven thousand seven hundred and forty-six.

This trap, at the time to which I alluded, absolutely divided the attention of the passengers; and for my part, it interested me quite as
much as did the steam-engine, because, perhaps, I could more easily

understand its mystery. To me, the steam-engine was Greek; the trap was plain English. Not so, however, to Jabez Doolittle. I found him studying the engine with great avidity and perseverance, insomuch that the engineer evidently became alarmed, and declined answering any more questions.

"Why, you needn't snap off so tarnal short," said Jabez; "a body would think you had not got a patent on your machine. If I can't meddle with you on the water, nigh as I calculate, I'll be up to you on land, on one of these days."

These ominous words fell upon my ear as I saw Jabez issue from the engine-room, followed by the engineer, who seemed evidently to have got his steam up.

"Well, Jabez," said I, "what do you think of this mighty machine?"

"Why," he replied, "if that critter hadn't got riled up so soon, a body could tell more about it; but I reckon I've got a leetle notion on't:" and then taking me aside, and looking carefully around lest some one should overhear him, he then and there assured me in confidence, in profound secrecy, that if he didn't make a wagon go by steam before he was two years older, then he would give up invention. I at first ridiculed the idea; but when I thought of the rat-trap, and saw before me a man with sharp, twinkling gray eyes, a pointed nose, and every line of his visage a channel of investigation and invention, I could not resist the conclusion that if he really ever did attempt to meddle with hot water, we should hear more about it.

Time went on. Steamboats multiplied; but none dreamed, or if they did, they never told their dreams of a steam-wagon, for even the name of "locomotive" was then as unknown as "locofoco." When about a year after the declaration of the last war with England—and may it be the last—I got a letter from Jabez, marked "private," telling me that he wanted to see me "most desperately," and that I must make him a visit at his place, "near Wilmingford." The din of arms and the destruction of insurance companies, the smashing of banks, and suspension of specie payments, and various other inseparable attendants on the show and "pomp and circumstances of glorious war," had, in the meantime, entirely wiped from memory my friend Jabez and his wonderful rat-trap. But I obeyed his summons, not knowing but that something of importance to the army or navy might come of it. On reaching his residence, imagine my surprise, when he told me he believed he had "got the notion."

"Notion? what notion?" I inquired.

"Why," says he, "that steam-wagon I told you of a spell ago; but it has pretty nigh starved me out:" and sure enough he did look as if he had been on "the anxious seat," as he used to say when things puzzled him.

"I have used up," said he, "plaguey nigh all the sheet-iron, and old stove-pipes, and mill-wheels and trunnel brads in these parts; and for fear some of those 'cute folks about here may have got a peep through the key-hole, and will trouble me when I come to get a patent, I've sent for you to be a witness, for you was the first and only man I ever hinted to; in fact," continued he, "I think the most curious part of this invention is that, as yet, I don't know any one about here who has been able to guess what I'm about. They all know it is an invention of some kind, for that's my business, you know, but some say it is a threshing-machine, some a distillery; and, of late, they begin to think it's a shingle-splitter; but they'll sing another tune when they see it spinning along past the stage-coaches," added he, with a knowing chuckle, "won't they?"

This brought us to the door of an old, clap-boarded, dingy, long, one-story building, with a window or two in the roof, the knot-holes and cracks all carefully stuffed with rags; and over the door he was unlocking, was written in bold letters, "No Admittance." This was his "sanctum sanctorum." I could occupy pages in a description of it, for every part exhibited evidence of its uses. The Patent Office at Washington, like your Magazine, Mr. Editor, may exhibit "finished productions" or "inventive genius," but if you could look into the folios of your contributors, in every quarter of the Union, and see there the sketches of half-finished essays, still-born poems, links and fragments of ideas and conception, which but breathed and died, you might form some notion of the accumulation of notions that were presented to my eye on entering the workshop of Jabez Doolittle.

But to my text again—"The first Locomotive." There it stood, occupying the centre of all previous conceptions—rat-traps, churns, apple-parers, bill-rollers, cooking-stoves, and shingle-splitters, which hung, or stood around it; or, as my Lord Byron says, with a reference to a more ancient, but not more important invention:

> "Where each conception was a heavenly gust,
> A ray of immortality, and stood,
> Star-like around, until they gathered to a God."

And there stood "the concentrated focus of all previous rays of inventive genius—'The First Locomotive.'"

An unpainted, unpolished, and unadorned, even-shaped mass of double-rivetted sheet-iron, with cranks and pipes, and trunnel-heads and screws, and valves, all firmly based on four strongly-made travelling wheels.

"It's a curious critter to look at," said Jabez, "but you'll like it better when you see it in motion."

He was by this time igniting a quantity of charcoal, which he had stuffed under the boiler. "I filled the biler," said he, "arter I stopped work here yesterday, and it hain't leaked a drop since. It will soon bile up, the coal is first-rate."

Sure enough, the boiler soon gave evidence of "troubled waters," when, by pushing one slide and pulling another, the whole machine, cranks and pistons, was in motion.

"It works slick, don't it?" said Jabez.

"But it don't move," I replied.

"You mean," said he, "the travelling-wheels don't move; well, I don't mean they shall till I get my patent. You see," he added, crouching down, "that trunnel-head there, that small cog-wheel? Well, that's out of gear just yet—when I turn that into gear, by this crank, it fits, you see, on the main travelling-wheel, and then the hull-scrape will move, as nigh as I can calculate, a little slower than chain lightning, and a darned little, too! But it won't do to give it a try afore I get the patent.—There is only one thing yet," he continued, "that I hain't contrived—but that's a simple matter—the shortest mode of stopping on her. My first notion is to see how fast I can make her work without smashing all to bits, and that's done by screwing down this upper valve—and I'll show you—"

And with that, he clambered upon the top with a turning-screw in one hand, and a horn of soft soap in the other, and commenced screwing down the valves and oiling the piston and crank-joints, and the motion of the mysterious mass increased until all seemed to be a buzz.

"It is nigh about perfection, ain't it?" says Jabez.

"Jabez," said I, elevating my voice above the buzzing noise of the machine, "there is only one thing wanting."

"What is that?" says he, eagerly.

"Immortality!" says I, "and you shall have it, patent or no patent!" And with that, I pulled the crank that twisted the connecting trunnel-head into the travelling-wheels, and in an instant away went the machine, with Jabez on top of it, with the whiz and rapidity of a flushed partridge. The side of the old building presented the resistance of a wet paper. One crash, and the "first locomotive" was ushered into this

Steam machines challenged horse-drawn transportation as the economic basis of the northern economy developed. Captioned "She see this wild and skairful machine approachin'," this comic illustration appeared in *Samantha Among the Brethren* (1890).

breathing world. I hurried to the opening, and had just time to clamber to the top of a fence, to catch the last glimpse of my fast departing friend. True to his purpose, I saw him alternately screwing down the valves, and oiling the piston-rod and crank-joints, evidently determined that, although he had started off a little unexpectedly, he would redeem the pledge he had given, which was, that when it did go, "it would go a little slower than chain lightnin', and a darned leetle, too!"

But a moment and he was here, a moment and he was there, and now where is he, or rather, where is he not? But that, for the present, is neither here nor there.

My task is done. All I now ask is, that although some doubt and mystery hang over the first invention of a steamboat—in which doubt, however, I for one do not participate, none whatever may exist in regard to the locomotive branch of the great steam family; and that in all future time this fragment of authentic history may enable the latest posterity to retrace, by the "back track and turn out," through a long railroad line of illustrious ancestors, the projector and contriver of the first locomotive, the immortal progenitor, "Jabez Doolittle, Esq., nigh Wallingford, Connecticut."

Picketing—an Affecting War Incident

Anonymous

While on my lonely beat, about an hour ago, a light tread attracted my attention, and, on looking up, I beheld one of Secesh's pickets standing before me.

"Stranger," says he, "you remind me of my grandmother, who expired before I was born; but this unnatural war has made us enemies, and I must shoot you. Give me a chaw terbacker."

He was a young man, in the prime of life, and descended from the First Families of Virginia. That is to say, his mother was a virgin. At least that's what I understand by the First Families of Virginia.

I looked at him, and says I—

"Let's compromise, my brother."

"Never!" says he; "the South is fighting for her liberty, her firesides, and the pursuit of happiness, and I desire most respectfully to welcome you with bloody hands to a hospitable grave."

"Stand off ten paces," says I, "and let's see whose name shall come before the coroner first."

He took his place, and we fired simultaneously. I heard a ball go whistling by a barn about a quarter of a mile on my right; and when the smoke cleared away I saw the Secesh picket approach me with an awful expression of woe on his otherwise dirty countenance.

"Soldier," says he, "was there any thing in my head before you fired?"

"Nothing," says I, "save a few harmless insects."

"I speak not of them," says he. "Was there any thing *inside* of my head?"

"Nothing!" says I.

"Well," says he, "just listen now."

He shook his head mournfully, and I heard something rattle in it.

"What's that?" I exclaimed.

"That," said he, "is your bullet, which has penetrated my skull, and is rolling around in my brain. I die happy, and with an empty stomach; but there is one thing I should like to see before I perish for my country. Have you a quarter about you?"

Too much affected to speak, I drew the coin from my pocket and handed it to him. The dying man clutched it convulsively, and stared at it feverishly.

"This," said he, "is the first quarter I have seen since the fall of Sumter; and had I wounded you, I should have been totally unable to have given you any quarter. Ah! how beautiful it is! how bright! how exquisite! and good for four drinks! But I have not time to say all I feel."

The expiring soldier then laid down his gun, hung his cap and overcoat on a branch of a tree, and blew his nose. He then died.

And there I stood, on that lonely beat, looking down upon that fallen type of manhood, and thinking how singular it was he had forgotten to give me back my quarter. The sight and the thought so affected me that I was obliged to turn my back on the corpse and walk a little way from it. When I returned to the spot the body was gone! Had it gone to heaven? Perhaps so—perhaps so; but I haven't seen my quarter since.

Henry W. Shaw (Josh Billings)

Amerikan Aristokrasy

Political ekonomists hav defined an aristokrasy as a power or government in which a privileged few hold dominyun.

I am not aware that sich a government exists, in a pure form, at the present day among the nashuns ov the earth.

But we kant be mistaken in the fackt that even in our own Republick thare are menny kandidates who would luv to participate in the peculiar privileges ov an aristokrasy.

We hav divided Amerikan Aristokrasy (jist for fun) into 3 piles—the moneyed, the mackrel, and the pedigree aristokrats.

Not having much time tew spare, we pitch into them a good deal as follers:

The moneyed aristokrats are like certain fine coated animals, worth just what their hides will bring.

The mackrels are remarkable for their numbers and the small kapital they dew bizziness on; and while arrayed in their false dignity, and straining hard tew cheat us in awl things, are like a drunken man trieing tew walk a krack.

The pedigrees hav mutch innosense and little courage. Content with the glory ov their ancestors, they are satisfied in holding under our noses a grandfather's fossils, and fondly beleaf that the bones make them smell ov greatness.

Finally, trieing tew be a fust klass aristokrat in America, just yet, appears tew us tew be almost as flattring an enterprise as climbing a greased pole. Thare is great doubt about our being able to reach the top, and if we dew succeed (and don't pull the pole up after us) we will soon hav the mortifikashun ov seeing some other sheumaker climbing up the same pole.

MORAL—Don't be an aristocrat if you kan help it.

Essays on Animated Nature
Meleagris Gallopavo—the American Turkey

Anonymous

Audubon and other scientific bushwhackers having discribed the habits, manners and personal appearance of this distinguished fowl, as it exists in its native thickets, I shall say little or nothing of the Wild Turkey of the Plateau and the Cover; but confine my remarks mainly to the Tame Turkey of the Platter and the Dish. In this connection, I will take leave to say, that the untraveled barnyard Ornithologist enjoys better opportunities for studying and digesting the subject than usually falls to the lot of his peripatetic confreres.

With all my partiality for the *Meleagris Gallopavo*, I must admit that in its domesticated state the creature is an idiot. The goose has generally been considered the weakest-minded of feathered imbeciles, but it has, at least, sense enough to make itself as disagreeable as possible to the human race by hissing at them most vehemently. But what does the Tom-fool of a Tom-turkey do when you approach him? With a simplicity that is next to miraculous, he gives notice of his own edibility by vociferating "*gobble! gobble!*"—imparting a sort of chuckling intonation to the suggestive syllables as if he were proud of the tenderness of his flesh and tickled with the idea of its delicate flavor. Fenelon's capons that ran about the streets of Cocaigne ready roasted, crying out "come eat me!" scarcely exhibited a greater lack of the self-preservative instinct.

The Puritan Fathers, self-denying saints though they were, could not hear that invitation to gormandize continually resounding through the woods of the Bay Colony, unmoved. It amounted, in their half-starved condition, to a cruel taunt, and moistened their sympathetic palates with epicurean tears. Yielding to their carnal appetites, they slew and ate, and although the Noble Savage, on discovering their taste for turkey, often lured them into the depths of the forest with imitative "gobbles," and by that means took many steeple-crowned scalps, the work went bravely on as long as the game lasted. I blame not those solemn gluttons for risking their lives to obtain such delicious fare. Under the same circumstances I should have done likewise.

Of our two national fowls—the Fourth of July Screamer and the Thanksgiving Gobbler—I prefer the latter. The eagle may be first in war, but the turkey is first in peace, and, if I mistake not, in the hearts of my countrymen. Fighting Falco moves in the highest circles, amid the flash and roar of Heaven's artillery; but, thunder and lightning! what is he good for practically. We brag of him, but can't utilize him. As to eating him—it would be as easy to masticate that metalsome uniped, the weathercock. He's well enough for a national "totem," but if the market were full of birds o' freedom, who would care to tote 'em home as provant?

Reader, it is not thuswise with our mutual friend Gallopavo. There is not a fibre in his structure from the arch of his merrythought to the top of the mis-located clerical nose of him, that isn't a tid-bit for June when she banquets. Could we offer up our November thanks with the requisite unction if turkeys were not? In tones of thunder the universal American epigastrium answers "No!"

The domestic turkey in its early youth being of a delicate habit of body, requires a stimulant, and the experienced breeder warms up its infant gizzard with peppercorns. Hard-boiled hen-fruit, intermixed with the Weathersfield vegetable—the whole being chopped fine—is considered its healthiest diet while in a state of down; but as it feathers out, its digestion becomes vigorous and comprehensive, and the full-fledged bird is so little particular about its *grub* that it will devour the most disgusting of all caterpillars—the tobacco-worm.

On the turkey farms of New England and in Pennsylvania and the West, there is, at this festive season a fearful massacre going on. The carotid-artery-cutting turkey-butchers are slaying their victims by the thousand and then sleighing them to the nearest markets. Christmas and New Year's, as well as Thanksgiving, are sad epochs in the history of all the gallinaceous tribes—but to the *Meleagris Gallopavo* they are ever-recurring St. Bartholomews. When turkey is twenty-five cents a pound it receives no quarter.

Yet the shedding of all this innocent blood touches not the heart or the conscience of that festive Ogre, the civilized Christian. As he treads the aisles of the Temples dedicated to Washington, Fulton, Jefferson and Franklin, walled on either side with the pale corpses of the Barn-yard Dead, he laughs ha! ha! like the mustang that smelleth the oats awaiting him in the corral. Visions of the boiled bird with celery sauce, of the roasted creature "filled in" with sausage meat, of devilled legs, wisely seasoned and flanked by segments of the *piquante* lemon, excite his inner-man and extinguish the better feelings of his nature. If he happens to be too poor to acquire a turkey honorably, he would have no objection, perhaps, to accept of one that had been *boned*, such is the effect of holiday hunger upon moral principle.

Fortunately for the festal piety of the American people, the wholesale and continuous slaughter of their favorite national fowl does not threaten its extermination. Procreation keeps pace with consumption. The turkey like the phenix appears to be irrepressible. Long may he wave!

Q.V.A.

Why She Could Not Be His Wife

Anonymous

Gwendolen, standing on the verge of womanhood, had received from Harold Nonesuch the greatest compliment that man can pay to woman—an offer to try and pay her board. Never for an instant had she suspected the deep, passionate admiration that this man's soul held for her, and of which he had just spoken in tones that were tremulous with hopeful expectancy. And then, mastering by a mighty effort the shock that his unexpected words had caused, she had answered him with the question, so weird in its realism as to be almost grotesque: "Do you like apple fritters?"

For an instant Harold seemed dazed by the girl's words, and stood silently beside a marble statue of Psyche, striving to repress the terrible grief that threatened to master every emotion of his being. As he stood there, the long evening shadows slanting across the sward, and the purple mists of Indian summer crowning the hills with their royal haze, he felt that life without the love of this woman would be a Sahara of grief, an endless desert of disappointed hope and crushed ambition over which the scorching winds of sorrow and anguish would ever blow with pitiless fury.

And then, just as a sob was welling up from his vest, he felt a pair of soft, warm arms twined lovingly around his neck, and close beside his own there was pressed a clear-cut cameo face that seemed in its spirituelle beauty like a vision from another world. There were tears in the violet eyes that looked into his so pleadingly, and the curves of the drooping mouth were tense with the agony of an all-powerful sorrow. For an instant neither spoke, and Gwendolen was the first to break the silence.

"You must have known, Harold," she said, in tones that were hoarse with agony, "that for months my heart has been in your keeping, and you must also have known that my love is no ephemeral passion—no let-me-take-your-slate-pencil-and-you-can-chew-my-gum-at-recess affection that is here to-day, and to-morrow where is it? And yet, despite this fact, which I so freely acknowledge, and of which I am more than proud, I can never be your wife."

"Why not?" he asks, in tones that are almost a sob.

"Because," answers Gwendolen, "I have cold, Boston feet."

✃ Bibliographical Essay ✃

Rich sources of northeastern humor remain largely untapped in newspapers, periodicals, jokebooks, hardcover reprints of the more transient popular pamphlets, and even such sources as elocution anthologies. The arbitrary division of American humor into Yankee, Knickerbocker, southwestern, and western schools obscures the responsiveness of northeastern humorists to their changing milieu. For example, the active group of Philadelphia writers, including Nicholas Biddle, Joseph C. Neal, Charles and Henry Leland, and lesser writers, attracted to *Neal's Saturday Gazette*, *Godey's*, and *Graham's* falls outside any of these previous categories. Even a comprehensive listing of the writers of the northern cities through the nineteenth century has yet to be done. However, many of the sources used to derive the selections for this anthology lead to still other writers.

Older anthologies of American humorists have provided the most obvious and broadest representation of American writers. Chief among these is William E. Burton's *Cyclopedia of Wit and Humor* (New York, 1858), which contains an extraordinary breadth of material produced from the 1640s through the 1850s. Burton's *Cyclopedia* is particularly helpful in its representation of northeasterners of the 1820–1850 period who are generally overlooked elsewhere. Evert A. Duyckinck and George L. Duyckinck's *Cyclopedia of American Literature* (2 vols.; New York, 1856) offers brief but useful headnotes with its range of selections from American authors, including numerous humorists. Thomas Chandler Haliburton, as "Sam Slick," edited a collection of comic stories, *Traits of American Humor* (London [1852]), which is valuable although it does not identify stories by author or date; a second volume, *The Americans at Home* (London, 1854), followed. *Mark Twain's Library of Humor* (New York, 1888), edited by William Dean Howells with Mark Twain's help, reflects lists of humorists in Twain's notebooks. Two later anthologies are extensive in their selections. A. R. Spofford's *The Library of Wit and Humor* (5 vols.; Philadelphia, 1894) has international selections, headnotes of varied quality, and a range of British humorists who bear on American humor; Marshall P. Wilder's *The Wit and Humor of America* (10 vols.; New York, 1907), like Twain's and Spofford's collections, has a good selection of post–Civil War writers. Edward T. Mason's *Humorous Masterpieces from American Literature* (3 vols.; New York, 1887) offers a large number of comic stories from conventional and sentimental writers in addition to the more obvious humorists of the era, and James Barr offers a well-rounded selection with an index to humorists in *The Humour of America* (London, 1909).

Collections of less value include the various volumes of *Yankee Drolleries* compiled by G. A. Sala (London, 1860s); *Half Hours with the Humorists* (New York, 1875); *American Wit and Humor* (3 vols.; New York, 1907); and collections by Eli Perkins [Melville D. Landon], *Kings of the Platform and Pulpit* (Akron, Ohio, 1906 [1890]) and *Library of Wit and Humor* (Chicago, n.d.). All of these cover fewer humorists and generally stick to the obvious post–Civil War newspaper comedians. Rufus Wilmot Griswold's early collections, *The Prose Writers of America* (Philadelphia, 1846) and *The Curiosities of American Literature* (New York [1843]), are valuable for Griswold's idiosyncratic judgments and for his reprinting of important earlier northeastern writers like Joseph Dennie and Lord Timothy Dexter of the earlier Federal period from 1776 to 1830.

A number of other commentators have made valuable contributions to the study of northeastern humor. Walter Blair's *Native American Humor* (San Francisco, 1960 [1937]) is definitive for modern students, although its terms differ slightly from those in this book. Walter Blair and Hamlin Hill also survey American comic literature fully in *America's Humor: From Poor Richard to Doonesbury* (Oxford, 1978). J. C. Derby, *Fifty Years Among Authors, Books, and Publishers* (New York, 1886), provides personal reminiscences about a range of popular and comic writers known to Derby as a leading publisher of such material. Will D. Howe's "Early Humorists" and George F. Whicher's "Minor Humorists," both in the *Cambridge History of American Literature* (4 vols.; New York, 1918), II, 148–59, III, 21–30, are good modern surveys as are chapters in the standard American literary histories, Robert Spiller *et al.*, *Literary History of the United States* (2 vols.; 4th ed.; New York, 1974), and Arthur H. Quinn (ed.), *Literature of the American People* (New York, 1951). Also noteworthy is "Yankee Humor,"

London Quarterly Review, CXXII (January, 1867), 111–24. Aaron Mendoza, "Some 'Firsts' of American Humor, 1830–1875," *Publisher's Weekly* (March 21, 1931), 1603–605, lists humorists without any discernible attempt at accuracy. B. P. Shillaber, "Experiences During Many Years," *New England Magazine*, IX (October, 1893), 153–55, also lists many northeastern writers not listed elsewhere. Other useful materials are provided in Blair's *Native American Humor* and in Blair's "The Popularity of Nineteenth-Century Humorists," *American Literature*, III (May, 1931), 175–94, which covers the national scene in the post–Civil War period particularly well.

The periodical literature of the Northeast is particularly productive of resources in northern humor, both in the presentation of original materials yet to be discovered and in the reproduction through the "exchange" system of jokes and comic stories that commanded national attention, as did many of Joseph C. Neal's "City Worthies." George P. Morris and N. P. Willis published a wide variety of comic and sentimental material in the New York *Mirror* in the first half of the century; the New York Sunday *Mercury* and Street and Smith's *New York Weekly* were equally active following the Civil War. Comic magazines as such included New England's *Yankee Blade* and *Carpetbag*, the latter edited by B. P. Shillaber, and New York's *Yankee Notions* and *Vanity Fair* among a number of other journals listed in Frank Luther Mott's *History of American Magazines* (5 vols.; Cambridge, Mass., 1938). Lewis Gaylord Clark's New York *Knickerbocker* requires special notice as a repository of northern humor before the Civil War, although Clark tended toward the refined rather than the roughhouse; the *Knickerbocker* might be taken as a companion of William T. Porter's *Spirit of the Times*, which also printed northern as well as southwestern humor. Norris W. Yates, *William Trotter Porter and "The Spirit of the Times"* (Baton Rouge, 1957), and Leslie W. Dunlap, "Biographical Introduction" to *The Letters of Willis Gaylord Clark and Lewis Gaylord Clark* (New York, 1940), are valuable studies of these periodicals. John Paul Pritchard's *Literary Wise Men of Gotham* (Baton Rouge, 1963) examines the critical theory motivating New York critics and editors prior to the Civil War. Other magazines, like the later *Judge* and *Life*, and *Graham's*, *Sartain's*, *Harper's*, *Galaxy*, and others, provided joke columns and comic stories on a regular basis.

Frequently, humor was recirculated through the newspaper exchanges to end up in joke books, which appeared throughout this era.

Not uncommonly a story originated in a source such as P. T. Barnum's *Life* or *Anecdotes, Tales, &C. Selected by a Debtor During His Confinement in Durham Jail* (Durham, 1800); traveled independently of its source, accumulating details not in the original; and ended up as a detached comic episode in one of the various collections of humor that appeared throughout the middle and later part of the century. Falconbridge [Jonathan F. Kelley], *The Game Cock of the Wilderness; or, The Life and Times of Dan Marble* (New York, 1851), and W. K. Northall (ed.), *Life and Recollections of Yankee Hill* (New York, 1850), along with Barnum, are particularly rich sources for Yankee comedy circulating in this manner. Among the most interesting of the joke books are Robert Kempt's *The American Joe Miller* (London, 1865) and *The Railway Anecdote Book* (New York, 1864); *The Spirit of the Farmer's Museum* (Walpole, N.H., 1801) contains interesting selections written prior to the period considered here; Frank Tousey's *Chill Blains* (New York, 1883) has jokes that reflect something more of the sense of modern urban neighborhoods than does the earlier humor. The list given here hardly scratches the surface of the collections of comic anecdotes available, and a full consideration would include English jest books as well as American joke collections.

A variety of critical studies deserve special note as resources for northeastern humor. Jennette Tandy, *Crackerbox Philosophers in American Humor and Satire* (New York, 1925); Walter Blair, *Horse Sense in American Humor* (Chicago, 1925); and Mody C. Boatright, *Folk Laughter on the American Frontier* (New York, 1949), are particularly insightful in showing American pragmatism at work. Keenly aware of the transmission and infusion of materials from one source to another in the Northeast, Richard M. Dorson offers a series of essays on the field in *American Folklore and the Historian* (Chicago, 1971) and *Jonathan Draws the Long-bow* (Cambridge, Mass.; 1946), which contains a long and valuable selection of Yankee anecdotes, including many particularly interesting ones from the *Yankee Blade*. Fred L. Pattee's *The Feminine Fifties* (New York, 1940) offers several chapters that help to place Phoenix, Cozzens, Shillaber, Whitcher, Curtis, and Willis, among others, in the context of their era. Van Wyck Brooks, *The World of Washington Irving* (New York, 1950), is equally good in defining a group of earlier writers including Dennie, H. H. Brackenridge, Simms, Paulding, and Irving. Daniel Royot's *L'Humour américain des puritains aux yankees* (Lyon, 1982) is a valuable study of

New England humor through Shillaber, with careful attention to the Yankee humorists and Haliburton, among others.

Specific Yankee sources include a number of anthologies. B. A. Botkin collected short anecdotes unsystematically in *A Treasury of New England Folklore* (New York, 1965 [1947]), one of a series of valuable collections by Botkin. Alton H. Blackington, *Yankee Yarns* (New York, 1954), and *More Yankee Yarns* (New York, 1956), reprints some of the yarns that he collected throughout New England and broadcast over WBZ in Boston from 1933 to 1953; he refers to masses of radio scripts then extant from which he took the small sampling. The books on Dan Marble and Yankee Hill, the first important stage Yankees, have already been cited, as has Dorson's book. William E. Burton's *The Yankee Amongst the Mermaids* (Philadelphia, 1843) is a collection of his longer pieces. V. L. O. Chittick's *Thomas Chandler Haliburton: A Study in Provincial Toryism* (New York, 1924) has a particularly comprehensive bibliography of primary and secondary sources related to Sam Slick and his creator. Later humor collections frequently devote a section to Yankee or New England humor, along with Negro, Irish, and western humor.

Boston was at the center of New England intellectual life, but other cities frequently spawned publications of their own, such as modest anthologies like New Haven's the *Tablet* (1831) with its one comic village story. Before the 1830s, Joseph Dennie's *Tablet* magazine and *The Farmer's Museum* from Walpole, N.H., stand out as particularly modern in their social and literary egalitarian sarcasm, a sample of which is reprinted in this volume. Yet the satiric Boston collection *The Echo, with Other Poems* (1807), a throwback to the coffeehouse London of the Augustan era, is overtly political and conservative in formal iambic verse. As elsewhere in the study of northeastern humor, focus on the main motivating force behind the comedians is easily lost. B. P. Shillaber of Chelsea and Boston was a leading figure as editor of the Boston *Carpet-bag* (1851–1853) and author of his Mrs. Partington pieces, among other comic writings and verse, for half a century; he has yet to be clearly placed in American humor as a seminal figure, if indeed he actually is one. Charles G. Leland's Boston *Continental Monthly Magazine*, during the months immediately preceding the Civil War and the first year of the war, offers a remarkable study of the political stance of the North in ironic and sarcastic prose and verse.

New York City as a publishing center naturally produced a lion's share of comic literature. Of the forty-six publishing houses listed in Madeleine Stern's *Publishers for Mass Entertainment in Nineteenth Century America* (Boston, 1980), the only significant comic publisher outside of New York City is T. B. Peterson and Brothers of Philadelphia. Even Alex E. Sweet and J. Armory Knox' *Sketches from Texas Siftings* (New York, 1882) bears a New York City publishing address and a dedication to Henry Clay Lukens of "Giddy Gotham." Washington Irving and James K. Paulding originated the Knickerbocker school of humor with their *Salmagundi* papers in the first decade of the nineteenth century. Brooks's study, *The World of Washington Irving*, has already been cited. The *Knickerbocker Magazine* took its shape under Lewis G. Clark in 1834 and lasted until the Civil War, during which time it was one of America's foremost humorous journals. *The Knickerbocker Gallery* (New York, 1854), a testimonial to Clark from his contributors, included Irving and Holmes, Donald G. Mitchell, John G. Saxe, C. A. Bristed, James T. Fields, George P. Morris, Charles G. Leland, George W. Curtis, George D. Prentice, and a host of others, all of whom figured in this study in one way or another. The circle of Bohemians and Civil War humorists assembled in Pfaff's Cellar on Broadway, including Aldrich, Stoddard, Artemus Ward, Henry Clapp of the *Saturday Press*—another leading comic paper—George Arnold, and more, has not been touched heavily in this anthology, although as a reporter Doesticks belonged to this configuration. Likewise, the humorists of the later part of the nineteenth century, because they are in many cases focused on the upper social classes to the exclusion of serious ethical and social commentary, fall outside the scope of this study. However, *Life*, *Puck*, and *Judge* deserve further analysis as the basis for the belles-lettres comic writers of the early twentieth century and, ultimately, the *New Yorker*.

Philadelphia was an active center of American humor, and from Benjamin Franklin's time on, a high degree of social commentary and urban description is evident. Joseph C. Neal, Lewis Godey, and a variety of other literary entrepreneurs fashioned a large number of newspapers and periodicals into popular and comic journals. *Neal's Saturday Gazette* brought forth the Widow Bedott, along with Neal's own writing, and Neal consciously encouraged western humorists even though he was cautious about their language because of his circulation "among the ladies." Most interesting in regard to Philadelphia is the publishing house of T. B. Peterson and Brothers, whose Library of Humorous Works as listed on the back cover of Neal's *Peter Faber's*

Misfortunes (1856) cited over thirty southern, western, and northern works. Some of the authors and books represented here have been studied, but others obviously invite analysis in the future.

A bibliography like this one necessarily omits far more resources than it includes. Comic songs comparing life in the various northeastern cities appear from the very beginning of the period in collections like *Nickerson's Humorous Sentimental and Naval Songster; or, Museum of Mirth!* (5th ed.; Baltimore, 1832). Even Britishers like William Aytoun, in "Bon Gaultier's" *Book of Ballads* (New York, 1854), out-frontiered the frontier in burlesques like "The Fight with the Snapping Turtle; or, The American St. George," "The Death of Jabez Dollar," and "The Alabama Duel." The influence of Aytoun and poets like Thomas Hood and "Barry Cornwall" on American humorists is an open question. Jesse Bier, in *The Rise and Fall of American Humor* (New York, 1968), his wide-ranging analysis of American humor from the Civil War era onward, suggests that a "vapid egalitarianism" leads to an excessive nonjudgmental, sentimental tolerance, a form of decay. Such a decay may well have affected the tradition under study here, leading to its dismemberment among local colorists, sentimental poets, and the revolt from the village sarcasts. H. L. Mencken certainly inherited some of the flamboyant language and manner of New England social critics in the Timothy Dexter tradition. The fact that many of the writers in this anthology are not even mentioned in Bier's book is evidence of their absentee status in the understanding of the development of American humor. The whole northeastern tradition offers a wide scope for study both in overall outline and in the contributions of the various subregions to its overall growth. Furthermore, numbers of writers worthy of at least passing attention are still waiting to be identified and placed in historical perspective. The field of study remains open.